Forgiveness and Remembrance

Forgiveness and Remembrance

Remembering Wrongdoing in Personal and Public Life

JEFFREY M. BLUSTEIN

OXFORD
UNIVERSITY PRESS

Oxford University Press is a department of the University of Oxford.
It furthers the University's objective of excellence in research, scholarship,
and education by publishing worldwide.

Oxford New York
Auckland Cape Town Dar es Salaam Hong Kong Karachi
Kuala Lumpur Madrid Melbourne Mexico City Nairobi
New Delhi Shanghai Taipei Toronto

With offices in
Argentina Austria Brazil Chile Czech Republic France Greece
Guatemala Hungary Italy Japan Poland Portugal Singapore
South Korea Switzerland Thailand Turkey Ukraine Vietnam

Oxford is a registered trade mark of Oxford University Press
in the UK and certain other countries.

Published in the United States of America by
Oxford University Press
198 Madison Avenue, New York, NY 10016

© Oxford University Press 2014

All rights reserved. No part of this publication may be reproduced,
stored in a retrieval system, or transmitted, in any form or by any means,
without the prior permission in writing of Oxford University Press,
or as expressly permitted by law, by license, or under terms agreed with the
appropriate reproduction rights organization. Inquiries concerning reproduction
outside the scope of the above should be sent to the Rights Department,
Oxford University Press, at the address above.

You must not circulate this work in any other form
and you must impose this same condition on any acquirer.

Library of Congress Cataloging-in-Publication Data
Blustein, Jeffrey.
Forgiveness and remembrance : remembering wrongdoing in personal
and public life / Jeffrey Blustein.
p. cm.
Includes index.
ISBN 978–0–19–932939–7 (hardback : alk. paper) — ISBN 978–0–19–932940–3
(pbk. : alk. paper) 1. Forgiveness. 2. Memory. I. Title.
BJ1476.B58 2014
155.9'2—dc23
2013035347

1 3 5 7 9 8 6 4 2

Printed in the United States of America on acid-free paper

CONTENTS

Acknowledgments   vii

Introduction   1

PART I   FORGIVENESS AND MEMORY IN PERSONAL LIFE

1. The Moral Psychology of Interpersonal Forgiveness   17

2. Forgiveness and Memory for Wrongdoing   70

3. Forgetting and Forgiving Revisited   99

PART II   FORGIVENESS AND MEMORY IN PUBLIC LIFE

4. Forgiveness, Commemoration, and Restorative Justice   143

5. Commemoration and the Moral Values of Remembrance   178

6. The Nature and Value of Memorialization as Symbolic Activity   227

7. Human Rights and the Internationalization of Memory   286

Index   340

ACKNOWLEDGMENTS

This book continues a project that I began several years ago when I was writing my last book, *The Moral Demands of Memory*. Both books examine the workings of memory from the standpoint of moral and political and social philosophy, a subject that I felt then, and continue to feel, is incredibly rich and could profit enormously from what philosophy can bring to it. There can be few tasks of greater practical relevance for philosophy than to understand the significance of memory in our personal lives as well as in the lives we share with others in a social and political sense. Memory has been studied from many different disciplinary perspectives: psychology, neuroscience, history, political science, comparative literature, and film studies, to name some. What is known as "memory studies" is a growing and exciting multi- and interdisciplinary field of study. But even when memory is not being studied philosophically, philosophical questions of all sorts naturally grow out of it. This book concerns itself with a subset of these questions.

I have many people to thank for help with this book, some of it in the form of written comments, some given in conversation. My colleagues in the Psychology Department at City College, Paul Wachtel and Jeffrey Rosen, generously shared their expertise as it related to some of the ideas presented in chapters 1 and 3. My colleague in Philosophy, Nick Pappas, an expert on Nietzsche, commented on the portion of the manuscript that deals with this philosopher, and a lively and very instructive conversation with Alex Prescott-Couch on Nietzsche's view of forgiveness shaped my interpretation of it in chapter 1. Colleagues at the City University of New York Graduate Center, Noel Carroll and John Greenwood, gave me helpful feedback on chapter 6, as did Jesse Prinz for chapter 1. Janna Thompson commented on a paper that I delivered at a conference on historical justice and memory that was expanded into chapter 6, and was kind enough to agree to comment on a draft of chapter 7. At the conference I had the good fortune of meeting Klaus Neumann and Robert Young, who made interesting observations about the introduction and chapter 7 respectively. The members of my longstanding philosophy discussion group, Michael Stocker, Christopher Gowans, and Jonathan Adler, read a number of chapters and discussed them with me over many hours in a relaxed, non-confrontational environment. John Davenport, a later addition to the group, shared his thoughts on my account of the relationship between forgiving and forgetting in chapter 3 and drew my attention to Kierkegaard's views on forgiveness and how they relate to my own. Charles Griswold had useful things to say about chapter 1, and Colleen Murphy's criticisms of an early paper influenced the substance and direction of arguments I advance in chapter 4. She also read and commented on a draft of chapter 6. Ernesto Verdeja, a political scientist working on issues related to justice in the aftermath of political violence, brought his real-world expertise in the politics of political reconciliation to a reading of chapter 7. I owe a special debt of gratitude to Margaret Walker, from whose books and articles I have learned so much. Her criticisms and suggestions and at least as important her encouragement of my work have been invaluable. Others whom I wish to thank are W. James Booth, Anna Gotlib, Dennis Klein, Ronald Salzberger, and David Wasserman. I also want to recognize the students in my graduate philosophy course on Memory and Morality, especially Ereshnee Naidu, who listened patiently but critically to my views on the subject.

Portions of this book were presented in a number of venues: at a panel on "Transitional Justice, Reconciliation, Identity, and Memory" at the 2009 Eastern Division meeting of the American Philosophical Association; the Humanities Seminar in Trauma and Testimony at the Graduate Center of the City University of New York; a joint Philosophy and Psychology colloquium at City College; a conference on "Historical Memory, Justice, and Reconciliation" at La Trobe University in Melbourne, Australia; the Philosophy Departments at West Virginia University and Brooklyn College; a panel on "Memory and moral repair" at the 9th Biennial Conference of the International Association of Genocide Scholars, in Buenos Aires, Argentina; and the Center for Bioethics at New York University. There were a number of useful comments at these presentations from members of the audience, but unfortunately I am unable to trace most of them back to their authors.

Two published papers were considerably expanded and reworked into chapters:

"Forgiveness, Commemoration, and Restorative Justice: The Role of Moral Emotions," *Metaphilosophy*, vol. 41, no. 4 (July 2010): 582–617, and "Human Rights and the Internationalization of Memory," *Journal of Social Philosophy*, vol. 43, no. 1 (Spring 2012): 19–32.

Introduction

1. Forgiveness, interpersonal and political

In May 2010, in a lecture on behalf of the Forgiveness Project, an organization that explores forgiveness and reconciliation through the personal stories of both victims and offenders, Desmond Tutu, former Archbishop of South Africa, spoke of the transformative power of forgiveness. Forgiveness, he said, made it possible for South Africa to avoid a "racial bloodbath" after apartheid, for the black victims of violently racist white rule to put bitterness and hatred behind them, and for the country to heal the divisions of the past. "Forgiving is never easy and it is never cheap," he acknowledged. "It isn't anything that you can demand of others. But when it happens it has an incredible capacity to change a situation." It is the best way to bring about lasting peace and move away from the conflicts of the past.

Sharing the platform with Archbishop Tutu was Mary Kayitsei Blewitt, a Tutsi who survived the Hutu-led genocide in Rwanda. She expressed a less sanguine view about the power of forgiveness to transform society for the better. The founder of a survivors' organization, Surf, she described how she had witnessed only pain, disillusion, and the retraumatizing of Tutsi victims who had to live next door to Hutus who had committed atrocities against them and their families. "The reason we still have violence in our community," she said, "is because it is so easy to forgive. I subscribe to the notion of forgiveness. But forgiveness without justice, to me, is delayed atrocity."[1]

I want to make a few observations about these remarks to introduce some of the themes of this book. First, what Tutu means by "forgiveness" is ordinary interpersonal forgiveness. It is the forgiveness that those who have been wrongfully harmed grant to those who have wronged them, and it consists in overcoming hostile negative emotions like bitterness and hatred and replacing them with more positive attitudes such as empathy. It is what I call "sentiment-based" forgiveness, in contrast to forgiveness that is more like forgiving a debt, where the debtor's feelings toward the indebted are of little consequence. Second, even though the forgiveness is interpersonal and involves overcoming very personal emotional reactions to wrongdoing, Tutu believes that it has enormous restorative potential socially as well as personally in circumstances of profound political transition. If widespread enough, it can bring about a lasting peace, renew civic values, restore the standing of victims, and reconcile former adversaries. Interpersonal forgiveness that achieves or promotes these objectives is political, not in the sense in which an official government pardon or amnesty is political, but in the sense that it has broadly political consequences for the society at large. Third, Blewitt distances herself somewhat from Tutu's position by focusing on the limitations of forgiveness as an approach to social reconstruction and political reconciliation. Psychologically speaking, forgiveness may not be easy, as Tutu says. But from the standpoint of its political significance, the problem as Blewitt sees it is that forgiveness is too easy. What she means, I take it, is that forgiveness might be too easy on the offenders, that it might not first demand that they take responsibility for their actions and make amends for what they have done. But forgiveness that does not demand this is forgiveness without justice, and without justice the claim that former adversaries are reconciled is a sham. This, the perpetuation of injustice, must also be included among the potential political consequence of forgiveness.

The three chapters of Part I and the first chapter of Part II deal with forgiveness, personal as well as political in the sense I have just explained. To some extent what I do there is reflect on the issues that surfaced in the debate between Tutu and Blewitt. That is, I explore both the contributions and limitations of forgiveness as a practice for achieving political reconciliation and justice in the aftermath of large-scale wrongdoing and collective atrocities. But my interest in interpersonal forgiveness goes beyond this, beyond assessing its political role in societies undergoing political transition. This is what I address in the first three chapters. There I critically examine some entrenched ideas that pervade much philosophical writing on the subject of interpersonal forgiveness. These ideas I refer to as part of the "standard" view. In particular, I discuss its emphasis on the importance of memory for forgiveness and its definitional requirement that forgiveness involves the overcoming of angry, hostile feelings. I offer an expanded emotive account of interpersonal forgiveness that contests and seeks to modify both these claims of the standard view. I do not offer anything like a complete theory of interpersonal forgiveness, however, for there are important issues that I do not address. For example, on the question of whether forgiveness can be virtuous if the offender does not repent and atone for what he has done, I have little to say. Nor do I discuss a distinction that some philosophers have thought important, between forgiving someone for what he has done and forgiving someone for being a certain sort of person. Another issue I do not pursue is whether persons other than the victim can forgive a wrongdoer. Nevertheless, it

Introduction   3

is my hope that the three chapters that make up Part I will not only yield a more complex and richer moral psychology of forgiveness than the standard view assumes, but that to some extent they can help illuminate interpersonal forgiveness as a political phenomenon in the context of a society in transition from authoritarian to democratic rule.

2. Remembrance of wrongdoing, personal and political

This book also deals with remembrance of wrongdoing, both personal and political, and the relationship between remembrance and forgiveness, considering each as an interpersonal as well as a political phenomenon. Memory is clearly foundational for forgiveness, since forgiveness is a means of confronting past wrongdoing that one holds before the mind, and it overcomes the emotions it engenders without relinquishing the judgment that one was wronged. There can be no forgiveness, as a conceptual matter, if one experiences amnesia with respect to the wrongs one suffered. But forgetting as an ingredient of forgiveness has not received nearly as much attention as remembering, and it is important for both individuals and societies to appreciate its value.

Remembrance as a political phenomenon in transitional societies is another major focus of this book. Transitional regimes often create some sort of memorial to the victims of past wrongdoing, perhaps because they are pressured into doing so by domestic or international actors; perhaps because they hope that it will promote political reconciliation; and perhaps because they regard memorials as a fitting tribute to the victims of wrongdoing. I am interested in what can be called the ethics of remembrance, both as it relates to remembering wrongs done to oneself and as it relates to memorials to the victims of wrongdoing in transitional societies and beyond.

The issues in the two cases are in some respects different and in others similar. One issue that arises in connection with both personal and political remembrance of wrongdoing is their relationship to forgiveness. It is a common assumption in much philosophical and nonphilosophical writing on forgiveness that to forgive one must wipe the slate clean and put the past behind one. But if this is what forgiveness accomplishes, then in the political domain it appears that forgiveness and remembrance are working at cross-purposes. For memorials are designed to keep the memory of wrongdoing and its victims alive, whereas forgiveness, allegedly, is completed in erasing that memory. There are two things one could do at this point. One is to accept this conception of forgiveness and oppose memorializing victims when offenders have been forgiven for their wrongdoing on the ground that it stirs up memories and emotions that forgiveness has put in the past. Or, and this is the approach I take, one could reject the conception of forgiveness that generates the difficulty for remembrance. This would not necessarily mean that memorializing victims under these circumstances is always politically safe and constructive. But it should make us more open to exploring ways in which it can be coherently combined with forgiveness, and I spend some time doing this.

3. An ethics of remembrance

One thing that an ethics of remembrance does is situate remembrance in the context of an ethics of forgiveness. Remembrance's relationship to forgiveness is complex: remembrance makes forgiveness possible and it can both facilitate it and impede it. Because of this, the moral evaluation of remembrance can be subordinated to questions about the moral justification of forgiveness or withholding forgiveness. If a particular act of forgiveness is morally commendable, then remembrance is a necessary condition of a morally commendable act, and a theory of forgiveness will tell us when it is morally commendable and what makes it so. On the other hand, remembrance is morally criticizable if it contributes to the victim withholding forgiveness without adequate justification, as I argue it sometimes can, and to decide this we need an account of when victims abuse their prerogative to set the terms of forgiveness.

Beyond exploring the moral relations between remembrance and forgiveness, an ethics of remembrance concerns itself with the moral evaluation of remembering and forgetting in general, and it does this at more than one level, about which I will say more in a moment: the individual as well as the collective. Now an ethics of remembrance, like any ethics, assumes that we are sometimes warranted or justified in crediting, praising, blaming, or censuring agents for remembering or forgetting, and arguably this assumes that they are morally responsible for these mental states. Of course one could take the hard determinist line that we should jettison free will and moral responsibility altogether and with it our blaming and crediting practices; alternatively, one could argue that these practices can survive the denial of moral responsibility. A third position, taken by P. F. Strawson, with which I am broadly in agreement, eschews metaphysical questions about responsibility and argues that judgments about being morally responsible are to be understood in relation to the role that attitudes like resentment, anger, and forgiveness—he calls them "reactive attitudes"—play in the practice of holding responsible.[2] According to Strawson, these attitudes are so inextricably bound up with human psychology and our way of life that it is pointless to ask whether we are "really" morally responsible for our actions if determinism is true. Our holding individuals and groups responsible for their memories and for whether they remember is also inextricably bound up with

Introduction 5

our way of life, so by the same reasoning, whether or not determinism is true individuals and groups can be liable to moral praise and censure for remembering or forgetting.

Moral language is often invoked explicitly or by implication in everyday contexts involving individual memory. For example, we say to someone who forgot to pick up his mother-in-law from the airport, as he promised he would, "You should have remembered"; or to my son on his mother's birthday, "You should be ashamed of yourself for not calling your mother;" or to the victim of a non-trivial wrong who put it out of mind, "You let that person walk all over you." These and like examples suggest that remembering is not only something that individuals do (or do not do) but that they have control over, something over which individuals can exert their agency. Moreover, terms of moral praise and blame are sometimes attributed to persons for remembering or forgetting, and they are regarded as appropriate. "You should have remembered," "You should be ashamed of yourself for not calling your mother," and "You let that person walk all over you" are all forms of moral criticism. On a collective level, in societies with recent histories of massive and systematic wrongdoing, audiences are enjoined, as a matter of duty or obligation, to remember the events and honor the victims and to establish memorials to keep their memory alive. (I do not distinguish here between duty, obligation, and responsibility.) This is partly so that the world does not allow anything like this to happen again, and partly simply to honor and pay tribute to those who suffered and died.

Duty is one of the moral terms used in connection with remembrance, and one way to explain why we are justified in applying it to remembrance is to link it to the general category of obligation. Individuals have moral obligations, and obligations of any kind transmit their binding force through time and can be acted upon only if the agent can appreciate that the reasons for discharging them that arose in the past persist into the present. This requires memory both of the generating source of the obligation and the existence of the obligation itself. Collectives also have obligations and these too require remembrance, in this case collective remembrance, for their fulfillment. In political communities that have functioning democratic institutions and where the public enjoys some systematic influence over political decision making, the legitimate actions of those who represent the people are binding on the people as a whole. Their legitimate actions are authorized by those they represent, and such authorization entails ownership of and moral responsibility for those actions. Of particular interest here is when the members of a political society collectively have an obligation to make reparation for the injustices committed by their political representatives and predecessors. Remembrance plays an essential role in relation to all of these collective obligations, as it does in relation to the obligations of individuals. The existence and force of these obligations is transmitted to individuals and collectives by remembrance. Indeed, without the capacity for memories of the relevant sort, it would be pointless to hold them to obligations of any kind, and even if there is a sense in which they could still have obligations, they could not be action guiding.

Remembrance is thus an enabling condition of the fulfillment of other obligations. However, a defense along these lines is only part of the task of an ethics of remembrance. This is so for two reasons. First, remembrance may be obligatory even though it does not enable the fulfillment of other obligations that are specified independently of it. Second, remembrance can be assessed morally from other standpoints than that of obligation. This is suggested by my remarks about the relationship between remembrance and forgiveness: forgiveness may be morally admirable though it is not obligatory, and in these cases remembrance would not enable or be a condition of the fulfillment of an obligation. Further, in concerning itself with a duty to remember, an ethics of remembrance articulates the values that are protected and promoted by the duty and the ends and interests served by it, and these can be discussed without adverting to the duty, or even committing oneself to it. This is what I do to some extent, although I also take these values to be sufficiently important to ground memorial duties in some situations.

3. From the individual to the collective

Since I have referred to remembrance and forgiveness as political phenomena, and since political phenomena have a collective dimension and do not just involve large numbers of individuals working separately, I need to explain how we can make sense of attributing these conditions to collectives.

Remembering and forgetting are not just states attributable to individuals. Groups of individuals also remember and forget in ways not that dissimilar from how individuals remember and forget. This may seem unsurprising. After all, the term "collective memory" is widely used in the discourses of the social sciences, and if asked, Can groups remember? the answer is likely to be affirmative. Nevertheless, despite its familiarity and currency, there is still some confusion about what collective memory means. Even more troubling are problems that arise in connection with another collective phenomenon: collective forgiveness. To the question, Can groups forgive? the answer may be more hesitant than the answer to the parallel question about memory. This is especially the case if we adopt a sentiment-based conception of forgiveness, for on this account, forgiveness is a process of amending one's negative attitudes and overcoming one's negative emotions, and it may seem that groups as such cannot have attitudes and emotions, let alone amend and overcome them.

We can approach both questions by distinguishing between different types of groups. The labels I use may depart somewhat from other terminologies, but the distinctions are familiar enough. I call these random assortments of individuals, nonrandom assortments of individuals, and collectives. As an example of the first kind consider the victims of a train wreck. The victims are a group only because they all happened to be on the train at the same time, and we may suppose that this is all that they have in common. They are not united by any relationship to each other or by an identity that they share. The survivors may come together in the aftermath of the crash in a community of loss and grief, but then their group is no longer random. An example of the second kind is the group composed of Jews in eastern Europe during the Holocaust. Here the members of the group were not just random victims—they had a specific identity as Jews and were targeted for extermination precisely because of this fact about them. However, although there were noteworthy instances of organized resistance by Jews, systematic Nazi persecution was extraordinarily successful in preventing them from being able to organize, to collectively make decisions about how to deal with their condition, and to come together to advance some common goal. The third kind of group has these features that both random and nonrandom assortments lack. Obvious examples include the military, special interest groups, and political parties. In each case the members of the group understand themselves as belonging to the same group, act in concert or solidarity to achieve some common goal, and do their part as individuals to advance this goal; and they all understand one another to be committed to the same thing. These are the marks of a collective as opposed to a collection.

It is only in relation to a group of the third sort that we can properly speak of either collective remembrance or collective forgiveness. Individual members of an assortment can remember and forgive those who wronged them, but they lack the capacity to make decisions jointly and to act in a unitary fashion as a single body, and this is necessary for collective remembering and forgiving. Collectives consist of individuals, of course, and ultimately when there is collective remembering and collective forgiving, it is individuals who remember and forgive. But collectives consist of individuals who are related to each other in various ways and who act together, and collectives can act in pursuit of a goal even if not every member of the collective has the pursuit of this goal as his or her individual project.

Even if a group of people constitutes a collective, it may be doubted that it can truly forgive. It may be thought that attributing attitudes and emotions to groups, as I sometimes do in this book, is a category mistake. To be sure, we do speak about Hutus as a group being filled with hatred for Tutsis, for example; about the American people as a whole being disappointed by the performance of their president; about the grief that a community feels in the aftermath of a devastating tragedy. This can't be taken literally, however, the objection goes. A *group* can't actually feel grief, disappointment, or hatred, only this individual and that individual and that individual, etc. can. It is of course a complex question how we can make sense of attributing attitudes, emotions, and other mental states to social groups, and I will say more about this later in the book. I would only point out here that resistance to the idea of collective attitudes and emotions may in part be traceable to a confusion about what collectivity commits us to in this context. It does not commit us to holding that a collective is a sort of ontologically distinct entity that feels emotions, that it is just the individual writ large with all the mental states that the individual has only magnified. On the contrary, these are still the emotions of individuals, only now they are collectivized. Like collective memories, these emotions are transformed by being communicated to and shared with others in the group, and they are collective because the emotions of each are adjusted to, shaped by, and integrated with the emotions of the others. Rather than *my* and *your* hatred, or disappointment, or grief, the emotion becomes *ours*.

4. Outline of the book

This book presents a set of overlapping and interlocking analyses that explore aspects of forgiveness and remembrance, and the relationships between them, in both interpersonal and political contexts. The trajectory of the book, in brief, is this. Part I, which is composed of chapters 1 through 3, deals with interpersonal forgiveness and remembering and forgetting as aspects of it. Chapter 4 of Part II is a bridge chapter. It situates forgiveness in the context of societies undergoing political transition and introduces public commemoration as a practice that, like forgiveness, is often said to exemplify a restorative approach to transitional justice. The nature and significance of commemoration are explored at greater length in chapter 5. Its contributions to political reconciliation are explained and certain problems concerning the relationship between it and forgiveness in transitional contexts are addressed. The rest of Part II, chapters 6 and 7, are given over entirely to memorialization. Chapter 6 focuses on the symbolic character of acts and practices of memorialization. It sets this in the context of a broader examination of the nature of symbolic value and its relationship to moral value and discusses some of the symbolic moral values with which memorialization is associated. The concluding chapter 7 analyzes memorialization from an international perspective and advocates a role for international actors in the memorialization practices of transitional societies. Here are the contents of the chapters in more detail.

Introduction

Part I: Forgiveness and Memory in Personal Life

Chapter 1: The Moral Psychology of Interpersonal Forgiveness

This chapter, a lengthy examination of interpersonal forgiveness from the standpoint of the victim's emotional responses to wrongdoing, is the heart of my expanded emotive account of interpersonal forgiveness. I argue that the moral psychology of response to wrongdoing that is tacitly assumed by standard philosophical accounts of forgiveness is not rich enough to encompass the wide range of negative emotions that those who are wronged experience. They do not just respond with anger or resentment, what I call retributive emotions, but also with grief, disappointment, hurt, and sadness, what I call non-retributive emotions, and the latter may or may not be accompanied by the former.

The argument against the standard view proceeds in a number of steps. At each step, I take one of its central claims and show that it supports a more capacious account of the emotional dynamics of forgiveness than the view offers. First, persons typically forgive others for wrongs that have insulted them, but the negative emotions that register insult are quite diverse, including but not limited to anger. Second, there is nothing to forgive someone for if he is not to blame for what he has done, but blame is not always accompanied by anger or some other retributive emotion. It might instead be registered as disappointment or even sadness. One can also forgive someone and continue to blame him, as I argue, but the negative emotions that register continuing blame must be non-retributive. Third, susceptibility to negative emotions in response to being wronged is an indication that the forgiver retains his self-respect, but a variety of emotions can signify this and be communicated to the offender and others in protest against wrongs suffered, including but not limited to resentment.

Chapter 2: Forgiveness and Memory for Wrongdoing

One cannot forgive by forgetting, as both the standard philosophical view and popular belief have it, but not all memories are alike. Some memories are purely declarative, with no emotional valence or tone, while others are infused with emotion, either negative or positive. The importance of this distinction is not generally recognized in the philosophical literature on forgiveness. Emotional memories of wrongdoing are especially evaluatively significant because the emotions that constitute them are, and this chapter gives two reasons for this: emotions of the right sort give the values that are negated by wrongdoing a weighty effect in the life of the one who was wronged, an effect that accords with the importance of the values and that nonemotional memories do not deliver; and susceptibility to emotional response is one of the criteria of valuing.

Emotional memories are not only ingredients of the process of forgiveness, however. They also continue even after the wrongdoer has been forgiven, as can blame, although their role in the life of the wronged party and their relationship to other aspects of his psychology will be different from what they were prior to his having forgiven the wrongdoer. I explain how they differ in my discussion of what I call the "differentiation problem."

Chapter 3: Forgetting and Forgiving Revisited

The standard view claims that memory is necessary for forgiveness, and I agree with this to some extent. But like its assumptions about the moral psychology of response to wrongdoing, its account of the role of remembering in the process of forgiveness is overly simplified. The chapter aims to correct this by arguing that remembering can actually impede forgiveness if it is such that the wronged party dwells on or ruminates on the wrongs that he suffered. Rumination magnifies the intensity of the emotions that respond to being wronged and makes it more difficult for the wronged party to overcome them. To counter the effects of rumination, one needs to forget by rendering memories of wrongdoing difficult to access, and various techniques of emotion regulation can help with this, which I call attentional deployment and cognitive reappraisal. If forgiveness is warranted or justified, then there is moral reason to employ these techniques. I also suggest that there is some parallel between personal and political cases with respect to the dangers of rumination and the value of emotion regulation.

Part II: Forgiveness and Memory in Public Life

Chapter 4: Forgiveness, Commemoration, and Restorative Justice

I now move from the interpersonal to the political, but the meaning that I give the word "political" explains why Part I continues to be relevant to the concerns of Part II. The notion of political forgiveness retains the primary sense of forgiveness as an emotionally transformative process but refers to interpersonal forgiveness on a large enough scale to have political consequences, including consequences for the achievement of political reconciliation between former adversaries. Political reconciliation is the aim of societies transitioning from authoritarianism to democracy, and in at least some of its different meanings it is the cornerstone of an approach to transitional justice that is known as restorative justice. Some have argued that forgiveness promotes restorative justice by helping to restore the dignity and civic standing of victims and that punitive approaches fail to do this. I take issue with both of these claims. However, forgiveness can assist in the moral reconstruction of political relationships under the

Introduction 11

right circumstances. In this connection I argue that there may be value in providing opportunities for forgiveness, at least as long as these opportunities do not become a vehicle for exerting pressure on victims to forgive. This mixed verdict on the value of forgiveness from a restorative standpoint also applies to another practice frequently mentioned in this context, commemoration or memorialization. Memorialization has significant restorative potential, but I caution that memorials can allow communities to forget the wrongs of the past and to consider past injustices to be over and done with. Ironically, instead of promoting justice by not allowing communities to bury the past, memorials can undermine memory and with it accountability.

Chapter 5: Commemoration and the Moral Values of Remembrance

Ethical norms of different sorts work together to inform and facilitate responsible deliberation and action with respect to memorializing the victims of wrongdoing. Consequentialist arguments for remembrance are probably the most familiar and the most frequently appealed to. We should remember the wrongs of the past, it is said, so that among other things we can change the social and institutional conditions that made these wrongs possible and take steps to prevent a recurrence before it is too late. But there are other norms as well to which an ethics of remembrance appeals, norms for the expression of intrinsically valuable attitudes, the possession and exercise of virtues, and the prescriptions of deontology, and in this chapter and the next these are my chief concern. My approach is eclectic rather than systematic. I am selective in my use of ethical expressivism, virtue theory, and deontology, drawing on each of them for assistance in developing a credible alternative to an exclusively consequentialist approach to an ethics of remembrance. Questions about which ethical theory is most plausible overall or best able to account for the widest range of moral phenomena can fortunately be set aside.

In this chapter I focus on three intrinsically valuable attitudes that figure in expressivist norms, self-respect, respect for persons, and fidelity to the dead, and I show how each of them provides part of an account of the moral value of remembering the victims of wrongdoing. Having thus established it as a moral practice, I next consider how remembrance can be made to endure so that the values it embodies are sustained over time. I call this the "sustainability of memory problem." Monuments, archives, museums, testimonials, and artifacts of various kinds, each created to memorialize some element of the past, are often  transient in terms of their memorial effects. Commemorative rituals, however, are able to help them withstand the forces that undermine and interfere with remembrance, and I explain this as a consequence of their ritualistic, repetitive, and emotive character. Here I draw on research in empirical psychology that shows emotional memories tend to be stronger and more long-lasting than non-emotional memories. Of course, if the emotions aroused by commemorative rituals are such as to impede the process of political reconciliation or prevent its consolidation, then the fact that memories of wrongdoing are sustained by commemorative rituals would not necessarily be a point in their favor. But this outcome is avoidable, I contend, if only non-retributive negative emotions are encouraged. Further, commemorative rituals of this sort are compatible with forgiveness since victims can continue to have non-retributive feelings toward wrongdoers even after forgiving them.

Chapter 6: The Nature and Value of Memorialization as Symbolic Activity

The moral values of remembrance are sometimes embodied in social practices of memorialization, which in its various incarnations is always essentially a type of symbolic activity. I begin therefore with remarks about the nature of symbolic activity and symbolic value, and give some examples to show that symbolic value is socially constructed and grounded in objective public norms. The central claim of the chapter is that the moral value of memorialization is realized symbolically, by activities and practices that have symbolic meaning. Symbolic value, however, is sometimes discounted on the ground that it is not a terribly serious sort of value as compared with the value of actually making a difference in the world. This is a view that I call the "thesis of lesser value," and much of this chapter is spent giving reasons why I reject it. Specifically, I argue that memorialization can express moral attitudes of respect for value as well as for persons, can embody a commitment to justice, and can exemplify virtues like courage and hope. Symbolic acts of memorialization are important for another reason as well: they can implicate a community's sense of what is integral to its collective identity. Sometimes identity and the claims based on it have moral force and deserve recognition and respectful consideration by others. When this is the case, I argue, when symbolic practices, including (some) memorial practices, are important to group identity and the identity-based claims of the group have moral force, the connection of these practices to identity magnifies the moral significance of the former.

Chapter 7: Human Rights and the Internationalization of Memory

Transitional justice covers a range of approaches to achieving justice in the aftermath of civil conflict and/or state repression. Transitional regimes confront massive and systematic human rights violations resulting from the breakdown of the rule of law, and they must respond to victims' demands for recognition, truth

Introduction

telling, and accountability. In light of the fact that the wrongs are of this grievous nature—that is, massive human rights abuses—their remediation is properly a matter of international and not just national concern. The aim of this chapter is to extend this argument to memorialization and to suggest how this concern can be demonstrated in actual political practice. Memorializing the victims of wrongdoing is one way of providing a kind of reparation for the wrongs they suffered and, as with other sorts of reparation, international actors have a legitimate interest in seeing to it that this is properly and effectively done by those who have primary responsibility for doing so. Those who have primary responsibility are the same political bodies as have primary responsibility for protecting human rights, namely states. I give a number of reasons why the primary responsibility for redress is lodged there: the state serves as proxy for citizens in the fulfillment of their reparative obligations; the state is uniquely capable of conferring political legitimacy on social projects and practices of memorialization; and the state that is a nation can appeal to national identity to generate widespread support within the political community for memorial measures. By the expression "the internationalization of memory" I do not mean to suggest that international actors ought to supplant individual states as the primary loci of memorialization efforts. Rather I mean that they have responsibilities to employ their resources to assist states in these efforts and to hold them accountable for fulfilling their memorial responsibilities. They have these responsibilities because, as a general matter, they have the moral responsibility to guarantee that those who have primary responsibilities for the protection of human rights and remediation of their violations are able and willing to fulfill them. I suggest how this can be done in the case of memorialization by using as illustrations actual cases of judicial and nonjudicial participation in human rights practice that show an awareness by international actors of an international role in memorialization.

Endnotes

1. www.independent.co.uk/news/uk/home-news/forgiveness-cannot-be-demanded-says-tutu-1972201.html
2. P. F. Strawson, "Freedom and Resentment," in John Martin Fischer and Mark Ravizza (eds.), *Perspectives on Moral Responsibility* (Ithaca, NY: Cornell University Press, 1993), pp. 45–66.

PART I

FORGIVENESS AND MEMORY
IN PERSONAL LIFE

1

The Moral Psychology
of Interpersonal Forgiveness

1. Revising the standard account of forgiveness

The moral psychology of interpersonal forgiveness has been under-theorized in the philosophical literature of forgiveness. By this I mean several things. First, the account one finds in this literature of the emotions that those who have been wrongfully harmed experience is too spare to do justice to the full spectrum of emotions and feelings evoked by wrongdoing. Second, the literature fails to provide a convincing rationale for limiting its account in this way. Third, it pays insufficient attention to the emotional state of the person who has forgiven and to its relationship to the emotional state of the person who has not or not yet forgiven. Fourth, the philosophical literature maintains that memory plays an essential role in forgiveness, but has said little beyond noting that memory is conceptually necessary for forgiveness. Specifically, it has not addressed, or adequately addressed, the question why it matters morally that and how we remember wrongs committed against us, both before and after we have forgiven.

My aims in this chapter are both critical and constructive. I point out the shortcomings of standard philosophical accounts of the moral psychology of forgiveness, and I offer an analysis of the relationships between forgiveness and emotional response to wrongdoing that attends to these concerns. Its central thesis is that it is a mistake to conceptualize forgiveness as these accounts do, namely as the overcoming of anger or resentment. On the contrary, there are good reasons, psychological as well as moral, for expanding the repertoire of emotions to include ones that function very differently than anger and resentment. This may be opposed on the ground that anger and resentment are the only morally appropriate or most adequate responses to moral affront or injury that results from culpable wrongdoing. However, this too is a mistake, and it accounts for the mistake about forgiveness. For if these are not the only or most morally appropriate responses, then we will have to modify our conception of forgiveness to accommodate others.

Since I take the position that there are problems with many philosophical accounts of forgiveness, I need to say more about what I take them to assert. Though there are some variations in these accounts, there are also significant commonalities, enough to constitute what, for the purpose of drawing a contrast with my own view, I will call the orthodox or standard account. Its main features can be traced back to Bishop Joseph Butler's seminal analysis.[1] One element of the standard account is a claim about the emotions that forgiveness overcomes: forgiveness is said to involve the overcoming of some type of angry or hostile emotion. If other emotions are involved at all, they play only a minor role. Here is a small sample of statements culled from the literature to give a sense of the prominence that angry or hostile emotions have in the standard account:

"The intuitive tie between forgiveness and the moral anger one feels at being unjustly treated is unbreakable.... The moral sentiment(s) given up by forgiveness must embody the features evident in resentment."[2]

"Forgiving means overcoming anger and vengefulness."[3]

"Forgiveness involves ... the overcoming on moral grounds, of the intense negative reactive attitudes that are quite naturally occasioned when one has been wronged by another—mainly the vindictive passions of resentment, anger, hatred, and the desire for revenge."[4]

"Forgiveness may be said normally to have two aspects. (i) a volitional aspect ... and (ii) an emotional aspect—that which has to do with the extirpation of such negative feelings as those of anger, resentment, and hostility."[5]

"I propose, then, that the emotion 'overcome' in forgiveness is anger, and that the fact of anger that makes it important sometimes to overcome it, even in its morally purest forms, is the 'view' of the offender as bad, alien, guilty, worthy of suffering, unwelcome, offensive, an enemy, etc."[6]

Many more examples could be adduced, since most discussions of forgiveness in the philosophical literature either follow Bishop Butler in holding that forgiveness entails the forgoing of resentment or amend this slightly to include forgoing negative emotions with a family resemblance to it. What anger, resentment, hatred, and vengefulness have in common is a particular desire and belief: the belief that the wrongdoer has some sort of punishment "coming to him," and the desire to hurt him and make him suffer.[7] For this reason, I call them "retributive emotions," emotions that have as their characteristic aim visiting retribution on wrongdoers. Retributivism is commonly understood, in the words of R. Jay Wallace, "as the view that it is intrinsically good that wrongdoers should suffer harm."[8] But there is an alternative definition as well, one that may be thought more morally palatable, namely that wrongdoers deserve to be condemned for their offenses, and making them suffer and imposing hard treatment on them is the only fully adequate way to condemn them.[9] Retributive emotions, then, are constituted by the belief that it is fitting the offender should suffer for what he has done, either because this is intrinsically good or the most appropriate means of condemning wrongdoing.

As I construe the standard account, forgiveness presupposes a view of the offender as having done something that warrants the wronged party's anger or resentment (or a related emotion) toward him. And what forgiveness involves is a renunciation of retributive emotions held to be appropriate and an overcoming of retributive emotions that results in an altered view of the offender as no longer an appropriate target of these emotions. In short, forgiveness, on the standard account and as often understood outside of philosophy as well, consists in moderating and ridding oneself of retributive emotions and renouncing the right to inflict pain or suffering on an offender. Various verbs are used to express the kind of emotional transformation that interpersonal forgiveness consists in: conquer, overpower, abandon, renounce, abort, let go, forswear, and overcome. Whichever verb is used, it must be understood to imply not just that one's negative emotions are moderated, but also that one regards moderating them as desirable or appropriate and is committed to doing this. The wronged party may also experience a range of negative non-retributive emotions alongside or intermingled with the retributive ones, but these are not thought to be directed at the wrong[10] or to be the core emotions that embody a sense of moral affront or moral devaluation. Nor is the disposition to respond to wrongdoing with these emotions, unlike the disposition to respond with retributive ones, thought to be part and parcel of the wronged party's having an accurate sense of his or her self-worth, an omission that I will try to remedy in this chapter.

Many accounts of forgiveness also have the following feature, although this is perhaps not as clearly favored by philosophers as the element of overcoming anger. It seems to be part of a popular conception of forgiveness that to forgive is to wipe the slate clean, and this is sometimes echoed in the philosophical literature as well. What I take "wiping the slate clean" to mean in these contexts is that the wronged party no longer has any negative or bad or hard feelings toward the offender because of what he did, or if she has any of these, they play an inconsequential role in her emotional life. To forgive is not just to renounce emotions like anger and resentment, but to renounce *any* negative emotions occasioned by the wrong. Why this is taken to be a mark of forgiveness—or of "genuine" or "complete" forgiveness—is usually not explained or explained very well. Perhaps the thought is that if any bad feelings linger and not all of them are renounced, their association with earlier angry feelings is likely to stir them up again. Bad feelings toward the offender keep the memory of wrongdoing alive, and by holding on to memories of wrongdoing one is liable to get angry all over again and revert to the former non-forgiving stance. (Of course if angry feelings are liable to emerge again, then one may question whether the wronged party has undergone the emotional transformation that is supposedly effected by forgiveness.) Or perhaps the thought is different, not that bad feelings will stir up anger and resentment, and so undermine forgiveness, but that bad feelings indicate that one still blames the offender for what he did and holds it against him, and one cannot continue to blame the offender for what he did if one has forgiven him for it. Forgiveness involves ceasing to blame, so it renounces any emotions that give evidence of blame, even of the non-angry sort. I will comment on this too.

There are, however, different interpretations of "wiping the slate clean," and these suggest different relationships between forgiveness and memory. One cannot wipe the slate clean if one does not (in some sense) disregard past offenses. Indeed, it is part of the standard view as I conceive of it that forgiveness is partly constituted by or leads to the disregarding of past wrongdoing. The notion of disregarding the past, however, is multiply ambiguous. One succeeds in disregarding the past if one forgets it. Alternatively, one can remember the past but treat it as a matter of no importance to oneself, as something one does not care about, so in this evaluative sense "disregard" it. Related to this, one can remember the past but not dwell on it or be preoccupied with it, keep it in the back of one's mind, so to speak. The memories might be emotionally neutral, arousing no feeling positive or negative; or they might be emotionally inflected but not be such as to attract and hold attention, and so be relegated to the periphery of one's ongoing concerns, occupations, and motivations. Memories of some sort may remain after the offender has been forgiven, but the emotional quality of one's engagement with the past will change. In short, the person who forgives might afterward not remember being wronged, but if she remembers it at all, it will not have the same emotional significance for her that it had initially. Wiping the slate clean can be understood in these different ways, but the standard account has not explored them.

In this chapter I set out and defend my version of an emotive account of interpersonal forgiveness that expands the range of negative emotions that need to be overcome if the wrongdoer is to be forgiven for his offense. I do not wish to deny that angry emotions are common responses to culpable wrongdoing and that they are frequently the very emotions that must be renounced if the wrongdoer is to be forgiven. What I do wish to deny, in what follows, is that the reasons commonly given for singling out these emotions show why other ways of responding to wrongdoing should be discounted. The connection between angry emotions and the judgment that one has been wrongfully harmed is not as tight as proponents of the standard account of forgiveness suppose, because the account of the phenomenology of response to wrongdoing that underlies it is more complex than supposed. The implication for forgiveness is this: if it is a process that involves overcoming emotional responses to the wrongdoer that express or communicate condemnation or censure that fits his offense, as I believe it is, then given the range of negative emotions that can do this, it is a mistake to suppose it is exclusively a matter of overcoming (forswearing, etc.) emotions that are retributive in nature.

My defense of an expanded emotive account of forgiveness has a number of components. One part is in sections 2 and 3. Here I argue that forgiveness is commonly a matter of overcoming or forswearing feelings of *moral insult*, but that contrary to the standard account there is a wide range of negative feelings that signify this, including but not limited to retributive emotions. The relationship between forgiveness and insult is introduced by considering one extremely unflattering portrayal of forgiveness, that of Nietzsche. According to Nietzsche, forgiveness is not an option for persons with superior characters—that is, for noble souls—and one way to explain this is that they are constitutionally incapable of being morally insulted by the alleged offenses that those with slavish natures commit against them. They have achieved a degree of perfection that makes them immune to attacks that would, among baser natures, constitute an attack on their self-worth. (Nietzsche is also important for my purposes because of what he says about the relationship between memory and forgiveness. For Nietzsche, only those "with a memory for insults and base deeds committed against" them can forgive, whereas noble souls lack this memory and so are not in a position to do so. Memory and its relationship to forgiveness is the subject of chapters 2 and 3.) Having defended a link between forgiveness and insult, I turn to various emotions that are associated with being insulted, and being wronged more broadly, emphasizing that these emotions are not only retributive but include non-retributive or partly non-retributive ones as well.

Section 4 presents another component of my defense of a modified emotive account of forgiveness. Here I challenge the claim that retributive emotions are the uniquely appropriate type of response to serious wrongdoing by examining the nature and moral functions of *blame*. The argument that I consider and reject goes like this. Agents responsible for serious wrongdoing are blameworthy for their actions and deserve to be blamed for them. Blame can be thought of as an internal evaluative state of the victim or as an outward expression of condemnation. If it is not expressed, it must at least be accompanied by hostile feelings, otherwise it will not rise to the level of blame. If condemnation is expressed, it should be of a sort that gets wrongdoers to appreciate the wrongness of what they have done. But the wrongness of what they have done is only brought home to them if the condemnation is expressed in terms of some sort of action that is hard on them, that punishes them. Retributive emotions have this as their aim; non-retributive ones, by definition, do not. My criticism of this argument challenges both of these claims, the one about the emotions that should accompany blame, and the other about the unique expressive and teleological functions of retributive emotions. What I propose instead is a conception of blame according to which the emotions that normally accompany it are diverse and not necessarily hostile or angry. With regard to which negative emotions adequately express and communicate condemnation, I argue that non-retributive negative emotions can this do this as well and that they have been unduly neglected.

The third part of my defense of a revised emotive conception of forgiveness is in section 5. Here I explore the connection between retributive as well as non-retributive negative emotional responses to wrongdoing and *self-respect.* Retributive emotions are commonly emphasized in discussions of the moral psychology of response to wrongdoing because some degree of hostility or anger toward the wrongdoer is thought to be necessary for the victim's self-respect or for the victim's assurance that she still retains it. As with the alleged linkages between retributive emotions and feelings of insult and blame, in my view too much emphasis has been placed on the link between retributive emotions and self-respect. Self-respect and the closely related notion of self-esteem do provide an explanation of the significance of resentment and other retributive emotional responses to wrongdoing. But they can provide an explanation of the significance of other negative emotional responses as well, specifically various non-retributive ones.

Retributive emotions are also commonly thought to have a special force or role as "protesting" other-directed emotions, and in section 5 I also challenge what I regard as the excessive attention given to them in this regard. Non-retributive emotions, and not only retributive ones, are capable of fueling, expressing, and communicating protest against mistreatment. And to connect this to the preceding discussion, protest and self-respect are linked: protest against mistreatment, or the ability to protest mistreatment if one so chooses, can be critical to the maintenance or recovery of self-respect, especially in the victims of serious and systematic wrongdoing. However, even if we expand our notion of protest so that it can embody different kinds of negative emotional responses, retributive as well as non-retributive, "protest" only seems appropriate as a description of the victim's stance prior to having forgiven his wrongdoers. If this is correct, then while forgiveness might not wipe the slate clean of all negative feelings, they would have no role to play in protesting wrongdoing once the offenders have been forgiven for their offenses. I conclude the section with some remarks about this.

By exploring the relationships between different types of negative emotional responses to wrongdoing and insult, blame, and self-respect, I aim to show the inadequacy of the moral psychological picture that underlies the standard account of interpersonal forgiveness. In so doing, I intend to challenge the hegemony of the standard account itself.

2. Nietzsche and the possibility of forgiveness

There is an often-quoted passage from the First Treatise of Nietzsche's *On the Genealogy of Morality* that I will fix on in order to explain his views on forgiveness. It comes in his discussion of how modern morality is born out of a peculiar condition and attitude that he calls "*ressentiment*":

> To be unable for any length of time to take his enemies, his accidents, his *misdeeds* themselves seriously—that is the sign of strong, full natures in which there is an excess of formative, reconstructive, healing power that also makes one forget (a good example of this from the modern world is Mirabeau, who had no memory for insults and base deeds committed against him and who is only unable to forgive because he—forgot). Such a human is simply able to shake off with a single shrug a collection of worms that in others would dig itself in; here alone is also possible—assuming that it is at all possible on earth, the true "*love*" of one's enemies.[11]

Among persons with "strong, full natures," noble human beings, there is a kind of self-sufficiency that enables them to shrug off the "insults and base deeds" that may be directed against them. They simply do not experience the insults and base deeds as moral injuries, or more specifically, they do not respond to them with *ressentiment* or with the anger and hostility that weaker natures are naturally prone to.

Ressentiment is a state of "suppressed . . . desire for revenge" (GM, I, 7) that arises when the "weak and powerless" (GM, I, 10) desire to lead a certain kind of life they deem valuable but come to recognize they are unable to achieve. They refuse, however, to accept their inability to realize it and attempt to compensate for their impotence by indulging a "lust to rule" (GM, I, 6). When the "human being of *ressentiment*" (GM, I, 10) is insulted or the target of base deeds, he does not forget it. Lacking "nobility" (GM, I, 5) of character, he adopts the posture and persona of a victim and harbors a grudge against those who have injured him. He may or may not be able to forgive his enemies. But if he does forgive, it is not because he overcomes *ressentiment*. *Ressentiment* in Nietzsche's account of forgiveness plays a different role than resentment in standard accounts: the forgiveness of the man of *ressentiment* is not the overcoming of *ressentiment* but an expression of the impotence that fuels his envy and vengefulness.[12] He will at any rate satisfy one of forgiveness' preconditions because he remembers the wrongdoing. We might say, in keeping with the spirit of Nietzsche's remarks, that he remembers it all too vividly.

By contrast, "strong, full natures" are unable to forgive, but not because they are too angry or vengeful to do so. Rather, they quickly "shake off" insults and injuries, so in a sense forget them. I say "in a sense" because they do not necessarily have amnesia when it comes to what was done to them. They may remember *that* they were insulted or, more accurately, that their enemies treated them in ways that they, the enemies, intended to be insulting or that count as insulting among them. But their memory, such as it is, does not have the same emotional quality as the memory of the man of *ressentiment.* They do not dwell on it at all, so it does not disturb, distress, aggrieve, or torment them. If they experience anger at all, it "runs its course and exhausts itself in an immediate reaction, therefore it does not *poison*" (GM, I, 10). Their values play a critical explanatory role here as well. The "noble manner of valuation" (ibid.) is revealed in how they remember the insults directed toward them, and being very different from the manner of valuation of the man of *ressentiment,* they do not have the sort of bitter, vengeful memory that makes forgiveness possible. Forgiveness is only possible among those who can react to wrongful injury as victims react—that is, only among weaker natures. Those with "strong, full natures" are incapable of forgiveness because they are beyond it. They do not forgive: they just forget.

The importance of this passage for my purposes does not lie in Nietzsche's distinction between noble and slavish value or in how it relates to his controversial account of the origin of modern morality. Rather, it lies partly in its suggestion that forgiveness requires a certain sort of memory of wrongdoing, and that for forgiveness to be possible, the one wronged cannot "simply shake off with a single shrug" what was done to him. For Nietzsche, *ressentiment* is the emotion or attitude that explains why some people cannot simply shake it off. But there are other emotions as well, other kinds of anger or hostility and the like that do not have *ressentiment's* particular mixture of envy and resentment that can serve a similar purpose. In addition, the passage makes connections between forgiveness and the value systems of the parties involved in wrongdoing that are worth exploring. The inability to experience *ressentiment* among those with noble natures reflects and is to some extent explained by their particular values (or modes of valuation); and their values, expressed in how they respond emotionally to wrongdoing, preclude certain ways of remembering the "base deeds" directed at them. Finally, the passage suggests that the possibility of forgiveness is linked to the emotional responses to wrongdoing that one is capable of and to the valuations they embody, both of which, to repeat, determine how or whether one will remember wrongdoing.

Nietzsche's remark that the masters are able to "shrug off" the base deeds committed against them can be further clarified by introducing the concept of *insult.* On a plausible interpretation of his view, the masters are able to forget so easily because they are incapable of feeling insulted by the actions and attitudes of the slaves. To explain, we can distinguish between two senses of feeling insulted:

The Moral Psychology of Interpersonal Forgiveness   25

(1) A feels insulted by B if A experiences some sort of pain or distress as a result of
     B's failure to show proper attention, respect, or deference to him personally;
(2) A feels insulted by B if as a result of B's actions, A believes that the ground
     of his sense of self-worth is under attack and is pained or distressed by this.

The word "pain" or "distress" in both cases is intended to cover a range of
emotional reactions to being wronged, "from wounded pride, to humiliation,
shame, embarrassment, guilt, anger, and so on indefinitely."[13]

The reason that a person can feel insulted in sense (2) has to do with the fact
that we are vulnerable to the views of others. The perception a person has of
her own worth is normally partly dependent on the treatment she receives from
others and the attitudes toward her that the treatment expresses. B, through his
actions, is telling A that she is not a person who deserves better treatment, and
this is an attack on the basis of her self-respect. This does not imply that A is
uncertain of her worth or that she fears B might be right after all. The treatment
she receives might not call her value into question in her own mind. But if she
is confident of it, she will resist the attack and reject the message of inferiority
implicit in B's actions. B's actions threaten A's self-respect in the sense that they
throw down the gauntlet: if she does *not* resist, she will seem in her own eyes
and that of others to lack it. (There are various ways to resist. Resistance does
not have to be aggressive or combative.) Further, A can feel insulted by B's actions in sense (1), even if she does not feel that she has to resist the message they
contain in order to retain her self-respect—in other words, even if she does not
feel insulted in sense (2).

It is uncontroversial that for Nietzsche, the masters cannot feel insulted
in sense (2). Their perception of their own superior worth is unshakeable
and immune to any suggestion that they might not have the worth they take
themselves to have. In particular, their self-respect is entirely independent of
the opinion of slaves. Whatever the slaves might think of them, and whatever
base deeds they might commit against them, the masters will not take this
as evidence that contradicts their perception of their own worth, so will not
need to show that they reject it and to assert their self-worth. The explanation,
I suggest, has to do with the radically different value systems within which
masters and slaves act and deliberate and that inform their reactions to others'
actions.

The following two non-moral cases might help to explain this:

Case #1: An adolescent says to his peer, you have terrible taste in music; you are
          so not with it, so uncool.
Case #2: An adolescent says to his parents, you have terrible taste in music; you
          are so not with it, so uncool.

I take it that the reactions of the second adolescent in case #1 and of the parents in case #2 could be very different. It would not be surprising if the second adolescent in case #1 felt insulted by the harsh judgment of his peer; after all, his taste in music, which presumably is a matter of pride for many adolescents, has been impugned. The parents in case #2 are much less likely to feel insulted by this, indeed would probably not feel insulted at all, unless they have reason to believe that their adolescent is a particularly precocious teenager when it comes to appreciating the merits of different sorts of music. The parents are likely not to take the accusation of lack of taste terribly seriously; or as Nietzsche put it, they are likely to shrug it off. And while they may be moved by their child's criticism to re-examine their own musical tastes, this need not be because they credit him with superior judgment when it comes to music. They may still think his opinions reflect his immaturity.

The reason they will not take it seriously is that they do not have the same standards for evaluating music as he does and, further, they believe their child's standards are not the right ones for them to use in evaluating music. (They might rely on something like Mill's "competent judge" criterion to support their position.) In other words, there is not sufficient overlap of aesthetic values and musical standards for the parents to be insulted by their child's impugning their musical taste. They may be insulted, of course, if their child rudely or disrespectfully challenges them in public. But that is another matter: they feel insulted by his rudeness or disrespect, not by his criticism of their musical judgment, and the insult will be of the first sort, not the second.

An analogous argument, I believe, explains why the masters in Nietzsche's account will not feel insulted (in sense (2)) by the actions and attitudes of slaves. The masters and slaves inhabit very different evaluative universes. Their moral values and principles do not overlap sufficiently for insult to get any traction among the masters. If a slave tries to send a degrading or demeaning message to the master by acting toward him in a certain way, the slave will not get the intended uptake from him. For the master is assured of the superiority of his own values and principles, and he will see the actions of the slave as amounting to no more than pathetically empty threats and futile attempts to prove his worth. He might be physically injured by the slave, so get angry at him because of this, but his self-respect will remain unscathed.

It would still seem to be the case, however, that a master could feel insulted in sense (1) by the actions and attitudes of a slave—that is, by the slave's failing to show proper deference and obedience to him. Perhaps the master will not able to shrug this off so quickly. However, even this possibility is foreclosed, presumably because Nietzschean noble souls hold the slaves in contempt, and so believe that they are not worth the trouble of being taken seriously. Were the masters to feel insulted by their lack of deference, they would credit the slaves

The Moral Psychology of Interpersonal Forgiveness   27

and their opinions with more significance than they deserve. Hence masters will not feel insulted in either of the above senses: they will not be pained either by a perceived attack on their sense of self-worth or by the failure of the slaves to recognize what they regard as their superior merits.

Note that in egalitarian societies, where individuals are believed to have equal rights and the sort of contempt that masters have for slaves is not a defining feature of the social ethos, feeling insulted by disrespectful treatment in something like sense (1) would be appropriate, even among those who are unshakably convinced of their moral worth. In this case, however, what one would feel insulted by would not be the lack of deference for superior moral character. Rather, it would be for the failure to acknowledge and show respect for one as a moral equal—that is, as someone to whom others have obligations and who can hold them accountable for complying with them.

To return to forgiveness: What place do insult and insulted feelings have in an account of the conditions of forgiveness? Does the capacity to forgive presuppose the capacity to feel insulted by what others do to you? Is forgiveness only of wrongs that insult or can one also forgive for wrongs that, while perhaps serious, are nevertheless not insulting? I believe the latter is possible and in a moment I will explain why. First, however, I want to say more about feelings of insult, specifically their causes and objects, in order to make the point that "insult" is a broad enough notion to encompass importantly different sorts of wrongs for which offenders may be forgiven.

Feelings of insult can embody or represent disappointed expectations of equal concern and respect, as I just noted, and forgiveness can involve the overcoming of such feelings. But if this were all that feelings of insult responded to, there would be wrongs, perhaps quite hurtful ones, for which the notion of insult would be inadequate. Consider for example the case of a parent who, despite having failed to express love for her child, nevertheless claims to deserve gratitude from him; or that of a husband who selfishly disregards his wife's feelings on a matter that touches her deeply. The wrongs involved here are not constituted by violations of other persons' entitlements to *equal* concern and respect but rather by the disappointment of their legitimate expectations of *special* affection and care from particular others. Hence, they would not count as insulting under the former definition. However, I do not restrict feelings of insult to violations of moral principles that pertain to persons as moral equals. On this more inclusive characterization, a person can properly speaking feel insulted by his friend's disregard of his feelings or his failure to share confidences with him as well as by a stranger's racist or homophobic comments. And in both sorts of cases, the personal and the impersonal, overcoming these feelings of insult can constitute forgiveness.

However, there may be wrongs that are not insulting in any of the ways just mentioned. As a conceptual matter, could one nevertheless forgive another for such wrongs? The answer is that we forgive persons for doing wrong to us, and that there are wrongs that insult us and wrongs that do not.

Some philosophers have argued that serious moral wrongs, those that are deliberate, are essentially communicative acts—that is, acts that communicate important moral messages, in particular the message "you can be treated by me any way I like, I am not accountable to you for my actions, and you are impotent to do anything about it." Jeffrie Murphy, a major writer on forgiveness, has this view. "Wrongdoing," he says, "is in part a communicative act, an act that gives out a degrading or insulting message to the victim—the message 'I count and you do not, and I may thus use you as a mere thing.'"[14] Now as with any communicative act, for this communicative act to be successful, it must secure uptake from its intended target.[15] The target must correctly interpret the expressive meaning of the act and perceive that the wrongdoer is conveying (intentionally or otherwise) a degrading message by it. She must, that is, recognize the objectively insulting character of the act. Moreover, to recognize its objectively insulting character is to believe that feelings of insult in response to the act would be appropriate were she to have them. She will also frequently have them, not necessarily because her conviction of her own worth has been disturbed but because she has been treated badly by someone who believes he is entitled to treat her this way.

In terms of a communicative conception of wrongdoing, the wrongs for which a person is forgiven convey a demeaning or insulting message to the wronged party. Even if the person who forgives does not feel insulted, she would nevertheless view the wrongdoing as rendering feelings of insult appropriate or fitting responses were she to have them. (Nietzsche's masters would not and could not have them: it would be beneath them to have them.) Of course, not all wrongdoing is deliberate or shows ill will, and not all insults are intentional. Some wrongdoing may be a result of thoughtlessness or negligence. But unintended wrongs of this sort can also be insulting, depending on the circumstances. They are insulting if they result from a failure to take due care to protect the rights and interests of others because they are thought not to be important enough to do so. Moreover, unintended culpable wrongdoing can be as insulting as fully intended wrongdoing, although more commonly it is wrongdoing of the latter sort that is the subject of forgiveness.

However, not all wrongdoing, even serious and fully intended wrongdoing, is communicative in this way, and while there is not always a sharp line between wrongs that insult and those that do not, there are some clear examples of the latter. R. A. Duff gives the example of tax evasion: tax evaders, he argues, do not normally insult dutiful taxpayers by their actions, though they wrong them.[16] After all, the individual dutiful taxpayer is not the specific target of the evaders' free riding. Another example is the thief who randomly breaks into cars parked on the street, mine included, and who thus does not single mine out because he has some particular grievance against me.[17] As Eve Garrard and David McNaughton are right to point out, I can be wronged by actions that do not confront me as their target:

> If my car is stolen by someone wholly unknown to me, it would be odd to say, without a special context, that I resent it, and this is because it would be odd for me to regard myself as being personally slighted [and wrong for me to think that the wrongdoer was communicating anything whatsoever—to me or to anybody else]. The unknown thief does not pick on *me* [or on anyone else] (any car would do, mine just happens to be there).[18]

I would add that for this reason these actions cannot insult me, since I am only insulted by actions that target me, even if only by way of targeting a group with which I identify. Nevertheless—and this I want to underscore —in these cases it is still perfectly intelligible to hold that if the tax evader or thief is caught and his identity made known to one of the parties he wronged, he might be forgiven by the wronged party for the wrong he committed. Forgiveness may commonly be for wrongs that insult—that is, for wrongs that in a direct way violate a person's entitlements to equal respect or disappoint legitimate expectations of special care and attention. But there is nothing in the logic of forgiveness that limits the wrongs for which one may be forgiven to these.

To conclude, we now have some elements of an account of forgiveness that is suitable for persons who are less perfect and more vulnerable to challenges to self-worth than Nietzsche's noble souls. I have suggested that in order to make sense of forgiveness we need to understand the role of insult in it, although I have not argued, and have in fact denied, that all wrongful acts insult the victim and that forgiveness always involves overcoming feelings of insult. On a communicative conception of wrongdoing, wrongdoing does insult, either intentionally (with awareness or perhaps malice) or unintentionally (through negligence, thoughtlessness, insensitivity, etc.). Even then, however, the victim may not *feel* insulted: she may recognize the insulting character of a wrongdoer's actions without having the feelings of insult that commonly attend that recognition. As we might say, wrongful actions can be *objectively* without being *subjectively* insulting. Often, of course, it is otherwise: disappointed expectations of concern and respect or an attack on one's sense of self-worth are felt as painful by the victim.

When a person who is wronged has none of the feelings regularly associated with and indicating recognition of insult, is it still possible for forgiveness to be an option for her? This question arises against the background of a certain conception of forgiveness, a sentiment-based conception according to which the overcoming or renouncing of negative feelings caused by wrongdoing is an essential part of what forgiveness accomplishes. If this is what forgiveness involves, and if there are no feelings of insult, then we might be tempted to conclude that whatever the victim does for the offender, it could not count as forgiveness. However, this assumes, mistakenly, that feelings of insult are the only negative feelings that are caused by and respond to wrongdoing. Even without feelings of insult, there is a wide range of negative feelings associated with wrongs that are not insulting, including anger, anguish, fear, and many more. Overcoming these can, under the right conditions, count as forgiveness as well.

3. Forgiveness and feeling wronged

(a) Being wronged and being insulted

I do not want to link forgiveness too tightly to a communicational account of wrongdoing and to the notion of insult that is associated with it. One can have negative emotional responses to being wronged that are not feelings associated with being insulted, and one can forgive an offender even if feelings of insult do not fit the nature of the wrong that is committed. Nevertheless, feelings of insult are what I focus on here, for two reasons.

First, feelings of insult respond to wrongs that "pick on *me*" and for this reason may be particularly hard for the wronged party to forgive. The wrongs that are committed have a personal and possibly an intimate character that wrongs not specifically targeting me do not have, and overcoming them may be difficult, especially when someone with whom I have had a close personal relationship rejects me, or is insensitive to my needs, or betrays my trust. Of course, grievous wrongs that are not directed specifically at me are normally more difficult for me to forgive than lesser wrongs that are directed at me, and this shows that whether a wrong is insulting or not is not the only factor that affects the intensity of one's emotional reactions to it. But it is an important factor nonetheless, and other things being equal—that is, as between two wrongs that do roughly comparable injury apart from the fact that one insults and the other doesn't —the former is likely to pose special psychological challenges for the wronged party. The personal nature of insulting wrongs is often salient for the wronged party and compounds the injury she suffers, and the wrongs that forgiveness addresses, at least in serious cases, are commonly thought to strike home in this way.

There is another reason to highlight insult that has to do with the role that insult implicitly plays in the standard account of forgiveness. In the standard account, forgiveness is defined as the forswearing or letting go of resentment in particular, or of some other negative emotions that "embody or perpetuate key features of resentment."[19] Though there are other varieties of moral anger that forgiveness overcomes, resentment is typically taken to be the central case. Moreover, resentment is an emotion associated with insult. It is not only a way of responding to insulting or degrading messages but an emotion that arguably doesn't make sense except as a response to insult. As Gerard and McNaughton note, it would be odd, barring some unusual context, to claim to resent being wronged by another if the wrong did not constitute a personal slight, which I take to mean if it did not communicate an insulting message aimed at the wronged party. Now as I have said, I want to amend the standard conception of forgiveness in certain ways. But preserving the connection between the emotions that forgiveness overcomes and insult is more in line with the orientation of the standard account than severing the link to insult, and I regard it as a selling point in favor of my revision that it takes the spirit if not the letter of that account seriously.

Still, it may be argued that the notion of insult fails to capture the seriousness of many moral wrongs. When we think of insult, we usually have in mind something like a violation of conventional norms of good manners or a display of some type of discourtesy or minor offense, and this doesn't get at the wrongness of serious wrongdoing at all. If we think of insult in this way, then we can appreciate how someone might say, quoting Jerome Neu, "In rape, or murder, the injury is so great that any insult involved may be the least of one's concerns."[20] Insult can also sometimes be added to or accompany injury (as in the expression "adding insult to injury"), and when it is, it compounds the distress caused by it. But in these cases, the argument goes, the injury is one thing, the insult something else, detachable from it. In response, I acknowledge that there are insults that fit these descriptions. There are insults that involve minor harms or mere offenses. Persons can also suffer injuries that do not insult, as when the mover accidently drops a box on my toe and breaks it or when my father who is suffering from Alzheimer's disease lashes out at me. However, insult, as I am here thinking of it, is different and not a contingent add-on to injury. Insults can be to a person's dignity as a human being, even if he is confident that he possesses it; they can violate a person's human rights; they can undermine trust in persons who have played a central role in one's life and damage valued relationships that have partially constituted one's identity. In short, serious wrongs can be morally insulting because they reach to core ingredients of the self and the bases of self-respect. Moreover, in cases of this sort where the wronged party is harmed, the insult is inseparable from the harm, an essential ingredient of the particular sort of injury that it is. The notion of insult is needed, therefore, to capture an essential aspect of the wrongness of a certain kind of moral harm. And as just noted, this kind of harm has played a central role in the standard account of forgiveness.

(b) Feelings associated with being wronged and insulted

Negative feelings associated with wrongs that insult overlap negative feelings associated with wrongs that do not insult, and overcoming feelings associated with either can constitute forgiveness. I mainly cast the following overview in terms of the former, however, since feelings of insult figure prominently in most discussions of forgiveness in the psychological and philosophical literatures. They either assume that the wrongs that can be forgiven are wrongs that target or concern specific individuals, so insult them, or treat these as the paradigm cases. The wrongs may be intentional or unintentional, a result of negligence or indifference, and the disrespect or insufficient respect they exhibit is objectively and possibly subjectively insulting.

Two preliminary points are in order. First, while these feelings can be of variable duration, they are generally not transient. It is possible to be vexed or unsettled or annoyed by some relatively inconsequential matter only for a moment, but feelings of insult—as well as the feelings that victims of serious wrongdoing experience—typically last for some time beyond the initial wrongdoing. Indeed, too rapid a recovery from these feelings may call into question whether this is a case of feeling insulted at all. The persistence of feelings of insult is explained by the fact that they arise because of disappointed expectations of equal concern and respect or special care from close others. In extreme cases, they arise in response to degrading messages that worsen the perceived evidence of one's self-worth. Even if it is not conceptual of insult, insults are typically not "shake[n] off with a single shrug." I may try to shrug it off, but the wrongdoing that insulted me is not so easily forgotten, and as long as I remember it, I may continue to feel insulted by it to some degree, even after I have forgiven the wrongdoer for it.

Second, most people respond to wrongs that insult as well as those that do not with some type of negative emotion. At a minimum, negative emotions are partly constituted by a particular desire: as Robert Gordon says,[21] when one has a negative emotion about the fact that p, one wishes it not to be the case that p. It is certainly possible to respond to wrongdoing and the wrongdoer with positive emotions—for example, to have compassion for the offender. But compassion, while important in explaining how the wronged party is able to forgive her offender, is not an emotion of insult—that is, an emotion that involves pain or distress in response to perceived wrongdoing directed at oneself. Nor is compassion an emotion that registers the wrongness of wrongdoing. Further, feelings of insult are painful or at least in some manner unpleasant. The degree of this distress can vary depending on the circumstances, from relatively subdued to intense. Finally, the pain or distress has a specifically moral dimension. I will say more about this later. For now, I note that the person feels pained or distressed by (moral) insult because another has done something morally wrong to *her* and because she understands it for what it is.

There is a rich phenomenology of feelings of insult. Annoyance and irritation are negative emotions that respond to minor offenses or inconveniences—Robert Solomon characterizes them as "trivial or minimally accusatory versions of anger"[22]—but they are too tame for the feelings associated with insult or with significant wrongdoing and too tepid for the kind of wrongdoing that people considering forgiveness often have to struggle with. Better candidates for the emotions associated with insult include, among others, resentment, hatred, vengefulness, and spite, a family of negative emotions that Paul Hughes labels "angry emotions"[23] and that I call *retributive emotions*. These are emotions that figure prominently in most accounts of forgiveness,[24] and they are understood to be natural responses to wrongful acts that have a retributive aim—that is, to *get back at* or *even with* the offender or to make him *suffer* for what he has done. Some of these emotions have non-moral as well as moral versions: for example, there is non-moral as well as moral hatred. However, the angry emotions that are mentioned in the context of forgiveness are typically constituted by the belief that a wrong has been done to oneself and that the offender deserves to pay for it. I may be indignant at a wrong done to others and believe the offender deserves to pay for it and even that I should be the one to make him suffer. But it is commonly assumed, even if it is not conceptual of forgiveness, that the party with the standing to forgive is in the first instance the victim. Third parties are considered potential forgivers only if they have some relationship with the victim such that harm to him is also harm to them or if the victim has authorized them to forgive on his behalf.[25]

The members of the family of retributive emotions differ from one another in important ways. The aim of hatred, Solomon asserts, "is to destroy or at the very least humiliate the other." Spite, says Solomon, has "a much more convoluted logic in which self-destruction is on a par with the damage to others."[26] Vengefulness or revenge also seeks to punish the offender and inflict harm on him, but there is often the suggestion that the harm is inflicted for the pleasure of inflicting it. According to Trudy Govier, revenge involves "the desire to bring harm to another so that one may contemplate with satisfaction that harm and one's role in bringing it about."[27] And so on. Characterizing the often subtle differences between these various negative emotions is a large task and surprisingly harder than one might think.

The feelings associated with insult are even more varied than this, and not only because there are other types of retributive emotions I have not mentioned. Neu observes the following:

> It is a commonplace that anger consumes the angry person. But why is that so? Surely part of the answer is that it consumes his thoughts. His attention is directed at the object of his ire, and he dwells on his

grievances and on thoughts of revenge ... The wound in feeling insulted can be similarly consuming. Does that make feeling insulted a species of anger? Not necessarily.[28]

Feeling insulted is not necessarily a species of anger because there are other emotional responses to wrongdoing and ways of feeling insulted by it that do not have anger's characteristic desire and aim, which is to get back at or even with the offender (accompanied by a belief that it is appropriate to do so). Neu mentions several, including feelings of dejection and hurt feelings. Feelings of disappointment should be included as well, as one sort of painful or distressed response to disappointed expectations of respectful regard and caring attention. These feelings of insult may occur along with or instead of feelings of anger and they may or may not cause the victim to get angry. There is in fact quite a variety of negative feelings associated with insult that have this psychological profile. In addition to disappointment and hurt, a partial list would include grief, sadness, mistrust, fear, dejection, and humiliation.

I propose to call the negative emotions and feelings that respond to wrongdoing in this way *non-retributive emotions*. They are, to use a contrasting expression to what Hughes labels "angry emotions," non-angry (or non-hostile) emotions. None of these essentially involves the desire to strike back at the offender that is characteristic of anger.[29] Take sadness, for instance. Patricia Greenspan notes the following difference between it and anger:

> Even impersonal anger, or what might be called "frustration-anger," seems to be essentially connected to desire, in a way that sadness at a perceived injury is not. It involves not just a wish that things were otherwise, that is, but also an urge to act to change them somehow ... to take some sort of aggressive action in response.[30]

Fear also differs from anger in not being essentially connected to the desire to take aggressive action, since "fear of something viewed as inescapable may simply involve a state of passive dread."[31] This is true of all non-retributive negative emotions, by definition: their connection to a desire to take aggressive action is only contingent and often lacking. Yet though they differ in various and many ways from retributive emotions, non-retributive negative emotions are painful feelings that can resemble anger in the respect that they are caused by not receiving the respect or attention or concern that one expects and believes one is entitled to. Anger is only one of the emotions that we feel when we feel insulted, and we can feel insulted even if we don't feel angry and even if we forswear angry feelings. Since there are many different ways to register the perception of insult emotionally—as well as the perception of serious wrongdoing that does not

The Moral Psychology of Interpersonal Forgiveness 35

insult—there are many different sorts of emotional response to wrongdoing that a wronged party might have to overcome in order to forgive his wrongdoer.

I do not mean to suggest by the distinction between non-angry and angry emotions, however, that people respond to wrongdoing with either one type of negative emotion or the other. The distinction is introduced for analytic purposes only and is not intended to track people's actual psychological responses to wrongdoing. These responses are more complex and multilayered than the simple distinction between angry and non-angry emotions suggests.

For one thing, there are negative emotional responses to wrongdoing that I call *hybrid* emotional responses, which involve the intermingling of both retributive and non-retributive elements. Consider disappointment, for example. Disappointment is not essentially a hybrid, since one can feel disappointed in someone for failing to live up to one's expectations without also being angry at him. However, it is sometimes—perhaps often—a hybrid of anger, hurt, and grief. In psychodynamic terms, the one who is wronged is or remains angry, but his anger hides behind his disappointment and is not fully owned. He is shielded by his disappointment from feeling the full impact of his anger. Fear, by contrast, seems less clearly an occasional hybrid emotion than disappointment, perhaps because it is a more primitive response than disappointment.[32]

Another example of non-retributive feelings of insult is hurt feelings, a term that sometimes refers to what a range of feelings of insult have in common and sometimes, more narrowly, to a particular type of such feelings with a particular etiology and cognitive content.[33] As to whether hurt feelings in the latter sense are true amalgamations of various negative emotions, there appears to be no conclusive psychological evidence that hurt feelings are synchronically complex rather than just feelings with complex emotional sequelae. According to psychologists Mark Leary and Carrie Springer, it remains an open question "whether victims experience hurt at precisely the same time they feel anxious, guilty, surprised, sad, or angry, or whether these reactions are experienced sequentially."[34] Nevertheless, they believe that "hurt feelings possess a unique subjective quality that differs from other aversive feelings,"[35] and they grant that hurt feelings are at least often "accompanied by" feelings of rejection, anxiety, and hostility.[36]

Further complicating the phenomenology of feelings of insult is the fact that there are causal relationships between non-retributive and retributive emotions. For example, feelings of humiliation and shame, which are non-retributive in nature, are among the emotions that are commonly associated with insult, and a natural response to the person who has humiliated or shamed oneself is to get angry. The causal relation can go in the other direction as well: a person can feel ashamed of getting angry at another if, say, she has been taught that anger is an unseemly emotion. Similarly, a victim who is grief-stricken at another's having robbed her of something or someone precious might well come to hate the offender as a consequence of this.

In short, there are the following possible patterns of emotional response to insulting wrongs: retributive emotions can cause or accompany non-retributive ones or be the only type of response to being wronged; non-retributive ones can cause or accompany retributive ones or be the only type of response to being wronged; and some emotional reactions are amalgamations of retributive and non-retributive negative emotions. Non-retributive and retributive emotions may be difficult to tease apart, experientially and experimentally, and it may be difficult to determine whether some non-retributive emotion is best understood as an amalgamation of various negative emotions or as separable from them. Nevertheless, the logic of the non-retributive emotions, and of the non-retributive components of hybrid emotions, is distinguishable from that of the retributive ones, so that neither type of emotion can do the work of the other.

The implications of these remarks on the phenomenology of emotional response to insult—and again I do not want to suggest that forgiveness only overcomes the emotions caused by insulting wrongs—for the moral psychology of forgiveness is obvious: since there is a variety of ways in which persons respond to insult, the negative emotions that forgiveness overcomes, if they are of this type, should include more than the angry emotions. Fundamentally, forgiveness works on how one responds emotionally to perceived wrongdoing, and more narrowly to wrongdoing that insults, and thereby on how one affectively regards the offender, not on what one wants to *inflict* upon the one who has committed the wrong. The latter is only a special case. To be sure, reactions to being wronged often involve such emotions as resentment, bitterness, anger, and hatred. But they might not, or might not only involve emotions such as these, and forgiveness could make sense in these cases because of the existence of non-retributive emotions that have or have not yet been overcome. Feelings of hurt, sadness, disappointment, and the like can be how the victim experiences insult and be so deep-seated that they impede her ability to forgive: they do not just linger *after* the offender has been forgiven. Even if anger is present, it may subside and be replaced by a more abiding feeling of hurt or disappointment or sadness, so that there remains work for forgiveness to do. For these reasons, we need a more capacious account of the emotional landscape of forgiveness than the standard account provides.

4. Forgiveness, retribution, and blame

(a) Blame and negative emotions

Retributive emotions like anger and resentment are punitive in that they aim for the offender to suffer in some way because of what he has done, and usually the more intense the emotion the more severe the suffering that is intended. They are also thought to be warranted in response to significant wrongdoing and, indeed, to be *the* right or virtuous type of response to it. There are at least two issues to consider in relation to these claims. One is whether it is good or fitting that a wrongdoer experience some type of suffering because of what he has done; the other is whether he should be punished for it and whether the uniquely appropriate sort of emotional response to it is retributive. An affirmative answer to the first question does not entail an affirmative answer to the second. That is, one could believe that there is value in the wrongdoer suffering because of his wrongdoing but not that hard treatment should be imposed on him in response to it. My argument here will be that while censure or blame can cause the wrongdoer deserved suffering, blame can be adequately expressed and communicated in other ways than by imposing hard treatment on the wrongdoer and without the hard feelings that seek to inflict it.

The fundamental retributivist idea is that culpable wrongdoers should be given what they deserve and that either they deserve to suffer or should be made to suffer so that they get what they deserve. This view about the appropriateness of making wrongdoers suffer may explain why retributive emotions are given a special place in the moral psychology of response to wrongdoing. But why should they be made to suffer? Some retributivists say it is because it is intrinsically good that they suffer. Others claim instead that it is intrinsically appropriate for wrongdoers to be blamed or censured for their actions and that imposing suffering on the wrongdoer is the best vehicle for conveying this. For retributivists of either stripe it is not sufficient merely to withdraw good will, respect, or recognition from the wrongdoer. Rather, the wrongdoer must be called to account for his wrongdoing. As Christopher Bennett puts it in his especially clear statement of the rationale for retributivism,[37] he ought to engage in some form of penance, "which is something one does to *expiate* wrongdoing" (113). The penance must involve suffering of some sort because this is the only way that one can truly expiate wrongdoing. Retributivists also claim that suffering is necessary for full understanding of the wrongness of one's actions. Bennett again: "certain specific types of suffering are necessary for wrongdoers to experience in the context of their coming fully to understand the significance of what they have done" (118). Getting them to understand the significance of what they have done may be all that retributivists aim for. But they may also have a further goal, namely the moral improvement of the wrongdoer. Imposing hard treatment on a wrongdoer is supposed to accomplish this by bringing home to him, in an especially powerful way, the wrongness of his actions.

There may be value in a wrongdoer's suffering as a result of what he has done. Suffering in the form of guilt or shame shows that the wrongdoer appreciates and takes seriously the moral significance of his actions, and it may motivate him to seek through moral improvement to become a better sort of person. But it does not follow that retributive censure—that is, censure that involves punishing the wrongdoer by imposing hard treatment on him—is the only fully adequate way to respond to serious wrongdoing, even if one aims at the moral improvement of the offender. We need to draw, and it is possible to draw, a distinction here between suffering as the aim of censure and suffering as a consequence or by-product of censure. Actions motivated by and expressive of non-retributive negative emotions may cause wrongdoers to experience pain and suffering even if the aim is not to punish them, and this can be valuable for the reasons just mentioned. Martin Luther King, Jr. and Mahatma Gandhi provide instructive counterexamples to retributivist claims about the unique importance of retributive emotions as responses to wrongdoing.[38]

King and Gandhi were not just filled with love and compassion for those who supported unjust laws and policies; and they did not hold their oppressors blameless for the injustices they perpetrated against their people. On the contrary, they blamed them and held them accountable for those injustices. Commonly, however, King and Gandhi are cited as examples of morally admirable individuals who, as R. Jay Wallace characterizes them, "demanded conformity with important moral principles but forswore malicious or punitive responses toward those who had flouted such principles in the past."[39] Their purpose in breaking the law was to nonviolently bring about a change in the laws and policies of the government, and they appealed to the sense of justice of the community and its officials and leaders to accomplish this. They believed not only that the community and people in powerful positions were capable of recognizing the legitimacy of their complaints, but also that it was reasonable to expect them to make the changes necessary to meet their demands. Further, to a significant extent their beliefs were vindicated, and not because those who upheld the status quo were the target of malicious or punitive responses motivated by retributive emotions. In fact it is doubtful that King or Gandhi would have accomplished what they did had they not forsworn malicious or punitive responses. At the same time, King and Gandhi did not forswear all negative emotional responses to the wrongs they were protesting, for they were deeply distressed by the injustices they confronted. Their responses were just of a different character from the retributive emotions that might have motivated others to retaliate with hostility and violence.

King and Gandhi clearly blamed those who supported and implemented an unjust system, but the dominant feelings that accompanied and drove their protests were not retributive. What this suggests is that even if we accept that blame always or typically involves emotional responses that go beyond a simple negative moral evaluation, we can nevertheless deny that these emotional responses must be retributive. In other words, we can hold that there is a close connection between blame and negative emotions but not that these emotions must be retributive: they might instead be non-retributive or what

I have called hybrid negative emotions. There is, of course, one difference between retributive and non-retributive negative emotions that should be mentioned here: retributive emotions like anger and resentment are intrinsically blaming emotions, whereas non-retributive emotions like sadness, hurt, grief, and dejection are not. (Disappointment is different from other non-retributive emotions in being both non-retributive and an emotion of blame or disapproval.[40]) But this difference is not as significant for an account of blame as it may appear, for non-retributive emotions may motivate one to take a stand against wrongdoing no less than retributive ones. In addition, non-retributive emotions may be communicated to a wrongdoer in a way that makes clear he is being held blameworthy for his actions. The victim of violence who communicates her grief to her offender with the intention of letting him know that he is the cause of it may be blaming him for it, even if she has no desire to pay him back for what he has done. By not keeping her grief to herself but communicating it to her offender, she may be expressing moral criticism of him for his objectionable actions. She needn't *show* anger, nor does she need to *get* angry or have retaliatory feelings in order for her attitude toward her offender to count as blame.

Two recent philosophical accounts of the nature of blame present somewhat similar views on the role of negative emotions in it. George Sher wonders if it is sufficient for blame that I believe another has acted badly and desire it to be the case that he not have acted badly.[41] It may seem not, for I can believe that someone has acted badly and desire that he not have done so even when I am not disposed to do anything about it or to have any emotional reactions to it whatsoever. I may desire that he not have acted as he did, but not be angry at him for acting this way, or disappointed in him, or indeed have any emotions of disapproval or bad feelings toward him at all. Perhaps this is because I think it's not my place to blame him and that this should be reserved for someone else, the one who was harmed by him. But if this is what I think, then I must believe that the relevant belief–desire pair falls short of blame.

Sher considers the possibility of "affectless blame" (88), blame that is not accompanied by hostile feelings or even a withdrawal of good will, and concludes that even without affect, an attitude can be one of blame, although he admits this claim is controversial. Nonetheless, he believes blame is not usually like this:

> When we blame someone, we may feel—among other things—anger, resentment, irritation, bitterness, hostility, fury, rage, outrage, disappointment, contempt, disdain, or disgust. Although these feelings differ in important ways, each is always negative and, when it accompanies blame, is always directed at a particular person. (94)

Blame, then, is usually if not always an attitude that engages our emotions, specifically negative emotions. It involves being disposed to have a range of negative feelings toward a wrongdoer that are rooted in the belief that he has acted badly, and when negative feelings accompany blame, they are directed at the wrongdoer. People are often angry with those whom they blame, but more properly understood, blame involves the withdrawal of good will from a wrongdoer, and there is no specific negative emotion, or one type of negative emotion, that indicates this.[42]

T. M. Scanlon's account of blame is similar[43]: negative emotions do not play a central role in blame, although blame is sometimes, perhaps often, accompanied by negative emotions. Blame not only doesn't essentially involve having hostile feelings toward the wrongdoer. It need not involve rebuking feelings of any kind. Rather, his account emphasizes the attitudes displayed by the wrongdoer toward the wronged party and how they affect the relationship that the wronged party can have with him. "To blame a person," he says, "is to judge him or her to be blameworthy and to take your relationship with him or her to be modified in a way that this judgment of impaired relations holds to be appropriate" (128). Blame is to be understood in relational terms, since judging someone to be blameworthy for an action "is to claim that the action shows something about the agent's attitudes toward others that impairs the relations that others can have with him or her" (ibid.), as a consequence of which it is appropriate for these others to revise their attitudes toward him or her. Individuals legitimately make certain demands of one another that are determined by the standards that are appropriate to the kind of relationship they participate in. When one of the participants displays attitudes toward the other that are incompatible with these demands, the relationship is impaired, and depending on the kind of attitude revealed, the wronged party may either end the relationship altogether or modify it to a greater or lesser degree. Presumably in the more serious cases the wronged party will want to cut off the relationship, to make clear that she blames the wrongdoer. Whatever happens to the relationship, what is central to blame, in Scanlon's view, is the revision of intentions and expectations that the wronged party has with regard to the wrongdoer, in light of the attitudes displayed by the wrongdoer toward her.

This revision may or may not be registered in emotional terms, but when blame is affective, the negative emotions are not always retributive, contrary to what is commonly thought. The wronged party might feel resentment or indignation, but there might be other negative emotions instead. According to Scanlon, "I might just feel sad" (136), "sad that the person has turned out to be such a reprobate."[44] Sadness, that is, may accompany the revision of attitude that is appropriate in light of the other's violation of the standards internal to their relationship. It can be the emotion that characterizes how the wronged party feels

The Moral Psychology of Interpersonal Forgiveness

about the attitude that the wrongdoer displays; and it can signal a disruption in their relationship and mark a change in the wronged party's attitude to the wrongdoer. When the feeling of sadness plays this role, when it accompanies blame, whether it is expressed outwardly or not, it targets the wrongdoer as its cause. The wronged party's sadness may also be communicated to him.

Some philosophers have more closely connected blame and negative emotions than either Sher or Scanlon do. R. Jay Wallace,[45] for example, has argued at considerable length that an adequate account of blame includes an emotional component. Fortunately for my purposes in this chapter it is not necessary to decide between a cognitive or conative account of blame and an emotive account according to which negative emotional responses are constituent ingredients of blame.[46] It is enough to have established that when there are blame-related bad feelings, the negative emotions need not be retributive, but include non-retributive negative (and hybrid negative emotions) as well. Blame is often experienced emotionally and displayed in behavior through which these feelings are expressed, and my argument for not limiting these emotions to retributive ones has the same structure as the argument I gave in the last section concerning the emotions associated with insult. Just as I can feel insulted in a wide variety of ways, there are diverse negative emotions that blaming someone can add to a cognitive assessment of fault. In fact, there is more than a parallel here: the list of emotions that accompany insult and the list of emotions that accompany blame overlap. But blame is not necessarily accompanied by negative emotions any more than insulting actions are necessarily felt as such.

(b) Two objections answered

There are two objections that might be raised to the implications of these remarks about blame for an account of forgiveness. One has to do with the alleged non-directedness of some of the non-retributive emotions mentioned above. Emotions like anger and hatred are directed at the wrongdoer, the argument goes, so they are responses to wrongdoing that best express one's appreciation of the wrongness of what he has done. They are also for this reason the emotions that ought to figure centrally in an account of forgiveness. The other objection has to do with the relationship between negative emotions and moral norms. The argument here is that only certain negative emotions—resentment, for example—are moral in the sense that they are intrinsically linked to morality, and this makes them especially appropriate as responses to wrongdoing. Moreover, this is why forgiveness ought to be defined chiefly in terms of overcoming or forswearing them. I will consider these objections in order.

The "directedness" of negative emotions that accompany blame has been noted by some philosophers as the key feature that differentiates negative emotions that forgiveness overcomes from those it does not. According to Glen Pettigrove, emotional responses to a blameworthy action or trait of character are quite varied and include, in addition to anger and resentment, "hatred, loathing, contempt, disgust, or sadness." However, he holds that not all of these are emotions that forgiveness overcomes. Sadness is one that is not. His argument runs as follows.

(1) Sadness is a negative feeling that "falls into a different conceptual class than anger, resentment, hatred, and contempt."

(2) Sadness is not "other-directed" in the way these others feelings are.

(3) Only emotions that are other-directed in this way are emotions that forgiveness overcomes.

Therefore, (4) sadness should not be included among the emotions that forgiveness overcomes.[47]

I grant premise (2): we are not sad *at* someone or *with* someone (not to be confused with sharing someone's sadness) or *toward* someone. But I reject premise (3). Sadness, when it accompanies blame, *is* other-directed, only not in the very same way that these other emotions are. In the relevant cases, A is made sad by B's wrongful act or by what his wrongful act shows B to be, and her sadness is how she emotionally registers her blame of B. It is therefore centered on B as its cause, so has him in its crosshairs, and this is sufficient reason to include it among the emotions that can be overcome by forgiveness. Moreover, A's sadness will likely be communicated in some way to B, as well as to others. When it is communicated directly to B, the implicit centering of A's sadness on B is made explicit. Even if A communicates her sadness to someone other than B, it is what B has done that makes her sad. Her sadness is not unmoored from a target but colors how she regards B.

The second objection is that while sadness and other non-retributive emotions can be our dominant feelings when we blame someone, resentment in particular—the emotion that plays a prominent role in the standard account of forgiveness—is not just one emotion among others that can accompany blame. Rather, it is a particularly apt response to wrongdoing, and it is so because it is a *moral* emotion, unlike other emotional responses to wrongdoing that I have mentioned. John Rawls characterizes moral emotions this way:

> In general, it is a necessary feature of moral feelings, and part of what distinguishes them from the natural attitudes, that the person's explanation of his experience invokes a moral concept and its associated principles. His account of his feeling makes reference to an acknowledged right or wrong.[48]

Resentment, for Rawls, is a moral feeling that is partially constituted by the belief that one has been wrongfully harmed. If a person is asked to explain why he feels resentful, he will normally invoke a concept of moral injury and appeal in some fashion to the principle that one should not be subjected to harm undeservedly, although he may not self-consciously embrace it as a principle or be able to fully articulate it. Herein lies a difference between resentment (and indignation too) and the non-angry negative emotions mentioned above: resentment is a moral emotion because it necessarily makes reference to moral concepts and principles, whereas this is not true of disappointment and the other non-angry feelings. I can be saddened by the fact that my daughter has taken a job in another city; disappointed that I did not make the college football team; hurt by my friend's spending a lot of time with other people instead of me; and so on. These sorts of feelings need not accompany blame, and I can also have them without feeling insulted. So sadness, hurt, disappointment, etc. are much less significant for forgiveness than resentment and other negative emotions that are intrinsically bound up with moral norms.

There is an obvious *tu quoque* response to this objection. The standard account of forgiveness does not just have resentment as the emotion that forgiveness overcomes. Rather, it admits many forms of anger, including animosity, malice, wrath, vengefulness, and so on, and a person's explanation of these feelings only sometimes invokes moral norms. So why exclude non-retributive emotions? The critic could bite the bullet and say he was wrong to admit other kinds of anger and that the only emotion that forgiveness overcomes is resentment (and some similarly morally constituted emotion). Or he could say, more plausibly in my view, that in order for a retributive emotion to figure as one of the emotions that forgiveness may need to overcome, it is not necessary for it to be an emotion that essentially invokes moral concepts and principles. It is enough that in the particular situation the wronged party confronts these emotions are explained by and embody her belief that she has been wronged. This belief both renders her susceptible to certain negative emotions and validates her having them. But if other forms of anger should be included when and only when they are partially constituted by the belief that one has been wrongfully harmed, the same could be said of non-retributive emotions like disappointment, grief, and hurt, or of retributive/non-retributive hybrids. These emotions are sometimes constituted by the required belief, so they should not be categorically excluded from the emotions that forgiveness overcomes or marginalized.

What makes some instances of negative emotions apt for inclusion in an account of forgiveness and some not can be explained in part by the presence of a particular grounding belief, the belief that one has been wrongfully harmed. Moral anger, moral disappointment, moral hurt, and moralized instances of other non-retributive emotions depend on and are partially constituted by the judgment that there has been a moral offense committed against oneself. Non-moral anger, non-moral disappointment, non-moral hurt, and so forth, do not arise in response to the violation of some moral norm. We experience them without judging that we have been wronged, and overcoming them is not what forgiveness is about.

There is an additional and related way to distinguish between moral and non-moral tokens of retributive, non-retributive, and hybrid negative emotion types, namely in terms of the appropriateness of feelings of guilt or shame. To illustrate, we can contrast two cases of disappointment: one is non-moral (e.g., disappointment at losing a fair race); the other is moral (e.g., disappointment that arises when we expect our friend to be honest with us and he is not). There is nothing to forgive anyone for in the first case (I assume that no moral objection can be raised to the circumstances and outcome of the race); in the second case there is something to forgive the friend for, although in the end he might not be forgiven. Further, in the first case, if the losing runner were to put himself in the shoes of the other contestants or race officials, he would not, looking at the situation from their perspective, have any reason to feel shame or guilt for having beaten him or for having organized the race as they did. But the second case is plainly different, for if the disappointed friend were to put himself in the shoes of the one who did not live up to the other's expectations of him and to assess what he had done from that perspective, he would have reason to feel guilt and perhaps shame as well. Thus, if one is uncertain how to classify what one is feeling, the following general test for whether the negative emotion is moral or only a non-moral analogue suggests itself: adopt the position of the one who caused you to react this way and, judging what was done from that position, consider whether you would be justified in feeling guilt or shame if you treated the other the way the other treated you. It is a moral emotion if you would be justified, non-moral if you would not be. If the wrongdoing is extremely minor or barely significant, the test might yield no definitive conclusion as to whether the negative emotion is moral or a non-moral analogue. But in many other cases, this sort of evaluative test will yield a clear verdict one way or the other.

(c) Blame after having forgiven

I want to close this section by returning to the subject of forgiveness and asking whether, on these different accounts of blame, forgiveness precludes blame. That is, once we have forgiven a wrongdoer, is continuing to blame him for his wrongful acts any longer appropriate or justified? The answer is often assumed to be no, but I want to argue for an opposing view.

According to Scanlon, blame consists in reorienting the relationship one had with a wrongdoer in order to better match attitudes held by the wrongdoer that

The Moral Psychology of Interpersonal Forgiveness   45

are precluded by the standards of that relationship. If, for instance, a friend has failed to act consistently with the basic demands of our friendship, "I might . . . cease to value spending time with him in the way one does with a friend and I might revise my intentions to confide in him and to encourage him to confide in me" (129–130). These and other modifications in our relationship are appropriate in light of the fact that my so-called friend has acted incompatibly with what is normative for friendship, so has impaired our relationship. The negative emotions that accompany this reorientation may be anger, disappointment, sadness, and so on. The question is whether, having forgiven the wrongdoer, some sort of reorientation in how I relate to him may be justified and appropriate. The answer, I believe, is yes. Forgiveness does not necessarily wipe the slate clean, and this means in part that it does not necessarily restore the relationship to its prior state, emotionally or behaviorally. Margaret Walker gives the following illustration:

> Consider the common case of a spouse betrayed by infidelity who forswears further recriminations, denunciations to others, and withdrawal from intimacies of sex and companionship with his wife; he may go forward with their joined lives with good will and resolution that the past is past. But he may be unable not to feel many things when the memory of his wife's unfaithfulness is stirred; and there may be, for all his resolution, some vibrancy and hopefulness, some playfulness and silly freedoms that he will not recapture. It seems entirely reasonable to think that he has forgiven on the basis of his rejoining the relationship, and the attempts he makes not to let residual feelings of anger, sadness, and fear get in the way of this.[49]

I do not see why the changes in the husband's feelings, attitudes, and behaviors have to be regarded as showing unreasonable stubbornness, a refusal to forgive, or an obsessive preoccupation with past wrongs. If this is correct, then cases of forgiveness can involve two sorts of emotional, attitudinal, and behavioral changes: there are those resulting from the wrongdoing when the wrongdoer has not been forgiven and those that persist after the wrongdoer has been forgiven. Moreover, both sorts of changes, on Scanlon's view, could count as responses to wrongdoing that are forms of blame. The character of the blame in Walker's example changes after the wife has been forgiven: the relationship between the spouses is no longer impaired in the way it was before the husband forgave her. But the important point is that it is still impaired. The remaining changes in attitude toward her, the alteration in the husband's feelings despite having forgiven her, arguably signify that he still blames her for her infidelity. Forgiveness does not necessarily wipe the slate clean of negative emotions or blame, nor is it necessarily evidence of some moral failing if it does not.

Sometimes, as in Walker's example, one cannot help but continue to blame another, despite one's best efforts to put the past behind one. It might be said in response that then it must be the case that one hasn't really forgiven the other person, since forgiveness overcomes negative feelings and repairs relationships. But this oversimplifies the moral psychology of response to wrongdoing. Forgiving another person doesn't mean that the relationship with him or her has been fully repaired or that they have reconciled. One might forgive another person because one believes that there is still something in the relationship with him or her that is worth salvaging, or in the hope that one can salvage it, but one might find that one cannot overlook the damage that has been done. Should we say then that one continues to blame the offender? To answer "no" is, I think, to subscribe to an overly idealistic picture of forgiveness.[50]

The standard view of forgiveness might be able to accept this explanation of how one can forgive and continue to blame. But in another respect, Scanlon's view raises a problem for it. According to the standard account, forgiveness entails or consists in a marked change of emotional response. The blame expressed in resentment or some other hostile emotion is overcome or forsworn, and if negative feelings that are not forsworn persist, they will necessarily be different in kind. For Scanlon, however, resentment is only one of the emotions that can accompany blame, and one can blame without feeling resentment at all. There may instead be any of a variety of negative feelings: I may feel angry, but also upset, disappointed, or just sad. And if a wronged party can continue to blame his wrongdoer even after forgiving her, this blame can also be accompanied by disappointment, upset, or sadness. The sharp distinction in the standard account between the emotional responses to wrongdoers before and after forgiving them, therefore, gets blurred in Scanlon's account of blame. I will have more to say about this in the next chapter when I discuss what I call "the differentiation problem."

Sher gives a different explanation of why forgiveness does not consist in renouncing blame. He claims that blaming is a two-tiered phenomenon. At the first tier there is a belief–desire pair: a belief that the wrongdoer acted badly or had a bad character along with the desire that he not have acted this way or had this character. Affectivity enters the picture at the second tier: this consists in dispositional mental phenomena that have as their source the frustration of the desire in the first tier. Sher uses this two-tiered account to explain how one can continue to blame the wrongdoer even after he has been forgiven: "we need only restrict the renunciation of which forgiveness consists to the dispositions in blame's second tier."[51] He says this is a "satisfying view," since it preserves the core of his account of blame, but it seems to me quite problematic. For even though one can continue to blame the wrongdoer if one has forgiven him, the blame will be dispassionate since forgiveness wipes the slate clean of all negative emotions elicited by his prior wrongdoing. The belief–desire pair remains in place: it's just the emotional and behavioral responses that are jettisoned. This, however, strikes me as too great a price to pay to salvage Sher's account. To be sure, this is a possible conception of forgiveness: it cannot be ruled out on conceptual grounds. But it mischaracterizes forgiveness from both phenomenological and psychological standpoints, so does not agree with our ordinary understandings and experiences of forgiveness.

5. Forgiveness, negative emotions, and self-respect

The final moral phenomenon I want to explore as it relates to forgiveness is self-respect. Specifically, I am especially interested in the role that negative emotions play as markers or signifiers of self-respect. First, however, some general remarks about self-respect.

Not all moral norm violations trigger the sorts of concern that center on self-respect, nor should they. There is, after all, such a thing as overvaluing one's dignity, exaggerating the seriousness of the wrongs committed against oneself, having too thin a skin, morally speaking. However, sometimes violations can only be "shrugged off" at some risk to one's self-respect, and it is norm violations of this sort that have figured in the standard account of forgiveness.[52] Serious moral norm violations that involve wrongs that personally target another person threaten in an especially clear way the basis of the wronged party's self-respect, and someone with self-respect will want to make it known that she cannot be mistreated with impunity. By adapting to or acquiescing in such norm violations when it is possible to take a stand against them, the wronged party tacitly confirms the opinion of herself that the wrongdoer's act expresses, namely that she is not worthy of or has no right to better treatment. A self-respecting person, however, will resist the imputation of moral inferiority. She will reject the message that the wrongdoer sends, namely that she is of little account and deserves no better, and she may protest against it in order to assure herself that she has not lost her self-respect. Self-respect is something that a self-respecting person values, so she will want to retain it, to claim it against those who would impugn it, and to give evidence to herself and others that she has it. What she does out of self-respect she does because it matters to her that she have and know herself to have self-respect, and also in order to affirm her commitment to values that are central to her personal and moral identity. So it goes according to a widely accepted account.

One sort of evidence that a wronged party has or retains self-respect is provided by the emotions, specifically negative emotions, with which she responds or is disposed to respond to the wrongs committed against her. A common view in the literature on forgiveness is that the negative emotion that best or most reliably or essentially does this is resentment. "Proper self-respect," Jeffrie Murphy says in support of this view, "is essentially tied to the passion of resentment . . . and a person who does not resent moral injuries done to him . . . is almost necessarily a person lacking in self-respect."[53] When our rights are threatened, we have to defend ourselves: we have to stand up for ourselves rather than let wrongdoers walk all over us. And *the* emotion of self-defense, he claims, is resentment. In later work, Murphy softened his stance somewhat on the relationship between resentment and self-respect. "Resentment of the wrongdoer," he subsequently claimed, "is one way that a victim may evince, emotionally, that he or she does *not endorse* this degrading message ['I count and you do not, and I may thus use you as a mere thing']; and this is how resentment may be tied to the virtue of self-respect."[54] Murphy allows here that someone may emotionally evince non-endorsement in some other way than by being resentful, and he admits that it is "more loyal to the actual texture of our moral lives" to include non-retributive feelings among "the variety of negative feelings that one might have toward a wrongdoer."[55] But his account of forgiveness still focuses on resentment.

Charles Griswold, in a major discussion of forgiveness, also thinks that resentment enjoys a special relationship to self-respect because resentment defiantly declares: "You *must not* do this sort of thing; for it is *not to be done*"[56] – specifically, it is not to be done to *me*. The close connection between resentment and self-respect is a frequent theme in the forgiveness literature, and the prominence given the former in that literature is partly explained by this alleged connection and by the evident truth that self-respect, when it is not overvalued or undervalued, is a virtue.

It is not my intention to question the connection between resentment and self-respect. Rather I want to consider whether other sorts of negative emotions, specifically non-retributive emotions, can, in Murphy's words, also "stand as emotional testimony that we care about ourselves and our rights."[57] I think the case for thinking that resentment enjoys some special standing in this regard is harder to make than it might seem. How might one argue for this special standing? Resentment is surely not the only negative emotion that announces "you must not do this sort of thing to me." Non-retributive emotions, like disappointment and hurt, can also announce this. They do not, of course, announce this in just the way that resentment does, because they are different sorts of emotions with different characteristic modes of expression and aims. Nevertheless, they may have a similar expressive and communicative function.

Perhaps, however, the differences are significant. Griswold claims that "protest . . . is part of resentment,"[58] and it may be thought that since resentment disposes one to show anger in defiant protest against wrongdoing, it has a special relationship to self-respect, since protest and self-respect are intimately connected. Non-retributive emotions, by contrast, do not seem as closely related to protest.

I will have much more to say about protest in the next section. But for now I will only note that attitudes and behaviors can embody protests of different sorts. The protest expressed and communicated by resentment is a particular kind of outward display of defiance, angry and possibly threatening in nature, and in certain contexts this sort of protest may be called for, even owed to oneself and others. For example, for individuals who are systematically treated as moral inferiors, who are oppressed and denied their basic rights, this sort of protest might be the only or the most effective way to assert their moral worth and to manifest self-respect. In other contexts, where the wrongdoing is not systematic and oppressive and where individuals do not fear that if they do not confront wrongdoing they will have no self-respect at all, a different sort of emotional protest might and might appropriately be forthcoming. Sometimes, just having a negative emotion might indicate that the wronged party has self-respect, even if he chooses not to outwardly express or communicate that emotion to others. This might count as a kind of "silent" protest that under different circumstances would be made manifest in one's conduct. (Perhaps the wronged party does not manifest it because it is too dangerous or costly for him to do so.)

To be sure, the emotion that protest expresses or communicates might not *essentially* be an emotion of protest. But this is not a good enough reason to conceptualize forgiveness in a way that excludes or marginalizes negative emotions that can in some circumstances function in this manner. The assumption that a proper analysis of forgiveness should focus on identifying emotional responses to wrongdoing that are essentially of a certain type—whether essentially moral emotions or emotions of protest—may have certain advantages from the standpoint of simplicity and neatness. But it can also lead us to overlook or discount emotions that, while not essentially of a certain type, nonetheless give us a more complete and realistic picture of the moral psychology of response to wrongdoing. We don't always outwardly protest wrongdoing, nor should we; and if we do protest it, we don't and shouldn't always protest it in the same way, in particular, angrily or hostilely.

How then does self-respect get engaged, how does it come into play, when one is the victim of wrongdoing? I said that one way it gets engaged is through emotional response. More fully, negative emotions, or better responding or being disposed to respond to wrongdoing with them, can reveal and constitute evidence that a person who is wronged has self-respect, or retains it despite being subjected to ill treatment. My suggestion is that they do this in virtue of the significance that they have, for oneself and others, of a repudiation of the insulting and degrading message conveyed by it that challenges one's sense of being a worthy human being. In these cases, what he announces by them, to himself and potentially to others, is that he will not accept, comply with, or submit tacitly or passively to being wronged.

Feeling resentment or indignation toward a wrongdoer because of his actions plainly repudiates the threatening message, and this explains why they are commonly thought to be intimately bound up with self-respect. But there are other emotions that can do this as well, other emotional responses to wrongdoing that in some circumstances are means and modes of what Joel Feinberg calls "symbolic nonacquiescence"[59] in wrongdoing. Feeling deeply hurt by my colleague's lack of gratitude for the favors I did for him; or profoundly disappointed in my son because he failed to live up to certain expectations that he gave me reason to have of him; or saddened by my spouse's repeated acts of infidelity, although they were hardly unexpected: these emotional reactions put a distance between me and the offender that can be evidence that I retain my self-respect, whether or not they are blended with anger.

When disapproval is emotionally laden in these ways, there is a change in the affective attitudes that the wronged party has toward the other. The other is now affectively regarded as a wrongdoer, and this normally involves the wronged party adopting a more self-defensive posture in relation to him. The realization that one must adopt such a posture is partly cognitive, but it may also have an emotional component or dimension. When it does, the emotions can be said to convey, although perhaps only to the victim herself, the following: "I am not okay with what you have done. You cannot do it to me and I will not go on with you as if nothing has happened." Although sadness, for example, often induces passivity or immobility in the one who experiences it and withdrawal from active engagement with others, it can also motivate a wronged party to take steps to distance himself from his wrongdoer, and withdrawal from active engagement with the wrongdoer might indicate not that she acquiesces in what he did but, on the contrary, that she is no longer willing or able to put up with it.

Of course sadness does not always have this expressive point. It can be an emotional response to being wronged that signifies resignation rather than disapproval or repudiation. It is only when sadness accompanies or, alternatively, is an ingredient of blame that it signifies repudiation of wrongdoing and, thus, is linked to self-respect. The same is true of other non-retributive emotions like hurt, disappointment, and grief. It is only when, or because, these negative emotions are blame-related, felt with or ingredient in blame, that they symbolically signify intact self-respect. Thus, Michael McKenna's comment about resentment and indignation could apply as well to a number of different non-retributive emotions:

> Blaming via resentment or indignation reveals itself in the altered means
> of interacting with the one blamed. Normal courtesies are withheld,

patterns of conduct are changed, expected social plans and arrangements are altered, and particular means of expressing one's moral anger in word and deed are found to be common in ways that are sometimes fitting and sometimes not.[60]

As I said before, non-retributive emotions like sadness, hurt, and grief are not *essentially* blaming emotions, and the non-retributive emotion of disappointment is not a blaming emotion in the same way that resentment and indignation are. Yet these non-retributive emotions can constitute the emotional dimension of blaming in certain situations, ways of affectively regarding the other as blameworthy and taking a stand against what he did. In these cases, one's non-endorsement of the degrading message conveyed by the wrong is still shown by one's negative emotional responses to it, only now these are not angry or vengeful ones. These emotions also inhibit or limit the wronged party's goodwill toward the wrongdoer so that she does not make herself vulnerable to further insult and harm.

The connection between these negative emotions and self-respect is most evident when they are communicated to and directed at the offender. McKenna usefully distinguishes between "private blame, overt blame, and directed blame,"[61] and parallel distinctions can be drawn between having a negative emotion but concealing the outward behavioral manifestations of it; making the emotion manifest in one's conduct; and manifesting the emotion to the wrongdoer. Directed emotion is emotion that is not only manifested in the presence of, but is outwardly directed at, the wrongdoer. A case of directed emotion would be when a wronged party overtly directs her hurt feelings at the one who caused them, in order to draw the wrongdoer's attention to them. The behavioral manifestations of these feelings will include speech acts, gestures, and bodily movements of various sorts. The intent of the wronged party in this case is not just to communicate *that* she is hurt but to make the wrongdoer *see* that she is hurt. Moreover, by showing him how she feels the wronged party may also intend that he understand himself to be the cause of her hurt feelings and, further, that he acknowledge his responsibility for having hurt her. The non-retributive emotion of hurt, outwardly manifested in this way and with this intent, sends the message that she, the wronged party, did not deserve to be hurt and will not just passively submit to it. In so doing, she manifests self-respect. But if the connection between hurt feelings and self-respect is shown especially clearly when the feelings are directed at the wrongdoer, there can also be a connection when the feelings are not manifested in conduct, let alone directed. Just reacting emotionally in this way can signify the presence of intact self-respect, even if the message of non-acquiescence is only conveyed by the victim to herself.

There are two objections to this line of reasoning. First, while these non-retributive emotions might be directed at the wrongdoer in the way I have described, what is left out of the story is that the wronged party would not be inclined to do so if she wasn't angry at him. In other words, the objection goes, it is anger, in addition to these emotions or as part of them if the emotion is a hybrid, that motivates a rebuking response directed at the offender. However, this supposition is unconvincing on several grounds. A wronged party may be moved to communicate her negative feelings to the offender out of anger, to put him "on notice that any next action will be costly."[62] Or she may communicate her feelings to the offender even if not angry, to make him understand why she cannot completely trust him any longer; or why she has decided to withdraw from any further contact with him; or to make it plain to him that he cannot expect to keep his offense secret and to flout moral norms with impunity; and so on. Rebuking displays of negative emotions can take various forms, from overt denunciation to turning a cold shoulder, and while the latter *might* have a punitive intent, anger need not be a factor motivating the rebuke. The wronged party might not be motivated by anger or hostility but by frustration with the other's repeated wrongdoing and by a feeling of hopelessness that the relationship with him can be salvaged.

The second objection is that non-retributive emotions do not take wrongdoing seriously enough because they do not show proper respect for morality, and this in turn shows a lack of respect for oneself. To properly care about morality, the objection goes, one must defend moral values and respect the objects that give rise to them. As Christopher Evan Franklin puts it,

> among the norms that govern how to properly care about morality is the requirement that we defend and protect moral values: we must stand up for and safeguard moral values against those who flout them.[63]

The victim of wrongdoing, on this view, only takes morality seriously if she takes steps to defend and protect the moral values that the wrongdoer flouted. Experiencing and expressing resentment and indignation show that the victim takes the wrongs seriously because they are defensive and protective emotions. Non-retributive emotions, or the non-retributive part of hybrid emotions, by contrast, cannot play the same expressive role. In addition, the victim who has non-retributive responses to being wronged fails to this extent to take the wrongs done to herself sufficiently seriously. Her repertoire of emotional responses reveals that she lacks proper concern both for morality and for herself. But this objection too is unconvincing. There are, after all, many ways to defend and protect moral values. If, without anger, a victim makes plain to her wrongdoer that she will not just passively submit to his wrongdoing, if she directs her

The Moral Psychology of Interpersonal Forgiveness   53

disappointment or grief at him to make this point, she has certainly done something to protect the moral values that he flouted. But perhaps it will seem that she has not done enough. Resentment and indignation, when directed at the wrongdoer, do more because they warn him that he had better not repeat his offense or he will pay a significant price. However, without saying more about the standards that require defense and protection of moral values, specifically why only the protection afforded by retributive emotions is adequate, the argument is hardly persuasive. Indeed, it is hard to see how any argument that purports to show this could avoid the charge of question-begging.

6. Protest and the emotions it embodies

(a) Protest and emotional response

I have argued that negative emotions of different types, namely retributive, non-retributive, and hybrid ones, can accompany blame, and I have also suggested that arguments singling out retributive emotions as *the* emotions that register blame are unconvincing. Moreover, I have argued that it is when and because they are associated with blame that these emotions reveal that the victim has sufficient self-respect to be distressed by the wrongs done to her and to resist the message conveyed by the wrongdoer's actions. (Shame and guilt impute fault to the self for engaging in certain acts, and both can serve as a kind of warning to the self not to repeat similar acts, a warning that is grounded in at least some remnant of self-respect. Of course, another response to feelings of shame and guilt is to expect less of oneself in the future.) When wrongdoing is unopposed by retributive or non-retributive negative emotions, the wronged party invites the charge that she lacks self-respect, and the wronged party who is not roused by wrongdoing to such emotions may herself doubt whether she retains it. However, by repudiating the wrongs done to her, emotionally and otherwise, the wronged party makes apparent to herself and others that the person she holds responsible treated her worse than she was entitled to expect. Her emotional responses provide evidence that she is a person who is cognizant of her moral entitlements and is unwilling to acquiesce in their violation.

Of course, it is not always possible or advisable for a victim to communicate her feelings to her offender by showing him how his wrongdoing has emotionally affected her. The offender may be unavailable or dead or hard to identify or find; or the victim may regard the costs of communication as prohibitively high. But especially when the offense is serious, the impulse to let the offender and others know that he cannot simply "get away with it," that it cannot be overlooked or treated as acceptable or harmless or just part of business as usual, is a natural one, and acting on it is a way of affirming one's moral worth. This is so even between very close friends and loved ones. Acquiescence to wrongs committed against oneself by a friend or loved one is not always a product of morally creditable impulses. On the contrary, it sometimes indicates overindulgence of the friend at the expense of one's self-respect, although obviously the existence of a prior relationship of care and affection will have a bearing on how the non-acquiescence is felt and expressed. Anger initially felt toward a friend for betraying our trust may give way to a feeling more akin to disappointment or sadness.

One explanation for why a wronged party's non-acquiescent emotional responses provide evidence of intact self-respect is that they constitute a kind of *protest* against the wrongs done to her. Protest and self-respect are closely linked, as I will explain shortly. To be sure, protests are often thought of as very public, attention-getting affairs, and viewed this way protest might not be a particularly prudent way to defend one's self-respect. For example, I can be hurt by what I regard as my boss' condescending treatment of me, and this feeling of hurt, even if not outwardly expressed, is important because it shows that I think enough of myself to be distressed in this way by his behavior. If I thought I didn't deserve better treatment, I might feel hurt, but not for this reason. It is a separate matter, however, whether I should go about publicly protesting what he has done. Other co-workers might not have experienced the same treatment, so I may not find a sympathetic audience for my complaints. Protesting might get me fired or prevent me from advancing in my job. Protesting might be an overreaction, because the wrong done to me, though not insignificant, is not weighty enough to protest. Perhaps there are less risky and more efficacious ways of dealing with my hurt feelings than publicly protesting how I've been treated. As a general matter, protesting of this sort can be extremely dangerous or counterproductive or otherwise a bad idea, and it may be best to keep my disapproval to myself. But protests don't have to be like this. There can be private protests, protests that have the same connection to self-respect as overt ones, but without the latter's outward behavioral manifestations. Moreover, protests, whether private or overt, can involve negative emotions of different sorts, including but not limited to retributive ones.

Nevertheless, I propose to start with anger, since this is what is likely to come to mind first when talking about protest. Anger, according to Philip Fisher, is an emotion of protest with significance for one's self-respect.[64] "The excitations of anger," he tells us, "mark out the places where self-worth or honor has been transgressed" (176). This is not true of all instances of anger, but only those where "injustice has been felt" (176–177), hence only what we can call moral anger. Moral anger does not simply convey to others that an injury has been experienced as a slight or insult, however. It also insists that I have "the right to be honored and not slighted" (184) and defends "a measure of self-esteem, or of endangered self-regard" through "a combination of external protest and warning" (195). As protest, it "insist[s] and declare[s] that I will maintain a certain perimeter of my own worth" (188). To get angry at injustice is to notice and insist on it and to go on record, as it were, that one is not willing to act "as though nothing just happened" (187). As warning, it puts "the other on notice that any next action will be costly" (187). Further, the relationship between moral anger and what one takes to be an injustice is bidirectional. Sometimes moral anger is a response to what one perceives is a violation of one's right to be honored and not slighted. On other occasions, the order of explanation is reversed: what one takes to be an injustice is revealed by what arouses one's anger:

> Because it is not predictable in advance, in many cases, whether or to what degree I will be angry, I in fact learn about the extent of the radius of self-worth that I am committed to maintaining (or not) by what can at times be the surprise of finding myself enraged. (188)

In these ways, anger "announces or discovers to me, insofar as I feel exactly this degree of anger, the contours or importance of my sense of self-worth" (193–194).

The various kinds of moral anger are not the only negative emotions that protest against wrongdoing, however. They are not the only emotions that can drive, infuse, and give shape to protest. Specifically, non-retributive emotions, and those that are part of hybrid ones, can do so as well. It is perhaps tempting to suppose that all protest *must* be angry and that people would not protest if they were not angry, but this is a temptation that should be resisted. It presumes an overly narrow conception of protest and its characteristic motivations. Non-angry protest, protest not out of anger but out of profound disappointment in the failure of others to live up to their professed ideals, for example, is arguably what Gandhi and Martin Luther King and many of their followers engaged in. They forswore anger, but the absence of anger did not prevent them from standing up for their rights or render them oblivious to the wrongs committed against them. Other negative emotions of the non-retributive kind played the same role for them.

What are the features of protest, as I understand it? First there is the threshold issue: I am only interested in moral and not non-moral protest. Moral protest is a deliberate response of a certain sort to perceived moral wrongdoing, whereas non-moral protest is protest against matters that do not fall within the domain of morality. Protests can be made for purely strategic reasons, to gain some advantage for oneself, although the protester might invoke moral language to gain respectability for his actions. These are not moral protests. Angela Smith tells us what moral protest is by noting that it has two aims, and I follow her in this:

first, to *register* the fact that the person wronged did not deserve such treatment by *challenging* the moral claim implicit in the wrongdoer's action; second, to prompt moral recognition and acknowledgment of this fact on the part of the wrongdoer and/or others in the moral community.[65]

It is possible that someone protests what he or she sincerely believes is wrong and is motivated by moral convictions, but that she is mistaken. What the other person did wasn't in fact wrong, or though it was wrong, there were extenuating circumstances. Nevertheless, such protests can still count as moral.

There are a number of other noteworthy features of protest. A protest consists in part in disapproval of what is being protested, but a person can disapprove of the treatment she has received without protesting it. This is not merely because disapproval can be private whereas protest is not. As I said, one can protest privately as well. Rather, the difference is that protest has as its point and purpose to *communicate* disapproval to an audience—the offender, assuming the offender is reachable, and to others in the community as well—whereas an act of disapproval might not be aimed at communicating anything at all. Further, while it is a communicative act, a protest is not essentially an invitation to dialogue, although dialogue may ensue as a result and ultimately reconcile the parties. It is rather a defiant announcement of one's refusal to remain passive in the face of continuing or unacknowledged wrongdoing, and typically one is defiant because argument and persuasion have not proven or are thought unlikely to be effective in securing relief or admission of responsibility. "Defiance," as I am using the term, may take a belligerent or combative form that threatens harm to the offender, but it need not. More broadly, it refers to an act or instance of "confront[ing] with assured power of resistance,"[66] and resistance, as the examples of Gandhi and Martin Luther King demonstrate, can be nonviolent.

Moral protest, according to Smith, aims for the wrongdoer to recognize that the wronged party did not deserve the treatment she received from him, and if it is successful in this it may bring about an end to the wrongdoing and prevent its repetition. The latter too is typically one of the aims of protest in its overt form. The sought-for recognition may include an apology from the offender and this may be accompanied by a promise to desist. In transitional contexts, as we will see in later chapters, protest may also seek compensation, material or symbolic reparations, and reform of the institutions that facilitated or supported wrongdoing. The protest declares that these matters are of great, perhaps the greatest, urgency and that further delay is unacceptable. And finally, those engaged in overt protest typically believe that injustice can be stopped directly or indirectly by means of the protest, that this is not entirely out of reach even if the chances are remote. This may in fact be more than just a description of the protesters'

The Moral Psychology of Interpersonal Forgiveness   57

beliefs, but a condition of the justification of their actions. Arguably, when moral protest takes the form of overt social protest that could have serious negative consequences for others or those involved, it is justified only if the protesters have reasonable grounds for believing that there is some chance that their protest will put an end to wrongdoing or have some other comparably worthwhile outcome—and, further, only if there are sound reasons for believing that the elimination of injustice outweighs whatever negative consequences the protest may bring about.

Protests may continue to have uses even after the initial injustice has ended. For example, the offenders may not really be convinced that what they did was wrong, so may not take responsibility for their actions. There is continuing wrong in the refusal itself to take responsibility for past wrongdoing, but protests can hold them accountable and make it difficult for them to deny their guilt. Even if the injustice has ended it might recur, but it may be less likely to do so if the offenders are opposed by a display of organized moral protest. (This could be particularly valuable in the early stages of a political transition, when the new regime has not yet consolidated its power and the threat of a return to violence and repression is quite real.) Another reason for protesting, about which I will say more in a moment, is not to end injustice, but to ensure that it is not forgotten. The object of protest in this case is not the wrongdoing itself, which has been acknowledged, but the forgetting of it that both dishonors the dead and may in the long run make a recurrence of wrongdoing more likely.

Protests, however, might fail to achieve these objectives. They might not prompt the appropriate moral recognition and admission of responsibility from wrongdoers; or put an end to injustice; or prevent injustice from recurring; or counteract the corrosive effects of forgetting. What, we may wonder, was the good of protesting if, in the end, it failed in these ways or perhaps was even counterproductive to some degree? Bernard Boxill's account of the relationship between protest and self-respect gives us an answer.[67]

Boxill's central claim is that "persons have reason to protest their wrongs not only to stop injustice but also to show self-respect and to know themselves as self-respecting" (59). There are three reasons, on his view, for protesting: to end injustice; to evince self-respect and assert moral worth; and to give the protester herself compelling reason to believe that she has self-respect. Let me say something about the third condition.

According to Boxill, there is a way in which a person can have an exaggerated sense of her self-worth, namely if she is confident that, come what may, she will never lose her conviction that she has it. A person who has appropriate self-respect, by contrast, is sure "that he has worth; not that he will always be sure of this" (67). As a person with a realistic sense of his own worth, he will recognize that it is vulnerable, that he may lose his confidence in his self-worth, and therefore that he may have to take steps to shore it up in order to show himself and others that he retains his self-respect. He will want to take steps to show *himself* this because he believes that it is important for him to believe it, so he will want to give himself reasons for holding on to this belief. And he will want others to know that he still has his self-respect and that he is claiming it.

In circumstances of persistent and serious wrongdoing—the sorts of circumstances that societies undergoing profound political upheaval confront—the loss of or injury to self-respect is a very real possibility: self-respect is not impervious to harm, even when the victim firmly believes that he was grossly mistreated. The degrading and demeaning treatment that an individual receives in these circumstances can destabilize and erode even the most confident conviction that an individual has of his worth. He may come to fear that "because of what he is doing or because of what is happening to him, he will become servile" (67). The fear is that because of persistent and serious wrongdoing, he will adjust downward his expectations of what he is due from others. But fear of servility is not the only motive for protest, and servility is not the only explanation of the lack of self-respect. Individuals may be so brutalized by wrongdoing that they lose a sense not only of their own value, but of any value in going on living at all. Those who find themselves in such situations may realize that this can happen to them if they do nothing to protest their mistreatment, and they may engage in protest to prevent it. The protest is itself a way of forcefully assuring themselves that they have not yet reached the point where they can be written off. As Boxill puts it, "the self-respecting person in such straits must, in some way, protest to assure himself that he has self-respect" (66). And though he is thinking here of overt forms of protest directed at wrongdoers, he could say the same thing about protests that are not manifested in outward behavior but that nevertheless involve the adoption of a defiant attitude.

The importance of asserting one's moral worth, and of reassuring oneself and letting others know that one still has it, explain why protest has moral value even if it is unsuccessful in ending injustice and in prompting recognition of the wrongness of their actions among the offenders. As Boxill suggests, protest can have a moral function even if the protester realizes that he has little chance of convincing others of his moral standing. In these cases it still has the important function of convincing himself and giving evidence to others that his commitment to his worth remains intact: "When he has to endure wrongs he cannot repel and feels his self-respect threatened, he will publicly claim it in order to reassure himself that he has it. His reassurance does not come from persuading others that he has self-respect. It comes from using his claim to self-respect as a challenge" (69).

Protest also has moral value in interpersonal, nonpolitical contexts and for much the same reason, although Boxill does not discuss this. It may be important,

The Moral Psychology of Interpersonal Forgiveness 59

even urgent, to assert one's moral worth in the face of serious wrongdoing by another individual, and to assure oneself and others, especially the wrongdoer, that one's self-respect remains intact. And it can be worthwhile to seek acknowledgment from the wrongdoer and others than one did not deserve to be treated this way, even if one's efforts are unsuccessful.

Finally, to turn the discussion back to the relationship between protest and negative emotions, emotions of different types play various roles in protest. The types of moral anger, with their constitutive desires to get back at the offender, are certainly common among the victims of violence and serious, deeply entrenched wrongdoing. But while moral anger challenges the moral claim implicit in the wrongdoer's actions through "a combination of external protest and warning," it is not just anger that can challenge it with "assured power of resistance." It is the conviction that one has been wronged that gives one this assured power, and this conviction can be expressed in and by negative feelings of different kinds. The feelings may be angry ones, but they may instead, or in addition, be negative emotions of the non-angry sort, including disappointment, hurt, grief, and humiliation, among others. Retributive, non-retributive, and hybrid negative emotions can motivate protest, can infuse it and keep it going, and can determine the particular shape and direction that it takes. There is no good reason to think that only retributive emotions can do these things, or that a person's non-retributive negative emotions can't be equally effective in prompting from wrongdoers recognition and acknowledgment of the wrongness of their actions.

(c) After forgiveness: self-respect and protest

I want to end these remarks about protest with a question that on some views does not belong to an account of forgiveness, properly speaking. The question is whether there is any role for protest, interpersonal or social, after wrongdoers have been forgiven for their offenses. This—indeed, not only this but also questions about the negative emotions and memories of wrongdoing that persist after forgiveness—will be thought to fall outside the scope of an account of forgiveness, if one thinks that for that all one needs to concern oneself with is what impedes forgiveness, how this is achieved, and the conditions under which it may appropriately or should be granted. However, one might look for something more from an account of forgiveness. One might look for some insight into its typical or frequent aftermath; the sense or senses in which, having forgiven, the slate is or is not wiped clean going forward; and the functions, moral as well as psychological, of any negative emotions and memories that may remain after the wrongdoers have been forgiven. These and other related matters I include in an account of forgiveness, because without a discussion of what follows forgiveness, its moral and psychological significance cannot be adequately understood.

One question that arises, then, is whether the remarks I made about the moral functions of protest and the emotions that drive it continue to have any force or even relevance beyond forgiveness—that is, beyond whenever it is that the offenders can properly be said to have been forgiven. I believe they do and will close with a few words about this.

Suppose that wrongdoers have been forgiven because they have acknowledged the wrongfulness of what they did, apologized for it, shown remorse, and followed this up with concrete steps to make amends for their actions. If one of the aims of protest is to prompt acknowledgment of the wrongfulness of his actions from the wrongdoer, then to this extent further protest would seem to be at the very least pointless, a kind of moral overkill. But protest has other aims as well, namely to register a belief about the wrongness of what was done and assert one's moral worth by repudiating the moral claim implicit in the wrongdoer's actions. So the above question can be sharpened by asking whether there could still be a place for this even after wrongdoers have been forgiven. I believe the answer is yes, and that there is a place for this both in interpersonal relationships and the larger social arena. There may be a need to continue to assure oneself and remind others that the treatment was undeserved, and to repudiate it, even after the wrongdoers have taken full responsibility for it. Protest, that is, can still have a point even if the wrongdoers have already been brought to acknowledge the wrongfulness of their actions and been forgiven for them. It can also have a point if moral recognition and acknowledgment by wrongdoers is impossible (say because they are dead). For recognition and acknowledgment can also be sought from others in the moral community, and continuing protest can be valuable for this reason.

Protest is not rendered otiose because the conditions for warranted forgiveness have been satisfied and forgiveness has been granted: protest is not merely preparatory to forgiveness. For one thing, even if the wrongdoer has promised not to offend again, has taken tangible measures to make amends, and has been forgiven, there may be more than the ordinary possibility that he will offend again. The wronged party might have forgiven him on the basis of his efforts to be worthy of her forgiveness, but his efforts may prove inadequate to the task, despite his good intentions, and she knows this. After all, the process of taking responsibility for one's wrongdoing is often difficult and painful, especially if the wrong was serious, since it involves standing before the victim and perhaps the community and exposing oneself to their scrutiny and censure. So some backsliding may occur, and the wronged party may not be entirely surprised if this happens. However, she will likely be at least disappointed in the offender because of this and will want to express her disappointment to him. She may even experience some resurgence of anger. But she will not necessarily hold his backsliding against him to the extent of returning to the state of mutual estrangement that existed before. She might instead see his efforts at amends-making and self-improvement, imperfect though they are, as evidence that he is trying his best to earn her trust and, on this basis, continue to extend forgiveness to him, with the understanding that there is still more to do to make up for what he has done. Here, though the wrongdoer does not need to be brought to recognize and acknowledge the wrongness of his actions, protest serves another purpose: it impresses on the wrongdoer the need to do more to be worthy of the wronged party's continuing forgiveness.

Second, protest has self-reparative and self-protective functions in cases where wrongdoing expresses an opinion of the wronged party that clashes with her belief in her own worth. Wrongdoing doesn't always do this: the victim might have no such belief about herself or the actions of the wrongdoer (suppose the wrongdoer is deranged) might not be implicitly making the claim that she doesn't deserve better treatment. However, wrongdoing, at a certain level of seriousness, often does express such an opinion, and then protest works to protect a person's dignity by producing evidence of her worth. This may be necessary because damage has been done to a person's self-respect that is not easily repaired, and it may require continued repair work to assure herself that she still retains it. It may also be necessary to let others in the community know that she still retains it because otherwise they may suppose that they now have license to mistreat her too. Protest may be part of this ongoing repair work and it can send a warning message to the community, and for these reasons it can play an important moral role even after the wrongdoer has been forgiven.

Third, protest after forgiveness can have two additional functions: to combat forgetting and, with forgetting, the weakening of moral restraints on conduct. As I will discuss in a later chapter, there are psychological, political, and social factors that contribute to the erosion of personal and social memory over time. In light of this, even if the offenders have taken full responsibility for their actions and been forgiven, there is still a use for protest: it keeps the memory of wrongdoing from fading or being manipulated by others and in so doing helps prevent repetition of the wrongs that were committed or denial that they ever occurred. The repetition and denial must be resisted if possible by those who were wronged if they are to retain their self-respect. Repetition aside, the forgetting itself dishonors the dead and is an insult to the victims that threatens their self-respect. In its political manifestations, protest mounts a challenge to the sort of social amnesia that, ironically, is all too common as a consequence of memorializing the victims of wrongdoing. Creating memorials to the victims does not ensure that they and what they suffered are remembered: it may instead give individuals and communities the license to forget.

Protests against wrongdoing, and against the forgetting of wrongdoing specifically, also help to reinstall and reinforce the moral standards whose authority was damaged by the wrongs being protested. When wrongs are systematic and widespread, forgetting has a corrosive effect on the social commitment to morality and erodes confidence in the ability of moral standards to regulate social life. Loss of faith in the effective authority of morality to govern how the members of society relate to one another, a kind of moral skepticism or cynicism, may result. Protest doesn't just challenge the specific moral claim about the victim that is implicit in the wrongdoer's actions; it can also express support for the principle that relations between persons should be governed by moral standards. For these reasons, protests *against* wrongdoing and its forgetting can also be considered protests *on behalf* of morality. And importantly, there is no incompatibility between forgiving wrongdoers and keeping the memory of their wrongdoing alive by protesting against whatever and whoever would undermine that memory. The latter can be a morally worthy activity even if forgiveness was fully warranted.

7. Conclusion

My discussion of the ways that moral insult, blame, and self-respect are emotionally experienced and expressed presents a more complex picture of how people respond to wrongdoing than is commonly found in the philosophical literature on forgiveness. In so doing it complicates the account of forgiveness as well, if forgiveness is understood as a process of emotional transformation in which certain negative emotions that are directed toward the wrongdoer and responsive to his wrongdoing are overcome or forsworn. Specifically, I did this by making a case for the relevance and importance of what I called non-retributive negative emotions, emotions that I claim have been neglected in standard accounts of forgiveness or treated merely as an afterthought by them. These I contrasted with retributive emotions or emotions of moral anger. I argued that the privileging of retributive emotions in an account of forgiveness is not supported by the various considerations adduced for it, because these apply as well to instances of non-retributive responses to wrongdoing. Emotions of both retributive and non-retributive sorts can be regularly associated with insult and blame; and instances of both types can be distressed reactions to wrongdoing that evince a refusal or inability to go on as if nothing untoward has given one reason to distrust the wrongdoer or to defend oneself against his offensive behavior.[68]

A few objections remain, however, and I would be remiss if I didn't say something in closing about them. One is that my account of the moral psychology of response to wrongdoing is psychologically unrealistic and implausible. The other is that the overarching distinction with which I framed the problem with

The Moral Psychology of Interpersonal Forgiveness

standard accounts of forgiveness is based on a misunderstanding of the nature of angry emotions. I will respond to these in turn.

Victoria McGeer makes the following observation that relates to the first objection:

> Is it possible for creatures like us to engage in such a process [of normative reflection on the appropriateness or inappropriateness of what someone has done] under the burden of perceived injury without feeling or expressing angry emotions, however mild these may be? My response to this is brief. Perhaps it is possible, at least for the saints among us. But however much we may suppose this is a preferable state of affairs, I doubt it is practically available to the common run of humanity.[69]

My response to this is also brief. I do not deny that angry emotions are commonly felt and expressed in response to being wronged. Even if we grant McGeer's point about anger, this does not force me to retract the claims of this chapter. For it is a too simple account of how people react emotionally to being wronged to suppose that they *only* respond with angry emotions. They also commonly respond with a mix of negative emotions, including angry and non-angry ones, and the latter can persist even after the former dissipate or are overcome. These persisting non-angry negative emotions, no less than the angry ones, can accompany insult and blame and can evince self-respect, as I have argued. Moreover, as regards forgiveness, sometimes it is the persistence of the non-angry emotions that explains why the wronged party is unable or unwilling to forgive her offender, not the persistence of angry ones. A person can continue to be distressed by what was done to her, indeed so distressed that she cannot bring herself to forgive her offender, even if she is no longer angry with him. McGeer may be right that one would have to be a saint not to respond to being injured with anger— she weakens her claim, however, by allowing "mild" anger – but this is compatible with a more complex picture of emotional responses to wrongdoing and their connections to forgiveness.

Now to the second objection. Retributive emotions, as I use the term here and elsewhere in this chapter, have as their characteristic desire and aim to retaliate against or get even with the wrongdoer, whereas non-retributive negative ones do not. It was this understanding of retributive emotions that I used to characterize the standard account of forgiveness. The standard account, I said, holds that forgiveness is or involves overcoming the desire to pay back or get even with the offender and the emotions in which this desire is embedded. I called these "angry" emotions and the objection is that I should not have used "angry emotions" and "retributive emotions" interchangeably, for not all angry emotions are retributive in this sense. Margaret Walker takes this view. She maintains that "an action that embodies anger at unacceptable behavior need not be violent, vengeful, or retaliatory, although it will be in some way confrontational or demanding." Anger, in her view, covers a range of responses that "pursu[e] a settling of accounts from offenders," and only some ways of settling accounts involve paying back or getting even with the offender.[70] It is not entirely clear on her view what constitutes angry rebuking responses as opposed to non-angry ones, but be that as it may. Similarly, Charles Griswold observes that "anger is a highly complex, polymorphous phenomenon," and while the focus of his analysis is something he calls "vengeful anger," there is the suggestion that there are non-vengeful forms of anger as well.[71]

Once again, as with the first objection, I can accept the point without having to substantially modify the claims in this chapter. There may be non-retributive forms of anger as well as retributive ones (again where "retributive" has the sense of paying back or retaliating). There are also non-retributive negative emotions of other sorts, as well as blended or hybrid negative emotions. Instances of any of these emotion types can accompany insult and blame and can emotionally evince intact self-respect. And instances of any of them may need to be overcome for forgiveness to be possible.

Endnotes

1. Sermons VIII and IX, in vol. 2 of *The Works of Joseph Butler*, ed. W. E. Gladstone, 2, vols. (Oxford: Clarendon Press, 1896).
2. Charles Griswold, *Forgiveness: A Philosophical Exploration* (Cambridge: Cambridge University Press, 2007), pp. 39, 41.
3. Avishai Margalit, *The Ethics of Memory* (Cambridge, MA: Harvard University Press, 2002), p. 192.
4. Jeffrie Murphy, *Getting Even: Forgiveness and its Limits* (Oxford: Oxford University Press, 2008), p. 13.
5. H. J. Horsbrugh, "Forgiveness," *Canadian Journal of Philosophy*, vol. 4, no. 2 (December 1974): 269–282, at 271.
6. Robert C. Roberts, "Forgivingness," *American Philosophical Quarterly*, vol. 32, no. 4 (October 1995): 289–306, at 293.
7. Paul Hughes refers to the emotions that forgiveness overcomes as instances of "moral anger," which he says includes "resentment . . . animosity, indignation, wrath, malice, contempt, and possibly even disgust." "What is Involved in Forgiving?" *Philosophia*, vol. 25 (1997): 33–49, at 37. Should contempt and disgust be included among emotions of moral anger? Anger may sometimes be a component of contempt, but there are important differences between these emotions. Anger is generally thought to involve a desire to hurt its object or to take some aggressive action toward it, whereas contempt is partially constituted by a very different desire, the desire to withdraw from its object. (See note 47 for more on contempt.) And disgust, according to Martha Nussbaum, "is very different from anger" (See *Hiding from Humanity* [Princeton, NJ: Princeton University Press, 2004], pp. 13–14, 99–101). I can be angry at someone who disgusts me, and perhaps because he disgusts me, but disgust is not an essentially angry emotion. Perhaps Hughes includes disgust among emotions of moral anger

The Moral Psychology of Interpersonal Forgiveness   65

because he is thinking of these cases; and perhaps he includes contempt because he is think-ing of cases in which contempt is accompanied by retributive feelings.

8. *Responsibility and the Moral Sentiments* (Cambridge, MA: Harvard University Press, 1994), pp. 59–61. Importantly, Wallace notes: "It certainly seems that I could blame someone for a wrong, and even engage in sanctioning behavior toward that person (avoidance and censure, say), without believing it to be intrinsically a good thing that the person should suffer harm" (p. 60). Later in this chapter, when I discuss forgiveness and blame, I will argue that one who forgives might overcome emotions that censure the offender but that are not constituted by the belief that it is a good thing to inflict harm on him in retribution for what he has done.

9. Lucy Allais offers this as an alternative definition of retributivism in "Restorative Justice, Re-tributive Justice, and the South African Truth and Reconciliation Commission," *Philosophy and Public Affairs*, vol. 39, no. 4 (Fall 2011): 331–363.

10. Griswold makes this argument in defense of defining forgiveness in terms of overcoming anger or resentment. Op. cit., pp. 40–41.

11. F. Nietzsche, *On the Genealogy of Morality*, M. Clark and A. Swensen (trans.) (Indianapolis: Hackett Publishing Co., 1998), p. 21.

12. Further, when the man of *ressentiment* does manage to forgive, it is not because he has overcome resentment either, for it is not resentment that he felt in the first place. Bernard Reginster puts the fundamental difference between resentment and *ressentiment* this way: "re-sentment appears to presuppose the condemnation of its object and constitutes a reaction of disapproval to its occurrence, whereas *ressentiment* rests on the implicit endorsement of the very values embodied by those towards whom it is directed." "Nietzsche on *Ressentiment* and Valuation," *Philosophy and Phenomenological Research*, vol. 57, no. 2 (June 1997): 281–305, at 296. See also Charles Griswold, op. cit., p. 15n21: "So forgiveness [for Nietzsche] is actually the expression rather than the forswearing of *ressentiment*."

13. Jerome Neu, *Sticks and Stones: The Philosophy of Insults* (New York: Oxford, 2008), p. 31.

14. Jeffrie Murphy, "Forgiveness in Counseling: A Philosophical Perspective," in S. Lamb and J. G. Murphy (eds.), *Before Forgiving: Cautionary Views of Forgiveness in Psychotherapy* (New York: Oxford University Press, 2002), pp. 41–53, at 44.

15. See J. Hornsby, "Illocution and Its Significance," in S. L. Tsohatzidis (ed.),*Foundations of Speech Act Theory: Philosophical and Linguistic Perspectives* (New York: Routledge, 1994), pp. 187–207, at 192.

16. R. A. Duff, "Justice, Mercy, and Forgiveness," *Criminal Justice Ethics*, vol. 9, no. 2 (Summer/Fall 1990): 51–63.

17. Similarly, Leo Zaibert claims that the communicative conception of wrongdoing is problem-atic, and that it fails even for some cases of fully intended wrongdoing. See "The Paradox of Forgiveness," *Journal of Moral Philosophy*, vol. 6 (2009): 365–393, at 378–379.

18. Eve Garrard and David McNaughton, "In Defense of Unconditional Forgiveness," *Proceedings of the Aristotelian Society* (2003): 39–60, at 42–43.

19. Griswold, op. cit., p. 41.

20. Neu, op. cit., p. 34.

21. Robert Gordon, *The Structure of Emotions* (Cambridge University Press, 1987), pp. 29–30. A negative emotion is not necessarily a bad emotion to have—take righteous anger, for example. What one wishes not to be the case is what aroused one's anger. If one is righteously angry, one does not wish it to be the case that one believes one's anger is unwarranted.

22. Robert Solomon, *True to Our Feelings* (New York: Oxford University Press, 2007), p. 40.

23. Hughes, op. cit., p. 38

24. Leo Zaibert claims that according to "the overwhelmingly standard view . . . to forgive is, explicitly, to overcome resentment." Op. cit., p. 388.

25. Glen Pettigrew argues for expanding the sphere of potential forgivers to include persons who do not meet these conditions, in *Forgiveness and Love* (Oxford: Oxford University Press, 2012), pp. 20–39. But see P. E. Digeser, *Political Forgiveness* (Ithaca: Cornell University Press, 2001), pp. 103–108.

26. Solomon, op. cit., p. 104.

27. *Forgiveness and Revenge* (London: Routledge, 2002), p. 13.

28. Neu, op. cit., p. 29.

66 FORGIVENESS AND REMEMBRANCE

29. John Kekes calls sadness and disappointment "quiet emotions," in contrast to "resentment, bitterness, anger, hatred, and indignation." See "Blame versus Forgiveness," *The Monist*, vol. 92, no. 4 (2009): 488–506, at 491.

30. Patricia Greenspan, *Emotions and Reasons* (New York: Routledge, 1988), pp. 50–51. She goes on:

If I am angry at X in response to his insult, that is—not simply hurt, or angry about his role in something unintended—I must view his insult as a wrong that I ought to repay. I must "feel as though" I ought to repay it at least partly because he is to blame for it—and because I am uncomfortable with that thought. (54)

31. Ibid., p. 51.

32. I thank Prof. Paul Wachtel for helping me to see that responses to wrongdoing cannot be neatly divided into retributive and non-retributive.

33. According to Lucy Allais, "hurt can be seen as a reactive attitude . . .it is a response to the way in which another manifests lack of good will towards you which it [sic] involves affectively seeing the other as valuing you less than you want her to." See "Wiping the Slate Clean: The Heart of Forgiveness," *Philosophy and Public Affairs*, vol. 36, no. 1 (Winter 2008): 33–68, at 59.

34. Mark R. Leary, Carrie Springer, et al., "The Causes, Phenomenology, and Consequences of Hurt Feelings," *Journal of Personality and Social Psychology*, vol. 74, no. 5 (1998): 1225–1237, at 1235.

35. Ibid.

36. Dennis Klein has suggested to me (personal correspondence 12/1/09) that anger itself may conceal the more primitive emotion of hurt, and he conjectures that all violations ultimately evoke hurt which gets expressed in different negative emotions, including mistrust, sadness, grief, and so on, as well as anger. If he is right and the emotion of hurt does underlie both retributive and non-retributive emotional responses to wrongdoing, this would require some minor adjustments in my sentiment-based account of forgiveness. The basic distinction between angry and non-angry feelings would have to be recast as the distinction between angry hurt feelings and non-angry hurt feelings.

37. Christopher Bennett, *The Apology Ritual* (Cambridge: Cambridge University Press, 2008). Page numbers are in parentheses in the text.

38. Bennett disagrees and thinks that the only adequate kind of moral censure for significant wrongdoing is retributive. His argument, in part, is this:

Subjecting all wrongdoers only to (strictly non-retributive) moral criticism makes no distinction between two importantly different sorts of cases: one in which the agent is non-culpably ignorant of the wrongness of her act; and another in which she did or could have been expected to know better. For the moral criticism approach the response in both of these cases is essentially the same: present the wrongdoer with the reasons why what she did was wrong, seek to get her to grasp the full force of these reasons, and thus to determine to reform her attitudes and conduct for the future. (101–102)

I agree that moral criticism in the two cases will be different, but I am not convinced that a moral criticism model that emphasizes moral education and moral persuasion is incapable of accommodating the difference. Bennett's reason for thinking otherwise is that "moral education would suggest that it was not the wrongdoer's responsibility to discover and decide for themselves how to meet their responsibilities within the practice" (ibid., 97). But mightn't even responsible adults sometimes need moral education? Southerners during Jim Crow were certainly responsible for their actions, but it is likely they would not have seen them as unjust had the protests of Martin Luther King and others not been addressed to their sense of justice in a spirit of nonviolence.

39. Wallace, op. cit., p. 72.

40. Jesse Prinz calls disappointment an emotion of blame, in "The Moral Emotions," in P. Goldie (ed.), *The Oxford Handbook of Philosophy of Emotion*, (Oxford: Oxford University Press, 2000), pp. 526–527. Nevertheless, the action tendency of disappointment, he says, is not "aggressive or punishment–focused," unlike anger.

41. *In Praise of Blame* (Oxford: Oxford University Press, 2002), pp. 78–91. Page numbers appear in parentheses in the text.

The Moral Psychology of Interpersonal Forgiveness 67

42. The expression "withdrawal of good will" comes from P. F. Strawson's discussion of the free will versus determinism debate in his enormously influential essay, "Freedom and Resentment," and my account of the moral psychology of response to wrongdoing is indebted to it. In this essay, Strawson speaks about a class of moral sentiments that he calls "reactive attitudes," such as resentment and indignation:

    [These attitudes] tend to inhibit or at least to limit our goodwill towards [their] objects ..., tend to promote an at least partial and temporary withdrawal of goodwill; they do so in proportion as they are strong; and their strength is in general proportioned to what is felt to be the magnitude of the injury and to the degree to which the agent's will is identified with, or indifferent to, it. "Freedom and Resentment," in *Free Will,* Derk Pereboom (ed.) (Indianapolis: Hackett, 1997), pp. 119–142, at 138.

    In my discussion of the emotions associated with blame, I do not limit them to the usual instances of Strawsonian reactive attitudes. So, for example, dejection and sadness can be the emotions I feel when I blame another, but dejection and sadness are not usually regarded as reactive attitudes. Nevertheless, if A's sadness is caused by B's wrongdoing and accompanies blaming him for it, some withdrawal of goodwill from B, or some impairment in A's relationship to B, is to be expected.

43. *Moral Dimensions: Permissibility, Meaning, Blame* (Cambridge, MA: Harvard University Press, 2008), chapter 4. Page numbers appear in parentheses in the text.

44. See also T. M. Scanlon, "Reply to Hill, Mason and Wedgwood," *Philosophy and Phenomenological Research,* vol. 82, no. 2 (September 2011): 490–505.

45. Wallace,op. cit. Also, "Dispassionate Opprobrium: On Blame and the Reactive Sentiments," in *Reasons and Recognition: Essays in Honor of the Philosophy of T. M. Scanlon,* R. Jay Wallace, Rahul Kumar, and Samuel Freeman (eds.) (New York: Oxford University Press, 2011).

46. Victoria McGeer asks how the dispute between those who favor a "cool" account of blame and those who favor a more emotive account can be resolved. She addresses the problem by distinguishing between "essential" features of a phenomenon and features that are "characteristic" of it. Her view is that blame is, characteristically, an emotion-laden psychological phenomenon, even if there are instances of blame that are emotionless. See "Civilizing Blame," in *Blame: Its Nature and Norms,* D. Justin Coates and Neal A. Tognazzi (eds.) (Oxford: Oxford University Press, 2013), pp. 162–188.

47. For Pettigrove's argument, see *Forgiveness and Love,* op. cit., pp. 6–7. Paul Hughes gives a similar reason for not including "heartache, depression, disappointment, misery" among the emotions overcome by forgiveness, "even when these emotional states involve the belief that one has been wrongfully harmed" (Hughes, op. cit., p. 39).

    In contrast to sadness, Pettigrove includes contempt among the negative emotions that forgiveness may overcome, since it is directed at another. Here he departs from the standard view as I have characterized it, since in the standard view forgiveness overcomes or forswears retributive emotions, and contempt is not essentially a retributive emotion. According to Michelle Mason, "although contempt might quite often be accompanied by retributive feelings, such feelings are not essential to contempt" ("Contempt as a Moral Attitude," *Ethics,* vol. 113, no. 2 [January 2003]: 234–272, footnote 16). My expanded sentiment-based view of forgiveness departs even further by including other sorts of non-retributive emotions among those that forgiveness overcomes. Macalester Bell also argues that overcoming contempt is a genuine form of forgiveness, in *Hard Feelings: The Moral Psychology of Contempt* (New York: Oxford University Press, 2013), pp. 227–271.

48. John Rawls, *A Theory of Justice* (Cambridge, MA: Harvard University Press, 1971), p. 481; see also p. 533.

49. Margaret Walker, *Moral Repair:Reconstructing Moral Relations after Wrongdoing* (New York: Cambridge University Press, 2006), p. 155.

50. Christopher Bennett also argues that one can forgive an offender while continuing to blame him, but his argument differs from mine. ("Personal and Redemptive Forgiveness," *European Journal of Philosophy,* vol. 11, no. 2 [2003]: 127–144.) Central to his account is the distinction between two types of forgiveness, what he calls "personal forgiveness" and "redemptive forgiveness." Though blame, he says, should not be overcome if the offender does not repent and atone for what he has done, forgiveness in the personal sense is unconditional: it can be

extended to an unrepentant offender because it involves overcoming "morally inappropriate attitudes to the wrongdoer," such as resentment, out of the conviction that one's moral status is undiminished by his wrongful action. Resentment is inappropriate because it reveals that one is insecure about one's moral worth, but one who is able to forgive in a personal sense does not let the other's wrongdoing interfere with her confident belief that she is entitled to respect. But—and this is the important point for my purposes—personal forgiveness is compatible with continuing to blame the offender. Redemptive forgiveness, on the other hand, is not since it is an acknowledgment that the offender has been reconciled with the moral community, and this is only proper if he has repented and atoned for what he has done, thereby rendering further blame inappropriate. As to why one should count forgiveness in the absence of repentance and atonement as any type of forgiveness at all, Bennett says this: "it is a form of forgiveness because, for one thing, it involves the overcoming of hostile feelings towards the wrongdoer occasioned by the wrongdoing; and for another, it involves the resumption of relations between two individuals, where the forgiver recognizes the appropriateness of putting the wrong behind her" (141).

There is much that I agree with here. I agree that overcoming hostile feelings toward the wrongdoer and reestablishing a relationship with him may be sufficient grounds for saying that the wrongdoer has been forgiven and, further, that this is compatible with continuing to blame him. I also agree that forgiveness may be extended under these circumstances in order to "inspire the wrongdoer to see, or to admit to himself, that what he has done was wrong" (141), and thereby to encourage him to rejoin the moral community. But I disagree with Bennett in part because I do not regard resentment as necessarily a morally inappropriate attitude, born of insecurity. One can resent another's acting as if one deserved no better treatment, even if one is confident of one's moral worth and one's ability to ward off any threat the other may pose. Moreover, I don't believe that repentance and atonement necessarily render continuing blame inappropriate. Redemptive forgiveness—that is, forgiveness that is only appropriate if the offender repents and atones for what he has done—is not necessarily an acknowledgment that he has "reconnected fully with the moral community" (133). There are different degrees of reconnecting. And at least from the victim's point of view, full reconnection with the moral community in the wake of serious wrongdoing may not be possible.

51. Sher, op. cit., p. 113, footnote 12.
52. It will be recalled that Nietzsche's masters are invulnerable to this sort of threat.
53. Jeffrie Murphy, "Forgiveness and Resentment," in J. G. Murphy and J. Hampton, *Forgiveness and Mercy* (Cambridge: Cambridge University Press, 1988), p. 25.
54. Murphy, *Getting Even*, op. cit., p. 77.
55. Ibid., p. 59.
56. Griswold, op. cit., p. 45.
57. Murphy, *Getting Even*, p. 19.
58. Griswold, op. cit., p. 45.
59. Feinberg, "The Expressive Function of Punishment," in *Doing and Deserving* (Princeton, NJ: Princeton University Press, 1970), p. 102.
60. Michael McKenna, "Directed Blame and Conversation," in *Blame: Its Nature and Norms*, op. cit., p. 126.
61. Ibid., p. 121.
62. Philip Fisher, *The Vehement Passions* (Princeton, NJ: Princeton University Press, 2002), p. 187.
63. "Valuing Blame," in *Blame: Its Nature and Norms*, pp. 215–216.
64. Fisher, op. cit., pp. 192–193. Page numbers appear in parentheses in the text.
65. Angela Smith, "Moral Blame and Moral Protest," in *Blame: Its Nature and Norms*, op. cit., pp. 27–48, at 43.
66. *Merriam-Webster's Collegiate Dictionary*, 11th Edition, 2005.
67. Bernard R. Boxill, "Self-Respect and Protest," *Philosophy and Public Affairs*, vol. 6, no. 1 (Autumn 1976): 58–69. Page numbers appear in parentheses in the text.
68. Like me, Macalester Bell wants to expand the definition of forgiveness to include more than the overcoming of resentment. She agrees with Jeffrie Murphy that the list of emotions that can be overcome by forgiveness includes, in addition to retributive emotions of resentment,

anger and hatred, "loathing, contempt, indifference, disappointment, and sadness." What all these emotions have in common, and what makes them all suitable as targets of forgiveness, she claims, is that they "constitute barriers between persons" and serve "to separate us from one another" (op. cit., pp. 232–233). This, it seems to me, is not a sufficient explanation of why we ought to expand the definition of forgiveness in this way. Emotions can constitute barriers between persons, or serve to separate them from each other, even if no wrongdoing was committed, so that the issue of forgiveness doesn't even arise. Further, without knowing more about *what* these negative emotions are barriers to and *how* they are barriers to it, Bell's explanation is incomplete. Perhaps, in line with her earlier remarks about contempt, what she means is that they constitute barriers to both "valuable interpersonal relationships" (112) and "moral relationships . . . relationships we have with all members of our moral community" (122). But then we need to know how they do this. Isn't some disappointment, sadness, even anger compatible with valuable interpersonal relationships?

69. McGeer, op. cit., p. 181.

70. Margaret Walker, "The Cycle of Violence," *Journal of Human Rights*, vol. 5 (2006): 81–105, at 93.

71. Charles Griswold, "The Nature and Ethics of Vengeful Anger," in *Passions and Emotions*, James Fleming (ed.) (New York: New York University Press, 2013), p. 81.

2

Forgiveness and Memory for Wrongdoing

1. Some important questions about memory

A psychologically realistic account of forgiveness as a sentiment-based phenomenon requires a psychologically realistic account of the moral psychology of response to wrongdoing.[1] However, as I argued in the last chapter, the standard view of forgiveness restricts the range of emotions that forgiveness overcomes to emotions of moral anger, and this fails the test of psychological realism. Emotional responses to wrongdoing are considerably more complex and multifaceted than this. In this chapter, I want to investigate another topic that I believe the standard account has not probed deeply enough, namely the nature and significance of memory in forgiveness and its aftermath. The next chapter will consider an allied topic, not addressed at all by the standard account: why it may be important to forget in order to forgive.

This is not to say that memory has been entirely neglected in the philosophical literature. On the contrary, the standard account insists on the importance, indeed necessity, of memory as a foundational element of the process of forgiving. We might be able to get rid of anger toward the wrongdoer by taking a pill that induces amnesia, but this way of dealing with one's anger is clearly not forgiving. Psychological therapy might also help us rid ourselves of anger by reinterpreting our past experience, but this would not necessarily enable us to forgive our offender. And there are other ways too of eliminating distressing memories of wrongdoing or blunting their impact that do not constitute or signify forgiveness. One cannot forgive by entirely forgetting that one was wronged or by refusing to pay attention to it or by coming to see that what one thought was wrong was not really wrong after all. Forgiving another person for the wrong that he has done does not involve retracting or setting aside or repressing the *judgment* that one was wronged by this person who was responsible for so acting. Rather, it consists in overcoming certain *emotions* that are occasioned by and accompany the judgment, and to retain the judgment one must, to some extent at least, retain the memory of having been wronged by this person.

I have no quarrel with any of this as far as it goes. But it doesn't go far enough. For one thing, it is important to know what kind of memory is involved in forgiveness, specifically whether the memory is affectless or infused with emotion. Memories of wrongdoing are generally filled with emotion for some period of time after the commission of the offense, and the emotionality of the memories is significant because it reveals evaluative connections between the wronged party and the wrongdoing. The standard account, however, doesn't draw a distinction between emotional and nonemotional memories of wrongdoing, and this suggests that it supposes nothing of moral significance rides on it. For another, while memory of wrongdoing is conceptually necessary for forgiveness, there are ways of remembering that may not in fact be conducive to forgiving. One can be obsessively concerned with or fixated on some aspect of the past and therefore be unable to put it behind oneself and move on with one's life. *How* one should remember so that forgiveness is not just, as a conceptual matter, possible but psychologically achievable, is also a topic that the philosophical literature of forgiveness does not address.[2] It should, however, for the moral psychology of forgiveness as it relates to remembrance of wrongdoing is a critical part of the philosophy of forgiveness.

There are other important questions about memory and forgiveness that are not taken up by the standard account. When a wronged party forgives her offender she may continue to remember both the offense and this particular person as the one who committed it. Neither wrongdoing nor wrongdoer is necessarily forgotten by the wronged party because she has forgiven him. What does change, however, is *how* she remembers them. One way to think about this is to ask how the memories of being wronged after the wrongdoer has been forgiven relate to the rest of the wronged party's emotional life and how, in this respect, they differ from the memories of wrongdoing before the offender has been forgiven. I will explore this possibility below. In any case it is clear what needs explaining: how the memories of being wronged that persist after the offender is forgiven differ from those the wronged party retained during the process of forgiveness.

Another question is whether and to what extent it might be good or morally desirable for the wronged party to hold on to her memories of being wronged even though her offender has been forgiven for it. It is not obvious that once you have forgiven your offender it is best to forget what he did, and in fact I suggested some reasons in the last chapter for taking issue with the sentiment expressed in that familiar bit of so-called folk wisdom, "forgive and forget." The standard view, insofar as it addresses the memories and emotions that remain after forgiveness, says only that the memories of being wronged must not reignite angry emotions if forgiveness is to be sustained. I agree with this. But once again this is not saying enough. Memories of wrongdoing and the wrongdoer commonly do linger after the wrongdoer has been forgiven, and it is not enough to be told that they can't be angry ones. For there are also reasons for holding on to them, reasons of self-protection, self-respect, and moral agency, and an account of the moral psychology of forgiveness must pay attention to these no less than to the reasons for holding on to the memories of wrongdoing until the offender has been forgiven.

This chapter is organized in the following way. In section 2 I distinguish descriptively between emotional and nonemotional memory and between different senses of emotional memory. Discussions of forgiveness in the philosophical literature generally do not go into these matters, but this is critical to my aims in this chapter. It is emotional memories that are my focus here partly, but only partly, because the memories we have of recent wrongdoing are typically emotion-laden. In addition, as I explain in section 3, emotional memories are or can be *evaluatively* significant because there are connections between emotions and evaluations and evaluative cognitions. I argue for this in the following way.

First, I argue that it is a criterion of properly appreciating the wrongness of being wronged that it have a significant effect in the life of the wronged party, and this effect obtains when one is disposed to respond to the mistreatment with negative emotions that one regards as justified by what they are responsive to. According to this explanation, emotional memories of wrongdoing, because of their emotionality, show that one has a grip on the evaluative significance of the wrongs done to oneself. Second, I examine the link between emotions on the one hand and values and valuing on the other. Valuing requires that we have some emotional attachment to the object of our valuing. It is in part a matter of being emotionally invested in and engaged with it, including being emotionally vulnerable in the sense that one is disposed to positive feelings if the object of one's valuing does well and negative feelings if it does not. Without this investment and the dispositions it involves, a person might believe that X is valuable, but he wouldn't value it. Or as we might put it, X would not be among this person's values. In this explanation, what emotional memories of wrongdoing reveal or can reveal about the one who was wronged is her valuing, specifically her valuing what was violated or damaged by the wrongful treatment she received, including her own dignity. If her memories, in virtue of their emotionality, are indicative of her devotion to and emotional engagement with objects of moral value, then the memories reveal her moral values.

In section 4 I take up the question of how memories of wrongdoing and their relations to other elements of a person's psychology are altered as a result of forgiveness. This is an interesting question for any account of forgiveness, but there is a particular need to address it in light of my revision of the standard account, since the emotional distinction between before and after forgiveness is considerably more clear-cut in the standard account of forgiveness than in the more complex picture of emotional transformation that I present. So I need to say something about how I conceive of the passage from the before to the after. Part of this will have to be about how the memories of wrongdoing are experienced by and integrated into the emotional life of the one who was wronged. For it is not only the wrongdoing that survives in the psychological and material effects it has on the life and well-being of the one who was wronged, but also the memories of it that she retains for some time after.

Finally, having set out various criteria for the emotional transformation that forgiveness effects, I briefly address two issues related to my account. The first is a normative question about the good of having emotional memories of wrongdoing even after forgiving the wrongdoer, and I add a few remarks to the discussion from the previous chapter about the moral psychological aftermath of forgiveness. The good that I focus on can be called prudential, since the reasons for continuing to remember are reasons of self-protection, but I do not want to draw a sharp distinction between these and moral reasons. The second has to do with the adequacy of an account of forgiveness that focuses exclusively on changes in the victim's emotions and emotional memories. I claim this leaves out the relational element of forgiveness, more precisely the element that consists in a decision or policy not to allow past wrongdoing to continue to impair, or to impair in the same way, one's relationship to the wrongdoer.

2. The nature of emotional memory

There is an obvious connection between the emotional responses to wrongdoing that forgiveness is concerned with and memories of that wrongdoing. The negative emotions that are the stuff of forgiveness relate to events that occurred in one's past, even if only the very recent past. These events to which the wronged party responds emotionally are normally retained in her memories of them and provide them with content and focus. The memories may be conscious or unconscious—that is, beyond the reach of conscious awareness because they are repressed. Repressed memories have their costs and their distortions in the emotional life of the individual, and these constitute a kind of emotional engagement in or with the memories despite their repressed nature. Both sorts of memories are important for a theory of forgiveness. Here, however, I focus on conscious memories. As in the standard account, I assume that forgiving another is an intentional act that requires consciousness of what one is forgiving him for. The memories that the victim has of wrongdoing concentrate her attention on something with respect to which the question of forgiveness arises and enable her to target past events for considered response. If her memories of wrongdoing have been repressed, then according to psychoanalytic theory forgiveness is only possible if she is able to "work through" the repressed material and to consciously express hitherto unconscious emotions. Thus, unconscious and conscious memories are important for a theory of forgiveness in different ways: unconscious memories can impede forgiveness, but the memories that are required for and that make forgiveness possible are conscious.[3]

In addition to unconscious memories, two other possibilities are worth a brief mention. There might be someone who reacts emotionally to being wronged but is able to overcome his distress almost immediately and with scarcely any effort. He is the sort of person who cannot hold a grudge for any length of time at all, and who, a bit like Nietzsche's noble souls, is able to "shake off with a single shrug" (or perhaps a few shrugs) even serious wrongs done to him. He does remember long enough to forgive, and he does forgive, but the memory may be vanishingly brief and once the offender is forgiven, his wrong is forgotten. A second possibility is when someone is *incapable* of remembering anything for more than a few minutes. The most famous example of this is the case H.M. After an operation for epilepsy, which had grown increasingly incapacitating over the years, H.M. experienced a profound and lasting change in his ability to remember. Eric Kandel describes it this way:

> What H.M. lacked, and lacked to the most profound degree, was the ability to convert new short-term memory into new long-term memory. Without this ability he forgot events shortly after they happened. He could retain new information as long as his attention was not diverted from it, but a minute or two after his attention was directed to something else, he could not remember the previous subject or anything he thought about it.[4]

Clearly a person with such profound memory impairment cannot remember long enough to forgive another for wronging him if he is wronged, for before he can even entertain the idea that there is something to forgive another for, he has forgotten that he has been wronged.

These are unusual cases. Most people, at least when the wrong done to them is serious, experience strong emotional reactions to it and cannot forgive the offender without some inner struggle or marked effort. The emotional reactions and the struggles that attend them depend upon and sustain their memories of being wronged. Moreover, it is quite extraordinary for someone to suffer such devastating damage to his capacity to remember that he cannot convert short-term to long-term memory. Ordinarily when people are wronged, or seriously wronged, they remember it for some period of time, although perhaps not consciously if the memories are too painful. These memories may also persist for some time after the offender has been forgiven. Forgiveness, as I have said a number of times, does not necessarily erase the wronged party's memory of having been wronged. It does, however, modify and blunt the memory so that she is able to recall the event without reliving or reliving in the same way the emotional responses that the original experience evoked. On the standard account of forgiveness, which emphasizes the retributive emotions, the memories that persist after forgiveness, if any, either do not reactivate angry feelings or, if they occasionally do, the wronged party disavows them as no longer appropriate. On both the standard account of forgiveness and my revised emotive account, there is a difference, emotional if not cognitive, between the memories that precede and the memories that follow forgiving. The latter is the subject of section 4 below. In this section I am setting aside the distinction.

How is wrongdoing remembered or, since forgiveness is the topic and minor offenses may not warrant forgiveness (being too trivial to get upset about), how are major offenses and *serious* wrongs remembered? I propose to approach this by drawing a number of distinctions among kinds of memory. Though it is beyond the scope of this book to undertake a philosophical study of the nature of human memory, I speak about it often enough to justify taking some time to disambiguate its various meanings. The resulting taxonomy demarcates more precisely the sort of memory that I claim has evaluative import and, incidentally, raises an interesting issue in the epistemology of memory.

The most basic distinction memory researchers draw is between declarative and nondeclarative memory: the former is explicit and expressible linguistically; the latter is not (e.g., remembering a skill, such as how to ride a bicycle). Declarative memory in turn is divided into semantic and episodic memory. The former refers to the store of general knowledge about the world, concepts, rules, and language that a person has accumulated. In addition, one of its characteristic features is that what is remembered contains no reference to the circumstances in which the knowledge was acquired or to one's having acquired it. Episodic memory, by contrast, refers to the recall of experiences and autobiographical events.[5] Here's an example of semantic memory: My teacher asks me when Columbus discovered America and I remember it was in 1492; an example of episodic memory: I remember being on my way to work when I heard about the attack on the World Trade Center. Since episodic memory refers to how stored information was acquired and the acquisition of this information may have been an emotional process, episodic memory is not infrequently emotionally inflected.[6]

Emotional memories are a type of declarative, typically episodic, memory, and it is these that are particularly significant for my purposes. However, beyond this general characterization, there are a number of things emotional memory might be taken to mean, so additional classifications are in order. An emotional memory$_1$ is a memory of an emotional event, but the memory does not involve the experience of an emotion. For example, I remember that some time ago I was angry at you for (what I now regard as) a relatively minor offense. I have some inferential evidence for this: perhaps I remember yelling at you or avoiding your company afterward. However, the memory of the offense, many months after the fact, arouses no emotion in me. An emotional memory of this type is a memory of an event that, at the time the subject witnessed or was involved in it, elicited some emotion in her, but where the present experience of it in her memory is without affect. Memories$_1$ of one's past emotional state are not appreciably different from emotionally neutral memories of other facts about one's past, such as what one did yesterday or where one was at a certain time.

An emotional memory$_2$ is a memory of an event that, at the time it occurred, did not arouse any emotion in the subject, at least consciously. However, now when she remembers it, she does so with emotion. This may be because the event she remembers is one that occurred before she was born. One can also have a delayed emotional reaction to events because one is not able to fully appreciate their circumstances and significance until sometime after they occur. In cases of this sort, the emotions the subject currently experiences are new emotions in the sense that they are directed toward past situations or events that did not generate any emotional responses in her when they originally occurred, even if she was involved in them.

An emotional memory$_3$ combines both past and present past-directed emotions. It is both a memory of an event that one witnessed or was involved in and that one reacted to emotionally at the time, and a present experience of an emotion directed at that event. There are two types: in emotional memory$_{3a}$ the currently experienced emotion is directed at a past event and is similar to the emotion originally experienced; and in emotional memory$_{3b}$ the currently experienced emotion directed at the past event and the emotion originally experienced are dissimilar. An example of the former: I remember being racially profiled and that I felt humiliated by it, and now, remembering it, I feel humiliated once again.[7] An example of the latter: I was angry at my parents when they told me that I have to move out and find my own apartment, but now looking back I am grateful to them for helping me to become a more independent person. I react to my parents' decision now in an emotionally different way than I reacted to it at first, and this is an integral part of my adopting a critical stance toward my earlier anger.

Given the similarity between *past-directed* emotion and *original* emotion that is a defining feature of emotional memory$_{3a}$, it might be supposed that memories of this kind provide us with a particularly direct kind of access to our own past emotions.[8] It might seem, in other words, that without relying on any process of inferential reasoning, the subject's past-directed emotions present her with how she emotionally experienced events in the past, and that for this reason emotional memory$_{3a}$ is an important source of knowledge about one's past emotions. Similarity of emotion, however, is not sufficient to establish this. Memories

Forgiveness and Memory for Wrongdoing   77

imbued with emotions similar to those originally experienced may seem to give us, by virtue of this similarity, direct access to the emotions themselves that were generated by those events. But the similarity may mislead. They may not give us direct noninferential access any more than memories imbued with emotions that are different from the original emotions do.

On an alternative view, past-directed emotions are *present, new* emotions, not *old* emotions recollected, and therefore in terms of giving direct access to past emotions, emotional memory$_{3a}$ is no different than emotional memory$_{3b}$.[9] Hence we would do better to talk about emotional memory$_3$ without attaching any particular significance to its subtypes. Nevertheless, as Dorothea Debus argues, emotions that are present, new ones can still play an extremely "important role in a subject's mental life" (773) because they contribute to self-understanding. They do this in different ways. Debus shows this by distinguishing between two types of "autobiographical past-directed emotions," "empathic" and "non-empathic." The empathic ones result from the subject's putting herself in the shoes of her former self and coming to react emotionally to past events in the same way she reacted emotionally when they occurred. For example, I can try to remember what it was like to have the feelings of disappointment that the situation originally provoked. If I succeed in this effort at empathy, my new emotion of disappointment is empathic and more or less matches the original one. The non-empathic ones involve emotional reactions to past events from a subject's present point of view. That is, the subject reacts emotionally to a past event as the past event *currently* provokes her to react. Non-empathic emotions can also help a subject develop an "evaluative stance," sometimes but not always critical, toward her former emotional responses to past events. She can, for example, remember an earlier disappointing event from a somewhat more detached standpoint and with new emotions that cast her earlier actions and emotional responses in a new light.

The distinction between empathic and non-empathic past-directed emotions is relevant to the concerns of this chapter because it can be used to characterize different responses to past wrongdoing, some of which may make forgiveness more difficult than others. One reason that forgiveness may be a difficult achievement, even after some time has passed since the initial wrongdoing, is that in remembering the wrongs done to them persons put themselves in the shoes of their former selves and feel again what they felt before. By empathically projecting themselves into an earlier situation as it was experienced by their former selves, persons may relive those emotions to such a degree that they are unable to forgive. Forgiveness becomes possible when, without forgetting the wrongs done to them and without thinking their earlier emotional responses were unwarranted, they are able to adopt a critical stance toward these responses and consider whether they are still warranted, given their present view of things.

This reassessment that is part of forgiving is not just a cognitive process, devoid of emotionality. On the contrary, the memories may still be imbued with negative emotions; only these are not simply the result of empathetic identification with the emotions of their earlier selves. Rather, the emotions change as those who were wronged confront their past experiences from their present point of view. This change in emotions does not just give them a standpoint from which to assess their past emotional responses: it is in fact a constitutive ingredient of a new evaluative stance that they have toward the wrong and the wrongdoers.

The process of forgiveness, therefore, is not only one in which the wronged party comes to see the offender in a new light. It is also one in which the wronged party comes to see her own past reactions to wrongdoing in a new light, to reflect on them from her present standpoint. And the perspective from which she reflects on them is itself an emotionally engaged one.

The distinction between empathic and non-empathic past-directed emotions is a fruitful one, but since my concern here is to set out the defining features of emotional memory, I will not pursue it further.[10] Emotional memories, by which I mean emotional memories$_3$ (leaving aside the question of their epistemic status), are memories for the emotional significance of experiences, and emotions figure into this in two ways: the memories are both directed at past emotional experiences and themselves emotional experiences. They are instances of a kind of memory in which the emotion is a constituent part of the memory and in which a distinct separation between cognition and emotion cannot be maintained. Emotional memories in this sense can be either occurrent or dispositional. For example, I may on a particular occasion have a memory of my strained relationship with my now-deceased father that is "filled" with regret: it is a regretful memory, not just a memory of regret or an amalgam in which the emotion of regret somehow gets hooked to an affectless recollection of missed opportunities. And when the memory is conscious, I am not just conscious *of* my regret but *consciously regretful*.[11] I may also be prone to remember my relationship with my father this way under certain circumstances. Emotions that are caused by memories can also then color these memories, so that the memories become imbued with the emotions that they cause.

To further clarify how I am using the term "emotional memory," I add a few words about the view of emotion on which I am relying. The theory of the emotions to which I subscribe is broadly speaking cognitivist—that is, it holds that evaluative cognition of some sort is essential to the emotions. The cognition, according to some versions, is an evaluative *judgment*, which consists in grasping and affirming a proposition. According to an extreme version of this view, emotions just are or are reducible to evaluative judgments. In other versions, the cognition is a sort of *perception*. In either case, whether the cognition is a judgment or a perception, it is intended to account for what has seemed to many to be an essential feature of the emotions, namely their intentionality, the fact that they have intentional objects and are not the same as feelings or sensations that register bodily changes. Mere feelings or sensations are not about anything; they have no import. But emotions are different, even if what they are about is somewhat vague and indeterminate. When I respond to a person's wrongdoing with anger, or fear, or disappointment, my emotion has an object: someone toward whom I am angry because he has harmed me; or whom I fear because I take him to be dangerous; or in whom I am disappointed because he has failed to live up to my expectations. And what determines the object of these emotions is a judgment or a perception.[12]

So the emotions that constitute emotional memory are themselves partly constituted by cognitions. They are not mere feelings without intentionality, for at least in the standard cases evaluative cognitions are essential to them. When I have an emotional memory of being wronged by someone, for example, negative emotions that are directed toward that person are integral to the memory, and this directedness is explained by the content of the evaluative cognitions that are integral to them. As we will see in the next section, the disposition to respond emotionally to objects can reveal one's values and embody one's valuing in relation to these objects, and this would be difficult if not impossible to explain if emotions were mere feelings or bodily sensations.

3. Emotions, valuing, and wrongdoing

(a) Taking wrongdoing seriously

Declarative memories can be neutral or lacking in emotional affect, or infused with and constituted by emotion. The latter are what I have been calling emotional memories, and they, or more precisely conscious emotional memories, are what I highlight in developing an account of memory's role in forgiveness. Traumatic memories may be repressed to avert mental pain, putting forgiveness at least temporarily out of the wronged party's reach. But wrongdoing is often consciously remembered with strong emotion for some time after the initial event, and even after the wronged party has forgiven her offender it is not necessarily unreasonable or pathological for her to continue to have negative emotional memories of it. Of course, after a prolonged period of time, regardless of whether she has forgiven her offender, the memory of the wrong done to her, if she has occasion to reflect on it at all, might no longer trigger any negative past-directed emotions in her. The memory and the emotions it triggers may fade, and as the emotions fade, the memories they sustain fade with them. She might remember *that* she was the victim of culpable wrongdoing, yet not care enough about it for it to cause her the slightest distress or upset. However, the persistence of conscious negative emotional memories of wrongdoing despite having forgiven the offender is not surprising from a psychological standpoint, nor is it ruled out by a plausible conception of forgiveness.

These remarks belong to the empirical psychology of remembering wrongdoing: the memories of serious wrongdoing tend to be emotionally charged and they often persist for some time after the offender has been forgiven. I now want to discuss what is shown about a person's evaluative relationship to wrongdoing by having memories of being wronged that are emotional in this way. I will argue that emotional memories in general, and emotional memories of wrongdoing in particular, can be evaluatively significant precisely because the memories are constituted by negative past-directed *emotions*, whether these are retributive or non-retributive in nature. (The distinction between these types of negative emotions, so important in chapter 1, does not play a central role here.) The wronged party's emotional reactions show that she appreciates the wrongness of what was done to her and how she appreciates it; and when the evaluations they involve reveal her moral values, they are morally significant. I start with the claim about appreciation.

We might approach it this way. Merely remembering that one was wrongfully harmed without having some negative emotional response to that wrong because it was wrong, it might be said, is not much different than denying that the wrong was actually wrong or than condoning the wrong. Paul Hughes seems to rely on a view like this in arguing against those who deny that forgiveness is compatible with the retention of negative emotions directed toward the wrongdoing and the wrongdoer. His claim is that "to hold otherwise is to assume that to forgive another is to utterly wipe the emotional slate clean; to 'feel,' that is, as if the misdeed were never committed."[13] Presumably one may continue to *believe* that the misdeed was committed. It is just that one lacks any negative emotion constituted by this belief. This is tantamount to "feeling" as if that wrong was not committed, Hughes suggests, and to feel this is to deny what really happened. Or it may be said that with respect to wrongdoing, having only nonemotional declarative memories is close to, perhaps too close to, condonation. Condoning a wrong is different from forgiving it. It is to overlook it or treat it indulgently, and the thought might be that one indication of condoning a wrong is that one is not bothered by it. To preserve the distinction between condonation and forgiveness, the argument goes, we must stipulate that the memories of wrongdoing (at least for a certain range of cases) are negative emotional ones and that one is distressed by them. My argument is different from this, although it has some resemblance to the point Hughes is trying to make.

Consider what we might say about the use of drugs to dampen memories of having been wronged.[14] Memory-dampening drugs, like the beta-blocker propranolol, are alleged to have the capacity to blunt the emotional impact of traumatic memories, such as memories of being raped, when taken shortly after the incident. Presumably a declarative memory of the trauma would remain to some extent, for a time. The victim would remember *that* something terrible happened to her, although her memories would likely be less detailed and vivid than they would have been had she not taken the drug. But she would be spared from the painful emotions that ordinarily accompany such events and that are part of the memories that people ordinarily have of them. The painful memories would not just be relegated to the unconscious and the dampening effect would not just be temporary, we may suppose. When she remembers the traumatic incident, she will simply not be distressed, and even such memories as she has will tend to fade over time without negative emotions to sustain them.

What should we say about the victim's relationship to the traumatic event and, specifically, to its wrongness? First, it may not be wrong of her to take the drug. The memories may cause her intense emotional suffering and she may need to gain control over her psychic life to return to normal functioning. Second, there seems to be an important difference between *judging* that what done to oneself was wrong and *affectively seeing* or regarding it as wrong, even if we can understand why a victim might not want to see it this way. The latter involves being disposed to ways of relating to the wrong and the wrongdoer—perceptual, emotional, deliberative, and behavioral—that one who only judges that it was wrong is not disposed to. And for this reason it seems that the one who takes the drug and dampens her emotional memory of a traumatic event is not fully engaged with the wrongness of what happened to her, understandable though it may be under the circumstances why she chooses not to be. Her lack of engagement with it, moreover, will condition her relations with the wrongdoer if she continues to have any. It would be wrong to say that after she takes the drug she condones the wrongdoing or denies that anything bad happened to her. But her condemnation of the wrong and the wrongdoer is muted to such an extent that it doesn't have much moral bite.

What gives condemnation moral bite is roughly speaking its emotionality, not the fact that it expresses a dispassionate moral judgment. We can say also that there is a sense of *appreciation* according to which a person who does not have or is not disposed to have negative emotional responses to wrongdoing does not really appreciate it for what it is. Or to put this another way, she does not have a grip on its evaluative significance. One's emotional responses may change, of course. One may come to see the wrongdoer, affectively, in a new light. But in the absence of these responses to his wrongdoing the trauma victim is not "taking in" its wrongness. To try to explain what I mean by this, I want to turn to a discussion that may seem at first to have little to do with the current topic but that actually has a connection to what I am gesturing towards here. I am referring to Robert Nozick's remarks on retributive punishment, specifically what he calls nonteleological retributivism.

According to Nozick, there are two sorts of retributivists, teleological and nonteleological. Teleological retributivists aim to bring about some change in the wrongdoer, his moral transformation through recognition of the wrongness of what he has done. Nonteleological retributivists, in contrast, view punishment as right or good in itself, not because of any further consequences to which it might lead. They do not aim to change the wrongdoer but simply to connect him with the correct values, and it is the connecting with correct values, because they are the correct values, that gives retributive punishment its intrinsic value. It is also this idea that may be of some use in expressing what is lacking in the person whose responses to wrongdoing are without affect. Nozick explains the idea as follows:

> Correct values are themselves without causal power, and the wrongdoer chooses not to give them effect in his life. So others must give them some effect in his life, in a secondary way . . . Through punishment, we give the correct values, qua correct values, some significant effect in his life, willy-nilly linking him up to them.[15]

It is not just any significant effect on the wrongdoer that nonteleological retributivists seek, however, but an effect commensurate with the "magnitude of his flouting these correct values" (377), as determined both by the importance of the values that are flouted and by how seriously he flouted them. Thus, even if a wrongdoer does not take up the correct values and conform his conduct to them, and even if the probability of his moral transformation is small or nonexistent, there is still a purpose to punishment. The purpose is just to give the correct values an effect in his life that is equal in magnitude to his flouting of them. It is right and good that the wrongdoer be connected in this way to correct values, qua correct values. This, we might say, is one way that those who punish take the correct values seriously.

What I want to suggest is that negative emotional responses to wrongdoing secure for the wronged party something like punishment secures for the wrongdoer according to nonteleological retributivism: they connect the individual to the correct values and give them some significant effect in her life. In the former case, emotional response secures the victim's connection to the values that the wrongdoer flouted and contributes to the moral quality of her life. In the latter, punishment secures the wrongdoer's connection to the values that he flouted and gives them significant effect in *his* life by "hit[ting] him over the head with them" (375). And in both cases, not just any significant effect in the individual's life is good enough: it must be roughly commensurate with his rejection of the correct values. What this means in the case of punishment is that it must fit the crime; what this means in the case of being wronged is that the victim should respond negatively and in such a way that her negative emotional responses fit the wrongness of the offender's action, his flouting of moral values and the values he flouted. Just as a slap on the wrist does not fit the crime of homicide, mere annoyance at having one's human rights violated, for example, does not fit the nature of this particular wrong. Mere annoyance would indicate that the victim does not have a grip, or only a very weak grip, on the evaluative significance of what was done to her. It would indicate a failure on her part to appreciate the wrong for the sort of wrong it is.

Finally, as the nonteleological retributivist says about punishment, the fitness of the emotions to the wrong to which they respond is good in itself, apart from whatever consequences it might lead to. We may hope that the victim will learn from her experience how to protect herself in the future or that if she is suffering from posttraumatic stress disorder she will seek professional help or that some other good outcomes will result. And if we were teleologists about the value of having emotional access to the wrong she suffered, we would have to conclude that if none of this happens, the emotions would simply cause the victim distress for no good purpose. But nonteleologists about emotional access would not say this, since for them effecting an emotional connection of the right sort to the wrong is intrinsically valuable. To be sure, it might be questioned whether, in the absence of certain outcomes, such as taking steps to protect herself, the victim actually *made* the right connection to the values that her wrongdoer flouted, or fully appreciated the wrongness of what he did. But it would be a mistake to think that there is no value in her responding emotionally to wrongdoing if her responding does not have further good consequences. What's more, even if consequences can provide some evidence of the character of the victim's connection to the correct values, this does not undermine the basic distinction between a teleological and a nonteleological account of the value of emotional response to wrongdoing.

If the comparison with nonteleological retributivism is apt, we have one explanation for why emotional memories$_3$ of wrongdoing are evaluatively significant: they effect a connection of the wronged party to the correct values, qua correct values, a connection that is fitting if the significance of the effect they have in the wronged party's life is commensurate, in both type and intensity of emotional response, with the significance of the values the wrongdoer flouted and his flouting of them. This result is important for a theory of forgiveness. If nonemotional declarative memories of being wronged are the only conscious memories the victim has of it, then in forgiving her offender she has not come to grips with, has not connected in this way to, the wrongness of what was done to her. There is something lacking in the wronged party's appreciation of the wrongness of what was done to her, and this carries over to the moral assessment of her forgiveness.

There may also be something lacking in the wronged party's appreciation of her own worth. To appreciate one's own value as a human being is not only to take steps to defend one's dignity when it is threatened by the actions of others. It is also, before this, to appreciate that one did not deserve to be treated this way because it is a wrong way for someone to be treated. There is, in other words, an impersonal aspect to the criticism one is leveling against the other's conduct: it is not to be done and it is for this reason, although not only for this reason, that it is not to be done to me. I am suggesting, therefore, that to appreciate one's own worth is partly to grasp the wrongness of what was done to oneself, to grasp it *as* wrong, and that this involves grasping it in a certain way, affectively. It is not just something about which one makes a dispassionate moral judgment but something to be or to be disposed to be exercised about. Otherwise, barring exceptional circumstances there are grounds for doubting whether one really takes one's dignity seriously.

I now want to turn to another explanation of the evaluative significance of emotional memories of wrongdoing, the connection between emotions and valuing. Here again the distinction between types of negative emotions does not play a prominent role. This additional explanation may be viewed as complementing or completing the one just discussed. The latter holds that negative emotional response constitutes a "significant effect" of the wrongdoing in the life of the victim and that it is appropriate or fitting for wrongdoing to have a significant effect there. It may still be wondered, however, why the significant effect has to be of this sort. The next explanation answers this question by investigating the conditions of valuing.

(b) Wrongdoing, emotions, and valuing

A connection between emotions and valuing is explicit in Samuel Scheffler's account of valuing. According to Scheffler, though normally we value what we judge to be of value, valuing something is not just a matter of *believing* it good or valuable or worthy. If this were all that there was to valuing, then everything that we believe is valuable we would value, which is manifestly not the case. I might believe, for example, that competitive sports have value, but since I have no interest in sports, not value them myself. Similarly for the relationship between believing something to have negative value and disvaluing it. Some kind of emotional vulnerability to how the things one values fare is necessary for valuing, and there must also be a disposition to endorse these reactions—that is, to believe that these emotions are merited or appropriate. Scheffler puts it this way:

> Valuing . . . comprises a complex syndrome of interrelated attitudes and dispositions, which includes but is not limited to a belief that the valued

item is valuable. Valuing something normally involves, in addition to such a belief, at least the following elements: a susceptibility to experience a range of context-dependent emotions concerning the valued item, a disposition to experience these emotions as being merited or deserved, and a disposition to treat certain kinds of considerations pertaining to the valued item as reasons for action in relevant deliberative contexts.[16]

According to this, valuing is a complex evaluative attitude that partly consists in being disposed to have a range of emotions concerning valued items in a range of circumstances. The particular emotions to which one is susceptible in virtue of valuing something vary, depending on the norms governing how one should feel in light of that value.[17] But generally speaking, one is susceptible to a range of positive emotions when the object of our valuing does well (or what one disvalues does poorly), and a range of negative ones when the object of our valuing does not fare well (or what one disvalues does well). If I value my friend, for example, I tend to rejoice for him when he prospers, to feel sad for him when he fails, to fear for him when he faces danger and relief when he escapes it, to grieve when he dies, and so on. If I value our friendship my positive and negative emotions concern the survival and flourishing of our relationship. If I value honesty, I tend to feel guilty for lying, to get angry at displays of dishonesty, to feel contempt for those who lie, to experience emotions of praise that reflect positive attitudes toward persons who act honestly, and so on. And there is a similar range of emotions relating to how well or poorly what one disvalues fares. There are also connections between valuing and memory: we tend to dwell on memories of valued objects that matter to us, in no small measure because we are susceptible to emotions concerning them.

Because valuing is an attitude that partly consists in being susceptible to a range of emotions concerning what one values, one's susceptibility to emotions regarding an object can reveal one's values in relation to it and how one values it. (I speak of values and valuing in the same breath: in my sense, a person's values are expressed by his valuings.) Consider, for example, that our emotional responses to some event or state of affairs may surprise us, because they show us that we value something that we did not suspect or even denied that we valued. Suppose I profess a belief in an open marriage, but nonetheless become extremely angry when I find my wife with another man. My anger not only shows that I value my wife's fidelity after all, but also just how I disvalue her infidelity. Or suppose I profess indifference to the outcome of the next U.S. presidential race. But when I find myself becoming extremely upset at the prospect of one of the candidates becoming the next president, I realize how very bad I think this would be. Thus, emotions sometimes enable us to become aware of our valuing something that we did not realize we valued. More generally, because susceptibility to emotional response is one of the constitutive components of valuing, emotions can contain and reveal our particular valuings, and they can do this both when we aware of what we value and when we are not. Some of the values that are revealed in this way are moral or have moral import, and these are the ones that interest me. But of course other sorts of values may be revealed as well—for example, aesthetic values or religious values.[18]

This gives us an explanation also of why being disposed to remember events and people with emotion is evaluatively significant, since then we are susceptible to emotional reactions of various sorts when we remember, and the pattern of these susceptibilities can reveal our values. To disvalue as well as value something is to be emotionally invested in it, although in opposite ways, and one is not emotionally invested if one is not susceptible to emotional response in relation to it. Thus, if one is not susceptible to negative emotions in response to being wronged, one cannot properly be said to disvalue being treated this way or to disvalue it any longer. Likewise, if one is not susceptible to such emotions when one remembers being wronged, then even if one's memories involve continuing to *believe* that one was wronged, one's memories do not or do not any longer show that one *disvalues* having been wronged. Valuing and disvaluing require (the right sort of) emotional engagement with their respective objects, and memories that are not constituted by susceptibilities to emotional response do not reveal our valuings. For this reason too memories that are constituted by such susceptibilities have significance for a theory of forgiveness that memories that are not so constituted lack.

There is a difference, obviously, between past events affecting us emotionally and past events affecting us emotionally because we have emotional memories of them: the former can happen without the latter. However, it is memory that is required for forgiveness, memory of past wrongs typically done to oneself, and what I am claiming is that if we are not susceptible to emotional reactions to the wrongs committed against us when we remember them, then these memories do not satisfy one of the defining conditions of valuing. I can now put in a somewhat different way what I said about the individual who takes a drug to dampen her memory of a traumatic event. When a person disvalues what was done to her in her memories of it, she is susceptible to negative emotions in regard to it and is disposed to endorse these reactions as merited or deserved. A victim of trauma, however, may have good reasons for resisting emotionally charged memories of it, if she could be retraumatized by them.

These general remarks about the relationship between emotions and valuing also apply to the wronged party after she has forgiven her offender, since forgiveness does not preclude continuing to harbor negative emotions. Some of the negative emotions that she experiences in response to being wronged, such as anger or profound disappointment and grief, may be so intense and deeply rooted that they will just never go away; she will never be able to work through them sufficiently to forgive him. But it is also possible that her negative emotions permit her to forgive, that she is able to moderate them and eventually to get rid of them altogether. The wronged party may continue to have emotional memories of being wronged and be disposed to remember the wrong with negative emotions, even after she has forgiven her wrongdoer. These memories, while they may not impede forgiveness, can nevertheless signify that she continues to disvalue how she was mistreated and by whom. In this case the moderation or forswearing of the emotions that prevented her from forgiving does not show that she has stopped disvaluing what before she had not forgiven her wrongdoer for. Nor does it show that she no longer cares about or values her self-respect. Moreover, these lingering negative emotional susceptibilities are not necessarily inappropriate or unwarranted since the norms for how one should feel about past wrongdoing do not proscribe continuing to disvalue it in one's memories after the wrongdoer is forgiven.

4. Memory and the differentiation problem

But if emotional memories remain, and may properly remain, after the wrongdoer is forgiven, forgiveness does something to them. What it does is the subject of this section. I will be asking how the memories of wrongdoing change emotionally once the offender has been forgiven. This is an important question for any sentiment-based account of forgiveness, including my own. However, it seems that my account has made it especially difficult to answer this question. Let me explain why by briefly reviewing the standard account and comparing my own to it.

According to the standard account of forgiveness as I have described it, the emotions that need to be overcome are angry ones, chiefly or paradigmatically resentment. While the victim has not yet forgiven her offender, she has not yet let go of her angry feelings or fully renounced them. There may be considerable ambivalence about whether she can forgive her offender, and even if she decides it is worth making an effort to do so, there is usually no steady unbroken progress toward forgiveness. Her angry feelings may be unruly and difficult to master, her management of them fitful and erratic. This, I take it, is more or less how the standard account would or could characterize the process of forgiveness. However, after she has forgiven him, the psychological picture is very different. She no longer views the offender through the lens of angry emotions. Anger may occasionally resurface, but she does not endorse it. Indeed, she views these occasional outbursts as unwarranted. If she is ambivalent about whether she should renounce them, then to that extent she is ambivalent about whether she should forgive him. Negative feelings concerning the wrongdoing may remain, but they will be predominantly non-retributive, and even then they are not likely to dominate the victim's emotional life in the way her anger may have done before she was able to forgive her offender. In these ways the standard account draws a relatively clear distinction, even if they can't always be sharply distinguished in practice, between how the wronged party is engaged or exercised by the wrongful action before she has forgiven the offender and how she is engaged after she has forgiven him.

My expanded sentiment-based account of forgiveness muddies this picture. I have argued that it is more in keeping with our actual experiences of forgiveness to think of it as overcoming or forswearing a variety of negative emotions toward a wrongdoer. There may be no hostile affects and desire to lash out. If there is anger it may be blended with non-retributive feelings in hybrid negative emotions; or, if there is such a thing as non-retributive anger, it may be non-retributive. The emotional reactions of the victim prior to forgiving her offender are complex, multilayered, and fluid. After forgiveness, there is change, but not as pronounced as it is in the standard account. The change is not as pronounced because the negative emotions that are felt by the victim prior to forgiveness, and that may have impeded her ability to forgive, may continue to be felt in some manner after she forgives her offender and to color her memories, and she may endorse this. In other words, there may be tokens of the same type of negative emotion before and after forgiveness. Sometimes the explanation for why the wronged party hasn't yet forgiven the offender is that she hasn't yet overcome or forsworn the nonangry feelings she has toward him. For example, it may be distrust that explains why the victim couldn't forgive her offender. Yet some distrust of the wrongdoer may remain even though she has forgiven him, because she has seen what he is capable of doing.

The problem that this presents for my account can be put this way: how do we distinguish the after from the before in terms of the character of the victim's emotional response to wrongdoing and the wrongdoer? Or alternatively, and relatedly, how do the emotional memories of wrongdoing change once the offender has been forgiven? Now I admit that this way of formulating the problem is not entirely satisfactory, especially since it suggests precisely what I want to deny, namely that forgiveness signifies some sharp discontinuity in the emotional responses of the victim. Nevertheless, I will continue to speak in this way for the sake of simplicity. The standard account, of course, also has to distinguish between before and after. But because the predominant emotional responses before and after are of different types, the problem seems more tractable. This may even be considered an advantage of the standard account over my amended version. Needless to say, I don't agree.

One proposal for how my account can distinguish between before and after turns on a feature of negative emotional response to wrongdoing that we can call *depth*. Using this notion we can distinguish the disappointment or the hurt that impedes forgiveness from the disappointment or hurt that remains after forgiveness on the grounds that it is only the former emotions that are deep or profound. As long as I remain profoundly disappointed in or hurt by the offender, I will have difficulty forgiving him; having forgiven him, if I am still disappointed in him or hurt by what he did, these emotions will be comparatively superficial or not deeply felt. And the memories will not be deeply painful either. The problem with this suggestion, however, is obvious: the criterion of the depth of a negative emotion that is employed seems to be nothing other than whether it impedes forgiveness. What we need is a specification of the notion of depth that explains the distinction between before and after forgiveness and that does not presume it.

Perhaps what distinguishes the emotional states of the wronged party before and after forgiving her offender is not or not only the depth of the emotions involved but something about their temporal character, what we might call their *persistence*. The negative feelings that need to be overcome in order to forgive the one who caused them may stay with the wronged party for a prolonged period and may be hard to shake off. Wronged parties may harbor grievances against those who wronged them for years and may never be able to forgive them. But once the offender is forgiven, the wronged party's emotions tend to dissipate quickly, as do her emotional memories of the offense. "Forgive and forget," it might be said, is not just a piece of advice but a description of what we expect to happen when people forgive: we expect as a more or less direct consequence of their forgiving that their memories of wrongdoing will be short-lived. However, this proposal fares no better than the previous one since it is wrong both about the before as well as the after. First, and quite obviously, persons who are wronged do not always bear a grudge for an extended period of time before forgiving their offenders. Second, the victim can have emotional memories of what her offender did to her for a considerable period of time after she has forgiven him, perhaps for the rest of her life. Forgiveness, as I have explained it, does not mean that the wronged party will not hold the offense against the wrongdoer any longer. It sometimes happens that memories of it are short-lived, but this is not a consequence of forgiveness per se. For what forgiveness signifies, and all that it signifies, is that the victim will not hold the offense against her wrongdoer *in the same way* she held it against him before she forgave him. His offense, therefore, may continue to play a role in how the victim affectively regards him and may continue to be held against him in some way indefinitely. (This is one of the messy consequences of my account.)

The first proposal, in terms of the depth of emotion, provides no useful criterion for identifying what is deep as opposed to superficial; the second, in terms of the persistence of emotion, is faulty as well. To be sure, it is sometimes the case that emotions persist for a long time until the one who was wronged is able to forgive her wrongdoer and that once she forgives him her emotional memories fade rapidly. But it is not persistence that explains how forgiveness alters the wronged party's emotional memories of wrongdoing. So let me try to get at this another way, by using a distinction between situational and background emotions to characterize the emotional transformation that forgiveness effects.

A background emotion differs from a situational emotion, according to Martha Nussbaum, in that "fewer concrete situations will call it to mind. That itself means that, even while it persists, its character will alter and it will be less noticed as troubling."[19] Over a given stretch of time, a background negative emotion might only occasionally occupy the foreground and might often be unattended to. This might be because the memories constituted by these emotions are repressed, but this is not the only explanation. It might instead be because the memories are subconscious, available to conscious awareness but infrequently entertained because there are relatively few retrieval cues triggering conscious memory. A further important point is that this distinction between background and situational emotions and the memories constituted by them should not be confused with the distinction between nondisruptive and disruptive memories. A background negative emotion, even though it is "only" in the background, may be capable of exerting considerable influence over a person's functioning and other parts of his mental life. It might be able to direct his life and relations to others from backstage, as it were, without his being consciously aware of how it does so. A situational emotion, by contrast, is an emotion that is triggered by some concrete stimulus and that one is aware of having, and being situational, it may be short-lived. To illustrate the difference, disappointment as a situational emotion is a direct response to a violation of expectations, and while it lasts it will be distressing to some degree to the one who responds this way. But it may not outlast, or outlast by much, the situational factors that triggered it. By contrast, disappointment, as a background emotion, is not as sensitive to changes in situational factors as its situation-specific counterpart. Moreover, as a background emotion, it can have a chilling effect on how one relates to the person in whom one is disappointed, even if one is only occasionally aware of one's disappointment.

There does seem to be something to the suggestion that the distinction between background and situational emotions can illuminate how forgiveness changes the way one remembers wrongdoing. Persons who have not forgiven their offenders often tend to be more susceptible to environmental cues that trigger conscious memories of their wrongdoing, or susceptible to more of them, than those who have managed to forgive them. Put another way, forgiveness seems to some extent to desensitize the wronged party to situations that might otherwise have revived her memories of wrongdoing. This also gives us a way of explaining how and in what sense forgiveness can enable the one who was wronged to get on with her life: there are as a result fewer situations in her life that serve as painful reminders of her wrongful injury. Nevertheless, the current proposal fails to adequately explain the emotional transformation that forgiveness brings about. Forgiveness doesn't just move negative emotions and the memories constituted by them to the background of one's mental life, for it is consistent with this that a victim can forgive her wrongdoer and still remain angry at him for what he has done, provided that her anger is repressed and seldom erupts into consciousness. But this hardly counts as overcoming anger or letting it go or repudiating it, and it is not the sort of emotional transformation that either I or proponents of the standard account of forgiveness envisage. In general, since background emotions can still exert considerable influence in the individual's life, it is questionable whether, on this view, the one who is said to have forgiven has really undergone a significant enough emotional transformation to qualify.

Though the distinction between background and situational emotions—and between the memories that are constituted by background and situational emotions—misses the mark for this reason, we might take a somewhat more charitable view of it. We might, that is, think of it as a flawed attempt to draw attention to another distinction that holds more promise as an explanation of the emotional transformation brought about by forgiveness: the distinction between intrusive emotions and emotional memories and nonintrusive ones. The problem with the situational/background distinction is that it doesn't track the emotional change resulting from forgiveness. Perhaps the intrusive/nonintrusive distinction can do a better job for the following reason. Negative emotions that are nonintrusive have been moderated, or rather their nonintrusiveness shows that they have been moderated, and moderation of negative emotions is just what forgiveness requires. In contrast, emotions that exist in the background may not have been moderated at all.

Let's examine this new proposal. The idea of intrusiveness is roughly this. Being on the receiving end of wrongful injury, at least when the injury is serious, commonly produces a kind of upheaval in the wronged party's beliefs and emotions. Expectations are shattered, trust in others is damaged, confidence in one's ability to successfully navigate the social world is shaken, and more. Wrongs are in this sense psychologically intrusive: they upset one's ordinary assumptions about oneself and others, assumptions with emotional implications and supported by an array of emotional dispositions. In extreme cases, the victim may be overwhelmed by the past-directed emotions she experiences. They may, in

Nussbaum's words, "violently tear the fabric of hope, planning, and expectation that I have up built up"[20] to sustain my life. Moreover, the memories the wronged party has of the wrongs she suffered are intrusive as well, to the extent that they upset her psychological equilibrium, and she may repress them because of this.

What, then, does forgiveness accomplish? Simply put, emotional reactions to wrongdoing that create upheaval in ordinary structures of belief and expectation are assimilated into new structures, and the memories that were once intrusive are rendered less salient. There is, in other words, a restoration of cognitive and emotional equilibrium through a reorganization of one's beliefs and expectations to accommodate the wrongdoing and the emotions that accompany it. With equilibrium restored, memories of wrongdoing after the wrongdoer has been forgiven tend to be less disruptive of the victim's psychological functioning than memories before. Consider, as an illustration, the grief one experiences when a loved one is murdered. It is highly intrusive, as are the persisting memories of the event. But when the wrongdoer is forgiven, if he is—and he may never be—the survivor manages to rearrange her daily structure of goals and occupations so that the memory of the loss, while still painful, is less wrenching. This reweaving of the fabric of her life to incorporate her grief does not leave her grief intact. Rather, by altering its relation to other parts of her mental life, it both changes its meaning and diminishes the extent to which she is preoccupied with it.

Of course, the intrusiveness of negative feelings is often diminished, and cognitive and emotional equilibrium restored, just because of the passage of time. What distinguishes the equilibrium that results from forgiveness from the settling that occurs with the passage of time is that forgiveness is never just something that happens to one. The "letting go" that forgiveness consists in is willed, a product of deliberation about the merits of continuing to feel toward the wrongdoer as one felt initially and of a commitment not to allow a resurgence of the negative feelings that one had to struggle with in order to forgive him. It is also partly the result of willed forgetting, as we will see in the next chapter. Forgiveness involves a commitment to change how one feels toward and relates to the wrongdoer, and on the current proposal, the change consists in arriving at a frame of mind in which the memories of being wronged become less discordant with other elements of one's psychology. This could not be a change brought about by *forgiveness* if one's thoughts, desires, and intentions were not engaged in bringing it about.

The current proposal, according to which the distinction between the emotions before and after forgiveness has to do with their relationship to other parts of one's mental content, is different from the previous proposal that draws a distinction between situational and background emotions. It is also the more plausible of the two. Reducing the psychologically unsettling effects of wrongdoing and the emotional memories of them by restoring psychological equilibrium is one thing; retaining the negative emotions caused by wrongdoing as background emotions is something else and not a satisfactory explanation of what forgiveness accomplishes. Relegating emotions to the background might create the appearance of forgiveness, and the individual whose negative emotions are in the background might manage to convince herself that she has forgiven her offender. But in the background these emotions can have wide-ranging effects on one's conduct and other elements of one's mental life such that any claim to have really forgiven is discredited. By contrast, under the current proposal, the emotions and the memories they constitute become less intrusive to the extent that the restoration of psychological equilibrium moderates their intensity.

In offering this as an explanation of the transformation of emotions and memories achieved by forgiveness, I don't mean to suggest that the restoration of psychological equilibrium after being wronged always shows that the wrongdoer has been forgiven. It may in fact show the opposite. Here's an example of that: the case of the deeply religious parent who breaks his relationship with his child in a categorical way because she has married outside the faith and he regards her failure to honor his most cherished beliefs as a personal affront. He may say that "she is dead to me," or "she no longer matters to me," and his subsequent conduct may fully bear this out. Here the willed establishment of a new psychological equilibrium that does not include disruptive emotions is not evidence of forgiveness. On the contrary, it shows intractable unforgiveness. So the intrusive/nonintrusive distinction does not yield a sufficient condition of forgiveness. Nevertheless, we can make this weaker claim: it is often though not always a sign that the wronged party has forgiven her wrongdoer that her negative feelings toward him have been worked into the fabric of her life to such a degree that their intrusiveness is significantly diminished.

There is an additional reason to be careful how we interpret this proposal. As I will discuss in the next chapter, forgiveness can be facilitated by a mental attitude that I call *not dwelling on* past wrongdoing. Not dwelling on wrongdoing reduces the intensity of the emotions the memories contain, so affects one's ability to retrieve them. The memories thereby become less intrusive. But here this does not show that the wrongdoer has been forgiven: it is rather a means of facilitating forgiveness. This, in addition to the possibility that memories become nonintrusive because one has taken stock of the past and decided *not* to forgive, is why the nonintrusiveness of emotions and emotional memories is not always evidence of forgiveness.

I said at the start of this section that one of the problematic features of my account of forgiveness is that it blurs the line between the emotional state of the wronged party prior to forgiveness and her emotional state after. According to the standard account, the one who forgives moderates and forswears resentment and vengefulness, whereas according to my account, not only might negative emotions linger after forgiveness, but the one who was wronged need not even renounce her right to continue to feel them. This left me with the problem of explaining how forgiveness, on my account, alters her past-directed emotional responses.

The proposals I have canvassed, of varying degrees of plausibility, assume or at least do not question that the negative emotions before and after forgiveness are tokens of the same type, and they try to explain how forgiveness can effect an emotional transformation that is nonetheless compatible with this. Sometimes, however, the emotional transformation is more accurately thought of as a genuine change in the makeup of the negative emotions that results in a different emotion. This happens when a hybrid emotion, consisting of retributive and non-retributive elements, becomes more singularly non-retributive. So, for example, one might not yet have forgiven the offender because one has been deeply hurt by what he did, where the hurt feelings, let us suppose, consist of a blend of feelings of rejection, anxiety, and hostility. Once the offender is forgiven, hurt feelings may remain, but any desire to punish the offender will have dissipated and any feelings of hostility will have been foresworn and overcome. This analysis of what happens when an offender is forgiven has some similarity to the standard account of forgiveness because it involves the foreswearing of angry feelings. But the angry feelings are part of a hybrid, and the introduction of hybrid emotions complicates the moral psychology of response to wrongdoing upon which the standard account relies.

There is another kind of emotional change that occurs in those who forgive: from an emotional state predominantly characterized by negative emotions that involve a withdrawal or limitation of good will toward the offender, to an emotional state characterized by a combination of negative and positive emotions or predominantly positive emotions toward the offender. This change may alter the intensity of the original emotion, but it does this by generating a new emotional complex. When we are disappointed in someone, or hurt by him, or grief-stricken by what he has done, we naturally tend to feel less favorably toward him than we might have felt had he not wronged us. There is usually some withdrawal or limitation of good will, prompted by our non-retributive emotional responses. We might want him to be distressed by what he has done, not for punitive reasons, but so that he repents his actions, seeks to atone for them, and is moved to try to become a different sort of person.

Forgiveness, however, may signify that the emotions that involve withdrawal or limitation of good will are to some extent counteracted or replaced by emotions that are expressive of good will toward the offender. These positive emotions include love, mercy, magnanimity, compassion, and, when it does not have a negative tone, pity. These emotions may displace the negative emotions altogether, but this may not and need not happen. Instead, the positive emotions may coexist with the non-retributive negative ones in a more or less stable combination. The latter remain, but their effects on our good will toward the offender will be tempered by the presence of positive ones.

This ordinarily happens with forgiveness. Forgiveness not only involves the moderation and forswearing of negative emotions, but the development and sometimes the restoration of positive emotions and pro-attitudes. If love for the wrongdoer was present prior to the wrongdoing, the wronged party's memories of her past feelings may make her more disposed to forgive him; and if she had no prior relationship with him, compassionate concern for his pain and suffering and an active regard for his good may be able to do the same. Moreover, the positive regard the wronged party shows the wrongdoer can help her regain a kind of psychological equilibrium that further testifies to the emotional transformation that she has experienced because she has forgiven him. When her memories of wrongdoing are colored by emotions of love and compassion for the wrongdoer, those memories may become less disruptive of her life.

5. The goods of memory and the limits of a sentimental account

I want to make two closing remarks about my account of forgiveness as an emotional and emotionally transformative process. The first returns to the question of the good of remembering wrongdoing after forgiveness, thinking of forgiveness as a process of this sort. The second is about what is crucially missing from this way of thinking of forgiveness.

I already addressed the first point to some extent in the last chapter when I discussed protest. Emotional memories of wrongdoing frequently provoke protests against it and, as I argued, protesting wrongs can be appropriate and valuable even after wrongdoers have been forgiven for them. It can motivate the wrongdoer to do more to be worthy of the other's continuing forgiveness; it can help the wronged party complete the work of rebuilding a damaged self-respect; and it can preserve the memory of wrongdoing and counteract forgetfulness. But emotional memories of wrongdoing can have important functions even if they do not motivate the wronged party to protest her mistreatment and even if protesting is thought to be futile.

The good of retaining emotional memories of wrongdoing after forgiveness is to a significant degree prudential, the reasons for doing so partly and importantly reasons of self-protection. Consider the following example. Suppose I trust my friend with some extremely sensitive personal information on the condition that he not divulge it to anyone else, but despite having promised not to do so, he can't resist disclosing it when pressed by his curious colleagues. When

I find this out, I feel betrayed and hurt. But presumably I have also learned some important lessons: about him, that he seems to attach less value to our friendship than I thought he did, and about myself, that I was unwise to trust him with sensitive information like this. Certain beliefs that I had about him, the closeness that I felt to him, and some of my hopes for our friendship will change in light of this evidence that he is not the kind of friend I took him to be. I will be more cautious around him in the future, more self-censoring in what I disclose to him about myself. This adjustment of our friendship in response to his offense protects me from putting myself in a similar position again, where I risk a new breach of confidentiality and the embarrassment it brings with it. I am not likely to revert to my earlier trusting relationship as long as I continue to have negative feelings toward him and the memories of his wrongdoing that they sustain. It is especially important to be on my guard if I don't trust him not to repeat the offense in similar circumstances. Moreover, the lessons I have learned about my friend have not lost their value, nor do my negative feelings toward him necessarily disappear, because I forgive him for breaking his promise. Indeed, I might forgive him and nevertheless continue to feel that I should keep up my guard.

My friend's betrayal may also trigger a more general self-reassessment. Perhaps, on reflection, I realize that I have been too trusting, not only of my friend, but of others as well. I may have made assumptions about others' trustworthiness without sufficient evidence and, as a result, exposed myself to abuse. After all, if someone I trusted so completely as my friend could abuse my trust, then others can too and I should be more cautious in my dealings with them. Maybe I'm not such a good judge of character. This is another reason why wiping the slate clean after forgiveness is not always salutary: negative emotions directed toward the offender, and the memories of wrongdoing that spark these emotions, can prime the wronged party to protect herself against further injury, not just from the offender but from others as well.

The second point concerns the inadequacy of an exclusively emotive or sentiment-based account of forgiveness. There is no simple way to describe the emotional transformation achieved by forgiveness or a single test for it. It may involve moderation of the intrusiveness of negative memories of wrongdoing by integrating them into the overall fabric of one's life, although the establishment of a new emotional equilibrium is not sufficient for forgiveness. If hybrid negative emotions were present, forgiveness involves the separation of its non-retributive from its retributive elements and renunciation of the latter. And ordinarily forgiveness involves the presence of a new emotional syndrome in which positive affective attitudes temper negative feelings toward the wrongdoer. But a description of the emotional transformation that is an integral part of forgiveness, however complex, does not yet give us a complete account of interpersonal forgiveness. Something is missing.

The problem in brief is this. The discussion in the last section has focused on changes in the emotions and psychology of the victim, but forgiveness also has a relational dimension. That is, there are changes in the relationship between the one who was wronged and the wrongdoer as well as in the attitudes of the wronged party toward him, and the former are not captured by an account that focuses only on internal changes in the one who was wronged. Forgiveness, as we might say following Avishai Margalit, is not just "a matter of psychology" but also "a policy or decision,"[21] a policy of not letting the wrongdoer's wrongful actions continue to impair one's relationship with him as it has before. We do not truly forgive, and overcoming our negative feelings toward the wrongdoer does not amount to forgiveness, if we do not also adopt such a policy, in addition to the changes that we experience in the emotional character of our memories of wrongdoing.

I will have much more to say about this policy feature in chapter 4. But before this, to finish my account of forgiveness as a "matter of psychology," I want to discuss how the process of forgiveness can be facilitated by a kind of forgetting of the wrong committed against oneself. To invert the usual saying, I will propose something like "forget and forgive" rather than "forgive and forget." Moreover, considering forgetting from the standpoint of its relationship to forgiving, the moral desirability or praiseworthiness of forgetting will depend on whether forgiveness itself is morally desirable or praiseworthy in the circumstances.

Endnotes

1. Forgiveness does not have to be thought of as exclusively a sentiment-based phenomenon, as I note in section 5 of this chapter. In chapter 4 I add a "policy" dimension to my account of forgiveness that is distinct from though dependent on sentiment.
2. I turn to this in chapter 3.
3. Unconscious memories are taken up again in chapter 3, section 4.
4. Eric Kandel, *In Search of Memory: The Emergence of a New Science of Mind* (New York: Norton, 2006), pp. 127–128.
5. The distinction between semantic and episodic memory is discussed by Endel Tulving in *Elements of Episodic Memory* (Oxford: Clarendon Press, 1983); and "Episodic and Semantic Memory," in E. Tulving and W. Donaldson, *Organization of Memory* (New York: Academic Press, 1972), pp. 382–403. See also Larry Squire and Eric Kandel, *Memory: From Mind to Molecules* (New York: Scientific American Library, 1999). The threefold classification of nondeclarative and declarative (semantic/episodic) memory corresponds to the distinction C. B. Martin and Max Deutscher draw between "direct memory of events, remembering information, and remembering how to do things." Declarative memory encompasses the first two. As for direct memory, Martin and Deutscher claim "that a person can be said to remember something directly, only if he has observed or experienced it." I am concerned in this chapter, in the first instance, with "direct memory" of having been wronged. See "Remembering," *Philosophical Review*, 75 (1966): 161–196.
6. According to Sven Bernecker, "When philosophers distinguish kinds of memory by their content they usually come up with a tripartite classification: experiential (personal), propositional (or factual), and practical (or procedural) memory." Some philosophers align propositional

memory with semantic, and experiential with episodic memory. For my purposes, however, the differences between these classifications are not critical. See *Memory: A Philosophical Study* (Oxford: Oxford University Press, 2010), pp. 12–19.

7. This seems to be common in the case of the memory of humiliating treatment. Remembering these experiences carries particular risks that remembering painful but nonhumiliating experiences may not. Avishai Margalit thinks so: "We do, in fact, remember the facts of physical pains to a remarkable degree, but we can hardly relive them. On the other hand, we can hardly remember insults without reliving them." Margalit, however, presents no empirical evidence for this claim. See *The Ethics of Memory* (Cambridge, MA: Harvard University Press, 2002), pp. 119–120.

8. This issue is raised by Bruce M. Ross. Discussing "memory for emotions," he asks how emotional memory works: "Do we remember emotions directly as emotions or only indirectly, with feelings being generated and attached to revived cognitions?" Most psychologists, he claims, take the second view, what he calls the "cognitive–intellectualist view of emotion." On this view, emotions are engendered by retained cognitions, not retained themselves. See *Remembering the Personal Past* (New York: Oxford University Press, 1991), p. 30.

9. These two views, the first that the past emotions themselves are directly recalled, the second that past-directed emotions are new emotions, are discussed and distinguished by Dorothea Debus in her paper "Being Emotional About the Past: On the Nature and Role of Past-Directed Emotions," *Nous*, vol. 41, no. 4 (2007): 758–779. She argues for the second view.

10. Debus makes a convincing case that emotional memories$_{3a}$ are not epistemically special. She concludes that "it is never reasonable for a subject to assume, without relying on any inferential reasoning, that an APD-emotion [autobiographical past-direct emotion] presents her with how she emotionally experienced things in the past" (ibid., p. 772).

11. The distinction between self-ascription of an emotion (such as regret) and the conscious experience of the emotion comes from Jonathan Lear, *A Case for Irony* (Cambridge, MA: Harvard University Press, 2011), pp. 52–53.

12. I am indebted here to John Deigh's excellent discussion of theories of emotion in "Concepts of Emotions in Modern Philosophy and Psychology," in Peter Goldie (ed.), *The Oxford Handbook of Philosophy of Emotion* (Oxford: Oxford University Press, 2010), pp. 17–40.

13. Paul Hughes, "What is Involved in Forgiving?" *Philosophia*, vol. 25 (1997): 33–49, at 40.

14. See M. Henry, J. Fishman, and S. Younger, "Propranolol and the Prevention of Post-Traumatic Stress Disorder: Is it Wrong to Erase the 'Sting' of Bad Memories," *American Journal of Bioethics*, vol. 7, no. 9 (September 2007): 12–20; Elizabeth Hurley, "The Moral Costs of Prophylactic Propranolol," ibid., pp. 35–36; and Adam J. Kolber, "Therapeutic Forgetting: The Legal and Ethical Implications of Memory Dampening," *Vanderbilt Law Review*, vol. 59, no. 5 (2006): 1561–1626.

15. Robert Nozick, *Philosophical Explanations* (Cambridge, MA: Harvard University Press, 1981), p. 375. Page numbers appear in parentheses in the text.

16. Samuel Scheffler, *The Afterlife*, lecture 1, New York University, August, 2010, p. 3.

17. Norms governing how one should *feel* in relation to valued objects are not the only norms governing how one should value something, although these are the ones I am focusing on here. According to Elizabeth Anderson, "To value something is to have a complex of positive attitudes toward it, governed by distinct standards for perception, emotion, deliberation, desire, and conduct" [*Value in Ethics and Economics* (Cambridge, MA: Harvard University Press, 1993), p. 2].

18. For more on how and when emotions reveal values, see Michael Stocker, *Valuing Emotions* (New York: Cambridge University Press, 1996), chapter 2.

19. Martha Nussbaum, *Upheavals of Thought: The Intelligence of Emotions* (Cambridge: Cambridge University Press, 2001), p. 80.

20. Ibid.

21. Margalit, op. cit., pp. 203–204.

3

Forgetting and Forgiving Revisited

1. The need to rethink the relationship between forgiving and forgetting

Forgiveness can be partly characterized as a process of working through the negative emotions one experiences in response to wrongdoing. There is no bright line, of course, separating the working through from the completed achievement, and even if in theory there were, psychological reality does not usually conform to neat analytic distinctions. Some ambivalence may remain in the one who has forgiven; some distrust of the authenticity of her own emotional transformation; and some concern that she may not be able to sustain, or continue to believe she has good reason to sustain, her forgiving attitude. In a few words, forgiveness, once achieved, is not necessarily achieved once and for all so that no additional work is needed to keep it going. Nevertheless, despite these difficulties, it is possible and, I would argue, useful to draw a *rough* distinction between the process and the end-state, between the efforts to confront and moderate one's negative emotions toward the wrongdoer, on the one hand, and the forgiving abandonment of those negative emotions, retributive as well as non-retributive, on the other.

The consensus within the philosophical literature on forgiveness is that remembering the wrong and the wrongdoer and remembering them accurately are necessary parts of the process, though not of the end-state. Forgetting may be a consequence of forgiving, it is said, but it cannot promote forgiving. One is not engaged in a process of forgiveness if, for example, one chooses to ignore the wrong, or allows oneself to be distracted from it, or represses it, or re-describes it in such a way that it is no longer wrong. One must retain the judgment that it is wrong and that the wrongdoer is responsible for it in one's memory for the duration of the process, and the impression that is usually conveyed is that the required memory is all or nothing: one either remembers or one forgets. In the standard account, there is rarely mention made of the role that forgetting might play in achieving forgiveness, rarely an admission that the capacity to forget

99

might be an element, let alone an essential element, of the capacity to forgive. We get the impression from this literature that forgetting is anathema to forgiving.

In this chapter, I want to complicate this picture just as in chapter 1 I complicated the standard account of forgiveness by challenging its understanding of the moral psychology of emotional response to wrongdoing. Here, in a nutshell, is what I will be arguing. One important and very common impediment to a person's ability to forgive is what I call *dwelling on the wrongs* that she has suffered, or what cognitive psychologists refer to as rumination. In order to be able to forgive, therefore, a person must not dwell on what was done to her, and if like most people she could succumb to this, at least when the wrong is serious, she must be able to influence how she experiences the negative emotions with which she responds to wrongdoing. There are various techniques for doing this, as I will describe below, all of which can be grouped under the heading of *methods of emotion regulation*. Specifically, the sort of emotion regulation involved in forgiveness consists in lessening or dampening the distressing emotional impact of an episode of wrongdoing, controlling one's reactions to it in such a way that it does not become the focus of ruminative thinking.

Further, this lessening affects the remembrance of wrongdoing: all of these methods of emotion regulation inhibit memory retrieval to some degree. They make it more difficult for the one who employs them to access her memories of wrongdoing because memories of a negative event are importantly sustained by the negative emotions it elicits and emotion regulation alters the emotional impact of a negative event, thereby affecting one's capacity to recall it. In one sense of this ambiguous word, to be explained below, they may facilitate forgetting, and in this sense, one may need to forget in order to be able to forgive, to disengage sufficiently from the past so that one can move forward with one's life without being dominated by memories of ill-treatment.

From the perspective of the standard account this may seem problematic. It seems to conflict with the very sound observation that we should not confuse forgetting with forgiving. How can forgetting facilitate forgiveness if forgiveness depends on not forgetting? To answer this, we have to take a closer look at how memory is implicated in forgiveness. The question for a theory of forgiveness is not whether the wronged party should remember past wrongdoing at all but *how* she should remember it, and this is where the notion of emotion regulation is relevant and helpful. To be sure, forgetting in the sense of regulating one's emotions so as not to dwell on the past makes it more difficult for an individual to access memories of past wrongdoing. But it does not prevent memory retrieval altogether, and it does not exclude belief in the culpability and wrongness of the offense or negative emotional responses to it. It is rather a mode of forgetting that enables individuals to retain memories of wrongdoing without being consumed by them. Emotion regulation also makes intrusive emotional memories of wrongdoing less intrusive, so it is a psychological mechanism that underlies the emotional change that the wronged party undergoes when she forgives, according to one account of this discussed in section 4 of the last chapter. Moreover, if there are good reasons why they should not be consumed by their memories of wrongdoing, as I take it there sometimes are, then this sort of forgetting enables individuals to remember properly when they do remember.

It is conceptual of forgiveness that a wronged party can only forgive if she does not cease to believe in the wrongness of what was done to her and the culpability of its agent, hence only if she remembers that she was the object of some culpable wrongdoing. This is correct as far as it goes, but like much else in the standard account, it doesn't go nearly far enough. We must also identify the kind of memory we are speaking about and explain why a theory of forgiveness should do this (issues I explored in the last chapter); and we should regard as significant the *quality* of one's holding on to the belief and examine its implications for the wronged party and her relationship with the wrongdoer. For example, one might hold on to the belief tenaciously or obsessively, so that one's thoughts about the wrongs done to oneself have a repetitive and rigid quality; or one might hold on to the belief in a more measured way, so that one is able to respond more flexibly. It is important to pursue these matters because it is possible for some ways of remembering wrongdoing or modes of belief adherence to be counterproductive to forgiveness, to impede rather than facilitate it. Additionally it is important because the philosophical literature on forgiveness does not have very much to say about the psychological processes and mechanisms that affect its realization.

One way to make the point that forgetting is an important or even vital part of the process of forgiving is to draw a distinction between remembering and remembering *well*. Forgiveness is only possible, it might be suggested, if one remembers being the object of culpable wrongdoing and does so well, and this presumes that there are good and bad, better and worse, ways of remembering. If, besides accuracy of memory, what partially distinguishes the good from the bad is their relationship to forgetting, then we will need to attend to methods of forgetting and their deployment in order to understand how the process of forgiving is advanced.

The claim that forgiveness may depend upon the capacity to forget (in some sense, to some degree) what was done to oneself is a psychological observation about the need for self-regulation of one's emotional responses to wrongdoing. But forgetting is also important for forgiving for moral or ethical reasons, because persons who are unable to forgive are often ruled by their memories of past transgressions, and because being so ruled is detrimental to human flourishing. I begin to argue for this in section 2 by turning once again Nietzsche, this time to his view of the relationship between remembering and forgetting. Since this is independent of his position on forgiveness, it is possible to draw upon the former without embracing the latter. What we learn from Nietzsche is that remembering in general, and the remembering that is relevant to forgiveness in particular (namely, remembering wrongdoing), is not an unqualified good. There are different ways of remembering badly and different ways of remembering well: for example, one might remember too often, too intensely, or for too long a time; or one might remember on the right occasions, in the right way, for the right amount of time, and so on. The latter recalls Aristotle and it is well that it should, since I will claim further that in some of his writings, Nietzsche adopts the rudiments of a virtue theory of remembrance—that is, he focuses on people's memory-related dispositions and evaluates acts of remembering in terms of them. According to such a theory, those who possess the virtue of remembrance are disposed to remember what, when, and how it is fitting or appropriate for them to remember. What's more, and this is something that Nietzsche stresses, this is a disposition whose contours are demarcated by its companion virtue, the virtue of forgetfulness. The latter virtue is implicated in the former and determines its shape, and my discussion of Nietzsche's remarks about them is intended to lend plausibility to my contention that remembrance in relation to forgiveness needs to be understood in a more nuanced way than the standard account does. I take Nietzsche as my launching pad for further elaboration of these virtues in section 3 and return to them in section 5.

I turn in section 4 to a more focused consideration of the role of forgetting in the psychology of forgiveness. The section, the largest of the chapter, contains three subsections. Subsection (a) presents a brief summary of empirical research on the psychological effects of rumination as a way of thinking about and responding to negative life events. What this has shown, with regard to anger and depression, is that ruminating about recent unresolved anger-eliciting or depression-causing events intensifies and prolongs the emotional experience of anger and depression, and that there are other ways of thinking about such events that have markedly more attenuated effects. Though the effects of ruminative thinking about events that elicit other sorts of negative emotions, like disappointment, hurt, and guilt, have not been empirically tested, the findings in the case of anger and depression strongly suggest that these and other negative emotions might also be prolonged and intensified by rumination. The relevance of these empirical studies to one of the issues I am interested in, namely the empirical psychological preconditions of forgiveness, is obvious. Rumination about negative emotion–arousing events, or dwelling on them, prolongs and intensifies the very emotions that one must overcome in order to forgive, so it impedes the ability to forgive. This also shows why, if forgiveness is to be possible, methods of emotion regulation may have to be employed that prevent or undo the emotional effects of rumination. These methods, I maintain, can facilitate forgetting of the negative emotion–arousing event.

Forgetting and Forgiving Revisited

Before considering some of the methods of emotion regulation in more detail, subsection (b) attempts to define more precisely what I mean by "forgetting." Roughly speaking, forgetting, in my sense, is a mental state located somewhere along a continuum of degrees of accessibility of memories. Freud famously thought that no experience, once committed to memory, is ever truly forgotten. Traces of it remain lodged somewhere in the mind, even if the memory is repressed and it resides only in the unconscious. But ordinarily we don't deny the possibility of forgetting in this way. Rather, the language of forgetting is part of the common currency of our personal lives and interpersonal relationships. At the same time, we do not necessarily suppose that one who has forgotten cannot consciously recall a past event, that it is buried beyond the possibility of recall, or that his memory bank is emptied out. Rather, we usually mean that, relative to some benchmark, it can only be recalled and articulated with difficulty, perhaps because of the operation of some psychological defense such as repression or dissociation or because the passage of time has piled layers of new memories on top of old ones. How difficult recall has to be in order to count as forgetting is not a question that can be answered in the abstract, since accessibility and our expectations concerning accessibility are determined by a number of factors, including the variable capacities of individuals. Those with well-trained and highly developed memories will have little trouble recalling events that others with more average memories may only be able to recall with considerable difficulty. So if difficulty of access is the test of forgetting, we should not expect it to be the same for both sorts of rememberers.

Subsection (c) describes some of the emotional regulation techniques that can modify the emotional impact of negative events and thereby affect memory retrieval and promote forgetting. I discuss two types, referred to in the emotion regulation literature as *attentional deployment* and *cognitive reappraisal*. One attentional deployment technique is mindfulness, a process that focuses nonjudgmental attention on the contents of one's consciousness in order to achieve distance from them. For example, one focuses attention on one's emotional reactions to an episode of wrongdoing in order to become less controlled by the thoughts and emotions that arise from it. Another more common technique is selective inattention, a process that involves a shift of focal attention away from negative emotions and features of the event that aroused them and toward other objects that are less upsetting or that arouse more positive emotions. Though selective inattention can be used in unhealthy and ethically objectionable ways, it can also be therapeutic and enhance moral agency. Cognitive reappraisal refers to a form of cognitive change that involves construing an emotion-eliciting situation in a way that alters its emotional impact and that can, as a consequence, moderate or negatively affect one's memory retrieval ability. Cheshire Calhoun's notion of "aspirational forgiveness," which involves placing an agent's wrongdoing in the context of a narrative that makes biographical sense of it, relies on cognitive reappraisal of the agent's action. Cognitive reappraisal is also used as one component in the management of anger, a process that involves, among other things, modifying the way an anger-eliciting situation is evaluated in order to decrease one's susceptibility to anger.

Section 5 takes up questions of moral value and returns to the Nietzschean virtue of forgetfulness (and of remembrance) in order to explore its relationship to the morality of forgiveness. Forgiving those who have wronged one is not always a virtuous or praiseworthy act. For example, a person may forgive because he thinks he deserves to be mistreated or because he has been taught to believe that harboring resentment or anger is a sign of some sort of moral failure or personal deficiency.[1] Insofar as forgiving or being a forgiving person conduces to one's moral credit, it does not consist in letting go of or being disposed to let go of negative emotions toward the offender for just any reason whatsoever. The virtues of remembrance and forgetfulness, similarly, consist in dispositions to remember and forget as appropriate, and what makes remembering and forgetting appropriate will vary according to the context and the ends promoted by them. The context might be one in which an individual has been the victim of culpable wrongdoing, and a particular blend of remembering and forgetting the wrongdoing might promote forgiveness. In order to determine whether the virtues associated with memory would be exercised in this way, we have to know whether forgiving the offender would be a morally good or virtuous act in the circumstances.

Section 6 ends the chapter with some remarks about possible parallels to the phenomena discussed here in the social and cultural domains. Can groups, as well as individuals, forget aspects of their past, and is accessibility the key factor here as well? Can groups as well as individuals forgive? And might groups need to forget in order to forgive—that is, so as not to become so preoccupied with wrongs committed against them that they are incapable of forgiving others for them? I will suggest that the psychological account can illuminate both the pathologies of social memory and the political uses of social forgetting.

2. Nietzsche and the virtues of memory

In chapter 1, I used Nietzsche's claim that noble souls have no use for forgiveness in order to explore the moral psychological conditions of forgiveness and to develop an account of forgiveness that is suitable for ordinary, vulnerable, and emotionally reactive beings like ourselves. Here I am interested in his views about the nature of remembering and forgetting, views that can be helpful in constructing a more complex psychological portrait of what is involved in the process of forgiving than the standard account provides.

Forgetting and Forgiving Revisited

To approach this, I begin by asking this question: why is forgetting thought to be incompatible with forgiving? Avishai Margalit gives an explanation in terms of a distinction between action and omission:

> If it [forgiveness] occurs through forgetfulness, it is not real forgiveness. Forgiveness is a conscious decision to change one's attitude and to overcome anger and vengefulness. Forgetfulness may in the last analysis be the most effective method of overcoming anger and vengefulness, but since it is an omission rather than a decision, it is not forgiveness.[2]

The idea seems to be that forgetting is passive because it involves omitting to take steps to remember. Without working to remember, memories will naturally slip from our consciousness and will become increasingly difficult to access over time. Forgiveness, by contrast, is an active process because it involves choices and decisions to let go of negative emotions. It is a process of deciding to free oneself of anger and vengefulness, and when one succeeds in forgiving, one has not just omitted to do something else. (Of course, trivially, whenever one does something there is always something else one has not done.) In short, for Margalit, one's agency and activity are not exhibited in one's forgettings but they are exhibited in one's forgivings. This argument is quite obviously flawed. First, just as one can omit to take steps to remember, and so forget, one can omit to take steps to forget, and so remember: claims about passivity and activity apply similarly to both forgetting and remembering. Second, and less obviously, "real" forgiveness can occur through forgetfulness: the distinction between "real" forgiveness on the one hand, and any sort of forgetfulness on the other, does not exhaust the possibilities. However, it is not my present purpose to critique this argument directly. Rather, I present it in order to draw a contrast with Nietzsche, who sees volition in both remembering and forgetting.

The ability to forget, according to Nietzsche, is a precondition of the possibility of any experience, thought, or learning whatsoever, and much forgetting is simply the result of the passage of time and the attendant fading of memories. (Perhaps this is how Margalit is thinking of forgetting.) But he also speaks about a forgetting that is willed and purposive and about a capacity for willed forgetfulness that enables us to live fully in the present by limiting our recollections of the past:

> Forgetfulness is not mere *vis inertiae* as the superficial believe; rather, it is an active and in the strictest sense positive faculty of suppression . . . To temporarily close the doors and windows of consciousness; to remain undisturbed by the noise and struggle with which our underworld of subservient organs works for and against each other; a little

stillness, a little *tabula rasa* of consciousness so that there is again space for new things . . . that is the use of this active forgetfulness, a doorkeeper as it were, an upholder of psychic order, of rest, of etiquette.[3]

The contrast between Nietzsche's description of "active forgetfulness" and Margalit's characterization of forgetting as a passive process is striking. Active forgetfulness is a reflective and purposive effort, the flip side of active remembering, which he describes as "an active no-longer-wanting-to-get-rid-of, a willing on and on of something one has willed, a true *memory of the will*."[4]

The capacity for active forgetfulness is not equally developed in everyone, however. In an early work, *On the Uses and Disadvantages of History for Life,* he writes:

> To determine . . . the boundary at which the past has to be forgotten if it is not to become the gravedigger of the present, one would have to know exactly how great the *plastic power* of a man, a people, a culture is: I mean by plastic power the capacity to develop out of oneself in one's own way, to transform and incorporate into oneself what is past and foreign, to heal wounds, to replace what is lost, to recreate broken moulds. There are people who possess so little of this power that they can perish from a single experience, from a single painful event . . . on the other hand, there are those who are so little affected by the worst and most dreadful disasters, and even by their own wicked acts, that they are able to feel tolerably well and be in possession of a kind of clear conscience even in the midst of them or at any rate very soon afterwards . . . Cheerfulness, the good conscience, the joyful deed, confidence in the future—all of them depend . . . on one's being just as able to forget at the right time as to remember at the right time; on the possession of a powerful instinct for sensing when it is necessary to feel historically and when unhistorically.[5]

This power, Nietzsche claims, can engender both too much and too little remembering: too much power, and one has no sense of history and feels only unhistorically; too little power, and one is overwhelmed by painful memories. In an admirable life, by contrast, active forgetfulness and active remembering are properly balanced and together shape the individual's relationship to the past and the future. In such a life, the plastic power of a man is well developed and well exercised, so that an individual's relationship to the past is life affirming rather than the "gravedigger of the present." Such an individual possesses the virtues of forgetfulness and remembrance, each doing its work in the right way and in balance with the other.[6]

Active forgetfulness, exercised in the right way about the right matters, is a "positive faculty of suppression," and only those with a capacity for active forgetfulness can have the virtue of forgetfulness. Similarly, those who possess the virtue of remembrance must have the capacity for active remembering. Each virtue involves *getting things right* with respect to forgetting and remembering. The virtue of forgetfulness in particular involves knowing how to forget so as to create "space for new things," which in Nietzsche's view means creating space "above all for the nobler functions and functionaries, for ruling, foreseeing, predetermining."[7] But one doesn't have to link the virtues of remembering and forgetting as closely to virtues of power as Nietzsche does in order to recognize the importance of the former.

3. Elaborating a Nietzschean account

If there are virtues associated with remembering and forgetting, they are so designated because of their contributions to a life well lived. And it seems clear that there are virtues associated with memory, dispositions to remember and forget the past in ways that have a positive impact on one's functioning and flourishing in the present. This is possible because persons who possess these virtues generally and characteristically strike the right balance between remembering and forgetting and do not exaggerate or underestimate their value. They strike the right balance in the sense that the possession of these virtues enables them to establish the right or an appropriate relationship to their past, a relationship that, among other things, avoids what Norman Care has aptly called "tyrannization by one's past."[8] This notion is essential to understanding the contribution that the virtue associated with forgetting makes to the goodness of an individual's life. Individuals who are, as Nietzsche describes them, deficient in plastic power are obviously tyrannized by their past. They "possess so little of this power that they can perish from a single experience, from a single painful event, often and especially from a single subtle piece of injustice, like a man bleeding to death from a scratch."[9] Tyrannization by one's past is not always so extreme as to cause an emotional meltdown. The strain that a painful event puts on one's psychological coping skills may be less severe. Still, in all of these cases, one is tyrannized by the past to the extent that, as Care explains it, there is "the overwhelming presence of the past in one's life, in a way that diminishes or eliminates one's capacity to move forward in one's life."[10]

But if the virtue of forgetfulness enables one to avoid tyrannization by one's past, the virtue of remembrance has an opposing effect: it keeps one from treating the past as of no consequence to one's current and future plans, projects, and relationships. Unlike the person who feels only unhistorically, as Nietzsche puts it, one who possesses this virtue is able to move forward in his life, not emotionally unburdened by the past, but burdened by it in the right way and to the right degree. With respect to being the victim of past wrongdoing, one's memories of it are moderated so that one is not consumed and debilitated by them. In this way, one tempers remembering with forgetting. One does not split off one's past from one's present self or deny that the wrong occurred. Rather, the past remains accessible to conscious awareness and is admitted to it, even if the wrong is not the object of focal attention and does not play a dominating role in one's life. One can then get on with one's life, primed to respond to indicators of new insults but not controlled or crippled by memories of past ones.

The virtues of remembrance and forgetfulness, if they are like other virtues associated with actions of a certain type, are what Rosalind Hursthouse calls "multi-track" dispositions, concerned "with many other actions as well, with emotions and emotional reactions, choices, values, desires, perceptions, attitudes, interests, expectations and sensibilities."[11] As multi-track dispositions, the virtues associated with memory are not constituted by action tendencies—that is, by tendencies to engage in acts of remembering or forgetting, even if only for certain reasons. They also dispose a person to attend to the ways in which remembering and forgetting can both enrich his life and restrict its possibilities, and to make choices that reflect this understanding. The person who possesses these virtues accepts that there are good and bad reasons for remembering and reasons for remembering different events in different ways, and his behavior reflects his acceptance of these reasons. He knows that sometimes he is better off forgetting unpleasant recollections rather than holding on to them, and he is able to differentiate between circumstances on this basis and to modulate his memories accordingly. And his emotions are properly engaged as well, in the sense that he is inclined to remember past events with emotions that are appropriate and fitting to them, whether the emotions are positive or negative or both, and to manage them in the right way. In short, the virtues of remembrance and forgetfulness are complex traits consisting of dispositions to accept a certain range of considerations as reasons to remember or forget, and whose exercise involves both a facility for situational appreciation and a flexibility of emotional response.

It is a general feature of all virtues that they are properties it is good for persons to have and that make their lives good or go well; so it is too for the virtues of remembrance and forgetfulness. We should not expect, however, that it is possible to specify exactly what combination of remembering and forgetting makes a person's life go well. These virtues, as Aristotle tells us about others, are not susceptible to such precise specification. If remembrance and forgetfulness were quantities that could be measured and combined, then we might have a sense of what it means for there to be an optimal quotient of remembering. But clearly neither is like this, so "what is the optimal quotient?" is the wrong question to

Forgetting and Forgiving Revisited

ask. The right question asks how well a person's life is going with respect to how he relates to his past, and to answer this, moreover, we can't just narrowly focus on the contents of his memories, any more than we can judge whether a person's life is good to the extent that he is honest by focusing only on his honest actions themselves. We also have to consider how a person's relationship to the past affects and shapes his current plans and projects, human relationships, and attitudes toward the future, and whether his remembering crowds out or defeats the enjoyment of other valuable activities that are otherwise within his reach. (See discussion of "effective agency" below.)

This way of determining the right kind of remembering and forgetting that a person needs to flourish is not consequentialist, at least not consequentialist in the same way as utilitarianism. It is rather teleological, in the sense that the standards of right and wrong for remembering and forgetting derive their authority from the ends or interests that the conduct guided by these standards serves. The relevant question here is not what combination of remembering and forgetting will make the individual happiest, but what attitudes toward and relations with the past are conducive to a well-lived life, and this is not a matter of maximizing some good, even the good of a well-lived life. The virtues associated with remembering and forgetting, like other virtues, have to be conceived in holistic relations with other elements of an individual's life distinct from them, with other virtues, relationships, ways of getting on, and so forth.

There is another reason why these views about remembering and forgetting are not consequentialist. The virtue of remembrance consists, among other things, in being disposed to remember events and people in the right way, and as I argued in the last chapter, one remembers in the right way in part when one recalls events with emotions that are fitting or appropriate to what one remembers. In the case of remembering wrongdoing, this involves having negative emotions that show one grasps the evaluative significance of the wrong: remembering an assault, for example, without any negative emotions whatsoever would not show that one has adequately appreciated the significance of being assaulted, even if remembering it with only negative emotions might also be grounds for criticizing one as unforgiving. There is, in other words, an intrinsic rightness to remembering being wronged if the memories fit the offense, and an intrinsic importance or rightness to feeling the emotions that the memories prompt, even if these are painful emotions to experience. On a teleological account of the standards of right and wrong with respect to remembering and forgetting, one remembers in the right way by having the right emotions and the patterns of remembering that sustain them, and this is in part to have emotions and memories that adequately express the moral truth of what took place.

It is obviously not an easy task to know how to exercise these virtues or to exercise them, and for these reasons some may feel more comfortable talking about *duties* of remembrance rather than a *virtue* of remembrance. But the impression that we are gaining some advantage by doing this is open to question, and for a thoroughgoing virtue theorist it is illusory. A virtue theorist about memory will claim that duties of remembrance are not antecedent to, but derivable from, the virtue of remembrance. This is because the virtue of remembrance involves practical wisdom, which in this instance consists in the ability to reason correctly about practical matters having to do with remembering and forgetting, and one of the practical matters we have to reason about is what our duties are in a given situation. To possess the virtue of remembrance, among other things, is to be reliably guided to know and do one's duty, as called for by the particular circumstances one finds oneself in. I say "among other things" because the virtue of remembrance is not just concerned with discerning and discharging duties of remembrance. For example, with respect to wrongs done to oneself, it is even questionable whether one has a *duty* to remember them at all. But even if one does, a person who possesses the virtue of remembrance will be concerned with a lot more than discovering what his duties are.

Finally, I said that the virtues of remembrance and forgetfulness are concerned with emotions and emotional responses—more specifically, with having the right emotions, to the right extent, toward the right objects, and for the right reasons. This is relevant to a discussion of forgiveness in two ways. First, those who possess the virtue of remembrance and have been the victims of culpable wrongdoing have memories that consist of emotionally appropriate responses to it., and these responses can involve both retributive as well as non-retributive emotions, as I argued at length in chapter 1. Second, those who possess the virtue manage their emotional responses to past wrongdoing well, and this involves some regulation of the emotions that constitute memories of it. Specifically, they do not focus repetitively on their internal negative emotional states in such a way as to give themselves no avenue of relief from their emotional distress. When distress caused by wrongdoing is so intense that memories of it take control of one's life, memories are not being regulated in accordance with the virtue of forgetfulness.

I will come back to the virtue of forgetfulness in section 5, after we have in place a fuller account of its psychological underpinnings.

4. Dwelling, forgetting, and regulating emotion

(a) Rumination

"Dwelling on" is the colloquial term for what psychologists call rumination. Rumination is a style of thought that, broadly construed, is characterized by "repetitive thinking that is difficult to control and difficult to terminate"[12] or by "repetitive thoughts around a common theme, absent immediate environment demands for those thoughts."[13] Echoing this, rumination is also said to be a type of repetitive thought that consists of "thinking attentively, repetitively, or frequently about oneself and one's world."[14] The most widely used definition of rumination, however, is "repetitive thinking about the causes, consequences, and symptoms of one's negative affect,"[15] and this is the definition I will adopt. As this definition makes clear, rumination has a number of different objects. One can ruminate about a negative event, for example some wrong that one has suffered or committed; about how the event makes one feel (i.e., one's feeling states); and about the consequences for various aspects of one's life of feeling this way. Usually when one ruminates, one's attention is to some degree focused on one's negative moods or emotional responses to some event, especially if it is distressing, and to the extent that this is the case, rumination is emotion-focused, self-directed thinking. Another much narrower definition limits rumination to "repetitive thinking about sadness, and circumstances related to one's sadness,"[16] but while this definition may be useful in some contexts, it is too restrictive for my purposes. Further, rumination is a style of thought that may be transient and circumstantial or, in more serious cases, characterological. Individuals may tend to ruminate about particular negative events only (for example, the occasion when they were humiliated or demeaned); or they may be prone to ruminate repeatedly about negative events of varying degrees of severity, from the consequential to the relatively insignificant, in which case rumination can be considered an ingrained personality trait. Individual instances of rumination may or may not be maladaptive; rumination as a general coping strategy generally is.

Two sequelae of rumination are particularly important to mention in the context of my concerns in this chapter. Rumination is connected both to a diminished capacity for a kind of Nietzschean active forgetting and to an intensification of the negative emotions that are the focus of the ruminative thinking. With regard to the former, Joorman and Tran claim to have demonstrated that "the tendency to ruminate is closely related to a reduced ability to intentionally forget emotional material,"[17] whether the emotional material is negatively or positively valenced. They also suggest that because of difficulties in forgetting negative events, cognitive and affective functioning may be adversely affected. Though Joorman and Tran do not discuss the psychological mechanisms underlying this close relationship, the association between rumination and reduced forgetting of negative material could be explained by appealing to the converging evidence from numerous empirical studies of memory that emotion slows forgetting and promotes retention and recall.[18] Rumination, it seems, has an impact on memory because it has an impact on emotion.

It is well established that emotionally arousing events are generally remembered longer and better than nonemotional events. Since the effect of rumination is not only to maintain the emotional response that was originally elicited out to strengthen it, an individual's memories will tend to be more enduring than they would be if he were less preoccupied with the emotion-eliciting event and his emotional responses to it. The psychological literature on rumination has shown in particular that the more one ruminates on an anger-eliciting event, the angrier one feels when the event is recalled.[19] Rumination on anger-eliciting events involves a focus of attention on and rehearsal of the causes of the anger, and this is likely to fuel the anger. These findings about the effects of rumination, combined with findings about the relationship between emotion and memory retention, suggest that ruminative thinking about anger-eliciting events results in increased anger and more persistent memories because the anger is intensified. Moreover, this would explain why rumination is closely related to a reduced ability to intentionally forget, since memories that are more persistent are more resistant to intentional forgetting. A similar effect has been observed with depressed individuals. Laboratory studies have found that when they are induced to ruminate about their depressed moods and their consequences, their negative moods worsen, becoming longer and more severe.[20]

While the effects of self-focused rumination on anger, vengefulness, sadness, and anxiety have been addressed by numerous empirical studies, its effects on other non-retributive emotions, such as disappointment and hurt, have not yet been explored. Nevertheless, it is plausible to suppose that the effects of rumination on these other emotions will be similar, although different emotions may respond somewhat differently to different emotion regulation strategies.[21] This is not merely an ungrounded supposition, but one that gains support from a group of theories suggesting that rumination should exacerbate a wide range of negative emotions. These are called associative network or spreading activation theories of mood, and Rusting and Nolen-Hoeksema summarize them as follows:

> According to these theories, emotions impose a fundamental organizational structure on information stored in a semantic network in memory. Each emotion is conceptualized as a central organizing node that links together causally related information. When an emotion node is activated, past events and beliefs associated with that emotion are brought to mind, prolonging or increasing the emotion. Rumination or self-focus on the negative emotion should enhance this spreading activation and therefore exacerbate the emotion.[22]

According to these views, negative emotions of all sorts are nodes in associative networks, and rumination on them activates the nodes and strengthens the connections between them and other beliefs and emotions, thereby intensifying and extending the former. Of course, this is an empirical hypothesis that further research will need to confirm. But the many studies of the relationship between rumination and negative affect that have already been conducted are strongly suggestive of such an effect.

What makes rumination on some past event problematic is not the fact that it takes the past seriously; rather, it is the way in which it does this. Negative emotions in response to past wrongdoing keep one connected to what was done in the past and to morality itself and, within limits, this is proper and fitting. However, when one dwells on or ruminates about an important past negative event and one's emotional reactions to it, the effectiveness of one's capacity to take charge of and move forward with one's life is placed in jeopardy, and the capacity is significantly impaired by persistent rumination. Rumination in these cases threatens to diminish elements of what Norman Care calls "effective agency," which is:

> the effectiveness of one's capacity to control the contents of one's life, including facing up to the next challenge that comes along in one's workplace or personal life. It concerns how far we can be, within realistic limits, masters of our fates, and, when we cannot in certain circumstances be masters, then how far we can be reasonable and constructive strategists when our circumstances go against us.[23]

Effective agency is needed to live any kind of productive, satisfying life. A person whose effective agency is severely diminished or disabled cannot take responsibility for forward-looking action or follow through on her commitments; cannot summon enough enthusiasm for projects and activities that could sustain a sense of self-worth; lacks hope and the motivation it provides to work toward achieving what she desires; and in general does not feel and believe herself to be in control of her life and the direction it takes. When this due to dwelling on some problematic part of her past, we may say she is in bondage to it; and if what she dwells on is some wrong that was done to her, then the wrongdoer has harmed her in two ways: by inflicting the initial wrong and, whether intentionally or not and whether he can be blamed for it or not, by weakening her capacity for effective agency.

Let me turn now to forgiveness and rumination's relationship to it. If rumination about the wrongs one suffered and one's negative emotional responses to them intensifies, strengthens, and prolongs these responses, then rumination is an impediment to forgiveness. This is because forgiveness involves overcoming or letting go of negative emotional responses to wrongdoing, and the more intense and durable these emotions are, the harder it will be to overcome or let go of them. Rumination, in other words, hinders forgiveness because it makes the emotional self-transformation that forgiveness consists in harder to achieve.

her, since, rumination has been shown to be closely related to a reduced ability to intentionally forget, in refraining from rumination one is more likely to be able to exercise active forgetting. Thus, refraining from rumination (compared with ruminating) is associated both with a lesser intensity of negative emotions and greater ability to actively choose to forget the wrongs to which those emotions respond. And, what is important, the techniques that diminish the intensity of negative emotions are the same techniques as those that enable one to more readily forget. Rumination is a barrier to forgiving because it amplifies the emotional response to wrongdoing, which makes forgetting the wrongdoing more difficult. On the flip side, techniques to counteract rumination can facilitate the process of forgiving by reducing the intensity of one's emotional responses, which makes memories of the wrongdoing more difficult to retain and the emotions that respond to it more responsive to attempts at moderation. The old adage "forgive and forget," therefore, should be complemented and supplemented by a new one: "forget and (or so that you can) forgive."[24]

But how does one refrain from ruminating? Or in the language of remembering and forgetting, what techniques of emotion regulation that keep one from ruminating enable one to forget? I will turn to this shortly, after I have said something about the concept of forgetting itself.

(b) What is meant by forgetting?

Margalit distinguishes between two conceptions of forgiveness in "present-day humanistic morality," which he claims derive from "two religious models of sin and forgiveness." One he calls "blotting out" a wrong—that is, "forgetting it absolutely." The other is "covering up" a wrong, which means "disregarding it without forgetting it." He claims that forgiveness based on covering up is "conceptually, psychologically, and morally preferable to the picture of blotting out."[25] In Margalit's terminology, it is morally preferable to think of forgiveness as involving disregarding and not forgetting past offenses. His reason for saying this no doubt at least partly derives from his understanding of forgetting, which I discussed and criticized in section 2: namely, forgetting is not voluntary, not the result of a decision. So if forgetting and disregarding are the only options, and forgetting is ruled out, forgiving must involve disregarding only. But setting aside Margalit's views about forgetting, his aligning of forgiving with covering up leaves out critical details. The problem is that there are cases in which one can be described as disregarding past wrongdoing, but where this mental state does not promote forgiveness. For example, a person may be able to disregard an injury for a short while, but be repeatedly and irresistibly drawn back to thinking about it. What we need, if we are to follow Margalit here, are finer distinctions between degrees or kinds of disregarding.

Forgetting and Forgiving Revisited   115

Nonetheless, I agree with Margalit that forgetting and disregarding are different: forgetting cannot be equated with disregarding either in the sense of paying no attention to something—which may have no judgmental component or not be purposeful at all—or in the sense of treating something as not meriting regard or notice. To show the difference, consider an example of motivated disregard—that is, deliberately avoiding thinking about something unpleasant: a struggling playwright who disregards the bad notices he received from the theater critics for his last play. He may do this because he has no respect for the critics and their opinions, or because he believes that if he lets the notices bother him, it will shake his self-confidence and hamper his ability to keep on working productively. For these or other reasons, he does not read the negative reviews or, if he reads them, summarily dismisses them. As so far described, however, the example may not involve forgetting, except in a very loose, unhelpful sense. The playwright is engaged in conscious thought suppression, but suppression may not be effective enough to do a great deal to block recall of unwanted material. There might be retrieval cues in a person's surroundings that put pressure on and weaken his resolve not to think about it. Moreover, there is empirical evidence that suggests suppression of unwanted thoughts may actually fuel the very emotions and thoughts one is trying to avoid.[26] When one forgets, by contrast, it seems that there should be some significant impediment to the recovery of one's memories, or some difficulty in bringing material to consciousness that consists in more than one's not currently thinking about it or even one's intentionally suppressing thoughts about it. In general, our everyday experience always involves paying attention to some things and disregarding others, and while forgetting is certainly common enough, the notion of forgetting would be much too capacious if we used the term interchangeably with disregarding or covering up. It would also be too encompassing if we just excluded all cases of covering up that were not due to the suppression of unwanted thoughts.

Still, if forgetting is not the same as disregarding, there may be instances of covering up that do amount to forgetting. Freud's early paper "Remembering, Repeating and Working-Through" focuses on such cases.[27] The aim of psychoanalysis, he says here, can be characterized in either of two ways: "Descriptively speaking, it is to fill the gap in memory; dynamically speaking, it is to overcome resistance due to repression" (148). Psychoanalysis fills in memory gaps by uncovering resistances that are unknown to the patient and that function as defenses against admission of repressed material into consciousness. Because of these resistances, "the patient does not *remember* anything of what he has forgotten and repressed, but *acts* it out. He reproduces it not as a memory but as an action; he *repeats* it, without, of course, knowing that he is repeating it" (150). The goal of therapy, simply stated, is therefore to turn the patient's compulsion to repeat into a motive for remembering. The repressed material is obviously not completely inaccessible to retrieval, since psychoanalysis would be pointless if it were. Rather, it can be accessible to conscious awareness if it is made less threatening to the patient. The trauma is "forgotten" in the sense that, although it continues to influence the patient's ongoing experience, thought, and action, repression renders it inaccessible to introspection and seriously impedes conscious recall of it.

Another interpretation of the effects of repression, suggested by Freud himself in the same essay, is that the patient does remember the past event, but the memories are of a particular type, namely unconscious ones. As he says, the patient's compulsion to repeat could be regarded alternatively as "his way of remembering" (150). However, the notion of repressed memories existing in the unconscious, though firmly entrenched in folk psychology and popularized in contemporary narratives of recovered memories, raises conceptual as well as empirical questions. Consider the following bare set of facts. Nancy's anxiety keeps her from entertaining thoughts of her traumatic experience and impairs her memory for it. However, with the help of an analyst, her anxiety is removed or lessened, and she is able to recall it. Now there are different ways of describing what is going on here. We might describe the process as the *recovery* of a certain type of memory, a repressed memory of the trauma she experienced. Memories of the trauma have been consigned to the unconscious, from which she is subsequently able to recover them. Alternatively, we might describe the process as the acquisition of a *new* memory of the experience: she acquires a new memory of it similar to the earlier one. Of course, memories that are conscious and subject to conscious control have effects on experience, thought, and behavior that are to some extent different from those of memories that are supposedly unconscious. But we can suppose that the content and perhaps the emotional tone of the new memory resemble that of the earlier one. The question then is which characterization to adopt—in particular, whether in the interim between initiation of repression and conscious recall some type of memory actually persists, such that it might be recovered.[28]

Compare a case of so-called unconscious memories with garden-variety cases of forgetting followed by re-remembering. I remember going on a vacation with my wife; time passes, the memory gets buried under an accumulation of layers of new memories acquired since the prior memory; then something triggers my recall of the vacation, perhaps the rediscovery of some photos, and I remember the vacation again. We would not, or need not, say that I had an unconscious memory of the vacation during the period when I forgot it. What is the difference between this case and one in which I allegedly retain an unconscious memory of some prior event? The difference, it seems, consists only in the explanation, the underlying mechanism, of the forgetting. With unconscious memories, there is repression or some other defense mechanism that explains

Forgetting and Forgiving Revisited

it. The term "unconscious memory," then, would refer to the potential to have a conscious memory that is similar in salient respects to a conscious memory that one had before, but where this potential is not actualized because of repression and the like. According to this, Nancy's memory of her traumatic experience is "unconscious" because, though having a conscious memory of the experience similar to the one she had before is not beyond her reach, her anxiety and distress prevent this from happening.

Even if a satisfactory construal can be given of it, I want to avoid using the term "unconscious" as applied to memories. The reason is that it obscures the view I want to advance here, which is precisely that prior to analysis Nancy does *not* remember her traumatic experience. (This is in line with Freud's remark that "the patient does not remember anything of what he has . . . repressed.") According to this view, her repression impairs her memory for the traumatic event to such an extent that we can properly say she has forgotten it.

The sense of "forgetting" that I am proposing depends upon two distinctions: one, between *availability* for conscious retrieval and *accessibility* to conscious retrieval; the other, between information about past events that is *highly accessible* and information that is *highly inaccessible* to conscious awareness.[29] Information about past events may be available and highly accessible; or available for retrieval but highly inaccessible to it; or neither available nor accessible. When information about past events falls into the last category, the event is clearly forgotten on anyone's definition. When information about past events falls into the first category and it is currently entertained, one has an occurrent memory of them; if it is not currently entertained, one has a dispositional memory of them. In either case, one remembers them. The category I want to focus on is the second. It is here that I locate a different sense of forgetting, namely forgetting as applied to information about the past that is, for one reason or other, highly inaccessible to conscious awareness.

My proposal is very close to the suggestion put forward by psychologists Jefferson Singer and Martin Conway, who argue that we should "substitute the idea of relative accessibility for forgetting."[30] They explain:

> Information that is encoded in long-term memory is available. This means it can potentially be retrieved and through the retrieval process might enter consciousness and so influence experience and behavior . . . However, because information (memories, facts, concepts, words, etc.) is available it does not follow that it is at any given time accessible. Accessibility is determined by many factors and, in general, information in memory, and we suggest in culture, is in variable states of accessibility with some items highly accessible and others highly inaccessible (but note, still available). Thus, we prefer to talk about the concept of

118   FORGIVENESS AND REMEMBRANCE

relative degrees of accessibility than to speak in terms of information being truly lost or forgotten. (280)

If by "truly lost or forgotten" we mean to refer, as Singer and Conway seem to, to some piece of information about the past that is *unavailable* for conscious retrieval, then, they suggest, it may be best to avoid talk of forgetting, presumably because there may be very few if any instances of information that gets into memory that is not available for recall. We should instead adopt a notion of degrees of accessibility that range along a continuum, from the highly accessible to the highly inaccessible, though still available. And we should not bother asking how highly inaccessible some information has to be in order to meet some predetermined standard of forgetting, since judgments of forgetting (if we continue to use the term) are *derived* from assessments of degrees of accessibility, not the other way around. The virtue of this approach, they claim, is that it allows for a more nuanced understanding of how memory works in individual and cultural contexts.

Singer and Conway are right to focus on questions of access and its determinants. Some piece of information may be forgotten in one context of memory but not necessarily in another, since degrees of accessibility and expectations regarding accessibility vary from context to context. And for purposes of social and psychological analysis, it is more helpful to look at the different critical factors that determine the accessibility of memories—factors that they label "emotion, meaning and goal relevance" (279)—than to ask whether past events have been "forgotten." Indeed, it is not at all obvious how we could answer this question without first considering the factors that impinge on access and the degree of difficulty in gaining access that they create. But none of this implies that we should stop referring to certain mental states as constituting forgetting—in particular, that we should refrain from referring in this way to cases that belong to the category of "available but highly inaccessible." Rather, we may continue to do so, as long as at the same time we acknowledge that there is no bright line dividing forgetting from remembering; that we need to be precise in specifying what is being forgotten; and that judgments of whether someone has forgotten something depend on consideration of the personal, psychological. social, and cultural factors that affect its accessibility to consciousness and on expectations for what should be remembered.

Forgetting, on this view, has to do with accessibility, and judgments of forgetting involve assessments of relative accessibility. One way to determine whether information about some aspect of the past is highly inaccessible for an individual is responsiveness to retrieval cues: if an individual does not consciously recall something from the past despite being presented with a wide range of relevant prompts, then we may be justified in saying that he has forgotten it, at least temporarily. (Of course forgetfulness is not always a serious problem. There are many small acts of forgetting that have little significance for the conduct of our lives. And sometimes forgetting is salutary.) Accessibility itself—what we are testing for—is affected by various factors. Among these are an individual's capacities, innate as well as developed, to remember, in general and with respect to different types of information and areas of experience. Those with generally highly developed powers of memory on the whole have less difficulty accessing information about past events or experiences than those with less well-developed powers, so that what the latter easily forget the former can easily remember. Or an individual may have highly developed powers of memory for certain types of information only, say people's names or dates, so that he rarely forgets information of that type but is more likely to do so in other domains. Particularly relevant to the concerns of this chapter, degree of accessibility is also conditioned by the emotional valence of the past experience for the individual. Thus, someone may have no trouble recalling pleasant experiences but erect defenses against recall of aversive ones, thereby rendering the latter highly inaccessible to conscious retrieval.

In addition to these psychological factors, social and cultural factors play an important role because they can either block or facilitate the process of retrieval. Singer and Conway give as an example a type of forgetting that Paul Connerton[31] calls "repressive erasure":

> totalitarian regimes remove the memorial cues that attach certain institutions and leaders to images of respect, authority, and power . . . and [institute] a new set of memorial cues to activate similar forms of deference and obeisance to the current authority. (281)

These repressive measures simultaneously obstruct and strengthen routes of accessibility: they induce a kind of forgetting of past objects of deference and, through indoctrination and other measures, transfer it to the new regime. Social forces can also affect accessibility in less malign ways, although these may still be manipulative. Cultural norms and social practices, including commemorative ceremonies and educational curricula, can facilitate and reinforce recall of beliefs and values that are integral to the preservation of particular ways of life and forms of political community. And they can inhibit recall of events that may challenge or erode commitment to a way of life or the institutions of a community.

These social and cultural factors have an impact on individual as well as collective memories, rendering certain elements of the past less accessible or even unavailable to the subject and other elements more accessible. We can distinguish between two kinds of collective *amnesia* on the basis of the distinction between availability and accessibility. One type of collective amnesia consists in past experiences and events being unavailable to the collective. To illustrate, imagine a newly installed political regime intent on removing all traces of the previous regime and social order in a massive effort to re-educate the public and redirect its loyalties. If it succeeds, the past is erased, since there is nothing left of it to enter the collective consciousness. A second type of collective amnesia does not consist in erasing the past but in making it more inaccessible. Singer and Conway give as an example what Connerton calls "planned obsolescence":

> When capitalism markets and advertises new products in order to make current products less desirable, it is not asking us to forget or lose awareness of the old. It is asking us to replace our desire for the current with a desire for the new; we are making less accessible the emotional appeal of what we have and replacing it with passion for what we have yet to acquire. (283)

The past is not "totally lost," hence not forgotten in this extreme sense. But there is nevertheless a kind of culturally induced forgetting in which elements of the past become harder to access because they are rendered less relevant to current consumer needs and desires.

Forgetting, according to my account, is not simply a value-neutral term. When we designate some condition (which may or may not be at the far end of the accessibility continuum) as forgetting, we may also be making a normative judgment of the one who forgets. It is sometimes a term of opprobrium. For example, we expect Harry to remember his wife's birthday, because these are the normative expectations that we have of husbands. If he doesn't remember, and has no legitimate excuse, we say he has forgotten, implying by this that his failure is blameworthy. In general, information that is too trivial or unimportant to remember we might not say is forgotten if it is not remembered; on the other hand, information that is important and that we expect someone to remember we might accuse him of forgetting if he does not recall it. These normative uses of the term forgetting do not always match judgments of the relative accessibility of memories. Harry in our example might have been able to recall his wife's birthday without difficulty (all he had to do was look at the calendar), but we might still blame him for forgetting it.

There are good reasons for using the term forgetting with respect to information that is highly inaccessible to conscious awareness. Ordinary usage sanctions this way of speaking, and we frequently refer to certain mental states and cultural manifestations as forgetting even though the information in question is not erased from the mind or made unavailable to the culture.[32] Moreover, we can better understand what Nietzsche means when he calls for more forgetting if we adopt this way of understanding it. As we have seen, Nietzsche's view of forgetting is that it is not simply a failure of memory but an activity of the will, what he calls "active forgetting." When properly exercised, active forgetting strikes the right balance between deference to the past and openness to the future: too much forgetting, and we lose our identities; too little and our futures are burdened by a past that unduly circumscribes our identities and life possibilities. To achieve this balance, individuals as well as groups must have a kind of resilience in response to traumas and disappointments, what he calls "plastic power," that enables a "man or a people or a culture" to absorb them without being crushed by them. And for this to happen, emotional response to negative events must be kept in check. But moderating the emotional response to past events does not result in these events becoming unavailable for recall by individuals or communities in an emotionally modified form. Indeed, it is critical for Nietzsche that it not have this result, for he urges us to dig more deeply into our past in order to develop new habits and patterns of action for the future, and for this the past must still be available to us to learn from. As he says, "sometimes ... this same life that requires forgetting demands a temporary suspension of this forgetfulness."[33] To live well, we must understand our history but not be dominated by it.

My interest in forgetting is not the same as Nietzsche's, of course: what concerns me but not him is the relationship between forgetting and forgiving, since Nietzsche is dismissive of the moral value of forgiveness. But for a theory of forgiveness that does not dismiss it, this relationship is worth further investigation. When negative events tend to arouse pronounced negative emotions in those who are wronged, they may have to engage in some type of emotion regulation activity if they are to forgive their wrongdoers. Rumination amplifies the victim's emotional responses, and it may do so to the extent that the one who is wronged can only view the wrongdoer through the lens of his wrongdoing and is psychologically unable to see him in a new light. Her negative emotions are experienced as too intense and dominating to permit her to disregard what the wrongdoer has done in the ways she relates to him. In this case, thoughts of her having been wronged enter her consciousness without restraint; indeed, they enter it too repetitively and insistently for her to be in a position to forgive.

Of course, not everyone who is wronged, even seriously wronged, ruminates or tends to ruminate on the wrong and his negative feelings. They may not, like Nietzsche's noble souls, simply shrug it off, because they take the demeaning claim implicit in the wrongdoer's actions to be deserving of protest. But they do not dwell on the wrong and their emotional responses to it in the way that those who ruminate do. Compared to the latter, there is a sense in which such persons are able to "forget" what happened to them with relative ease. In their case the relationship between ruminating and not forgiving holds counterfactually: were they to ruminate on the wrongs they suffered, it would be difficult, perhaps impossibly difficult, for them to forgive.

Finally, it may be asked how it is possible for emotional memories of wrongdoing to linger after forgiveness (which I claimed in chapter 1 is not uncommon) in those cases where forgetting was necessary to get to where one could forgive. I would explain it this way. The emotional intensity of the memories of wrongdoing may impede forgiveness, and when this happens the emotions will have to be moderated to permit it. The moderation of these emotions facilitates a kind of forgetting, and this undoes or prevents rumination and removes obstacles to forgiveness. But if one does forgive, any negative emotional memories of wrongdoing that remain will also not be the focus of rumination; they will be tempered so that whatever distress they cause will not threaten to subvert one's effective agency. Thus, the forgetting that was necessary for forgiveness made possible a different way of remembering the wrongdoing, precisely because it opened the way to forgiveness. Simply put, one may need to forget in order to forgive, but once having forgiven, one becomes more comfortable with one's memories. Of course, by becoming more comfortable with one's memories of wrongdoing one may also become more forgetful of it. But there are various memory aids that can jog one's memory and counteract forgetfulness after the wrongdoers have been forgiven. Among these are private and public commemorative rituals, the latter of which I will discuss at length in chapter 5.

(c) Techniques of emotion regulation

Emotion regulation, according to James Gross, a leader in the field, "refers to the processes by which individuals influence which emotions they have, when they have them, and how they experience and express them."[34] As used here, emotion regulation refers more narrowly to processes or techniques that moderate the intensity of negative emotional responses to wrongdoing—that is, diminish how powerfully they are felt and the extent to which they monopolize one's field of consciousness. Such techniques can be employed with conscious awareness but need not be, as Gross notes: one need not be conscious that one is engaged in some emotion regulation activity. However, for those who are prone to ruminate, processes of emotion regulation will be conscious and relatively effortful and controlled. (Repression can explain forgetting, but repression is deployed unconsciously.) This should not be taken to imply, of course, that the extent to which one ruminates on the past is subject to one's immediate voluntary control. It is not. The forgetting induced by deliberate use of emotion regulation techniques does not occur all at once, in response to the desire to forget: it is essentially a process that takes place over some more or less extended period of time. We may be able to disregard some unpleasant information by simply willing ourselves to do so. But as I noted earlier in discussing Margalit, forgetting and disregarding are not the same.

Two preliminary points will help clarify the focus of my discussion. First, there is a distinction between the emotion one is experiencing, on the one hand, and the intensity, duration, and frequency of the experience of the emotion, on the other. Emotion regulation techniques can prevent the occurrence of an emotion as well as create the conditions that cause a change in these experiential qualities and decrease the emotion's impact. This distinction, though not always easy to make in practice, is important. The use of these techniques can sometimes result in the extirpation of one emotion and its replacement by another—for example, anger may give way to disappointment or sadness. But for emotion regulation to promote *forgetting*, it is not enough that the identity of the emotion-type changes. It is not enough because one intense emotion may give way to a different but equally intense emotion, and the new emotion may dominate one's attention to the same extent as the old one did. Thus, it is also necessary that whatever new emotion results from emotion regulation, it is of such diminished intensity that conscious recall of the associated event is adversely affected. In either case, whether the type of emotion changes or not, negative emotions that are associated with memories of past wrongdoing and that have kept them from fading are weakened and no longer able to sustain them to the same degree. Since these techniques aim to lessen the emotional intensity of our memories, and since emotions have a significant impact on the strength and durability of our memories, we can expect that when the techniques are successfully deployed the memories will be harder to consciously retain (in comparison to when the techniques are not used or fail), absent some other way of shoring them up.

Second, some writers include in the notion of emotion regulation not only changes and modulations of the experience of the emotions associated with certain events but also the suppression of their expression in external behavior. Here, however, I will follow Eisenberg and Spinrad in distinguishing between "emotion regulation" and "emotion-related behavioral regulation."[35] Emotion-related behavioral regulation might eventually lead to changes in what and how the emotions are experienced (that is, to a decrease in emotion experience), although this is uncertain. But their immediate target is not to bring about such changes: it is rather to decrease expressive behavior.

How can one change the emotions that are generated by and directed at past wrongdoings and moderate how they are experienced? Gross distinguishes between two broad categories of emotion regulation activity, attentional deployment and cognitive reappraisal, and I will follow him here.[36] Attentional deployment encompasses various processes for deploying one's attention to lessen the emotional impact of negative events, including (a) selectively diverting one's attention from aspects of a situation that arouse negative emotions or from the immediate situation altogether and (b) focusing one's attention on one's memories, thoughts, and emotions so as to render them less overwhelming or frightening. The first sort of process is extremely familiar and widely practiced.

Patrick Boleyn-Fitzgerald, in a rare acknowledgment by a contemporary Anglo-American philosopher of the importance of forgetting for forgiving, describes it as follows:

> To cool down, we must move our attention away from angry thoughts long enough for our acute physiological arousal to subside. When individuals are angry, they often read, watch television, drive, walk, or use some other means of moving their attention away from angry thoughts. This is an attempt to forget about an anger-provoking event while the individual is still in a state of physiological arousal. These methods of forgetting are indispensable for managing anger.[37]

To the extent that these methods work, it is because shifts of attention alter the motivational strength of one's initial emotional reactions. Angry feelings, for example, tend to generate thoughts and actions that can be significantly influenced by shifting one's attentional focus away from them to less distress-provoking occupations. According to Boleyn-Fitzgerald's explanation, the shift of attention gives one's physiological arousal a chance to subside, and as it does so one's anger and angry thoughts subside as well. The degree of deliberate effort that this shift requires, and the particular self-control measures that are likely to be most effective, depend on the intensity of one's emotional reaction, on how one characteristically deals with slights and insults, and on the meaning and importance that one attaches to the emotion-arousing event. Using anger again as an example, mild anger about an acknowledged minor offense is not likely to seriously disturb one's equanimity or require much effort to overcome. In these situations, one may simply find one's attention drawn to pleasing or calming thoughts and activities, without the need for much effortful control. However, a great deal of anger is plainly not like this, especially when the anger of the moral sort. Anger of the moral sort is anger over a perceived violation of one's right to equal respect or expectations of special regard, and dampening it may require a focused intention to change emotion and strenuous efforts to distract one's attention from the anger-arousing event.

Another process that involves attentional deployment but in a very different way is mindful attention or mindfulness.[38] Mindfulness is a highly concentrated and structured mode of attention to experience that seeks to alter the impact of, and response to, thoughts, emotions, and feelings. More specifically, it is a mode of awareness that involves attending moment by moment to the contents of one's consciousness and adopting a stance of openness to and acceptance of one's thoughts, emotions, and sensations. Practices that employ mindfulness, including variants of exposure therapy for the treatment of post-traumatic stress disorder (PTSD) and other conditions,[39] are grounded in the belief that by

Forgetting and Forgiving Revisited   125

regulating the focus of one's attention in this way and bringing these attitudes to it, one will become less closely identified with these mental states, hence less controlled by them and better able to clearly and objectively perceive them. In the mindfulness literature, this attentional process is called "reperceiving," and Shapiro and colleagues describe its effects as follows:

> to the extent that we are able to observe the contents of consciousness, we are no longer completely embedded in or fused with such content. For example, if we are to see *it*, then we are no longer merely *it*; i.e. we must be *more* than it. Whether the *it* is pain, depression, or fear, reperceiving allows one to dis-identify from thoughts, emotions, and body sensations as they arise, and simply be with them instead of being defined (i.e. controlled, conditioned, determined) by them.[40]

Reperceiving or mindfully attending to one's memories and emotional states separates the self from them, allows an individual to stand back from them, and teaches her that they are not to be feared or avoided. Putting some distance between herself and her negative emotions, she is then less likely to respond to negative events in stereotypic reactive ways and more likely to adopt a wider, more adaptive range of coping strategies. She is, in this sense, liberated from bondage to the past—that is, from patterns of response to it that are automatic, habitual, and reactive. Further, as this description suggests, reperceiving is not a process of dissociation or a kind of thought suppression. Rather, as Bishop and colleagues characterize it, it involves "becoming more aware of thoughts and feelings, relating to them in a wider, decentered field of awareness, and purposefully opening fully to one's experience."[41] Mindfulness involves the adoption of a decentered perspective that is said to prevent or release one from ruminative thinking, and this differs from the detachment characteristic of dissociation and from the avoidance characteristic of suppression.

The two types of attentional deployment deploy attention in opposite ways: in one case, *diverting* attention from negative experiences and the thoughts and emotions associated with them; in the other, *focusing* attention on the thoughts and emotions associated with negative experiences. In both cases, however, attentional deployment, if effective, moderates the impact of negative emotions so that memories of the incident become less insistent and frequent, to the extent that they depend on these emotions. Strong emotions generally make for strong memories, and memories that are strengthened and maintained over a long period of time by strong emotions are not as strong or long-lasting once these emotions lose their intensity, unless there is some other mechanism that supports recall. In these circumstances one tends to forget negative emotion-arousing events more easily and forgetfulness of them is more likely. Moreover, for modes of attentional deployment to promote forgiving, a minor change in the accessibility of memories of wrongdoing, brought about by a minor reduction in the intensity of the emotions they provoke, may be insufficient. Some more substantial effect on accessibility may be required, substantial enough to count as forgetting.

The second category of emotion regulation activity is cognitive reappraisal, and here too there are various strategies that employ it. Cognitive reappraisal differs from attentional deployment, even from mindful attention, because it does not just involve regulating what one directs one's attention to or how one attends to negative events. Rather, it involves revising the story one tells about these events in ways that alter their meaning and significance for the storyteller. There are different ways of doing this. One is to attach a different, more positive or less negative meaning to particular emotion-eliciting aspects of a situation: for example, "he is preoccupied with his own troubles" instead of "he doesn't care about my feelings." This method is also commonly used in the therapeutic management of anger where individuals are trained in cognitive coping skills so that they can experience anger without being overwhelmed by it. Among the skills that assist them in this is "the ability to alternatively construe provocation."[42] Anger management techniques do not just aim to teach individuals how to suppress behavioral expressions of anger, nor do they aim to extinguish feelings of anger altogether. Rather, their goal is to enable individuals to moderate the intensity of their angry feelings so that angry thoughts do not cause unmanageable emotional distress or maladaptive behavior.

This sort of cognitive reappraisal may facilitate the forgetting of emotion-arousing experiences, but whether it facilitates forgiveness is another matter. Attaching a more positive or emotionally neutral meaning to seemingly negative events may in fact displace forgiveness if it consists in reinterpreting what another did so that there is nothing to feel hurt about or to resent. As the example "he is preoccupied with his own troubles" suggests, another person's apparently insensitive or demeaning behavior may be construed in such a way as to mitigate blame, and this would constitute excusing rather than forgiving. So if cognitive reappraisal is not only to assist forgetting but to assist forgetting in a way that facilitates forgiveness, it must not have the result that the offender is not or not as blameworthy for his actions after all. This would not be forgetting as I have been concerned with it here: that is to say, it would not be forgetting that facilitates the process of forgiving, but rather forgetting that obviates forgiving. The next suggestion recognizes the importance of this distinction.

A more elaborate version of the same method of cognitive reappraisal involves taking a more sympathetic attitude toward a person's actions by placing them within a biographical narrative that explains why he acted as he did. Cheshire Calhoun discusses this in the context of defending a novel and unorthodox view of forgiveness that she calls "aspirational."[43] According to her, aspirational forgiveness forgives another for his wrongdoing by making sense of it, and it does this by telling a story about his life that explains why an action of that sort might have seemed to him as the thing to do. This story cites earlier formative experiences and attachments that can plausibly have shaped his patterns of judgment and disposed him to act in selfish and destructive ways. A story of this sort is aspirational because it is burdensome to construct and there is no obligation to do so, and it does not condone or overlook what the wrongdoer did:

> because the aim of the aspirational story is to make sense of *culpable* wrongdoing by understanding how it might be a sensible way of continuing a biography, such stories cannot "wipe away" sins ... The aspirational story confirms our perception of the past. The injury is here to stay. It cannot be wiped away, because the agent's true self meant it and will not retract what she did. She would do it again. (95)

The forgiveness that the wronged party may then extend to the wrongdoer asks little of him, on Calhoun's conception: it accepts him as he is, does not demand that he express remorse or disavow what he has done, and apparently imposes no other conditions on granting forgiveness, such as requiring the wrongdoer to make some sort of amends.

The notion of an aspirational story is relevant to the issue of emotion regulation because of the possible effects that a story of this sort can have on the emotional responses of the individual who constructs it. Such a story about another's actions cognitively reappraises them, by appealing to a biographical narrative that gives them an alternative more sympathetic construal, and this is one way to intentionally modulate one's emotional reactions to negative emotion–eliciting events. Actions that before elicited anger and resentment might now elicit sympathy and compassion instead, and there might also be a corresponding reduction in the intensity of one's negative feelings. It might also be harder for the one who was wronged to remember what the offender did because emotions that are the focus of ruminative thinking and generate particularly strong reactions become less preoccupying and less psychologically compelling.[44]

How can constructing a biographical narrative facilitate forgiveness in this sense? The explanation, once again, is this. A narrative of another's life that revises the wronged party's understanding of it may have the potential to modify her emotional responses to the wrongs committed by the other, to de-intensify them. It can help her avoid ruminating about past transgressions, which is associated with reduced forgetting of emotional material. By removing this hindrance to forgetting—viz. the impulse to ruminate—or preventing the wronged party from falling under its sway, the construction of a biographical narrative creates conditions that assist her to forget. And by doing this, it may also assist her to forgive if what was preventing her from forgiving is the strength of her emotional responses to the treatment she received.

In Calhoun's account, if one can position a person's misdeeds within a biographical narrative that makes (non-moral) sense of them, then one may be prepared to forgive the offender for them, to forgive in an aspirational sense. She means by this in part "that one stops demanding that the person be different from what she is . . . that she improve" (95). But the importance of this kind of cognitive reappraisal for the possibility of forgiveness is not dependent on accepting Calhoun's particular conception of forgiveness. Indeed, one can endorse a very different conception, according to which one does not cease to demand that the offender become a different, better person, and still hold that explaining a person's actions in terms of her history has the potential to promote forgiveness, because it can reduce the potency of one's memories sufficiently to put them beyond the reach of ready accessibility. According to this different conception, forgiveness is granted to those who take responsibility for their wrongdoing, who feel and show remorse for it, repent of it, and seek to make amends. It is a kind of forgiveness that does not just accept the person as she is, warts and all, but on the contrary expects her to disavow her previous behavior and give evidence that she is making an effort to become a different sort of person for whom repeating the offense is less likely.

In forgetting, the person who was wronged avoids being consumed or debilitated by memories of past transgressions. But she does not *only* forget the wrongs; she remembers them too—indeed, she must remember them and their agent if forgiveness is to be possible. Active forgetting is an intentional strategy that can aid the wronged party in forgiving, not a substitute for forgiving, and as such it can only be one element in a complex interplay of psychological reactions, of episodes of forgetting and temporary suspensions of forgetfulness, that characterize her response to a problematic past. As Calhoun acknowledges, there can only be such a thing as forgiveness if the wronged party holds on to the judgment that she was inexcusably and unjustifiably wronged, and for this she needs to remember. But she can do more than remember that she was culpably wronged, and on the standard account of forgiveness, she will. She is not precluded from adopting this more demanding type of forgiveness because she has constructed an explanatory biographical story that makes sense of the offender's wrongdoer. Still, what I want to emphasize here is that meeting these conditions of responsibility taking to her satisfaction may only be part of the explanation of her forgiving the offender. It may also be that she has been helped to do so by deploying active forgetting.

As I said earlier, cognitive reappraisal is not necessarily conducive to forgiving, even if it is conducive to forgetting. Let me underscore this point in the

Forgetting and Forgiving Revisited

following way. Sarah Stroud, discussing the epistemic dimension of friendship, describes the partiality that friends tend to extend to one another in interpreting reports about their so-called questionable conduct:

> What is distinctive in this domain [when processing new data about our friends] is that we tend to devote more energy to defeating or minimizing the impact of unfavorable data than we otherwise would ... We deploy a different or at least a heightened array of cognitive activities in response to unfavorable information which concerns our friends.[45]

Stroud sees this as posing a serious challenge to the hegemony of standards of epistemic responsibility, and this is what her essay addresses. My purpose in bringing it up here is very different, however: it is to draw a contrast with what I have argued so far. The first thing to note is that there is a basis of comparison with my remarks about cognitive reappraisal because the kind of epistemic partiality that Stroud says is characteristic of good friends can also determine how a wronged party interprets and responds to the actions of her wrongdoer. That is, a person who was wronged might interpret her wrongdoer's conduct and motivation charitably, in the way that friends do, perhaps because the wrongdoer is her friend or because their relationship, though not a friendship, discourages harsh judgment of his conduct. Moreover, charitable interpretations of this sort employ an array of cognitive activities that can undercut whatever anger or disappointment the victim may initially feel by generating less damning explanations of the other's conduct than would otherwise be warranted. With her emotions affected in this way, her relationship with her friend would not be adversely affected. But there are different ways that this can come about, some a consequence of forgiving and some not. The important point is that in this case it is not. It is instead made possible by an interpretation that retracts any initial impression of culpability and that does not condemn the wrongdoer for what he has done. It amounts to giving the wrongdoer a pass, and however conducive to forgetting this might be and however advisable it might be for other reasons, it cannot promote forgiveness.

5. The virtue of forgetfulness and the ethics of forgiveness

If there are wrongs that are truly unforgivable, then refusing to forgive another for his wrongdoing is not always morally objectionable. The heinousness of the act can be a psychological barrier to forgiveness and might justify withholding it. But dwelling on these wrongs, so that memories of them intensify in their emotional impact and recur repeatedly, becoming at times unmanageable, is another matter. It too can be a barrier to forgiveness, but it does not follow from the fact that the wrong is too grave to forgive that ruminating on it is morally unproblematic or unobjectionable. On the contrary, rumination is not only linked to a heightened risk for the onset of various mental disorders, but it can also threaten the efficacy of a person's agency in ways that do not necessarily manifest as specific diagnosable mental illnesses: by compromising his autonomy and capacity for self-direction; by impairing his sense of his own value; and by eroding his confidence in his ability to fulfill his intentions and plans. Ruminating on the wrongs committed against oneself can hinder forgiveness, as can reflection on the seriousness of the wrongs committed. But it is important to distinguish between these two responses to wrongdoing and to evaluate them separately. Acts that are properly regarded as unforgivable, if there are any such, are not therefore acts that one may ruminate on without raising serious psychological and moral questions about its effects on one's life. It follows that to assess rumination from a moral standpoint, we have to do more than consider the moral quality of the act that is its focus.

I have argued that there are various techniques of emotion regulation that can facilitate release from or avoidance of ruminative thinking and, further, that their intentional employment can actively assist the individual to forget what he might otherwise ruminate on. But I have not said much about the conditions under which one may properly use such techniques to facilitate forgetting. Since one (only one) of the possible effects of forgetting is to facilitate forgiving—indeed, this is why I have been interested in forgetting in the first place—there is a more narrowly focused question about forgetting in relation to this end: when is it morally appropriate or desirable to facilitate forgetting when forgiveness is thereby promoted? The answer to this, obviously, will depend on our assessment of the moral warrant for forgiveness in particular cases. In addition, if we turn our attention from individual acts of forgetting to what I earlier called, drawing on a reading of Nietzsche, the virtue of forgetfulness, then this too will necessarily implicate the ethics of forgiveness. The victim of wrongdoing who possesses this virtue is disposed to engage in techniques that promote forgetfulness of wrongdoing, when forgetting can advance morally desirable or virtuous forgiving or some other morally worthy end. He is not disposed to forgetfulness that facilitates forgiving, when forgiving is morally objectionable or would exhibit a vice. In relation to forgiving there are good and bad uses of forgetting, and these conditions must be specified as part of a full account of the virtue of forgetfulness. They must be specified because forgetting can make it easier to forgive.

The person who possesses the virtue of forgetfulness hits the mean between obsessive rumination on the past on the one hand and a dismissive or indifferent attitude toward the past on the other. She is able to learn from the past, without being crushed by it; if the part of the past at issue involves wrongs committed against her, her memories of them will not be so debilitating that they prevent her from enjoying life goods that would otherwise be available to her if her agency were intact. The virtue of forgetfulness, however, like other virtues, is not invulnerable to external factors that can undermine it and deeply compromise or negate an individual's well-being. Susan Brison, for example, powerfully describes the effects of traumatic injury on the memories of the victims:

> Traumatic memory also perpetuates the loss of control experienced during the traumatic events. Traumatic memories are intrusive, triggered by things reminiscent of the traumatic event and carrying a strong, sometimes overwhelming, emotional charge . . . Such a loss of control over oneself—one's memories, one's desires—can explain, to a large extent, what a survivor means in saying "I am no longer myself." Trauma victims long for their former selves not only because those selves were more familiar and less damaged, but because they were controllable, more predictable . . . In order to recover, a trauma survivor needs to be able to gain control over traumatic memories.[46]

Trauma victims, as thus described, ruminate on the causes of their trauma, and under these circumstances it is neither possible to forget the traumatic events nor likely that they will be able to forgive the perpetrators, even if it would be a morally admirable thing to do. They are haunted by memories of their ordeal, and the process of gaining control over them involves overcoming cognitive and emotional barriers to the exercise of capacities that are constitutive of the virtue of forgetfulness. In general, there is a connection between the virtue of forgetfulness and the ability to exercise control over one's memories, whether or not they are traumatic, but with traumatic memories, the barriers are significant. The victims need to learn not only how to forget but also how to remember without incurring the fragmentation of self caused by their trauma. For these reasons, recovery *from* trauma is in part recovery *of* what is needed for the virtue of forgetfulness.

Forgiveness too is a virtue that involves hitting the mean between deficiency and excess: between an obdurate refusal to forgive on the one hand and, on the other, an excessive readiness to forgive that betrays a failure to take the wrong or oneself sufficiently seriously. Forgiving, obviously, does not always speak well of the forgiver and is not always a virtuous act or unconditionally good. Moreover, this carries over to forgetting, to the extent that it promotes forgiving: forgetting wrongdoing, to the extent that it disposes one to forgive, is not always a virtuous activity or unconditionally good. An individual who does not dwell on the past, who employs various techniques of emotion regulation to dampen his memories, might thereby exhibit a vice, precisely because of the role that these

132   FORGIVENESS AND REMEMBRANCE

techniques play in helping him to forgive his wrongdoer. Therefore, any recommendation of forgetting in relation to forgiving has to be conditional: the moral value of forgetting will depend on whether the forgiveness that it facilitates exhibits a virtue or is morally warranted or desirable.

The relationship between memory and forgiveness, it should be clear by now, is more complicated, both psychologically and morally, than what is suggested by the simple dichotomy of forgiving versus forgetting often adopted in the philosophical literature. Forgetting is not only a possible outcome of forgiving but can also be a means to forgiving, if the explanation of why one cannot forgive is that one cannot free oneself from one's memories of wrongdoing. Not all acts of wrongdoing may be forgivable. However, there may be acts of wrongdoing that are in principle forgivable, but where the victim is prevented from considering the merits of forgiving because his emotional responses will not permit him to do so. If the victim dwells on the past with an ever-present sense of grievance or victimhood, or if out of self-pity he wallows in his hurt feelings, then objective assessment of reasons for forgiveness will likely be beyond his reach, at least without the help of a skilled professional.

Moreover, the philosophical literature generally does not attribute any moral value to forgetting prior to forgiving. Yet there is a distinctive virtue related to forgetting (and a companion virtue related to remembering) whose status as a virtue can partly be explained by its relationship to acts of virtuous or morally praiseworthy forgiveness. Acts of forgiveness may be commendable even if they are not obligatory, and given the psychological relationship between forgetting and forgiving, forgetfulness can have an important moral function in relation to forgiveness. Knowing when and how to forget is an aspect of the *virtue* of forgetfulness in part because there is a connection between forgetting and forgiving, because forgetting can promote forgiving and because sometimes one has good reason to forgive.

6. From interpersonal to collective forgiving and forgetting

Is there an analogy, on the larger social or cultural level, to the intra- and interpersonal phenomena I have been discussing in this chapter? Is there a phenomenon that we might call social or cultural forgetting, and is there some basis for linking it to the promotion of collective forgiveness? I believe that there is, although we should be careful not to push the analogies too far.

We have already seen, in discussing Singer and Conway's response to Connerton (section 4b), that there are cultural and political processes that can manipulate accessibility and render particular collective memories obsolete or relatively inaccessible to the members of a group. An analogy with intrapersonal inaccessibility as the criterion of individual forgetting seems plausible, and Singer and Conway exploit it in moving freely from individual memory to the larger cultural one. Arguably, large groups as well as individuals can forget, just as large groups and individuals can remember, and this can be explained without having to appeal to some sort of group mind that operates according to psychological principles of its own. The parallels in terms of accessibility between the two cases are convincing enough on their own without this. In one, forgetting has to do with an individual's ease of access to what has been encoded and stored in her long-term memory; in the other, with a group's ease of access to its own history, including group values and sources of group identity embodied in the products of social life. In both cases, efforts to recall are hampered, although for different reasons: either because of psychological defenses or the passage of time (individual), or because of deliberate manipulation by those in authority or processes of cultural transformation (social).

But if groups of people can forget, they can also remember in ways that are the social analogue of psychological rumination. Groups, like individuals, can be hostages to their past; their agency can be crippled by it. Sometimes this is because there are intense and widely shared emotional reactions among the members of a group to what they have suffered as a group, or among the perpetrators and their descendants to the wrongs for which they are responsible. Further, as in the individual case, it is important to distinguish between reasons for not forgetting and reasons for ruminating: good reasons to remember do not entail that there are good reasons to ruminate on what is remembered. Charles Maier notes the distinction in his discussion of the controversy in post-war Germany surrounding German memory of the Holocaust:

> There may indeed be a difference between maintaining a decent quotient of collective memory and being obsessed by it. Few responsible Germans would deny the obligation of the former, but many think that what critics really want is the latter . . . [Some of these] commentators have also implied an analogue of neurosis: fixation with earlier guilt apparently precludes a productive maturity.[47]

The analogy between individual and collective is not perfect, of course, and with respect to emotion regulation techniques, not everything that could prove useful in interpersonal cases has an analogue in the domain of collective memory: mindfulness seems to have no parallel, for example, but cognitive reappraisal does. Nevertheless, the idea that there can be such a thing as collective rumination on a burdened past that prevents a society from moving on to a productive future is not implausible. Benchmarks of a healthy society can be formulated; the effects of collective memory on the health of a society can be gauged; and assessments of social preoccupation with the past can be generated.

134   FORGIVENESS AND REMEMBRANCE

And something analogous to emotion regulation may assist a society in avoiding the perils of rumination.

What about forgiveness? Can forgiveness be promoted by socially deployed techniques that instill a kind of collective or shared group forgetting? To answer, we first need to define terms: what is meant by forgiveness as a social (as opposed to a personal) phenomenon? A type of forgiveness that is appropriate to this setting is political forgiveness, and there are different ways to understand this. It can refer to something that is dispensed by persons (e.g., political leaders) who have not themselves been wronged on behalf of persons who have been (e.g., those they officially represent). Forgiveness in this sense has no essential relationship to emotion: it is just a decision that releases the offender from the obligation to make further amends.[48] What's more, shared group forgetting may have only some indirect relevance to the process of political forgiveness conceived in this way.

However, political forgiveness can be conceptualized differently, and this might allow a greater role for forgetting. Thus understood, it is political not because it is forgiveness dispensed by *political officials*, but because it is forgiveness that has broadly speaking *political consequences* and that matters from a political standpoint. Conceived in this way, forgiveness might be aided by techniques that facilitate group forgetting, techniques that are the social analogue of the techniques of emotion regulation discussed above. Of course, victims and victim groups are not always willing or able to forgive those who have wronged them; their hatred of the perpetrators may be too profound. In these cases, we should not expect forgetting, nor should we expect the forgetting that can lead to or promote forgiveness. However, suppose there is such a thing as group-based emotion regulation. Emotion regulation on a group level could make political forgiveness possible, and this would be for the good if it promotes the right sort of political reconciliation, which it might do even if many victims are not able to forget or to forgive those who wronged them. Of course, forgiveness is possible without reconciliation and a kind of reconciliation is possible without forgiveness. But the failure of victims to forgive and the failure to reconcile with offenders could have the same type of cause, namely excessive preoccupation with the wrongs of the past.

In arguing that group forgetting can promote group forgiving, I have assumed that we can intelligibly speak about groups forgiving, and therefore, on a sentiment-based account of forgiveness, about groups having emotions like resentment, grief, and so on. But in what sense can we attribute emotional (and other mental) states to groups? According to an aggregate view, a group emotion is not truly a collective emotion; it is merely the sum total of the individual emotions experienced by a certain portion of the group's members. A holistic view, by contrast, maintains that, with respect to emotions, there is a collective level

Forgetting and Forgiving Revisited 135

different from, though dependent on, the individual level. It takes group emotions to be a feature of the collectivity of a collective. This view, however, might seem implausible and objectionably anthropomorphic. Can it be defended?

Margaret Gilbert believes it can, and her plural subject theory of collective agency shows how. Central to her theory is the notion of a joint commitment, since it is this that explains the difference between an assortment of individual attitudes, feelings, etc., even those that belong to members of the same group, and collective attitudes and feelings of the group. Persons initiating a joint commitment, according to her account, "do not each create a part of it by making a personal decision. Rather, they participate in creating the whole of it along with the other parties. A joint commitment does not have parts, thought it certainly has implications for the individual parties. That is, each is committed through the joint commitment."[49] Plural subject theory explains group phenomena as the product of a joint commitment on the part of individuals to do or experience certain things as a body, a single unified agent or subject of the phenomena. When they are jointly committed to this, they constitute themselves a plural subject.

This, then, would be the plural subject theory's account of a collective emotion: for us to collectively feel an emotion E in relation to action A (our own or another's) is for us to be jointly committed to feeling E as a body in relation to A. Note that being jointly committed to do, feel, or express something does not entail that individuals do, feel, or express it individually: they can commit themselves to this though none of them feels the emotion as his or her own. Further, by making a joint commitment, whether to do or feel or experience something as a body, individuals bind themselves to one another, and they make this mutual binding known to all. The creation of a plural subject entitles members to make claims upon one another to follow through on what they have jointly committed themselves to—in the case at hand, to follow through on their commitment to feel an emotion. They can make normative claims upon one another in virtue of their belonging to a single unified body.

Assuming that we accept this way of distinguishing between collectives and aggregates, we next have to ask about the relationship between collectives and their individual members. This is a problem any account that subscribes to holism about groups will have to address, for if social phenomena are irreducibly holistic properties of groups, their relationship to properties of the individuals who make them up requires explanation. Two questions need attention. First, must each and every member of the group be a party to a joint commitment to feel an emotion in order for there to be a collective emotion? Second, how will individual members act if they act as required by their joint commitment?

As for the first question about inclusiveness, it may seem that individuals should be free to opt out of a joint commitment in some circumstances. But plural subject theory doesn't deny this. It doesn't say that individuals who do not want to participate in a joint commitment to feel as a body may nevertheless be forced to do so. It says rather that only those who participate belong to a single unified collective, and that certain subsidiary responsibilities flow from belonging to a body of this sort. As for the second question about the content of these responsibilities, there are various things that the members of a plural subject of emotion might and sometimes should do. For example, remonstrating with a group member who denies that there are any grounds for the group to have a certain emotion could count as one way of seeing to it that the joint commitment to experience this emotion as a body is adhered to. Perhaps little more than refraining from disparaging or expressing contempt for those who think there are grounds for such a commitment, or not obstructing those who wish to express this emotion, is all that is required of some who belong to a single unified subject of emotion. In general, the joint commitment to feel an emotion as a body obligates those who are parties to this commitment to act in ways appropriate to it, so they are required to help support or at least not to interfere with that commitment.

Plural subject theory is a well-developed philosophical response to skeptical claims that collectives as such cannot have emotions, but there is at least one problem with the account as applied to emotions: it seems a rather bloodless explanation of a collective emotion to say that it is *just* a joint commitment to feel emotion as a body. What is missing is the phenomenological component of emotion.[50] Nevertheless, it may be possible to provide a fuller account of collective emotions that builds on and does not upend plural subject theory, and this would be appealing if one believes, as I am inclined to, that plural subject theory is a critical part of an adequate theory of social phenomena of all sorts, including collective emotions. According to this fuller account, a collective as such has an emotion only if it widely shared within the group. However, this addition raises a difficulty of its own to which there is no clear-cut solution: how widely shared must the emotion be for it to be an emotion of the group as a whole? On the one hand, if only a very few members of a large collective share an emotion, then it is quite misleading to say that the emotion is collectively experienced. On the other, if only a few in a very large group do *not* share the emotion, then it seems equally unacceptable to say that the emotion is not collectively experienced. There is obviously no magic number that takes us over the threshold from the former to the latter case. Analogous difficulties appear in other contexts as well. For example, it is indeterminate what percentage of the members of a political community must agree with an apology delivered by their leaders for that apology to count as supported by the community as a whole. Problems of line drawing are common with respect to social phenomena of various sorts, and efforts to draw bright lines where bright lines do not exist only obscure rather than illuminate the issue.

In the next chapter, I will say more about a kind of forgiveness that is political in the sense of having broadly political consequences and taking place in a political context. Political forgiveness of this sort is often (though not always) a collective process in which individuals jointly commit themselves as a body to forgive those who wronged all or some of them. I will also consider the role of political forgiveness thus construed in the achievement of transitional justice—that is, in securing the peculiar kind of justice that pertains to societies transitioning from periods of large-scale wrongdoing that was often aided and abetted by government action or inaction. More specifically, I will discuss how forgiveness figures in the advancement of transitional justice understood as a process of restoration, restoration both of victims and of the political and legal order. In relation to this, I will also briefly comment on the practice of commemoration, which is the central topic of chapter 5.

Endnotes

1. See Thomas Brudholm, *Resentment's Virtue* (Philadelphia, PA: Temple University Press, 2008).
2. Avishai Margalit, *The Ethics of Memory* (Cambridge, MA: Harvard University Press, 2002), p. 193.
3. Friedrich Nietzsche, *On the Genealogy of Morality* (M. Clark and A. Swensen, trans.) (Indianapolis: Hackett Publishing Company, 1998), p. 35.
4. Ibid., pp. 35–36.
5. In *Untimely Meditations* (R. J. Hollingdale, trans.) (Cambridge: Cambridge University Press, 1997), pp. 62–63.
6. It might seem strange to characterize Nietzsche as a virtue theorist with respect to the faculties of remembering and forgetting since he has some very derogatory things to say about virtue. But many philosophers have thought it plausible to construe Nietzsche as a virtue theorist of some kind. The first to popularize the notion in Anglo-American philosophy was Walter Kaufmann in *Nietzsche: Philosopher, Psychologist, Antichrist* (New York: Vintage Books, 1968). According to Kaufmann, "Nietzsche's debt to Aristotle's ethics . . . is considerable." For a recent article defending this interpretation, see Christine Swanton, "Outline of a Nietzschean Virtue Ethics," *International Studies in Philosophy*, vol. 30, no. 3 (1996): 29–38. Mark Alfano, in "The Most Agreeable of all Vices: Nietzsche as a Virtue Epistemologist" (forthcoming in the *British Journal for the History of Philosophy*), argues that "Nietzschean virtues differ from neo–Aristotelian virtues because they are sophisticated versions of Nietzschean drives."
7. *Genealogy*, op. cit., p. 35.
8. Norman S. Care, *Living with One's Past* (Lanham, MD: Rowman and Littlefield, 1996), p. 81.
9. *Untimely Meditations*, op. cit., p. 62.
10. Care, op. cit., p. 81.
11. Rosalind Hursthouse, "Virtue Ethics," in the online *Stanford Encyclopedia of Philosophy*.
12. J. Joorman and T. B. Tran, "Rumination and intentional forgetting of emotional material," *Cognition and Emotion*, vol. 23, no. 6 (2009): 1233–1246, at 1234.
13. R. D. Ray, F. H. Wilhelm, and J. J. Gross, "All in the Mind's Eye? Anger Rumination and Reappraisal," *Journal of Personality and Social Psychology*, vol. 94, no. 1 (2008): 133–145, at 133.
14. S. C. Segerstrom, A. L. Stanton, L. E. Alden, and B. E. Shortridge, "A multi-dimensional structure for repetitive thought: What's on your mind, and how, and how much?" *Journal of Personality and Social Psychology*, vol. 85 (2003): 909–921, at 909.

15. The quote is from Jeanette Smith and Lauren Alloy, "A roadmap to rumination: A review of the definition, assessment, and conceptualization of this multifaceted construct," *Clinical Psychology Review*, vol. 29, no. 2 (March 2009): 1–30, at 2, who are describing Nolen-Hoeksema's Response Styles Theory. See also Cheryl L. Rusting and Susan Nolen-Hoeksema, "Regulating Responses to Anger: Effects of Rumination and Distraction on Angry Mood," *Journal of Personality and Social Psychology*, vol. 74, no. 3 (1998): 790–803.
16. Smith and Alloy, p. 2; and M. Conway, P. A. R. Csank, S. L. Holm, and C. K. Blake, "On assessing individual differences in rumination on sadness," *Journal of Personality Assessment*, vol. 75 (2000): 404–425.
17. Joorman and Tran, op. cit., p. 1241.
18. See Linda J. Levine and David A. Pizarro, "Emotional Valence, Discrete Emotions, and Memory," in *Memory and Emotion* (Bob Uttl, Nobuo Ohta, and Amy Siegenthaler, eds.) (Malden, MA: Blackwell Publishing, 2006), pp. 37–58.
19. See M. McCullough, C. G. Bellah, S. D. Kilpatrick, and J. L. Johnson, "Vengefulness: Relationships with Forgiveness, Rumination, Well–Being, and the Big Five," *Personality and Social Psychology Bulletin*, vol. 27, no. 5 (May 2001): 601–610; Ray, Wilhem, and Gross, op. cit.; Rustig and Nolen-Hoeksema, op. cit. Jennifer Goldman and Peter Coleman argue that rumination can increase the emotional experience of anger as well as strengthen intentions to engage in aggressive behavior: "In contrast to catharsis theory (which states that expressing negative emotions diffuses them), these studies suggest that the more individuals ruminate, the angrier they feel and the more aggressively they behave" ("A Theoretical Understanding of How Emotions Fuel Intractable Conflict: The Case of Humiliation," at http://humiliationstudies/org/documents/GodlmanNY05meetingRT2.pdf).
20. M. J. V. Fennell and J. D. Teasdale, "Effects of distraction on thinking and affect in depressed patients," *British Journal of Clinical Psychology*, vol. 23 (1984): 65–66; S. Lyubomirsky and S. Nolen-Hoeksema, "Self-perpetuating properties of dysphoric rumination," *Journal of Personality and Social Psychology*, vol. 69 (1994): 176–190; S. Nolen-Hoeksema, J. Morrow, and B. L. Fredrickson, "Response styles and duration of depressed moods," *Journal of Abnormal Psychology*, vol. 102 (1993): 20–28; T. Pyszczynski, K. Holt, and J. Freenberg, "Depression, self-focused attention and the negative memory bias," *Journal of Personality and Social Psychology*, vol. 52 (1987): 994–1001; J. V. Wood, J. A. Saltzberg, J. M. Neale, A. A. S. Stone, and T. B. Rachmiel, "Self-focused attention, coping responses, and distressed mood in everyday life," *Journal of Personality and Social Psychology*, vol. 58 (1990): 1027–1036; R. E. Thayer, J. R. Newman, and T. M. McClain, "Self-regulation of mood: Strategies for changing a bad mood, raising energy, and reducing tension," *Journal of Personality and Social Psychology*, vol. 67 (1994): 910–925.
21. On the possibility that different mood regulation strategies might be needed for different emotions, see J. A. Russell, "A circumplex model of affect," *Journal of Personality and Social Psychology*, vol. 39 (1980): 1161–1178.
22. Rusting and Nolen-Hoeksema, "Regulating Responses to Anger," op. cit., p. 791.
23. Norman Care, "Forgiveness and Effective Agency," in *Before Forgiving: Cautionary Views of Forgiveness in Psychotherapy* (S. Lamb and J. Murphy, eds.) (New York: Oxford University Press, 2002), pp. 217–218.
24. For support of this view, see McCullough, et al., "Vengefulness," op. cit.; L. Cosgrove and V. Konstam, "Forgiveness and Forgetting: Clinical Implications for Mental Health Counselors," *Journal of Mental Health Counseling*, vol. 30, no. 1 (January 2008): 1–13.
25. Margalit, op. cit., pp. 188–189, 197.
26. On the relationship between thought suppression and forgetting, see Daniel Schacter, "Suppression of unwanted memories: repression revisited?" *The Lancet*, vol. 357, no. 9270 (June 2001): 1724–1725. On the relationship between thought suppression and rumination, see Daniel Gold and Daniel Wegner, "Origins of Ruminative Thought: Trauma, Incompleteness, Nondisclosure, and Suppression," *Journal of Applied Social Psychology*, vol. 25, no. 14 (July 1995): 1245–1261.
27. *The Standard Edition of the Complete Works of Sigmund Freud*, J. Stachey (trans.), vol. 12 (London: Hogarth, 1914), pp. 147–156.

Forgetting and Forgiving Revisited

28. I do not address here the controversy surrounding whether there is sufficient scientific evidence to support the authenticity of claims of repressed memories. See G. A. Bonanno, "The Illusion of Repressed Memory," *Behavioral and Brain Sciences*, vol. 29 (2006): 515–516; H. Hayne, M. Garry, and E. F. Loftus, "On the Continuing Lack of Scientific Evidence for Repression," *Behavioral and Brain Sciences*, vol. 29 (2006): 521–522.

29. On the distinction, see E. Tulving and Z. Pearlstone, "Availability versus Accessibility for Information in Memory for Words," *Journal of Verbal Learning and Verbal Behavior*, vol. 5 (1966): 381–391.

30. Jefferson A. Singer and Martin A. Conway, "Should we forget forgetting?" *Memory Studies*, vol. 1, no. 3 (2008): 279–285, at 280.

31. In Paul Connerton, "Seven Types of Forgetting," *Memory Studies*, vol. 1, no. 1 (2008): 59–78.

32. As evidence, see, for example, Paul Connerton's recent book, *How Modernity Forgets* (Cambridge: Cambridge University Press, 2009).

33. *Untimely Meditations*, op. cit., p. 76.

34. James Gross, "The Emerging Field of Emotion Regulation: An Integrative Review," *Review of General Psychology*, vol. 2, no. 3 (1998): 271–299, at 275.

35. Nancy Eisenberg and Tracy L. Spinrad, "Emotion-Related Regulation: Sharpening the Definition," *Child Development*, vol. 75, no. 2 (March–April 2004): 334–339.

36. The distinction is presented in a series of papers by Gross. See "The Emerging Field of Emotion Regulation," op. cit.; "Emotion Regulation: Past, Present, Future," *Cognition and Emotion*, vol. 13, no. 5 (1999): 551–573; with Jane M. Richards, "Emotion Regulation and Memory: The Cognitive Costs of Keeping One's Cool," *Journal of Personality and Social Psychology*, vol. 79, no. 3 (2000): 410–424; "Emotion regulation: Affective, cognitive, and social consequences," *Psychophysiology*, vol. 39 (2002): 281–291; with Oliver John, "Healthy and Unhealthy Emotion Regulation: Personality Processes, Individual Differences, and Life Span Development," *Journal of Personality*, vol. 72, no. 6 (December 2004): 1301–1333.

37. P. Boleyn-Fitzgerald, "What Should 'Forgiveness' Mean?" *The Journal of Value Inquiry*, vol. 36 (2002): 483–498, at 490.

38. Mindfulness has its roots in Eastern contemplative traditions and is commonly associated with the practice of Buddhist meditation, but it can also be developed as part of a variety of psychotherapeutic approaches. Here I am only discussing mindfulness as a *technique* of emotion regulation. In Buddhism, of course, mindfulness is much more: it is an integral part of a philosophy that challenges Western conceptions of the self. In the Buddhist view, there is no self or agent, only a bundle of psychological phenomena, including beliefs, desires, and emotions. Of particular concern to many Buddhists is the emotion of anger, which they regard as bad and to be avoided even in the most extreme circumstances. It is an interesting question why anger specifically should receive such negative attention. Could part of the explanation be that anger is different from other negative emotions in somehow keeping one wedded to the belief in a persisting self, so that in order to give up the latter one must release oneself from the former? For the Buddhist view of anger, see Peter Vernezze, "Moderation or the Middle Way: Two Approaches to Anger," *Philosophy East and West*, vol. 58, no. 1 (January 2008): 2–16.

39. See Barbara Rothbaum and Ann Schwartz, "Exposure Therapy for Posttraumatic Disorder," *American Journal of Psychotherapy*, vol. 56, no. 1 (2002): 59–75.

40. Shauna Shapiro, Linda Carlson, John Astin, and Benedict Freedman, "Mechanisms of Mindfulness," *Journal of Clinical Psychology*, vol. 62, no. 3 (2006): 373–386, at 378.

41. Scott Bishop, Mark Lau, Shauna Shapiro, Linda Carlson, Nicole Anderson, James Carmody, Zindel Segal, Susan Abbey, Michael Speca, Drew Velting, and Gerald Devins, "Mindfulness: A Proposed Operational Definition," *Clinical Psychology: Science and Practice*, vol. 11, no. 3 (Autumn 2004): 230–241, at 237.

42. From R. W. Novaco, "The Functions and Regulation of the Arousal of Anger," *American Journal of Psychiatry*, vol. 133, no. 10 (October 1976): 1124–1128, at 1126.

43. Cheshire Calhoun, "Changing One's Heart," *Ethics*, vol. 103, no. 1 (October 1992): 76–96.

44. Certain models of emotion identify anger as a high-activation negative emotion and sadness as a low-activation negative emotion. This might partly explain why anger is often a more potent threat to forgiveness than sadness is, although sadness can be profound enough to

140   FORGIVENESS AND REMEMBRANCE

impede forgiveness also. Other negative emotions, like disappointment and hurt, might also be low-activation emotions. See J. A. Russell, "A circumplex model of affect," op. cit.

45. Sarah Stroud, "Epistemic Partiality in Friendship," *Ethics*, vol. 116, no. 3 (April 2006): 498–524, at 505–506.

46. Susan J. Brison, "Trauma Narratives and the Remaking of the Self," in *Acts of Memory: Cultural Recall in the Present*(Mieke Bal, Jonathan Crewe, and Leo Spitzer, eds.) (Hanover, NH: University Press of New England, 1999), pp. 39–54, at 45.

47. Charles S. Maier, *The Unmasterable Past: History, Holocaust, and German National Identity* (Cambridge, MA: Harvard University Press, 1999), p. 15.

48. For a discussion of this notion of political forgiveness, see P. E. Digeser, *Political Forgiveness* (Ithaca, NY: Cornell University Press, 2001); and Charles Griswold, *Forgiveness* (New York: Cambridge University Press, 2007), chapter 4.

49. Margaret Gilbert, "Collective Guilt and Collective Guilt Feelings," *The Journal of Ethics*, vol. 6, no. 2 (2002): 115–143, at 126.

50. This is what Burleigh Wilkins argues in his comment on Gilbert, "Joint Commitments," *The Journal of Ethics*, vol. 6, no. 2 (2002): 145–155.

PART II

FORGIVENESS AND MEMORY IN PUBLIC LIFE

4

Forgiveness, Commemoration, and Restorative Justice

The previous three chapters explored aspects of the complex moral psychology of forgiveness in interpersonal cases, including its relationship to remembering and forgetting. I presented an expanded emotive account of forgiveness that contests a number of entrenched assumptions pervading philosophical approaches to this topic: that forgiveness essentially consists in the overcoming or forswearing of resentment and other angry emotions; that to forgive one must wipe the slate clean, in the sense that one no longer blames the wrongdoer or has any hard feelings toward him or negative emotional memories of him or the wrongdoing; and that even if one may forget the wrongdoing after one has forgiven the wrongdoer, there is no place for forgetting it in the process leading to forgiveness. I argued, against these assumptions, that victims commonly experience a range of negative emotions in response to wrongdoing, including both angry and non-angry emotions, and that forgiveness may involve the overcoming of non-angry emotions, in addition to or instead of angry ones; that negative emotions often linger after the offender has been forgiven and that there are reasons of self-respect, self-restoration, and self-protection that explain and justify their continuation; that one can continue to blame the wrongdoer even after forgiving him; and that forgetting can actually facilitate a morally appropriate forgiveness. Moreover, while I agree with the standard philosophical account in emphasizing the importance of memory for forgiveness, there is another respect in which its treatment of this issue oversimplifies the phenomena. Memories are not all of one type. They can be emotional as well as emotionless, and the former have evaluative significance that the latter lack.

The moral psychology of forgiveness has a long history in philosophy. Recently, however, it has attracted considerable attention as a possible response of victims to perpetrators in the aftermath of violence and widespread or systematic human rights abuses. The literature on what is called *transitional justice* is filled with discussions of forgiveness, some advocating it as the best means

143

of achieving political reconciliation and reconstituting societies torn apart by conflict and some expressing skepticism that forgiveness can play a morally and politically constructive role in this process. There are also differences in this literature concerning how forgiveness itself is understood. Some regard it, as I have done in the previous chapters, as involving an emotional change in the wronged party and thus as emotionally constituted; others treat it as a formal political act that does not depend on the emotional or internal states of the forgiver.

Corresponding to these two approaches are two conceptions of *political forgiveness*—that is, of forgiveness *as* political. According to one, political forgiveness refers to the emotional transformations that victims undergo when they forgive, considered from a political standpoint. Thinking of it this way, we would be interested in assessing the political consequences of sentiment-based forgiveness, for example whether it promotes morally grounded political reconciliation, respect for human rights, and justice. According to the other perhaps more familiar conception of political forgiveness, it is a kind of public performance conducted by political officials who may not themselves have been wronged, typically on behalf of those who were. Thinking of it this way, we would be interested in determining the sorts of institutional forms that forgiveness can take, the various official acts through which forgiveness is granted and their moral, political, and social implications.

If political forgiveness in the second sense is independent of sentiment and does not consist in the overcoming of negative emotions directed at the wrongdoer, it must nevertheless involve some modification in the relationship between forgiver and forgiven; otherwise an act of political forgiveness is no more than an empty political gesture. Consider an analogy: if A claims to have forgiven B his debt but continues to press him for repayment, we would hardly take the claim seriously. Even on a sentiment-based account of forgiveness, at least as I conceive of it, there is more to forgiveness than just a change in how one feels about the offender. A sentiment-based account regards the overcoming or forswearing of negative emotions as essential to forgiveness, but it need not see forgiveness simply as an internal state of the victim. To be sure, a change in the way the wronged party emotionally sees or regards the offender will usually lead to a change in the way the former relates to the latter. But one can imagine a scenario in which the wronged party comes to feel differently about the offender but this change is neither communicated to him nor responsible for a change in the way the wronged party relates to him. The wronged party's so-called forgiveness is here an entirely private, intrapersonal matter. This is not forgiveness as I understand it, however.

So both uses of the term political forgiveness—politically significant sentiment-based forgiveness and forgiveness as an official act divorced from sentiment—have this in common: a relational component that consists in a

Forgiveness, Commemoration, and Restorative Justice 145

change of policy toward the wrongdoer, communicated to him, that henceforth the wronged party (or the wronged party through its representative) will not hold his past offenses against him, either at all or in the same way they were held against him before he was forgiven. The difference between these different notions of political forgiveness lies in the importance and relevance each attributes to sentiment. In one, the right sort of change of sentiment is definitional of forgiveness. In the other, change of sentiment is not necessary at all and the model is forgiving a debt, where one can forgive even if there is no moderation of one's negative feelings toward the erstwhile debtor.

My chief interest in this chapter is political forgiveness in the sense of sentiment-based forgiveness functioning in a political context with political consequences, so my account of interpersonal forgiveness in the previous chapters is obviously going to be relevant to a full understanding of it. That account can illuminate the emotional responses of victims of wrongdoing in politically charged cases; the conditions that make political forgiveness possible; and the emotional sequels of political forgiveness, thus conceived. In so doing, the account provides the basis of a psychologically informed and realistic picture of the process and outcome of politically significant sentiment-based forgiveness.

Of especial concern here is the extent to which forgiveness should be considered a practice of transitional justice or, more precisely, an element of one approach to transitional justice, what has been called reparative or restorative justice. Forgiveness has attracted considerable attention in transitional justice circles, due in no small measure to the work of the South African Truth and Reconciliation Commission. Bishop Desmond Tutu, chair of the TRC, even used the term "restorative justice" as a synonym for forgiveness in response to serious and widespread rights violations. I will want to examine this usage and to inquire whether forgiveness deserves the prominence it has been given.

Transitional justice can be characterized roughly as the conception of justice associated with periods of substantial political change in the wake of large-scale human rights abuses and widespread injustice. It has several dimensions, including retributive punishment and compensation. Another approach is restorative, and it is here that forgiveness is sometimes located in explicit contrast with retributive measures to redress past wrongdoing. Restorative and retributive approaches have certain aims in common, at least when these are described in very general terms.[1] Both seek to restore and reaffirm the dignity of the victims of wrongdoing and to hold perpetrators accountable for their wrongdoing. However, the two approaches have different understandings of how these aims are achieved and, fundamentally, what it means to affirm the dignity of victims and hold offenders accountable. Perhaps the most striking difference between the two approaches is the commitment of restorative justice to political *reconciliation*, which in one of its senses refers to the establishment or reestablishment of relations of respect and trust between former adversaries. In contrast to retributive justice, creating institutional and social conditions that support such relations and respect for human rights is a central feature of restorative justice. The focus of retributive approaches is different, since they aim to condemn wrongdoing by imposing hard treatment on wrongdoers, and even if the guilty are punished, this may do little in a larger sense to repair the relations of respect and trust that were damaged by serious and persistent wrongdoing.

Forgiveness, if it is classified as a practice of restorative justice, would have to be grounded in and justified by the same set of commitments that characterize restorative justice more broadly. But once we view it this way, we see how problematic it is to regard forgiveness as a practice of this sort. For forgiveness may not help to restore the dignity of victims, hold offenders accountable, or address the conditions that made injustice and oppression possible. In fact, forgiveness may actually render victims more vulnerable to wrongful harm, if it is granted for the wrong reasons or if it is coerced. There are two reasons for this. First, there is a kind of vulnerability that results from attitudinal change. Negative emotions directed at the offender can help protect important interests of the victim, and letting go of those emotions could have serious consequences for the victim by removing a safeguard against wrongdoing. Second, since there is a relational component to forgiveness that involves the forgiver adopting and communicating to the offender a policy of not holding his past offenses against him, forgiveness can render the forgiver perilously defenseless against further assaults to her dignity. In interpersonal contexts, the wronged party may forgive her wrongdoer even if the wrongdoer has not repented, and she may be prepared and able to protect herself should the offender offend again. But against the background of social institutions that have either failed to protect some members of society or have been used to harm them, making oneself vulnerable to further harm by forgiving offenders (if that's what forgiving offenders does) can almost be suicidal.

There is a restorative justice practice that seems relatively benign by comparison with this, however, and I want to say something briefly about it in this chapter as a kind of introduction to a much lengthier treatment of the subject in later chapters. This is the practice of memorialization whose aim is to promote and sustain remembrance of wrongdoing, wrongdoers, and their victims. Memorialization as a process or mechanism that can help a society come to terms with a legacy of large-scale past abuses is a largely unexplored topic; it certainly has not received nearly the degree of attention that forgiveness has received. Questions about whether and how remembrance can further the task of rebuilding society after large-scale wrongdoing; about how, if most or the most important offenders have been forgiven by their victims, it is possible for public remembrance of wrongdoing not to be politically regressive; and about how public practices of remembrance can be sustained over time have not been asked, let

Forgiveness, Commemoration, and Restorative Justice   147

alone addressed. Of course, insofar as forgiveness has been regarded as a response to wrongdoing that can have value in transitional settings, memory has also, if only implicitly, been folded into discussions of the challenges transitional societies face. However, the moral significance of remembrance in transitional settings is not completely explained by its conceptual connection to forgiveness. Even if wrongdoers are not forgiven, or even if it is unlikely that they ever will be forgiven, political reconciliation of a sort may still be within reach, and remembrance may be important for this. Apart from forgiveness, memorialization can be an approach to transitional justice that transitional states adopt to confront past regime offenses. In doing this, it helps to secure justice in the peculiar and valuable way that remembering those offenses does, by symbolically reaffirming the dignity of the victims and at least making certain that past events cannot be denied and do not fade from public consciousness.

Remembrance that is part of a political transition can take different institutional forms and can be part of a retributive or non-retributive process of transitional justice. Judicial proceedings against members of the previous regime responsible for rights violations represent one approach to transitional justice that governments may adopt. Remembrance of wrongdoing is clearly involved here, partly because the success of these criminal prosecutions depends on the testimony of victims, who must rely on their memories, and partly because the deliberations and findings of trials can inform the collective memory of society. A contrasting approach is the establishment of truth commissions to investigate the truth about past abuses and to acknowledge the suffering of the victims.[2] Truth commissions are forums for remembering, and they also provide a historical record for posterity that serves as a kind of memorial to the victims of those abuses. Other practices of memorialization include erecting monuments to the victims of human rights abuses; creating memorial museums and archives to document their suffering and thereby render it undeniable; and naming public spaces after them. These various types of memorialization activities not only represent different ways of remembering the victims of past wrongdoing but are also facilitators of communal self-reflection that influences a community's sense of its collective past. Of particular interest to me are *commemorative rituals*, and I will take them up in the next chapter.

This chapter is organized in the following way. Section 2 distinguishes between different ways of thinking about forgiveness, as the overcoming or forswearing of negative emotions or, alternatively, as an act of releasing the wrongdoer from further obligations to the wronged party that reflects the latter's commitment not to hold his wrongdoing against him. On a sentiment-based conception, the former is essential, although this doesn't preclude the relational element of releasing the wrongdoer from further obligations. I also critically examine the adoption by transitional regimes of policies that discount the importance of sentiment-based forgiveness or subordinate it to policies of national reconstruction. In section 3 I discuss the aims, values, and techniques of restorative justice and the various meanings of political reconciliation, and section 4 examines forgiveness from the standpoint of restorative justice. Here I argue that forgiveness can only be considered an ingredient of restorative justice under certain conditions and that even morally warranted forgiveness may fail to promote a more just society. It may fail in part because forgiving perpetrators for their offenses may do little to prevent wrongs that are structural or systemic in nature, as is commonly the case in transitional societies.

At the same time, I contend that it would be a mistake to suppose that forgiveness is necessarily incompatible with the aims of restorative justice or with political reconciliation. As I discussed in chapter 1, the emotions occasioned by wrongdoing might be constitutive of a kind of moral protest, and protest directed at wrongdoers helps repair the harm caused by their wrongdoing. If victims have opportunities for forgiveness that also give them opportunities for protest, forgiveness can promote social goods in transitional societies without compromising the moral integrity of the forgivers. What's more, forgiveness can do this without putting them or others in a position where they are vulnerable to future rights violations.

Finally, in section 5 I make a few remarks about memorialization. The efforts of transitional societies to repair damaged political relationships and to establish relations of trust and respect certainly involve more than creating memorials to the victims of wrongdoing as a kind of collective acknowledgment that they were harmed unjustifiably. But as I will suggest here and in the next chapter, remembrance can be restorative and rituals of commemoration have a special relationship to it. Such rituals have features that may actually help to strengthen and sustain the memory of wrongdoing over the long term. What's more, as I assert in section 6, it is a consequence of my account of interpersonal forgiveness that they may be able to do this without undermining whatever good forgiveness of wrongdoers has achieved.

2. Two conceptions of political forgiveness

Forgiveness, according to Charles Griswold's wonderfully succinct characterization, "attempts to free the future from being determined by the injuries and resentments of the past."[3] Forgiveness cannot undo the past—that is, cannot make the wrongs of the past disappear. But it can alter how the victim affectively regards her wrongdoer, how she understands her life in relation to that part of the past, and the impact that these wrongs and memories of them have on other elements of her psychology and behavior. These are some of the changes that constitute and accompany forgiveness. Here I want to broaden the inquiry. As I will explain, the notion of freeing the future from the injuries of the past has two dimensions, an internal and an external: one involves a process of emotional change, as described earlier; the other, a purposive act something like releasing others from debt. Each is taken up, moreover, by a different conception of political forgiveness.

The dominant conception of interpersonal forgiveness in the philosophical literature is essentially *sentiment-based*. It construes forgiveness as the forswearing, overcoming, giving up, or letting go, for the right reasons, of angry or retributive emotions that are naturally directed toward offenders in virtue of their culpable wrongdoing. For the wronged party to forgive, she must loosen the grip of these powerful hostile emotions and see or regard the wrongdoer through the lens of a transformation in her feelings toward him. The account I developed in chapter 1 shares with the standard account the belief that the continuation of unforsworn or unmoderated angry feelings is incompatible with forgiveness but extends the account to include a range of negative emotions that embody or convey censure. (The standard account of forgiveness, of course, also attaches significance to emotional changes in the offender: he should feel remorse for what he has done and shame, possibly even self-contempt or self-loathing. Here, however, I want to continue looking at forgiveness from the standpoint of the victim.) Political forgiveness, in one sense of the term, is not radically divorced from forgiveness thus understood. Rather, it consists of a set of processes like this, only with the additional features that they are carried out in a political context and have political meaning and repercussions.

Much of the literature on restorative justice views forgiveness this way as well. But in the larger literature on transitional justice, of which restorative justice is only a part, one also finds a very different conception according to which the moral significance and primary effect of forgiveness are independent of sentiment. This is a purely relational view of forgiveness, according to which sentiment is irrelevant.[4] Even sentimental views, of course, can include a relational *element*. That is, they can allow that there is an aspect of forgiving another that does not involve emotional change on the part of the one who was wronged (or the wrongdoer, for that matter). They just have to add that this cannot be the entire story. Purely relational views are generally reserved for political contexts; less commonly and less plausibly, they may also apply to interpersonal cases, in which case any overcoming of negative emotions that might also take place there is not what forgiveness is about.

Let me say more about the relational view. According to it, A forgives B when and just because A releases B from his obligation to make (any further) amends for his wrongdoing and communicates this to B. Forgiveness is a kind of relinquishment by A of a certain claim to moral authority over B. In releasing B from further obligations, A commits herself to refrain from using the offender's wrong-doing as justification for continuing to make demands of him related to it, such as that he should repent his actions and take steps to repair the damage caused by them. In releasing B from obligations of redress and communicating this fact to B, A effectively announces to B that he no longer needs to think of himself as exposed to and vulnerable to A's harsh judgment and treatment of him.

Avishai Margalit uses the notion of an exclusionary reason to characterize the relational aspect of forgiveness. Forgiveness, he says, is "a policy of adopting an exclusionary reason with regard to someone who has wronged us."[5] An exclusionary reason—here Margalit follows Joseph Raz—does not count in favor of or against an action in the way first-order reasons do; it is rather a second-order reason against acting on certain first-order reasons.[6] In the case of forgiveness, the first-order reasons in question are those that justify acting toward a wrong-doer in ways that negative feelings would make appropriate. Margalit's policy conception of forgiveness does not require that the victim actually have negative feelings toward the wrongdoer that she chooses not to act on. Rather, the victim adopts an exclusionary reason not to use his wrongdoing as a reason for acting toward him as it would be natural and appropriate to act *if* she had certain negative feelings toward him.

Further, if this is truly a relational view, the policy must be conveyed to the wrongdoer, so that he is given reason to believe that the one who forgives him will no longer hold it against him as she did before in the way she relates to him. (Blame may persist, however, as I argued in chapter 1.) Forgiveness, on a relational view, requires the publication of, and the offender's recognition of, the victim's intention not to use his wrongdoing in this way. In this respect, forgiving someone resembles saying "I do" as part of a wedding ceremony: success in marrying requires publicizing one's intention to be married and the other's recognition of this intention.[7] There is an additional similarity: just as more than publication and recognition of the speaker's intention to get married is required for the utterance to count as actually sealing the marriage, so more is required for forgiveness. If, for example, A claims to forgive an offender B in the name of victim C, but A has no standing to represent or speak for C in this matter, then A cannot forgive B, even if A makes known to B his intention to forgive and B recognizes his intention. I will say more about this below.

Thus, viewing forgiveness relationally, to say "I forgive you for having wronged me," or "I forgive you on behalf of those you wronged" is not to imply that I have a change of heart (which may or may not happen) and no longer harbor hostile or negative feelings toward you. It is also not to imply that I ever had such feelings. The overcoming of anger or other negative emotions that I may have had may come about incidentally as a result of the adoption of the exclusionary policy, but this is not what forgiveness means relationally. What matters is how the wronged person—or the person representing or speaking for the wronged person—acts toward the wrongdoer going forward and the reasons she has for acting this way. Hard as it may be to stay angry at someone toward whom one has adopted a forgiving policy, the moral psychology of forgiveness is only of peripheral or derivative interest from a relational standpoint.

These points concern the logic of forgiveness, not the conditions under which it is appropriate to release B from his obligations or to adopt an exclusionary policy. It is certainly possible for A to exercise her prerogative to release B inappropriately, if, say, B has not done enough by way of redress to properly warrant forgiveness, or if there are no grounds for hope that he will not need forgiveness again in the future. A can also abuse her prerogative to release B by making unreasonable demands of B before she communicates to him her readiness to release him. Similar points can be made about forgiveness when it is conceived as the overcoming of negative emotions directed at B.

The most plausible account of interpersonal forgiveness, I would argue, is sentiment-based but partly relational. Typically when we think of forgiveness, we think of the individual's emotions being centrally involved and of an emotional change in her that consists in overcoming or forswearing them. Official, ceremonial, or ritualistic expressions of forgiveness, offered in a political context and for political purposes, require a different analysis. They are explainable in terms that resemble those of forgiving a debt, where what forgiveness is *about* is not the overcoming of negative emotions by the forgiver. After all, one can forgive a debt even if one continues to harbor negative feelings toward the debtor. This is not to say, however, that interpersonal forgiveness has no relational component. A complete account of interpersonal forgiveness, in my view, has both sentimental and relational elements: interpersonal forgiveness is not *only* relational, since it essentially involves a change in emotion, but it is not only sentimental either. Thus, there are uses of the expression "I forgive you," even in interpersonal contexts that mean something like "I won't hold it against you going forward" and not "I'm not angry with you anymore." However, without some emotional transformation in the forgiver that accompanies and motivates this relational change, this cannot be considered a central case of interpersonal forgiveness.

These different aspects of interpersonal forgiveness are associated with different conceptions of sincerity on the part of the one doing the forgiving. With regard to the relational aspect of forgiveness, sincerity means correspondence between word and deed, between professed commitment not to count past wrongdoing against the wrongdoer and its actual implementation in practice. By contrast, sincere forgiveness with regard to the sentimental aspects of forgiveness consists in the correspondence between word and emotion, between an announced change of heart and a new way of feeling toward and affectively regarding the wrongdoer. Sincerity in the first sense pertains to political forgiveness understood as solely relational or as having a relational component.

I do not want to leave the impression that the sentimental and relational aspects of interpersonal forgiveness as I conceive of it are easily disentangled from each other. They are not: changes in sentiment can lead to the adoption of a policy to exclude certain reasons as reasons to treat the offender in certain ways; and conversely, once the victim has adopted the policy, this can lead to further downstream changes in the victim's emotional responses to her offender. It can also happen that certain negative emotions, including but not limited to angry retributive ones, prevent the victim from actually adopting or following through on a policy of forgiveness toward the offender. It can be difficult to refrain from acting on reasons for holding the wrongdoer's past conduct against him if one can't moderate one's anger toward him, or is overwhelmed by grief at what he has done, or is profoundly hurt by his treatment of oneself. Thus, overcoming or at least moderating these emotions might be necessary to facilitate the adoption and carrying out of desirable policies of not taking into consideration the offender's wrongdoing as a reason for acting toward him in certain ways.

It is important to note that insofar as we think of forgiveness in relational terms only, as a policy rather than a change in the mental state of the wronged party, this is the only reason that negative emotions can be morally significant. Sentiment-based views, however, are not wedded to thinking about negative emotions in instrumental terms and are free to explore other explanations of their moral import. I did this, for example, in chapter 1 when I explored the relationship between various negative emotional responses to wrongdoing and the self-respect of victims. And I did it again in chapter 2 when I discussed the evaluative significance of negative emotional responses to wrongdoing and the emotional memories constituted by them.

Political forgiveness as an official act, likely by persons not themselves harmed, releasing perpetrators from reparative obligations, is entirely relational, but this is not the only way to understand the phenomenon. Political forgiveness, as I have said, can also refer to acts of sentiment-based interpersonal forgiveness that, collectively or in the aggregate, have political significance. Sentiment plays no essential part in political forgiveness conceived in the first way; conceived in the second way, it does. In circumstances of profound political upheaval, a transitional regime might engage in political forgiveness in the first sense in order to promote political reconciliation; it might not concern itself with interpersonal forgiveness, and thus not grant it political significance. It might still have political significance, however, precisely because insufficient attention has been paid to it by those with political power. In another possible scenario, perpetrators are forgiven by official acts of the regime, but it also takes its reconciliatory task to include encouraging or trying to convince victims to overcome or forswear the negative feelings that they have toward them. Either way, the conduct of the regime raises serious concerns, of both a moral and a political nature.

An illustration of a policy on the political level that involves efforts to convince victims to forgive by renouncing negative emotions is the one adopted by the South African Truth and Reconciliation Commission. These efforts, critics have noted, went beyond providing victims with opportunities to forgive to applying pressure on victims to forgive.[8] Here is how Richard Wilson describes the hearings before the Human Rights Violations Committee of the TRC:

> The hearings were structured in such a way that any expression of a desire for revenge by victims would seem out of place. Virtues of forgiveness and reconciliation were so loudly and roundly applauded that emotions of vengeance, hatred and bitterness were rendered unacceptable, an ugly intrusion on a peaceful, healing process.[9]

Forgiveness was explicitly linked to a process of political reconstruction and national reconciliation, and while some of the members of the TRC accepted that victims would continue to harbor feelings of vengeance and hatred despite efforts to convince them that these feelings should be renounced, this was not taken to discredit the non-retributive political approach of the TRC. This is because "reconciliation operated at a more abstract, transcendental and national level"[10] than the concrete, on-the-ground, personal responses of victims to their perpetrators. Political reconciliation was chiefly understood to be a matter of furthering a national political agenda, and the victims themselves and their emotional readiness to forgive, while certainly not irrelevant, were secondary concerns, in practice if not in theory. For Tutu, in fact, forgiveness was "not conditional upon the wrongdoer expressing remorse or asking for forgiveness, but a duty incumbent upon all victims."[11]

In general, there are a number of problems with thinking of political reconstruction in the aftermath of serious and systematic wrongdoing in this way—that is, as first and foremost the pursuit of nation building and an agenda of national healing, with interpersonal forgiveness and personal reconciliation between individual victims and perpetrators treated as secondary. I will briefly mention a few of these now and others concerning forgiveness under these conditions in section 4. The problems largely stem from the fact that overcoming negative emotions directed toward perpetrators does not necessarily keep pace with the pursuit of a political agenda aimed at rebuilding social institutions and promoting national unity. Brandon Hamber puts the point this way: "political processes are fundamentally different from the personal healing process: a country and its politicians may be ready to move on before victims have come to terms with the magnitude of their personal pain . . . a gap between the individual (micro) and collective (macro) process of dealing with the past is generally present."[12]

One problem with this is that the relative neglect of victims' feelings and personal reconciliation might damage the prospects for success of national reconciliation. If the readiness of victims to forgive (in an emotive sense) is seriously out of step with the larger reconciliatory agenda of the nation, especially if this discrepancy is widespread, the success of the agenda could be in put in jeopardy. Victims may feel that the legitimacy of their anger and grief is not being acknowledged by the country and its political leaders. Commenting on what he calls forgiveness "boosterism," Thomas Brudholm notes how this can backfire: "instead of facilitating the overcoming of resentment, the advocacy of forgiveness can create new and justified resentments among victims as well as observers."[13] These new resentments cannot be entirely isolated from the nation's pursuit of political reconciliation and may prove difficult to contain, possibly leading victims to resist or subvert official policies. In the context of large-scale political violence and serious rights violations, it is politically shortsighted to relegate forgiveness as a sentiment-based phenomenon to the sphere of "merely" interpersonal interaction. Doing so is likely to have negative political repercussions, in that it threatens to derail the process of political and social reconstruction.

Another problem is whether this approach to reconciliation secures justice for the victims. According to a restorative conception of transitional justice, about which I will say more in a moment, the needs of the victims, including moral and emotional needs, have primary importance. However, a conception of political reconciliation that invalidates displays of negative emotion by victims, or effectively ignores or marginalizes the emotional readiness of victims to forgive or their feelings of mistrust and insecurity, can hardly be said to make the satisfaction of their moral and emotional needs a centerpiece of its reconciliatory program. From the standpoint of a restorative conception of transitional justice, political reconciliation with these features does not further but fails to take seriously justice for victims.

An additional critical question relating to political forgiveness as the adoption by public officials of a policy of remitting reparative obligations is whether they have the *standing* or authority to forgive.[14] Here it is important to distinguish between an act of political forgiveness that releases perpetrators from obligations to the political association and an act that releases them from obligations to the victims. The question of standing, as I am raising it now, concerns the standing of public officials to release perpetrators from obligations of the latter sort. It might seem that *only* the victims themselves have the standing or authority to do this. This, however, is an extreme view. P. E. Digeser argues that others may have the standing to forgive vicariously, if and only if the victims have transferred their right to forgive to them. Such transferences can be explicit or tacit, but explicit transferences are probably rare, he argues, and what counts as sufficient for purposes of tacit transference is controversial. A case in point is the TRC. Tutu claimed that the TRC had the credentials to speak on behalf of the victims, and arguably he meant, among other things, that it had the credentials to forgive for them.[15] Yet the evidence he provided that the victims had in fact transferred their rights to forgive is unconvincing.[16]

Nothing I have said in this section is intended to deny the legitimacy of collective processes of dealing with past wrongdoing that are not fully responsive to the emotional and moral needs of victims, simply because they have not been fully responsive. The advancement of political reconciliation obviously cannot wait for all or even almost all of the victims of wrongdoing to be ready to forgive those who wronged them, nor should it. That said, important questions, political as well as moral, remain about how far victims' emotional responses should be given scope for expression in light of other transitional goals, and to neglect victim sentiment is to oversimplify complex decisions about the role of forgiveness in promoting political reconciliation. From the standpoint of justice, societies in transition should respect the victims' rights not to let go of whatever negative emotions might be impeding their ability to forgive. They should do this because respecting this right is a necessary condition of respecting *them* as victims. (Respecting them as victims also involves respecting survivors who speak on their behalf when they cannot speak for themselves, as I argue in chapter 6, section 4.)

3. Transitional justice, restorative justice, and reconciliation

The 2004 Report of the U.N. Secretary General entitled "The rule of law and transitional justice in conflict and post-conflict societies" defines transitional justice as comprising "the full range of processes and mechanisms associated with a society's attempt to come to terms with a legacy of large-scale past abuses, in order to ensure accountability, serve justice, and achieve reconciliation."[17] Among the processes and mechanisms mentioned in the report are criminal prosecutions of perpetrators responsible for past wrongdoing; truth commissions; and reparations for victims, material as well as symbolic. Each of these measures potentially makes a contribution to the three goals of ensuring accountability, serving justice, and achieving reconciliation, and each does so in a distinctive way. Other transitional justice measures have a longer timeframe, notably strengthening the rule of law and reforming legal institutions, including the judiciary and the legislature, to prevent recurrence of serious violations and impunity. These provide the infrastructure for reconciliation, without which the other measures are likely to have only limited impact.

These are examples of processes and mechanisms, but what kind of justice is transitional justice? We might begin by locating it in that part of a theory of justice that Rawls calls "non-ideal theory." Ideal theory, according to Rawls, pertains to the design and operation of the basic structure of society. It "assumes strict compliance and works out the principles that characterize a well-ordered society under favorable conditions." Non-ideal theory "is worked out after an ideal conception of justice has been chosen ... This division of the theory has ... two rather different subparts. One consists of the principles for governing adjustments to natural limitations and historical contingencies; and the other of principles for meeting injustice."[18]

Non-ideal theory is concerned with how to achieve or work toward a fully just society, and Rawls imposes three conditions on the policies adopted for this purpose: they must be morally permissible, politically possible, and likely to be effective as parts of a strategy for the realization of such a society. With these as conditions, there is a sense in which justice in nonideal theory *is* transitional justice. This is how A. John Simmons understands Rawls:

> a good policy in nonideal theory is good only as transitionally just—
> that is, only as a morally permissible part of a feasible overall program
> to achieve perfect justice, as a policy that puts us in an improved posi-
> tion to reach that ultimate goal.[19]

Discussions in the transitional justice literature, however, typically have a narrower focus, as in the Secretary General's report, and use the term to refer to measures a state takes to address past human rights abuses in the transition to a (more) democratic regime and a period of peace, stability, and the rule of law.

There need be no conflict between transitional justice as commonly understood and the transitional aspect of Rawlsian non-ideal theory. The policies adopted by transitional regimes are transitionally just if they deal with past abuses justly and facilitate a process of political reconciliation grounded in relations of trust and respect between individuals. These policies might involve efforts to secure redress for specific acts of wrongdoing, for example, by prosecuting those responsible for them or providing compensation to victims. But in addition, transitional justice policies can have a more far-reaching effect. Past abuses are usually systemic in nature because basic legal, social, and political institutions have been corrupted to make them possible. If transitional policies are directed at eliminating these abuses, they put the society in a better position to reach the goal of achieving ideal justice. That is, the policies can be transitionally just in Rawls' sense.

The "principles for meeting injustice" during extraordinary periods of political transition are of three sorts—principles of retributive justice, compensatory

Forgiveness, Commemoration, and Restorative Justice

justice, and restorative justice—and the policies implementing them are distinguished from one another by their characteristic aims and procedures and the values they embody. The focus here is transitional justice in its restorative dimension and what sets it apart from the others, particularly the retributive. Ultimately I will want to consider whether forgiveness (that is, forgiveness as a political phenomenon) should be classified as a practice of restorative justice.

Much of the literature on the topic of restorative justice places it in the context of contemporary crime policy and criminal justice and advocates it as a constructive alternative to the dominant punitive/retributive ways of viewing and responding to crime. Restorative justice is championed by its proponents because of its distinctive goals and methods, such as restorative conferencing and face-to-face victim–offender meetings, and because of the values that guide it, values that differ from those that underpin conventional criminal justice.[20] But interest in restorative justice has not been limited to the arena of criminal justice for ordinary crimes: its goals, methods, and values have also attracted considerable international attention as constituting a promising approach to conflict resolution in transitional societies. Societies that are attempting to rebuild political relationships in the aftermath of widespread and systematic wrongdoing and human rights abuses have adopted processes and mechanisms grounded in restorative justice principles, including truth commissions, public apologies, and commemorations. These initiatives have supplemented, not supplanted, criminal prosecutions of perpetrators and their supporters.

Advocates of a restorative justice approach to wrongdoing, in both the criminal justice and transitional justice contexts, favor it in part because it is victim-centered. As they describe it, it focuses on repairing the harm caused by wrongdoing and on meeting the victim's various needs—material, moral, and emotional—that result from it, rather than on the offender and what should be done to or with him. This shift in orientation from offender to victim is reflected in a number of practical recommendations. Victims should be able to be actively involved in the process of securing justice for themselves (assuming that their involvement is not more harmful than beneficial to them); they should have available to them a forum in which they can directly confront the offender, vent their feelings of bitterness and hurt, and demand clarification from him; and they should play a part in helping to determine the form in which the offender will make reparation. This participation is said to empower victims and through this to help restore their dignity and standing in the political community. The process of criminal prosecution fails to empower victims and make them the focus of efforts to secure justice, critics claim, because it typically marginalizes victims and effectively renders them voiceless, passive observers of criminal proceedings that are conducted with limited input from them.

Further, unlike punitive and material compensation approaches to wrongdoing, restorative justice advocates insist that the offender actively take responsibility for, and be genuinely accountable for, what he has done—or rather be accountable for his misdeeds in a different way. Taking punishment or paying compensation is one way of being accountable, but advocates insist on much more: for them, true accountability involves facing the victim and understanding concretely how one's wrongdoing has affected her; explaining (in other words, giving an account of) oneself and one's conduct to the victim; helping decide how one will repair the harm one has caused; and undertaking appropriate reparative acts. These ways of being accountable for one's crimes also empower offenders.

Related to this, unlike punitive approaches, a restorative justice approach eschews stigmatization and ostracism of offenders and aims to facilitate their reintegration into the community on a basis of mutual respect and trust. Finally, in addition to involving the direct victim and offender in the handling of their own conflict, restorative justice involves a wider range of people in the justice process as interested parties. These include family members of the victim and the offender, neighbors, and members of the community. The involvement of this larger circle of people as key stakeholders in the doing of justice reflects the belief that serious wrongdoing harms families and communities as well as the direct victims and that therefore it is not only victims confronting offenders that repairs wrongdoing. This is an additional difference between restorative justice, on the one hand, and punitive and compensatory approaches, on the other.[21]

An example of a political practice with restorative potential, with complex relations to political forgiveness, is the issuing of public apologies by or on behalf of perpetrators. Public apologies can be issued on behalf of perpetrators by public officials or political bodies acting as proxies for individuals or a collectivity.[22] Here the apology represents or symbolizes individuals' or the collectivity's undertaking to make amends for wrongdoing, and it is typically not accompanied by the usual feelings of regret or remorse that characterize apologies in the interpersonal domain. Given that these feelings are absent, it might be objected that public apologies of this sort are not really apologies at all, properly speaking. But Janna Thompson gives the following convincing rejoinder:

> If we take personal apology as a paradigm case of apology . . . and insist
> that a true apology must have the features of such apologies, then any
> apology that fails to have them becomes a doubtful case . . . But like a
> personal apology, taking responsibility for a wrong and making a commitment to avoid similar wrongs in the future are central to it [political
> apology]. If we take these features to be central to apology, then a political apology becomes as good an example as a personal one.[23]

Forgiveness, Commemoration, and Restorative Justice 159

Apologies are not just expressions of remorse or shame: they centrally involve a commitment to make amends for wrongful injury by providing means of redress appropriate to the offense, and a commitment that isn't demonstrated in action isn't a commitment at all.

Apologies can be "public" in a different sense. It might refer to apologies issued by perpetrators in their own name and on their own behalf in a public forum, addressed to the victims and the communities to which they and the perpetrators belong. These public apologies can express the collective sentiments of a group or the sentiments of individuals. In the latter case, the more numerous the perpetrators who issue public apologies of this sort, or the more important the perpetrators who issue them, the greater the political impact the apologies are likely to have. But even when the apologizers are numerous, each apology still consists of a bilateral relation between perpetrator and victim, between the one who owes an apology and the person to whom it is owed. Moreover, because these apologies are issued *in* public, not *by* a public official, they are not dissociated from sentiments like remorse, regret, shame, guilt, and sorrow the way the latter are. These emotions, expressed publicly to the victim and in the presence of the relevant communities, have the same functions as those expressed in personal, nonpolitical apologies between individuals: they show that the offender does not take his action lightly and that he cares enough about it to suffer for what he has done.

Because public apologies of this sort are interpersonal apologies with political consequences, they share other features with the latter. Wrongdoing targeted at specific individuals is a communicative act that conveys to them that they matter less as persons than the offenders, that they need not be treated with the respect to which a moral equal is entitled, and that they have no basis for complaint because of this. Apology (if sincere) conveys a counter-message: it recognizes the victims as having equal dignity and moral worth to whom the offenders must account for their actions. They reach out to the victims for understanding, sometimes for forgiveness,[24] but always with the intention of making known to the victims that they, the offenders, recognize their moral failure, are appropriately distressed about it, and are trying to atone for it. In the end, of course, victims might not accept an apology even from genuinely repentant offenders, might not release them from the burdens of self-reproach and reparative obligations by forgiving them, and might not reconcile with them. The choice to refuse the apology by remaining unforgiving is up to the victim, although the moral appropriateness of the refusal is not simply up to her.

Public apologies are characterized as practices of restorative justice chiefly because of their potential to restore and affirm the dignity of victims. This comes about as a consequence of the offender taking responsibility for his wrongdoing and holding himself accountable to the victim for it. By holding himself accountable to the victim, the offender treats the victim as someone to whom an accounting is owed—that is, as a moral agent to whom reasons may and must be given and who is worthy of being addressed by the offender accordingly. In apologizing, the offender also commits himself to accept the authority of the moral standards that were violated by his actions. He thereby expresses allegiance to the values at stake, attempts to establish his credentials as trustworthy, and vindicates the victim's sense of grievance and abuse. Reaching out to the victim in this way, the apology has potential to repair the damage done by his wrongdoing, and while the "repair" that is undertaken may be symbolic, it is no less morally significant than material reparations. Indeed, the reparative potential of material reparations itself depends on the symbolic message or messages that they convey. Another factor in the success of reparative efforts is the emotional component of the apology. This bears on its sincerity, and sincerity is important because apologies that are suspected of being insincere are not just ineffective, but insulting. Public apologizing is noteworthy in countering the suspicion of insincerity since it is often especially painful and humbling for the offender to admit his culpability in a public forum, and this can provide evidence of a particularly heartfelt desire on the offender's part to acknowledge responsibility for his actions and make amends.

Public apologies can also help bring about another end, political reconciliation, and while the point of apologizing is to repudiate past wrongdoing and acknowledge the legitimacy of the victim's grievances, political reconciliation can be one of the valuable outcomes of public apologies. Political reconciliation refers to the rebuilding of relationships in their political—as opposed to personal—dimensions in the aftermath of authoritarian rule, widespread violence, and abuse of civil and human rights. The relationships at issue are those between members of the same political community or state considered as such, between perpetrators, supporters, and passive bystanders, on the one hand, and victims, their families, and communities, on the other. In order to understand how public apologies, as well as other restorative justice practices, can promote political reconciliation, we need to take a closer look at what "reconciliation" means in this context and at the different ways in which political relationships can be rebuilt.

Lawrence Crocker usefully distinguishes between three conceptions: community solidarity, non-lethal coexistence, and democratic reciprocity.[25] The first of these is the most robust conception, and the one least likely to be achieved in the aftermath of serious wrongdoing. It refers to a political condition consisting of comprehensive social harmony; procedures for eliminating or minimizing dissent about matters of social or political importance; and attitudes of acceptance and care for others not very different from those that friends have toward one another. At the opposite extreme is non-lethal coexistence. It consists in adherence to injunctions against killing, torturing, or forced relocation of peoples and the renunciation of violence to settle social disagreements and conflicts. Reconciliation of this sort establishes a kind of wary trust among former adversaries, sufficient for peaceful coexistence but not for peaceful cooperation. Moreover, although limited in its ambitions, reconciliation conceptualized in this way is nonetheless a significant accomplishment in societies torn apart by civil conflict. Political reconciliation, according to the third conception, involves the establishment of relations of respect and sustained trust among perpetrators, victims, and bystanders, and democratization. This conception is less utopian than the first but more demanding than the second, and some version of it is most attractive for just these reasons.

There are a number of features of reconciliation as non-lethal coexistence that reveal its limitations as a normative account of political reconciliation and that point to a more adequate account. First, insofar as peaceful coexistence is the overriding goal, it does not focus on redressing past wrongs, and so avoids issues of perpetrator accountability and responsibility taking. Second, it does not attach special significance to the victims' needs for recognition of their undeserved suffering. Third, it does not necessarily acknowledge the critical importance of reforming the institutional political and legal order. And fourth, it is unstable, because the perpetrators may accept the going scheme only prudentially and provisionally, as the best they can do for now. The first and second features point to what is lacking in this conception of political reconciliation from the standpoint of transitional justice, for transitional justice demands that perpetrators be held accountable and that the entitlements of those harmed by wrongdoing and violence be addressed. Reconciliation that fails to address perpetrator accountability or the victims' feelings of disparagement and marginalization may be all that can realistically be hoped for under certain social conditions. But without a commitment to seeing that justice is done for the victims, the account of political reconciliation at issue can hardly be a normatively satisfactory one.

The third and fourth features explain why non-lethal coexistence cannot be relied on to produce civic trust and a lasting and stable political reconciliation. Reform of institutions that support and facilitate injustice and repression make their resumption less likely, thus enhancing trust in public officials and among fellow citizens. Further, well-grounded trust in a political arrangement requires assurance against fluctuations due to shifts in the alignment of power or changes in strategic considerations. In placing one's trust in another, one has expectations of the other that he will act as he should act and entrusts some aspect of one's well-being to his care. But if the basis for expecting this is just that conformity with a political arrangement accords with the other's consideration of current advantage, as is generally the case in a state of non-lethal coexistence, trust can leave one vulnerable if one is not vigilant. It can leave one vulnerable because changes in social and political conditions may render peace a less attractive alternative for some than the resumption of conflict. A stable reconciliation is only possible if parties to the reconciliatory arrangement are not tempted to defect from it and it is common knowledge that they will support it even when they are in a position to exact new terms more favorable to themselves. Reconciliation of this sort presupposes widespread belief in the value or goodness of the arrangement as something worthy of supporting, for then former adversaries will honor, and can be relied on to honor, its basic terms even when opportunities for extracting greater rewards for themselves present themselves. However, reconciliation conceptualized as non-lethal coexistence does not depend on, nor does it see particular value in, this sort of allegiance to the reconciliatory arrangement—that is, an allegiance that is not merely based on strategic or self-interested reasons. The tenuousness of civic trust grounded in the latter sort of allegiance can also be regarded as a failure of transitional justice.

What is also lacking in this conception of political reconciliation is respect for persons as moral equals, which, as I am understanding it, consists in the acknowledgment by each of the other's authority to hold oneself accountable to him for what one has done and to demand an accounting of it to him.[26] Political reconciliation in the third sense, by contrast, is defined as the establishment or reestablishment of relations of respect (thus understood) between former antagonists.[27] This respect is mutual for two reasons. First, it is between moral equals, and moral equals reciprocally acknowledge each other's authority to demand compliance with moral norms that affect them. Second, in societies characterized by conflict or repressive rule, wrongs and crimes may have been committed by victims as well as perpetrators. Though one side may be more blameworthy than the other, so that there is no moral equivalence between their actions, political reconciliation is only possible if each side takes responsibility for the wrongs it committed and accepts the authority of the other to demand an accounting of them.

In addition to mutual respect, Crocker includes democratic deliberation as one of the constitutive features of his third conception of political reconciliation, democratic reciprocity. Formal processes of democratic deliberation are institutional expressions of mutual respect: they both presuppose and strengthen it. They also presuppose and strengthen the rule of law, although forms of repressive rule are compatible with the rule of law as well. Pablo de Grieff argues that there is a close connection between recognition of victims as citizens with equal rights, civic trust, and democracy, all of which are associated with the third sort of political reconciliation:

> If transitional justice measures are to succeed in providing recognition to victims and promoting civic trust . . . this calls for the establishment

of participatory procedures. A minimum level of respect for democratic, participatory rights is a precondition of the successful implementation of these measures.[28]

Democratic institutions are likely to respect civil and human rights more consistently than nondemocratic ones, and they treat persons as free and equal citizens deserving of equal representation. If the aim of political reconciliation is to rebuild political relationships on a basis of mutual respect and trust among former enemies, then ideally democracies are better justified by these considerations than nondemocratic ones. Reconciliation of a sort (i.e., nonlethal coexistence) is possible without democracy, of course. In post-genocide Rwanda, for example, one of the most frequently discussed and intensely studied examples of a transitional society, reconciliation has chiefly meant ending the slaughter, punishing perpetrators, and addressing the harms done to victims through *gacaca* courts. Democratic participation has not been one of the objectives of its post-conflict recovery.[29] More important, arguably democratization is not always an appropriate goal of political transition, at least in the short term. Political transitions in societies whose histories and political cultures favor nondemocratic forms of governance, or whose citizens are barely subsisting, might be unstable if efforts to institute democratic reforms are undertaken by the transitional regime.

To sum up, a distinctive feature of the restorative approach to transitional justice is its emphasis on reconciliation. Other conceptions of transitional justice do not highlight this, although retributive and restorative conceptions do have some aims in common. This is clear from the following comment by Jaime Malamu-Goti on the role of criminal trials of military personnel responsible for human rights abuses in transitional societies:

> Submitting to the criminal law nullifies the supremacy of those who previously enjoyed a dominant position to it and turns them into ordinary, accountable citizens. In this way, criminal proceedings restore dignity to the citizenry and also demonstrate respect for victims in a broad sense.[30]

Restoring dignity and ensuring perpetrator accountability, aims of restorative justice, are also generally speaking aims of retributive justice. In contrast, criminal prosecutions do not have reconciliation as a defining aim, nor, for that matter, do measures to compensate victims for their losses. That said, however, political reconciliation is capable of being understood in more than one way, and the meaning of restorative justice varies with the particular conception of reconciliation that is adopted.

Suitably interpreted, holding perpetrators accountable for harms caused by their wrongdoing and restoring and affirming the dignity of victims can be thought of either as aspects of a restorative approach to transitional justice or as constitutive ingredients of political reconciliation. If we think of them in the second way, then the political reconciliation of which they are ingredients is not non-lethal coexistence, as usually conceived. It is less clear whether the political reconciliation at issue can be community solidarity, as Crocker describes it. This is in part because forgiveness plays a critical role in political reconciliation thus conceived, and the relationship between politicized gestures of forgiveness, accountability, and restoration of dignity is deeply problematic.

4. Forgiveness and restorative justice

(a) When forgiveness is not a restorative justice practice

Can forgiveness be properly regarded as a prime mechanism for achieving political reconciliation conceived in terms of relations of mutual respect and trust among equal citizens? Is the political outcome of sentiment-based forgiveness political reconciliation in this sense? There are a number of reasons to doubt that forgiveness can play this role.[31]

One reason might be that forgiving those responsible for harm fails to hold them accountable for their wrongdoing and to insist on their taking responsibility for their actions. It lets perpetrators off the hook too easily, benefiting them rather than upholding the just ethical demands of victims, so is unlikely to promote respect for the ones who forgive. Put this way, however, this criticism is unconvincing. Whether forgiveness fails in these respects depends, after all, on the conditions under which forgiveness is granted. If forgiveness is granted only after and because the offender has fully taken responsibility for his wrongdoing, faced the wrongdoing honestly and without evasion, shown remorse, and taken steps to make amends, then it is hard to see why forgiving him amounts to a denial by the victim of the moral legitimacy of her grievance or a discounting of its significance. Forgiveness is not necessarily granted because the victim lacks self-respect or fails to take her own rights seriously enough to insist on their recognition, nor does it necessarily fail to insist on respect for the one doing the forgiving. It may in fact be a morally justified response to wrongdoing under certain conditions. Viewed in this way, forgiveness does not signify a failure of justice for victims but a recognition that the conditions of justice have been satisfied.

This assumes that forgiveness occurs when the victim assesses the offender's sincerity and the reasons that she, the victim, has for forswearing her negative feelings, and based on this arrives at her decision free of controlling influence. She may be mistaken in believing that forgiveness is justified, and her reasons for

Forgiveness, Commemoration, and Restorative Justice 165

forgiving may be questionable, but the assumption is that she has decided to forgive without being pressured or bullied into forgiving, or threatened if she does not forgive. Forgiveness under these conditions is not likely to be sentiment-based, so not interpersonal forgiveness as I conceive of it but a matter of policy only. New and troubling ethical issues arise, however, when forgiveness becomes official state policy, or when the political climate within the transitional society is such that forgiveness is expected from victims. For then victims who do not forgive may be branded as morally deficient in some way, lacking in compassion or understanding, or unreasonably obstinate. Already wronged by their perpetrators, their self-respect already assaulted, the victims are wronged again and their self-respect is assaulted again, this time by being blamed, even if only tacitly, for withholding forgiveness. The blame might be both for obstinately holding on to their negative feelings and for refusing to communicate to the wrongdoers that they are released from further reparative obligations to them.

Political pressure to forgive can thus send the message that the victim's negative emotional responses to wrongdoing do not deserve official recognition, or at least that their recognition is less important than the reconciliation of former enemies. But the message is an invidious one, and not only because of its impact on the victims themselves. This is because the victims' emotional responses register their appreciation of the wrongness of what was done to them, and by discounting or disparaging these responses, the moral conscience of society at large is put in jeopardy. Paul Muldoon makes a similar point:

> The problem being outlined here is as much political as it is personal . . .
> an uncritical celebration of the morality of forgiveness has the potential
> to undermine the political integrity of the society as a whole. When
> victims fail to protest against injury or are too quick to forgive their oppressors, it is not simply their suffering which is devalued, but the principle of equal value itself.[32]

Due regard for the emotional responses of victims of wrongdoing has a powerful influence on the formation and maintenance of a society's moral conscience. A society that devalues the former or subordinates affirmation of their emotional responses to "loftier" social aims thereby risks the erosion of standards of mutual respect and trust as guiding aims of political reconciliation.

Despite this, it may seem that the benefits of pursuing forgiveness as a matter of public policy outweigh the potential costs. One argument for this rests on the assumption that forgiveness overcomes anger and resentment. Anger and resentment are regarded as socially divisive and destructive forces that imperil the prospects of political reconciliation, and so should be repressed if not extinguished, and this is the aim of public policies encouraging or insisting on forgiveness. There are at least two things wrong with this argument, however. First, as I argued in chapter 1, forgiveness is not best conceived of as a process of overcoming hostile or retributive emotions only. Other negative, non-retributive emotions may need to be overcome and forsworn, along with or instead of the former, and non-retributive negative emotions are not as easily branded as socially divisive and destructive as retributive ones. This lessens the appeal of policies promoting forgiveness in transitional societies, insofar as it is based on these concerns, since it is not only these socially disruptive emotions that forgiveness wards off or mitigates. Second, as suggested above in section 2, even if retributive emotions do impede political reconciliation, arguably it is important from the standpoint of justice to allow their expression and not to encourage their suppression. The sort of political reconciliation that can be achieved by devaluing or discounting victims' retributive responses would therefore not be a just one, even if in other respects, such as restoring peace and stability to society, it is successful. Encouraging victims to abandon resentment and anger through a process of forgiveness might fail to satisfy their sense of justice and weaken the commitment to justice across society.

Forgiveness is here contrasted with retributive justice, and I am suggesting that retributive responses to wrongdoing may be legitimate responses that society should not seek to discourage. This may seem to conflict with the argument in chapter 1 that retributive emotions do not deserve the place of honor they have been given in standard accounts of the moral psychology of response to wrongdoing, hence in standard accounts of forgiveness. Not all emotional responses to wrongdoing that evince self-respect or that accompany moral blame are retributive in nature, I argued there, and here I am suggesting that political projects of forgiveness may undermine rather than restore the dignity and self-respect of victims by denying their entitlement to anger specifically. The conflict can be resolved, however, if we recognize that retributive emotions have a somewhat different function and importance in transitional political contexts than in ordinary interpersonal ones.

The difference is that by affirming the victims' entitlement to anger, political officials acknowledge the legitimacy of punishing perpetrators as a response to wrongdoing, and punishment may be an especially appropriate response to the sorts of grievous wrongs that the victims of violence and repression have suffered. Joel Feinberg has noted the expressive function of punishment:

> punishment is a conventional device for the expression of attitudes of resentment and indignation, and of judgments of disapproval and reprobation, on the part either of the punishing authority himself or of those "in whose name" the punishment is inflicted. Punishment, in short, has a *symbolic significance* largely missing from other kinds of penalties.[33]

Forgiveness, Commemoration, and Restorative Justice

I would add to this that it has a symbolic significance in transitional contexts that may be missing from non-punitive modes of censure. Punishment, as an authoritative expression of attitudes of resentment and indignation, forcefully expresses the community's condemnation of wrongdoing, and it may be necessary for the community to do this in order to do full justice to the victims' sense of personal violation. Angry reactions to the sorts of horrific and systematic wrongs that transitional societies inherit are natural, widespread, and within limits appropriate. Legitimizing them through the social sanctioning of punishment of perpetrators is a way of acknowledging this. In addition, it can help the new regime earn the trust and respect of victims, and this can enhance the prospects of political reconciliation. Because punishment has special significance in transitional contexts, retributive emotions properly occupy a more prominent place in theories of transitional justice than they do in accounts of the moral psychology of response to wrongdoing. At the same time, these remarks about the importance of validating specifically retributive emotions in transitional circumstances are consistent with my earlier denial that these emotions are the only fitting or most appropriate responses to being wronged. Even in transitional contexts where victims confront grievous wrongs, appropriate emotional responses are not only retributive in nature but include non-retributive emotions such grief, shame, humiliation, fear, and mistrust.[34]

I have argued so far that when interpersonal forgiveness becomes state policy rather than a voluntary undertaking of victims confronting their perpetrators, it risks blaming the victim and subordinating the moral and emotional needs of victims to the pursuit of (a morally flawed) political reconciliation. The politicization of forgiveness in public policy also risks encouraging victims to forgive perpetrators regardless of whether the latter have taken full responsibility for their past wrongdoing. In these ways, the value of forgiveness itself is debased, insofar as the forgiveness that is encouraged is not consistent with the self-respect of the victims and their faith in the authority of shared moral norms.

There is a further problem as well: not the debasement of forgiveness but the very interpersonal conception of political reconciliation that forgiveness represents. One of the criteria of taking full responsibility is whether the perpetrators have endorsed reform of the institutions and social and political conditions that facilitated and supported their wrongdoing, or at least have committed themselves to not obstructing such reform. Without this, perpetrators give themselves an escape hatch to repeat their wrongdoing, or at least are perceived to do so, and their professed commitment to make amends for it is not entirely credible. Even if the perpetrators endorse such changes and take full responsibility for their offenses, and forgiveness and some renewal of trust follow as a consequence, forgiveness is an incomplete and insufficient response to systematic or structural injustice and oppression. This is so however we construe forgiveness, whether as a sentiment-based phenomenon or as a policy of adopting an exclusionary reason with regard to treating those who have wronged us in certain ways. Human rights abuses of the sort that transitional regimes confront are generally the result of systematic or structural injustice, pervasive social and political conditions that foster abuse and basic institutions that fail to protect citizens. Such injustice might eventually be ameliorated if state policies promoting forgiveness are implemented, but their amelioration is not the focus of forgiveness, and injustice and oppression are likely to persist if they are not directly addressed. Moreover, if establishing or reestablishing political relations of respect and trust between former antagonists is the aim of political reconciliation in transitional contexts, then reform of the background social and institutional conditions that made wrongdoing possible must be one of its principal aims. As long as their reform is neglected or postponed, perhaps because forgiveness is promoted instead, the status of former victims as citizens with equal rights will remain insecure.

(b) Forgiveness and political reconciliation

In agreement with a number of writers on the relationship between forgiveness, political reconciliation, and transitional justice, I have argued that policies that make forgiveness a political project are too problematic to be the driving force behind a political reconciliation that satisfies the requirements of transitional and restorative justice. However, this doesn't mean that forgiveness has no role to play in public discourse or policy regarding how the wrongs of the past should be addressed, or that forgiveness is simply incompatible with the moral reconstruction of social and political relationships. There is a difference between making forgiveness a political project in the way I have been describing, on the one hand, and creating conditions for forgiveness that are responsive to victim desires and needs, on the other, and criticism of the former does not justify neglect of the positive political contribution that forgiveness can make in transitional societies. I want to say something about the conditions under which forgiveness can make such a contribution and about why forgiveness is not necessarily incompatible with a just political reconciliation.

First some remarks about the conditions. Forgiveness can make a contribution to restorative justice and to the rebuilding of political relationships if state-recognized mechanisms are established that provide "structured opportunities for forgiveness"[35] that are also structured opportunities for moral protest. I emphasize moral protest because of its connection to self-respect: restoring and affirming the dignity of victims is one of the principal aims of restorative justice and what is done out of protest is done out of concern for one's dignity. Loss of or injury to self-respect is a very real possibility in circumstances of civil conflict

Forgiveness, Commemoration, and Restorative Justice

and repressive rule, since the self-respect of even confidently self-respecting individuals is not immune to injury from the degrading and demeaning treatment they receive in these circumstances. As I explained in chapter 1, protest can be both a way of asserting one's moral worth and of reassuring oneself and letting others know that one's self-respect is still intact, and it has especial restorative potential in these circumstances. If structured opportunities could be provided to victims to confront their offenders and protest the wrongs they suffered, and if these were among the conditions under which forgiveness was granted, this could help in the moral reconstruction of damaged political relationships. The opportunity to protest can itself be restorative, but if the protest receives the right uptake from the offenders, this could also help build trust between former adversaries.

One of the aims of the restorative justice movement is to replace the conventional processes of criminal justice with various types of victim–offender conferencing, and among other things, these can provide victims with such opportunities for forgiveness. These are social spaces in which victims can confront offenders face-to-face and offenders are called upon to actively participate in determining justice in their case. A primary aim of these practices is to enable victims to show offenders that they retain their self-respect, and also to reassure themselves that they retain their self-respect despite having been abused and brutalized. They provide structured opportunities for challenging the claims of moral impunity implicit in the offenders' actions and for prompting their recognition and acknowledgment of the wrongness of what they have done. They are, as such, vehicles for moral protest and possess the values associated with it. Gerry Johnstone comments on the value of meetings between victims and offenders:

> Face-to-face meetings can be a forum where victims can 'vent feelings of bitterness and hurt directly to the one who caused them'. While advocates of restorative justice insist that victim-offender meetings or restorative conferences should not become forums for the simple vilification of offenders, they do see one of their chief advantages over formal legal procedures as being their ability to act as mediums for emotional expression . . . [they] can also help victims to recover a sense of personal power.[36]

These victim–offender meetings create opportunities for offenders to recognize their victims as moral equals (and vice versa) and may compel the former to acknowledge the legitimacy of the latter's complaints. This is what protest typically aims at and what it can sometimes succeed in doing, although as noted in my discussion of Boxill in chapter 1, its moral value is not entirely dependent on whether it actually establishes or reestablishes relations of respect and trust between victims and offenders. It also has moral value as an assertion of moral worth, and the value of victim–offender meetings derives in part from this, from the fact that they are forums in which victims can declare their refusal to accept the wrongs they have suffered without complaint. This is a kind of empowerment, moral in nature, that restorative justice practices aim to promote. And if the protest of the victims receives uptake from the offenders, the victims might forgive them, and this might promote reconciliation between them. But if this happens, it is not because victims have abandoned their entitlements or been pressured or shamed into forgiving.

Further, as the quote from Johnstone suggests, advocates of restorative justice do not believe that these practices have to be merely forums for the vilification of offenders. The emotional reactions involved in the victims' defiance can be "bitterness and hurt" and these may be mixed together or the latter might occur without any retributive feelings. As I have argued, retributive, non-retributive, and hybrid negative emotions can prompt victim protest, can infuse and sustain it, can determine the particular shape and direction the protest takes, and can communicate disapproval to offenders. Anger may be a common response to particularly grievous wrongs and avenues for its expression should be available, including victim–offender conferencing. This can mitigate anger, although it does not necessarily erase all hard feelings for the wrongdoers.

The idea of protest captures one of the central legitimating features of restorative practices that are alternatives or supplements to the punitive practices of the criminal justice system: the moral empowerment of victims. Protests are not always successful in getting offenders to take responsibility for their wrongdoing, and victim–offender meetings do not always succeed in this either. But such meetings can lay the groundwork for morally warranted forgiveness. They do this by enabling victims to confront their offenders with a judgment of wrongdoing; by encouraging offenders to face their wrongdoing honestly and take responsibility for it; and by promoting joint problem solving about how to address the wrongdoing that models the reintegration of offenders into the community. In addition, an extension of victim–offender conferencing involves families of the victims and offenders and members or representatives of the local community, and the involvement of others besides the offender and victim can promote forgiveness. When families and communities are involved in these structured processes, this may provide the victim with additional assurance that the offender will actually follow through on his commitment to change and make amends. Since fear that the offender will strike again is often an obstacle to forgiveness, assurances from the community can dispose the victim to be more forgiving.

There is a remaining objection to consider. It might be argued that even if these are only opportunities for forgiveness and victims are not pressured into forgiving, making these opportunities available and sanctioning their use lends support to a pernicious idea. This is so because these measures promote forgiveness as the path to reconciliation, and the political reconciliation that is based on forgiveness is morally flawed. Forgiveness teaches victims to make peace with their oppressors rather than continue in a defensive posture against further assaults to their dignity, the objection goes, and this is not a kind of political reconciliation that we should be willing to endorse in circumstances in which the resumption of wrongdoing remains a realistic possibility.

There are two responses to this. First, one can endorse structured opportunities for forgiveness without at the same time endorsing forgiveness as the best or only satisfactory normative approach to reconciliation. Second, and more important, the claim that forgiveness necessarily teaches this sort of passivity is simply mistaken. Forgiveness does not disable protest against wrongdoing, or against forgetting wrongdoing, but can in fact coexist with a readiness to protest wrongdoing if and when the need arises. This is clearest where there is a considerable time interval between the forgiving and the subsequent protesting. Transitions are not completed merely with the transfer of political or military power from one regime to another. It takes time to consolidate a new democratic order, sometimes several generations, and while forgiveness of the original perpetrators may have been fully warranted, whatever political reconciliation has already been achieved may be threatened by a return of political repression and violence. Past forgiveness does not hinder organized resistance to these new threats, however. This is because forgiving does not entail forgetting and past wrongdoing can continue to leave a scar on the collective memory that past forgiving does not or cannot remove. This is true even within the span of a single generation. There is no incompatibility between forgiving wrongdoers, on the one hand, and the public being both alert to the possibility that they will offend again and ready to protect itself in the event that they do, on the other. The alleged passivity of forgiveness, therefore, is not a feature of forgiveness per se, but only of a kind of forgiveness that is rightly condemned, the sort that leaves one defenseless, impotent in the face of further assaults to one's dignity. Thus, we are not necessarily encouraging capitulation to injustice by creating conditions that facilitate forgiveness.

5. Commemoration and restorative justice

Though forgiveness has often been characterized as a practice that advances the aims of restorative justice, I have argued to the contrary that there are a number of reasons to question its restorative value as a political project. Public policies encouraging forgiveness risk damaging the self-respect of victims, subordinating their needs to a larger national goal of political reconciliation, and permitting perpetrators to evade responsibility for their actions. This is not to imply that forgiveness can't be restorative. But whether it is or not depends centrally on a number of factors, including the relative power of victims and perpetrators; the reasons for which the perpetrators are forgiven; the voluntariness of the forgiving; and the involvement of communities of victims and perpetrators in ensuring that the terms under which forgiveness is granted are adhered to. This is a significantly qualified defense of forgiveness from the restorative justice standpoint.

I now want to briefly introduce another practice often associated with restorative justice, namely memorialization, and offer a similarly qualified defense of its value from this standpoint. As with forgiveness, the restorative value of memorialization depends on numerous factors, and it can be problematic for reasons similar to those relating to forgiveness. It may seem that public policies promoting memorialization are relatively unproblematic morally and politically compared to ones promoting forgiveness. But this is mistaken. Policies of memorialization do not necessarily facilitate the rebuilding of political relationships and the establishment or reestablishment of relations of respect and trust. Part of the explanation for this is that memorialization can provide support for partisan political interests, which can prevent political reconciliation. But even memorialization that is relatively free of these difficulties and that is nondivisive can have consequences that are not reparative. I will say why in a moment.

There are various modes of memorialization. One common way to memorialize is by means of artifacts designed draw attention to people or events from the past, such as memorial plaques and monuments. The naming of public spaces, streets, plazas, etc., after important persons or historical events also has memorial intent; and museums, archives, and truth commissions can be established in part for this purpose as well. When these activities facilitate the sharing of memories, they count as activities of commemoration or memorialization. More precisely, memorialization, as I am using the term, refers to public practices that give communal or collective shape and focus to memories of a shared past. These practices I often refer to with the umbrella term "memorials." They might receive public funding or not, and the memories might be widely shared across the entire society or only or predominantly within a particular group, such as Native Americans or, more narrowly still, the descendants of Thomas Jefferson and Sally Hemings, for example. Since the point of memorialization practices is to provide a space and context for the *sharing* of memories, they are distinguished from individual acts of remembrance by their overtly communal and communalizing character. In other words, they are intended to be practices of commemoration or co-remembering, activities of experiencing a connection

Forgiveness, Commemoration, and Restorative Justice   173

to the past in a communal activity of co-remembrance. "Whenever commemo-rating occurs," Edward Casey observes, "a community arises. Not only is some-thing communal being honored, but the honoring itself is a communal event, a collective engagement."[37]

Jacob Klapwijk construes commemoration quite broadly:

> Commemoration is effected in rituals, wakes and celebrations, in masses and vespers, parades and protest demonstrations . . . Commemoration also transpires as a collective event, in the cherishing of our language and culture, in the respecting of our traditions and social institutions, in the rites of passage surrounding birth, marriage, sickness and death. Remembrance also manifests itself in the public domain, in memorial services and special days named Independence Day, Revolution Day, Remembrance Day, and the like.[38]

I am interested in commemoration in a more narrow sense (so for present pur-poses I exclude, for example, "respecting social institutions"). Commemoration in this sense often takes the form of rituals, of memorial services and remem-brance day ceremonies, and the ritualistic character of these commemorative activities will be of particular importance in the next chapter. Specifically, what interests me is the use of rituals of commemoration to promote and preserve the remembrance of wrongdoing and its victims. Further, I want to distinguish between commemoration and its products: to commemorate is to engage in a communal event (with or without a ritualistic dimension), but the products of such communal activity may survive even if they no longer inspire collective en-gagement. These products are devoid of memorial interest and lack the capacity to galvanize public reflection on the social meaning of past events.

It may not be difficult to understand how commemoration could promote the aims of restorative justice and help rebuild political relationships in the af-termath of civil conflict and repression. Commemorating wrongdoing can itself be a reparative gesture to some extent. It can be one way for those who are re-sponsible for wrongdoing to *take* responsibility for it, to (symbolically) stand up for those who were wrongfully harmed, and to provide some measure of moral validation for them. If it is an activity that is endorsed by the entire political com-munity, it can give assurance to victims that they are full members of it and help further political reconciliation. Commemorations can also reinforce other initia-tives aimed at repairing the harm done to victims by providing a powerful sym-bolic expression of the rationale for these initiatives, namely to make amends for wrongdoing. Victims also, with or without the support of the larger community, commemorate the wrongs they suffered, but here the purpose is not to take re-sponsibility for wrongdoing, for they are not or at least do not regard themselves as the guilty party. It is rather to assert their self-respect, to announce to others in the society that they still possess it, perhaps to convince themselves that they still possess it, and to derive strength from reflection on their shared past.

But commemoration, of course, is not an unqualified good, when judged from a restorative standpoint. One reason, as I said, is that commemorative activities can be socially polarizing. They can heighten antagonisms between former enemies by underscoring and reinforcing loyalties and political identities that fueled social exclusion and discrimination. Rather than restore trust and help rebuild political relationships in which all persons are treated as equals, commemorations might only perpetuate the intolerance and mistrust that transitional societies are trying to overcome. We need only think of the yearly Protestant marches through the Catholic neighborhoods of Northern Ireland, a country that endured 30 years of sectarian political violence, to appreciate the socially destructive potential of public commemorations.

But there is another reason to be cautious in embracing commemoration as a practice of restorative justice. This, I take it, is part of what Paul Connerton is getting at when he says that "the relationship between memorials and forgetting is reciprocal: the threat of forgetting begets memorials and the construction of memorials begets forgetting."[39] Ironically, the creation of memorials, even if not overtly polarizing, can stand in the way of full engagement with the wrongs of the past. It is as if the thought were: "there, we have remembered, so now we can put the past behind us."[40] Commemoration, misused and misdirected, may in fact be one aspect of a policy of burying the past, part of a deliberate effort by those in positions of political power to divert attention from those responsible for past wrongs and from the need for basic political and institutional change. The motivation for creating memorials might not be cynical like this, and the forgetting that commemoration makes possible and facilitates might not be its aim. Nevertheless, this can be its effect, especially if the political will to redress the wrongs of the past is limited. Like public policies encouraging forgiveness, public policies of commemoration that are not overtly divisive can nonetheless leave intact the structures of violence and oppression whose reform should be a primary focus of political reconciliation. And by leaving them intact, these policies can be complicit in failing to protect those already victimized and those still to be victimized from further wrongdoing.

6. The compatibility of forgiveness and commemoration

Though the restorative potential of forgiveness and commemoration is limited and dependent on several factors, each can play a role in the moral reconstruction

Forgiveness, Commemoration, and Restorative Justice 175

of political relationships. We should only be careful not to exaggerate their significance in this regard. However, even if our hopes for forgiveness and commemoration are appropriately restrained, it may be thought that the two cannot coexist easily in a transitional society in which victims have forgiven their perpetrators. For forgiveness ideally culminates in forgetting, it may be said, and forgetting and commemorating are mutually exclusive. To promote commemoration is to risk stirring up emotional memories of wrongdoing that the victims may have struggled long to overcome and that they were able to overcome in forgiving the perpetrators. So as not to endanger the stability of political reconciliation and the good that forgiveness has accomplished, it would be best for the state to avoid commemorations of wrongdoing and its victims, or to give them only a very low social profile, and to discourage such commemorative activities by segments of civil society.

I have already given part of my response to this argument. Forgiveness does not necessarily wipe the slate clean of negative emotional memories of wrongdoing. Non-retributive emotions and the memories they constitute can linger after offenders have been forgiven. What's more, these can have an expressive point and moral significance similar to the point and significance of those negative emotions that the victim needs to overcome in order to forgive. Thus, the fact that commemorations may keep negative emotional memories of wrongdoing from fading is not sufficient reason for supposing that where perpetrators have been forgiven, public policies supportive of commemoration are unwise and politically retrograde. The real problem, therefore, is not that commemorations sustain memories of wrongdoing, but rather concerns how they sustain them and what sort of memories they sustain.

To elaborate this, I will examine in detail the nature of commemoration, specifically commemorative rituals, and I will also argue for their particular value in transitional settings and beyond where memory is morally imperative but tenuous. This is the subject of the next chapter.

Endnotes

1. As noted by Elizabeth Kiss in "Moral Ambition Within and Beyond Political Constraints: Reflections in Restorative Justice," in *Truth v. Justice* (Robert Rotberg and Dennis Thompson, eds.) (Princeton, NJ: Princeton University Press, 2000), pp. 68–98, at 79.
2. There is a vast literature, mostly outside of philosophy, on the functions and rationale of truth commissions. An indispensable source of information about the types and purposes of truth commissions in Priscilla B. Hayner, *Unspeakable Truths: Facing the Challenge of Truth Commissions* (New York: Routledge, 2002). See also Amy Gutmann and Dennis Thompson, "The Moral Foundations of Truth Commissions," in *Truth v. Justice*, op. cit., pp. 22–44; Martha Minow, "The Hope for Healing: What Can Truth Commissions Do?" in *Truth v. Justice*, pp. 235–260; and Margaret Walker, "How Does a Truth Commission Work? Recognition, Accountability, and a Preventive Pedagogy of Human Rights," ICTJ Research Project "How Things Work," forthcoming.

3. Charles Griswold, *Forgiveness: A Philosophical Exploration* (New York: Cambridge University Press, 2007), p. 145.
4. A purely relational view of political forgiveness is defended and developed by P. E. Digeser in *Political Forgiveness* (Ithaca, NY: Cornell University Press, 2001). He claims that political forgiveness should be thought of as an illocutionary act:
   > Using J. L. Austin's terminology, we can say that political forgiveness must not only be a locutionary act but also an illocutionary act. Something must not only be said or somehow conveyed, but what is said must have the effect of releasing the debtor or the transgressor from the debt. (p. 28).
5. Margalit, *The Ethics of Memory* (Cambridge, MA: Harvard University Press, 2002), pp. 202–203.
6. See Joseph Raz, *Practical Reason and Norms* (New York: Oxford University Press, 1999), p. 39.
7. For a useful discussion of illocutionary acts and what the author considers to be a sub-class of them, namely communicative acts, see Ishanti Maitra, "Silencing Speech," *Canadian Journal of Philosophy*, vol. 39, no. 2 (June 2009): 309–338.
8. See Thomas Brudholm, *Resentment's Virtue* (Philadelphia: Temple University Press, 2008), chapter 5; Brandon Hamber, *Transforming Societies after Political Violence: Truth, Reconciliation, and Mental Health* (Dordrecht: Springer, 2009), pp. 187–188.
9. Richard A. Wilson, *The Politics of Truth and Reconciliation in South Africa: Legitimizing the Post-Apartheid State* (Cambridge: Cambridge University Press, 2005), p. 120.
10. Ibid., 108.
11. Ibid., p. 120.
12. Hamber, op. cit., p. 188.
13. Brudholm, op. cit., pp. 50–51. Brudholm is here discussing what he claims is the forgiveness boosterism of the South African Truth and Reconciliation Commission, but the observation clearly has wider implications.
14. Both Griswold, op. cit. (p. 119) and Digeser, op. cit. (pp. 92–108) discuss this issue.
15. Desmond Tutu, *No Future without Forgiveness* (New York: Doubleday, 1999), p. 57.
16. Digeser argues this, op. cit. pp. 105–106.
17. "The rule of law and transitional justice in conflict and post-conflict societies," Report of the Secretary General, United Nations Security Council, August 23, 2004, p. 4.
18. John Rawls, *A Theory of Justice* (Cambridge, MA: Harvard University Press, 1971), p. 246.
19. A. John Simmons, "Ideal and Nonideal Theory," *Philosophy and Public Affairs*, vol. 38, no. 1 (Winter 2010): 5–36, at 22.
20. For a discussion of all aspects of the theory and practice of restorative justice, see Gerry Johnstone, *Restorative Justice: Ideas, Values, Debates* (Portland, OR: Willan Publishing, 2006); and *A Restorative Justice Reader: Texts, Sources, Contexts* (Gerry Johnstone, ed.) (Portland, OR: Willan, 2003).
21. This brief summary of characteristics of restorative justice is drawn from numerous sources, including chapters and essays in Gerry Johnstone's two books (footnote 20) and the following: Christopher Bennett, *The Apology Ritual* (Cambridge: Cambridge University Press, 2008), esp. pp. 20–24, 125–151; Kiss, op. cit.; Linda Radzik, *Making Amends: Atonement in Morality, Law, and Politics* (New York: Oxford University Press, 2009), esp. pp. 153–174; Margaret Walker, *Moral Repair: Reconstructing Moral Relations after Wrongdoing* (New York: Cambridge University Press, 2006), pp. 191–229; "Restorative Justice and Reparations," *Journal of Social Philosophy*, vol. 37, no. 3 (Fall 2006): 377–395; "The Cycle of Violence," *Journal of Human Rights*, vol. 5 (2006): 81–105. The literature is vast and I have necessarily had to be selective.
22. This is how Charles Griswold understands political apology, op. cit., pp. 135–146.
23. Janna Thompson, "Is Political Apology a Sorry Affair?" *Social and Legal Studies*, vol. 21, no. 2 (2012): 215–225, at 223. For a critical view of the contemporary practice of government apologies for past wrongs, see Jeff Spinner-Halev, *Enduring Injustice* (New York: Cambridge University Press, 2012).

Forgiveness, Commemoration, and Restorative Justice 177

24. Not all offenders who apologize necessarily see it as a request for forgiveness or have any hope or expectation of forgiveness. Linda Radzik makes the point, op. cit., p. 96.

25. Lawrence Crocker, "Punishment, Reconciliation, and Democratic Deliberation," in *Taking Wrongs Seriously: Apologies and Reconciliation* (Elazar Barkan and Alexander Karn, eds.) (Stanford, CA: Stanford University Press, 2006), pp. 50–82. Other useful discussions of reconciliation are: Trudy Govier, *Forgiveness and Revenge* (London: Routledge, 2002), pp. 141–157; Griswold, op. cit., pp. 167–171; Colleen Murphy, *A Moral Theory of Political Reconciliation* (New York: Cambridge University Press, 2010); Linda Radzik, op. cit., chapters 4 and 5; and Ernesto Verdeja, *Unchopping a Tree: Reconciliation in the Aftermath of Political Violence* (Philadelphia: Temple University Press, 2009).

26. This is second-personal respect, and I discuss it at greater length in chapters 5 and 6.

27. Other accounts in which mutual respect is central to political reconciliation are: Murphy, op. cit.; Janna Thompson, *Taking Responsibility for the Past* (Cambridge: Polity, 2002), pp. 50–53; Verdeja, op. cit.; Walker, *Moral Repair*, pp. 207–218.

28. Pablo de Greiff includes democracy as one of the aims of transitional justice in "A Normative Conception of Transitional Justice," *Politorbis*, vol. 3, no. 50 (2010): 17–29.

29. See, for example, Timothy Longman, "Limitations to Political Reform: The Undemocratic Nature of Transition in Rwanda," in *Remaking Rwanda: State Building and Human Rights after Mass Violence* (Scott Straus and Lars Waldorf, eds.) (Madison: University of Wisconsin Press, 2011), pp. 25–47.

30. Jaime Malamud-Goti, "Transitional Governments in the Breach: Why Punish State Criminals?" *Human Rights Quarterly*, vol. 12, no. 1 (February 1990): 1–16, at 13.

31. A number of authors have addressed the inadequacy of forgiveness as a mechanism for political reconciliation or restorative justice more broadly. See Thomas Brudholm, op. cit., pp. 50–56; Paul Muldoon, "The Moral Legitimacy of Anger," *European Journal of Social Theory*, vol. 11, no. 3 (August 2008): 299–314; Colleen Murphy, op. cit., pp. 9–13; Rebecca Saunders, "Questionable Associations: The Role of Forgiveness in Transitional Justice," *The International Journal of Transitional Justice*, vol. 5 (2011): 119–141; and Ernesto Verdeja, op. cit., pp. 12–20. For a very different view, see Mark R. Amstutz, *The Healing of Nations: The Promise and Limits of Political Forgiveness* (Lanham, MD: Rowman and Littlefield, 2005).

32. Muldoon, op. cit., p. 308.

33. Joel Feinberg, "The Expressive Function of Punishment," in *Doing and Deserving* (Princeton, NJ: Princeton University Press, 1970), pp. 95–118, at 98.

34. See Walker, op. cit. "The Cycle of Violence."

35. The term comes from John Gehm, "The function of forgiveness in the criminal justice system," in *A Restorative Justice Reader*, op. cit., pp. 280–285, at 284.

36. Johnstone, op. cit., *Restorative Justice*, p. 77.

37. Edward Casey, *Remembering: A Phenomenological Study*, 2nd edition (Bloomington: Indiana University Press, 2000), pp. 235–236.

38. Jacob Klapwijk, "Commemoration: On the First and Second History," *Philosophia Reformata*, vol. 74 (2009): 48–69, at 51–52.

39. Paul Connerton, *How Modernity Forgets* (Cambridge: Cambridge University Press, 2009), p. 29.

40. The novelist Robert Musil remarks on this paradoxical outcome in writing about the glut of First World War monuments in the 1930s:

The most striking feature of monuments is that you do not notice them. There is nothing in the world as invisible as a monument. Doubtless they have been erected to be seen – even to attract attention; yet at the same time something has impregnated them against attention [Quoted in Marina Warner, *Monuments and Maidens: The Allegory of the Female Form* (London: Picador, 1985, p. 21)].

5

Commemoration and the Moral Values of Remembrance

1. Valuing and sustaining remembrance

Assuming that the victims of wrongdoing have forgiven, or might yet be able to forgive, those who have wronged them, and that there is pressure from some quarters to commemorate the victims of that very wrongdoing, transitional regimes confront the following political problem: how can they promote or even sanction memorial projects without risking a resurgence of the hard feelings that victims were able to or might in time be able to overcome? We can also ask, from a moral standpoint, why it should matter whether they are successful at avoiding this. Why or to what extent is this a moral and not just a political challenge? The full answer to this question depends on a better understanding of the values that memorialization recognizes and to which it responds, and this is what I aim to provide in this chapter.

The discussion of forgiveness has already given us part of the explanation of the moral significance of remembrance. Remembering that one was wronged by another is a necessary condition of the possibility of forgiving him (although as I argued in chapter 3, remembering can be excessive, so may need to be tempered by forgetting), and it can also keep one from forgiving, if the memory of what he did is too painful to permit it. So if it is a good thing to forgive, memory makes this good thing possible, and if it a good thing not to forgive, memory can make this possible too. To be sure, it sometimes happens that a wronged party decides to forgive another person for having done something so long ago that the wronged party can no longer remember what it was. But even here, it is the nature of his wrongful act, not his having done something wrong, that is forgotten. In addition, the type of memory involved, in particular its emotional character, bears on whether the victim's self-respect is engaged by the wrongs for which she does or does not forgive another, and this is an explanation not just of why it matters, morally speaking, *that* one remember, but also *how* one

178

remembers. However, the morality of remembrance is not fully explained by its connections to forgiveness. There are a number of other considerations that fill out the picture, quite apart from whether victims think offenders are worthy of forgiveness or are psychologically able or prepared to forgive them.

I introduce some of these additional considerations in section 2 by turning to a version of an expressivist theory of morality, according to which actions are judged by the appropriateness and adequacy of the attitudes they express. One of the attitudes that remembrance expresses is a kind of *respect*, both respect that survivors have for themselves and respect for victims generally, including those who did not survive. (The attitude of respect for persons is taken up again at some length in chapter 6.) A second attitude that remembrance expresses is a kind of *fidelity*. Specifically, it is a way of keeping faith with the victims of wrongdoing and not allowing their deaths to weaken or dissolve the attachments of the living to them, not only the attachments of families to their relatives but also the attachments of survivor communities to their own members. These are among the moral values of remembrance, and they serve as justifying reasons for remembrance not only in periods of political transition – my focus here – but also while conflict is still ongoing and after peace has been restored.

Finally, there are consequentialist considerations. Remembrance of wrongdoing, while itself an ingredient of a restorative approach to transitional justice, is also instrumentally valuable in helping to promote the work of political transition in other ways and to prevent backsliding. Commitment to transitional justice and to the various programs and policies that implement it may wane or become too narrowly focused on the goal of national reconstruction if memories of wrongdoing and its victims are suppressed or allowed to fade.

If remembrance is important for the reasons I adduce, then other things being equal, key actors within transitional societies should support and promote processes of memorialization that embody its values. Moreover, absent some compelling reason to the contrary, the resulting memorials ought to endure. If, for example, a community shows its respect for the victims of wrongdoing by remembering them, this is a significant enough value that its embodiment in memorial practices should have some permanence. This brings me to the topic of section 3, what I call the problem of the *sustainability* of memory. The weakening of memory over time is a familiar phenomenon, and it happens both with private and public, individual and collective, memory. Private and individual memory for even intensely emotional experiences tends to fade as a result of the passage of time and the accumulation of new memories in the interim: the more time that elapses between the original event and the memories of it, the weaker these become and, unless steps are taken to shore them up, the more difficult it becomes to retrieve them. In the case of public and collective memory for wrongdoing, there are factors at work in addition to those affecting individual

180   FORGIVENESS AND REMEMBRANCE

recall: social, political, and economic processes that erode collective memory by diverting public attention and interest away from the past and toward the present and future. These factors, combined with changes in individuals' psychological capacities for recall over time, present a problem, however. For while there is no precise way to formulate a moral statute of limitations for how long individuals, groups, and societies should continue to remember past wrongdoing, it seems clear that, from a moral standpoint, collective memory often does not survive as and for as long as it should. What should be remembered is forgotten sooner than the moral importance of what is remembered warrants. The section ends with a discussion of the relationship between emotion and the duration of memories and a suggestion about the role that emotion, tethered to past wrongdoing, may be able to play in safeguarding memory in transitional societies.

I turn next in section 4 to the nature and moral functions of one type of memorial activity, commemorative rituals, partly because I find in them a solution to the sustainability problem. I argue that two features of ritual—their repetitiveness and emotionality—can help sustain memory for wrongdoing as other ways of memorializing cannot. Section 5 presents some examples of commemorative rituals in transitional societies and discusses what I call "the dark side" of commemoration. Engaging in or providing authorization for the commemorative marking of past wrongdoing in ritualistic form could revive and give new energy to the resentment, hostility, grief, fear, and other negative feelings with which the victims responded to the earlier wrongdoing and that it provoked in others. Remembrance is not necessarily reparative, nor does it always promote reconciliation and forgiveness. On the contrary, it could undermine whatever trust has been established between former adversaries and the possibility of forgiveness as well. Nevertheless, other outcomes are possible, although they are far from assured where relations between former adversaries remain precarious. As I argue in section 6, commemorative rituals can link past wrongdoing to negative emotions different from the retributive emotions that commonly attend the perception of being wronged. Since negative non-retributive emotions can, and often do, surface or linger after offenders have been forgiven, there is no in principle incompatibility between forgiveness and commemoration, understood in this way.

2. The moral values of remembrance

There is a certain view about forgiveness, encapsulated in the maxim "forgive and forget," that raises serious questions about the wisdom of commemorations dedicated to the victims of the very acts for which the offenders have been forgiven. The maxim is not just making the empirical claim that forgiving generally leads to forgetting. It may be true that those who forgive no longer dwell on the past, that memories of past wrongdoing become harder to access, and that forgetting of a sort sets in. However, not infrequently the maxim is also understood to be asserting something else, or possibly two other things. It is sometimes thought that forgiveness is generally preferable to other ways of dealing with wrongdoing (a view some advocates of "restorative justice" seem to embrace); and it is quite commonly thought that once having forgiven others for their wrongs, there is no longer any good reason to remember those wrongs or those who committed them. Remembering wrongdoing may be necessary for the victim to be able to forgive, since one can't forgive *by* forgetting. But once the offender has been forgiven, according to a popular view, remembering his offenses, and remembering him as the one who committed those offenses, no longer serves any useful or valuable purpose. Indeed, it may indicate that one hasn't really forgiven him after all.

Now if this is one's view of the aftermath of forgiveness, it is obvious that memorialization will and should be worrisome, and that some types, those that are more likely to have an enduring social impact, will be more worrisome than others. For commemoration does just what the maxim advises us not to do: it keeps the memory of wrongdoing alive by not allowing us to forget the victims and their suffering, contrary to the maxim's recommendation.

I will eventually turn to questions about the sustainability of memory and the compatibility of forgiveness and commemoration in post-conflict, post-authoritarian transitional societies. But this is not the place to begin. First it is necessary to discuss the values of remembrance, for without a good understanding of the moral dimension of remembering wrongdoing and its victims, we will not be able to fully appreciate what is at stake in answering those questions.

(a) Consequentialist and non-consequentialist arguments

There are, broadly speaking, two sorts of moral considerations that are invoked in support of remembering wrongdoing and its victims.[1] The most promising way to vindicate the idea that there is moral value in remembering the victims of wrongdoing, perhaps even a moral duty to do so, seems to be with some type of consequentialism. Consequentialism is usually the theory of choice for defending various practices concerning the deceased, such as honoring wills and testaments, and a similar approach could plausibly be taken with respect to remembering people after they die, and in particular those who died as a result of wrongdoing.[2] It seems clear that the belief that one will be remembered after one's death motivates and sustains much that is valuable in human affairs and averts much that is not. For example, if it were believed that individuals in general or a particular person would not be remembered after death, then that person might not undertake valuable long-range projects that are likely to require efforts beyond his lifetime to complete. Since the continuation of those projects after his death is often done in his memory, they would not in that case come to fruition if he were forgotten. Or concern for posthumous reputation, a powerful deterrent for many from misconduct, would no longer act as a constraint on current behavior. As with honoring wills and testaments, remembering the dead has considerable utility for the living, and its overall beneficial effects for the living give us strong reason to institutionalize practices of remembrance. Reasons of the same general sort showing that remembrance has utility for the living could be brought to bear on behalf of remembering those who died from wrongdoing.

What social utility might public memorial practices dedicated to the victims and survivors of wrongdoing have, particularly in the context of post-conflict, post-authoritarian societies? In these circumstances, the justification of these practices could proceed by drawing connections between them and the achievement of various desirable transitional goals. These include building or restoring civic trust between former enemies; preventing a recurrence of wrongdoing; and helping to strengthen the rule of law and democratic values. Democratization promotes a culture of respect for human rights, and memorial practices can play a constructive role in this process by stimulating community involvement in dialogue about the past and fostering transparency with respect to assigning responsibility for past wrongdoing.[3] In addition, insofar as they assist in restoring the political status and legal standing of victims, memorial practices assist in restoring the benefits that victims were denied because they were not treated as equals in the political, social, and economic life of the community. Memorial practices are also important because they help meet the victims' emotional needs, emotional needs for their suffering to be remembered and acknowledged, and not just material needs for financial compensation for their losses. In this way memorialization can help promote the victims' psychological healing.

So much for consequentialist reasons to remember wrongdoing and its victims in the setting of a society in transition. Other reasons are non-consequentialist and they can be drawn from ethical theories of different sorts, including two I discuss in the next chapter, deontology or a duty-based ethic and virtue ethics, and ethical expressivism. (I borrow elements from each without adopting any one of them in its entirety and without trying to combine all these elements into a single theory.) Here I focus on expressivist elements of a moral theory of the value of remembrance because this goes a long way toward justifying what I believe is our intuitive sense that there is more to the morality of remembrance than its consequences. Activities and practices of remembrance express attitudes toward the victims of wrongdoing, although not all of the attitudes that might be expressed thereby, or the ways in which these attitudes are expressed, contribute to the moral value of those activities and practices. Expressive norms help us to distinguish those that do from those that don't.

Expressivism, in Elizabeth Anderson's formulation of the view, is both a theory of rational action and, derivatively, a theory of value. As she understands the former, "an expressive theory defines rational action as action that adequately expresses our rational attitudes toward people and other intrinsically valuable things."[4] As a theory of value, it holds that "something is valuable if and only if it is rational for someone to value it, to assume a favorable attitude toward it" (17). For example, persons are valuable just because it is rational to adopt certain favorable attitudes toward them. Attitudes that it is rational to adopt are modes of valuing that are appropriate to their objects, and they include the following:

> Use, respect, appreciation, consideration, and love are five different ways of valuing things. A little reflection suggests more modes of valuation, such as honor, admiration, reverence, and toleration ... To value or care about something in a particular way involves a complex of standards for perception, emotion, deliberation, desire, and conduct that *express* and thereby communicate one's regard for the object's importance. (10–11)

Expressivist theory is non-consequentialist: claims about value, in Anderson's view, are translatable into claims about what it is rational to value, and this is turn is determined by "principles for *expressing* rational attitudes toward people."[5] There are favorable attitudes that it is rational to adopt toward persons who are intrinsically valuable, and it is good to act toward persons in ways that express these attitudes. Acting in these ways may be likely to bring about good consequences, but this is not what makes the actions good or gives them their moral value, on an expressivist account. Of course, the consequences of our actions do matter. But this is only because they cannot be ignored if we are to adequately express the appropriate attitudes toward persons. I especially want to note the emotional dimension of these attitudes, since I will have more to say about this later. In Anderson's words, "a mode of valuation includes distinctive emotional responses to the apprehension, achievement, and loss of things related to what is valued" (11).

The question of value that I am mainly interested in pertains to remembering people for what they have suffered from wrongdoing, i.e. remembering them as victims, which entails remembering the wrongdoing and often involves remembering the wrongdoers as well. (Remembering people for what they suffered includes remembering oneself as a victim or remembering one's own suffering if one has been the victim.) We can think of this from an expressivist standpoint as follows: whether or not there is value in remembering the victims depends on whether it is rational to value them in the manner in which we remember them—that is, on whether our remembering them expresses favorable attitudes toward them that it is rational for us to adopt. But what favorable attitudes satisfy this condition? This is what I turn to next.

(b) Rational attitudes and remembering

Self-respect. Self-respect is a favorable attitude that is a rational response to one's dignity as a person, and it is especially salient when one has been the victim of an unjustified and unexcused moral injury or is threatened with it. By "favorable attitude" I do not mean to suggest that the person who has self-respect will necessarily think that he deserves some special credit for maintaining it. Gabriele Taylor rightly criticizes this idea:

> To respect oneself is to have a sense of one's own value, and this requires a degree of self-confidence, a belief that he has got his expectations right. But a person who has such confidence in himself and whose relevant expectations are fulfilled need not therefore have a favourable attitude towards himself, for if he thinks of the matter at all he may just think that to behave in such ways or to be so treated is the least a person can expect, and so is not something to be proud of.[6]

The point is well taken if the thought that one has exceeded expectations is the favorable attitude in question. But self-respect is a favorable attitude in another sense, since "it includes a perception of one's own worth as being to some extent adequate and intact."[7] Someone who perceives his worth to be adequate and intact will normally feel good about himself, and have a favorable view of himself, because of this. As Taylor says, "retaining one's self-respect always supplies a ground of reason for self-esteem."[8] Though self-respect is not identical to self-esteem, retention of self-respect provides a reason for self-esteem, for the particular favorable attitude to oneself that self-esteem consists in.

Not all situations in which someone is harmed by another pose a threat to rational self-respect. Expressive norms would state that one lacks adequate grounds to "stand up" for oneself in these cases, so self-respect would not be an attitude that is always rationally triggered when one is harmed. If someone inadvertently and non-negligently harms you, or a young child or profoundly cognitively disabled person does something that harms you, it would not be rational to believe that they threaten your dignity or call into question your perception of your positive worth. To take offense and see these actions as demeaning would be to attribute to them an expressive meaning they do not have. However, when the harm results from culpable wrongdoing, from flagrant negligence or deliberate malice, it has a very different expressive meaning. Protesting, censuring, and claiming self-respect would then be appropriate expressions of an attitude that it is rational to have.

What is the relationship between remembering wrongdoing and self-respect? I want to answer this by first going over some familiar terrain. In chapter 1, I argued that negative emotions, retributive as well as non-retributive, can be linked to the virtue of self-respect and derive moral significance from this relationship. In some circumstances, victims might be moved to communicate their negative emotions to the wrongdoers in protest of the wrongful treatment they received at their hands, and then the expression of emotion defiantly announces that their self-respect will not permit them to acquiesce in the treatment. I also claimed that some negative emotional responses to wrongdoing can remain after forgiveness has been achieved and granted, and that the connection between them and the self-respect of victims is not necessarily severed because the wrongdoers have been forgiven. Memory, clearly, is implicated in these various possibilities. Concerns about past wrongful treatment and the assault on the bases of one's self-respect can influence the behavior, thoughts, and feelings of victims only if there is a memory of that wrongdoing; and if victims are conscious of that influence, they must also have conscious memories of the wrongs and their undeserved mistreatment. And so they commonly do, at least for a time and at least when the wrongs are serious. These memories are not adequately characterized in terms of their propositional content alone: they also have a particular emotional tone and coloring. Wrongdoing, especially when it is serious and recent, is naturally and frequently remembered by its victims in various negatively emotional ways. In these cases, the very emotions experienced in response to the past wrong at the time it was committed are commonly transmitted in some form to the memories the victims retain of it.

When the memories of wrongdoing are partially constituted by negative emotional responses to it, the memories derive moral value from the moral value of those emotions. For example, if the emotional responses constitutive of resentful or angry memories have moral value because they are appropriate responses to being wronged, then to that extent the memories themselves have moral value. This is not to say that it is always appropriate to remember being wronged with the same emotions that the wrongdoing originally and appropriately provoked, or that it is always appropriate to retain an emotional memory of it, or even any memory at all. These would be absurd claims. For one thing, wrongs to which victims responded emotionally at the time may be extremely distressing to them if they are remembered, and this reason may be sufficient to outweigh whatever reasons there may be to remember them or at least to remember them as they were remembered before. Or the wrongdoing might have occurred in the distant past, so that continuing to harbor negative feelings about it gives it greater importance in one's life than it deserves. The point is only that we can explain the value of emotional memories, assuming they have value, in terms of the value of the emotions with which they are intertwined.

Here is where self-respect can do some explanatory work. If these emotions have moral value because they are linked to the virtue of self-respect and indicate what actions one's self-respect will not permit one to do or acquiesce in or be complicit with, then memories of wrongdoing imbued with these emotions will also have moral value insofar as considerations of self-respect in relation to the wrongdoing remain relevant and appropriate.

Self-respect is a rational or fitting attitude to adopt in response to the unconditional value or dignity that one possesses as a person. When one is the victim of moral injury, self-respect acts as a defense against the demeaning or degrading message that it conveys and provides one with reason to resist the imputation of inferiority. Remembering wrongdoing is connected to this attitude by the emotions that are constitutive of the memories, and it can take different forms, including participation in commemorative activities that serve as a vehicle for expressing and asserting self-respect.

Self-respect operates on a communal level as well, and communal participation in commemorative activities can express and assert it. This is particularly important in the context of transitional societies, where entire communities may have been the victims of violence and repression. Self-respect motivates a community's assertion of its own value and self-protective actions when its integrity as a community is threatened. Communities as well as individuals are capable of self-respect, can have their self-respect assaulted, and can rightly resist the imputation of inferiority implicit in the actions of those who have harmed them as a community. Admittedly a community does not possess dignity as persons do: it is not a person writ large, with the very same moral properties as persons, only on a larger scale. So the self-respect of a community has a different moral grounding than the respect that individual persons have for themselves. Claims of community self-respect are warranted if there is an injury or threat to the integrity of a community or its way of life and the community or way of life is worth preserving. Even so, it is a mistake to suppose that community self-respect pertains to an entity that is ontologically distinct from the individuals who make up the community. Claims of self-respect are always made by individuals: the difference between individual self-respect and communal self-respect is that in the latter case the claims are made *collectively* by individuals whose self-respect is bound up with their membership in the community. The value of collective memory, moreover, can be explained in this way.

This gives us one answer to the question: In virtue of which rational attitudes is remembering wrongdoing and its victims intrinsically morally good? Remembering persons as victims can display and assert an attitude of self-respect;

that is, it can be what those engaged in remembering do out of respect for themselves and to maintain a grasp on their self-respect. It is in these cases a means by which individuals as well as communities express their rational regard for their own value as individuals and as communities.

Respect for persons. Individuals and communities might also remember victims other than themselves and, as in the previous case, remembering them can be rationalized as involving a response to the dignity of persons and can express the respect that is due it. In the specific circumstances of transitional societies, it can be undertaken to make amends for past wrongdoing by symbolically reinstating the respect that they were denied by those who mistreated them. Insofar as this is one of its aims, remembrance has a reparative purpose. Both those who have and those who do not have anything to make amends for can express respect for the victims in remembering them.

The respect at issue here is what Stephen Darwall calls "recognition respect," which he distinguishes from "appraisal respect."[9] "Appraisal respect is esteem that is merited or earned by conduct or character" (122); recognition respect is not a kind of esteem at all, but a response to the "dignity or authority" (123) of persons. "We respect something in the recognition sense," he says, "when we give it standing (or authority) in our relations to it" (123). The difference between the two kinds of respect is intuitively clear: it may be irrational to esteem a thoroughly despicable or totally incompetent person in virtue of his badness or incompetence, but he may nevertheless have dignity as a person and be entitled to recognition respect because of this. Further, recognition respect is not merely an inner sentiment or a way of feeling about a person. It is also manifested in one's deliberations concerning the object of respect and what one regards as appropriate and inappropriate ways of relating to him; and it entails the performance of various actions that express that respect. Both attitude and expression, sentiment and action, are important on an expressivist account.

Respect for the dignity of persons can mean different things, however, depending on one's account of the source or basis of dignity, and this is where Darwall's account makes a particularly valuable contribution. Forms of recognition respect differ, he argues, according to whether they are or are not fundamentally second-personal. Accounts of recognition respect that are not second-personal locate the source of dignity in some non-relational property of persons, such as the capacity for autonomous choice or the possession of human rights, rights that they have simply in virtue of their humanity. They are non-relational in the sense that they do not entail *the authority to demand* that others support their autonomy or accord them their rights. As Darwall puts it, "someone might accept the first-order norms that structure the dignity of persons and regulate himself scrupulously by them, without accepting anyone's authority to demand that he do so."[10] The sense of respect that Darwall adopts, and the one I adopt as well, is second-personal: it is grounded in the authority to demand that others comply with these norms and to hold them accountable for failures to adhere to them. Respect that is not second-personal, he claims, is not as respectful of persons as respect that is.

Perpetrators of serious wrongdoing are doubly disrespectful: they do not adhere in their conduct either to the first-order norms that structure the dignity of persons or to the second-order norm according to which persons have the authority to demand compliance with the first-order norms. Perpetrators deny the dignity of their victims both by violating their rights and by refusing to acknowledge that they are accountable to them for these violations. At the same time, perpetrators typically regard *themselves* as having the right to treat others in ways that they do not allow others to treat them. They regard themselves as entitled to make demands of those they victimize and to hold them accountable to them for failures to defer to their authority, but they regard others as not entitled to make the same demands of them. So accountability is not reciprocal. This is the full meaning of the disrespect that perpetrators show their victims. In societies fractured by violence and repression, exclusion of some from the social, political, and economic life of the community is also exclusion from, as Darwall puts it, a moral "community of mutually accountable equals."[11]

How is the value of respect for victims implicated in remembrance and the public practices that embody it? Memorialization, especially when combined with other measures to address the needs and rights of victims, can be a powerful and effective means of publicly showing respect. It does this in part by signifying recognition of the importance of taking responsibility for the mistreatment of those being memorialized. It does this as well by constituting, symbolically, an actual taking of responsibility for this mistreatment. Memorialization is also restorative in a moral sense, insofar as it symbolically rehumanizes victims, acknowledges that they were wrongfully treated, and—belatedly—gives them standing in the political community from which they were wrongfully excluded. Willful forgetting of the victims of wrongdoing is itself a denial of the moral significance of their suffering, and to some extent memorialization shows respect for the victims simply by keeping their suffering from fading from the public consciousness. However, all of this can be true even if there were nothing particularly second-personal about respect. Since I conceive of respect as a second-personal attitude, this raises the additional question of how this can be incorporated into practices of public remembrance.

The answer might seem to be that when the victims who are memorialized are dead, as is often the case, it can only be incorporated by a kind of fiction, by pretending that they are not dead and that it still makes sense to think of them as having the authority to demand compliance with norms of respectful treatment. But even conceding that there is a kind of fiction at work here, which is not obvious, the fiction is supposed to have some effect on the practice of memorializing, and the question is what sort of effect it can have and how it can have it. Here I think there is an obvious answer: it can have a practical effect on how the dead are memorialized if practices of memorialization incorporate second-personal respect for those living persons who have standing to represent and speak for the dead. Doing this, *as it were*, accords the dead the respect they were denied by recognizing the second-personal authority of their proxies. But it is not enough for memorial practices to incorporate this. These practices are, after all, only one ingredient in a package of initiatives, policies, and laws that should address the abuses of the past. Those with standing to speak for the dead, as well as for themselves, should be recognized as having authority to hold others accountable for how they remedy these abuses more broadly. To limit their authority to memorialization alone is unacceptably arbitrary.

I will have more to say about remembrance, memorialization, and respect for persons in chapter 6, since I regard respect in the recognition sense as having a special symbolic role in transitional societies. Respectful memorialization is something that all segments of the political community, and not only survivor communities and their members, can and should participate in. For this reason, it has greater potential to facilitate political reconciliation than practices of memorialization that engage and express the self-respect of victims but that others in the community might chiefly relate to only as outsiders.

I now want to move to a third attitude, different from self-respect but arguably interwoven with it as well.

Fidelity. I spoke just now of standing to speak for or represent the dead, and this leads me to the final attitude implicated in remembrance, namely fidelity or loyalty.[12] There is a connection between fidelity and the standing to represent, in that what grounds the loyalty of the living to the dead can also be what authorizes the living to speak for them.

There are, Brandon Hamber notes, "important connections between the dead and the living after political atrocity."[13] He emphasizes the therapeutic value of the living making a "psychological pact" with those they care about who have been killed:

> It is now widely accepted among bereavement theorists and practitioners that an ongoing relationship to the deceased is normative and necessary for adaptation to loss . . . Work on the notion of a continuing bond teaches us that bonds to the dead are important in dealing with loss, and that it is a misnomer to think of the relationship between the dead and the living as ever being severed.[14]

Michael Ignatieff calls this "keeping faith with the dead,"[15] and this is the third attitude that can be expressed in remembering the victims of wrongdoing and in the practices that embody it. As I think of it, keeping faith with the dead has moral not just psychological import, because there is a virtue of fidelity and remembrance can both express and exemplify it. There are also obligations associated with fidelity, obligations that remembrance can partially fulfill. Survivors of violence and human rights abuses commonly believe it to be imperative for them to remember relatives and community members who did not survive because they feel bound to keep faith with them, and arguably these feelings track actual obligations to remember, grounded in fidelity. Since fidelity to the dead plays such a central role in the thinking of survivors both during and after periods of conflict and repression, it is important to say something about what fidelity is and about how remembering the dead can both express and exemplify the attitude of keeping faith with them.

Fidelity, a term that I am using interchangeably with faithfulness, is a kind of attitude that, like respect, one can adopt toward objects that are valued for their own sake, and like respect can be rationally endorsed. It is possible to be faithful to objects of all sorts, including promises, individuals, social groups, organizations, intimate relationships, and causes. In each case, fidelity enlarges the field of one's concern beyond the narrow confines of self-interest, since one cannot be faithful to something or someone if self-interest determines the extent to which one devotes one's energies to it. Some of these objects, such as individuals and groups, can be said to have interests, and fidelity to them involves a commitment to protect and further their interests. Faithfulness also calls for a certain persistence in one's attachment to the object, by which I mean that one sticks to one's commitment despite inconvenience, temptation, or the difficulty of doing so. Finally, there are expressive requirements related to fidelity. One can only be counted as faithful to someone or something if one expresses this in action, deliberation, and emotion. Fidelity to another person involves the performance of many actions that express this particular way of valuing or caring about her, actions that will not be identical to those that demonstrate admiration, for example, since one can admire someone without being loyal to her. It also entails that in one's deliberations about the other person, one will give greater weight to her interests than to those of persons to whom one is not so attached in cases of conflict. Finally, faithfulness is expressed in one's sentiments or emotions: with respect to objects of fidelity of various sorts, it would be anomalous if not simply incoherent to claim that a person can be faithful even if he lacks any affective attachment to them. The attachment may involve strong feelings of intense devotion, as when the object is a loved one or close friend or a cause to which one dedicates one's life. Or it may be more subdued and not as powerfully motivating, yet still capable of exciting one's attention. In any event, since one is emotionally invested in the flourishing of the objects of one's loyalty, one will rejoice when one's efforts on their behalf succeed by whatever standard success

Commemoration and the Moral Values of Remembrance

is measured in the particular case, and one will be pained when one fails in this endeavor or is prevented from engaging in it. Loyalty to an object is a way of valuing it, and like other ways of valuing, it has its own characteristic standards for how that valuing is experienced and expressed, and when it is appropriate or warranted.

Keeping faith with the dead involves all of these elements. It is a bond between the living and the dead, a way of valuing them that involves a sentimental attachment to them and a prioritizing of their interests in deliberation and action. The dead, as such, have no interests, of course. But posthumous interests need not be understood as interests that the dead have *as dead*, but as interests they had while alive and that can be furthered or set back by actions taken by others after their deaths, what Janna Thompson calls "lifetime-transcending interests."[16] Among these interests are those that the living have in being remembered posthumously, interests in how, by whom, and with what accompanying narrative they will be remembered. These interests they have while alive are set back later, after their deaths, if they are forgotten, or if those they had reason to expect would protect their posthumous reputations do nothing to counter slanders or misrepresentations about them. Among other things, survivors who keep faith with the dead in social conditions of violence against certain members of society will, if necessary, act to protect their reputations and wrest control of their memories from those who would dishonor them by shifting the blame to them for creating the conditions that led to their deaths. The relation between these actions and keeping faith with the dead is constitutive. In other words, this is partly what keeping faith with the dead consists in. Moreover, survivors who do not keep faith with the dead when loyalty is owed are subject to moral criticism for being unfaithful to the antemortem persons who are now dead.

Keeping faith with the dead involves keeping faith with persons one had some sort of relationship with while they were alive, and obligations of fidelity are responsive to this fact. That is, they are also in part obligations to be faithful to the character of the antemortem relationship. Survivors are called upon to keep faith with the dead, when they are, because this is a moral implication of the prior relationship they had with the victims, so keeping faith with the dead ought to reflect the kind of relationship they had. To illustrate the role of relationship, consider the case of the death of a loved one. While she is alive, loving her consists in part in manifold expressions of care and affection for her, and the one who loves her is properly criticized if he is insufficiently attentive to her needs and interests. Crucially, however, the reasons that love gives him to show special regard for his beloved do not end with but survive her death. To be sure, the death of the loved one will have a significant impact on how he can express his love, since ways of showing love are informed and shaped by responses from the one who is loved, and she can no longer respond. But there is still much that he could do to express his continuing devotion to and affection for her, and there are ways of deliberating and feeling that would show this as well. For example, he could cherish the plans and projects she had while alive by making them his own after her death, and in other ways he could express his continuing love for her by cherishing her memory. This close identification with her and hence with her surviving interests would naturally and appropriately find expression in actions and emotions that differ from those involved in furthering the surviving interests of those to whom one is related more distantly.

There are various sorts of relationships that survivors can have to the victims and that entail particular norms that govern what the survivors must do to keep faith with them. The victims might be fellow countrymen or they might be related to the survivors as members of the same religion, ethnic group, professional association, family, village, and so on. To keep faith with the dead one must be faithful to many things: to how one knew them, to the character of the prior relationship one had with them, and to the particular importance they had for oneself because of this. An appropriate expression of fidelity to another is significantly determined by the moral and other standards governing the particular relationship in question, from the intimate to the familiar to the relatively impersonal, and this remains true after the other's death.

Another factor that bears on how one keeps and should keep faith with the dead has to do with how the person died, whether under more or less normal circumstances or, as in the cases that are typical of many transitional circumstances, in extraordinary circumstances of government-orchestrated or -tolerated human rights violations or civil conflict. In general, keeping faith with the dead who are known or presumed to have been murdered (presumed in the case of the "disappeared") involves actions and emotions that are specific to and reflect the circumstances of their deaths and that differ from usual emotional and behavioral reactions to loss in more ordinary circumstances. Within the former group there are further distinctions as well. When those who were murdered or disappeared are loved ones, as opposed to, say, fellow community members, keeping faith with them is distinguished by the emotions and ways of deliberating and acting that flow from the nature of the love relationship.

These then are three attitudes that, when expressed in activities and practices of remembering wrongdoing and its victims, make that remembering an intrinsically valuable activity: self-respect, respect for persons, and fidelity (to the dead). As such they contrast with the reasons for remembering that focus on the expected utility of doing so. Moreover, these attitudes are not only expressed in and through the actions, emotions, and deliberations of individuals considered apart from the communities to which they belong. They are also expressed by persons whose identities are bound up with their membership in particular communities and who, in expressing them, ally themselves with others in their community. When these attitudes are *shared* among the members of a community and *jointly* expressed by them, they partially constitute the community to which they belong and become the attitudes of the community itself. They become collective attitudes, collective because they arise from the way members of the group understand themselves in relation to one another; from their shared emotional reactions to events in their common experience and history; and from their commitment to join with others in expressing attitudes as a single body.[17]

The claim that there can be collective attitudes of self-respect, respect for persons, and fidelity might be thought to be merely metaphorical extensions of their literal application to individual cases. But they are no more metaphorical than comparable claims about collective memory or collective intentions and, I take it, there is substantial philosophical support for nonreductive accounts of these phenomena.[18] Further, the notion of collective attitudes, which can be vindicated philosophically, is an integral part of an adequate account of memorial practices in both transitional and ordinary circumstances: it helps to explain the character of many of the practices dedicated to the victims of wrongdoing. These are practices not only of individuals considered severally but of groups and communities of individuals, and they are valuable as collective phenomena. A nonreductive account of collective attitudes, along with a defense of the intrinsic value of these attitudes, can explain why they are.

To sum up, there are several moral reasons to remember wrongdoing and its victims. They can be categorized as consequentialist or non-consequentialist; they operate on an individual as well as a collective level; and they explain why it is good and also why it is imperative to remember. But the values of remembrance have to be embedded in social practices, projects, and institutions with memorial intent and effect if remembrance is actually to promote the work of restorative justice and political reconciliation in transitional societies. This embedding is what I regard as the moral work of memorialization. Practices, projects, and institutions of remembrance have moral value because remembrance itself has moral value, and processes of memorialization ought to reflect and serve the values that give remembrance its distinctive moral significance. But when and how people and events should be memorialized is also a political judgment, and political judgments are not based, nor should they be based, on moral considerations alone.

3. Problems of compatibility and sustainability

There are two main problems related to remembrance that I take up in this chapter: one has to do with the compatibility of forgiveness and memorialization, the other with the durability of remembrance in public memorials. I will here only flag the first issue and will return to it after I have discussed the nature of commemorative rituals. I spend most of this section on the second.

Remembrance of wrongdoing and its victims, and the memorial practices and institutions in which it is embedded, are deeply moral phenomena, and they have several purposes. Commonly, remembrance, even if offenders have been forgiven, is for some time imbued with negative emotional energy, with emotions that victims—and possibly offenders—are susceptible to because of their evaluative attitudes toward themselves and others. In particular, emotions evincing self-respect can color and inform remembrance of wrongdoing, individually as well as collectively, and they can do the same after offenders have been forgiven. In other words, the negative emotions implicated in remembrance and those that may remain after forgiveness can be morally significant for the same reason. Commemorations can provide a context and vehicle for the assertion of self-respect, and one way they do this is by means of the negative emotions they elicit and sustain, negative emotions that are not necessarily wiped clean by forgiveness or rendered of no particular moral value because of it.

However, the self-respect that commemorative practices signify can be carried too far. As Lester Hunt says, "it is quite possible to rate too highly the importance of the things that are the concerns of self-respect."[19] One consequence of rating this too highly, or indication that one has rated it too highly, might be that commemoration imperils forgiveness—that is, threatens to undo whatever fragile reconciliation forgiveness has been part of and to put forgiveness farther out of reach if it has not yet been attained. The larger problem here has to do with whether forgiveness can be compatible with memorialization and the conditions under which this is possible, and I will return to it later in this chapter.

The second issue has to do with the duration of remembrance. The issue here is whether and how memorialization can be an effective restorative justice practice and help prevent the recurrence of wrongdoing over the long term. Different kinds of memorial projects and practices are in theory compatible with forgiveness. But compatibility with forgiveness is not the only criterion for judging their appropriateness and moral value, and not all of them score equally well when other criteria are taken into account. Other criteria include whether the memorial is actually able to influence the collective memory of the community and to stir its collective conscience. It would be important to know if the memorial is capable of generating strong interest among its participants and members of its intended audience in the plight of victims and of motivating them to redress and repudiate the wrongs of the past. Memorials are also ranked better or worse, not just from an aesthetic but a moral standpoint, on the basis of how long they can be expected to continue to do these worthwhile things, to express respect for the victims, to foster self-respect among the survivors, to enable them to keep faith with the dead, and to promote critical reflection on past wrongs. Duration is a moral criterion for judging the adequacy of memorial practices that presupposes but is distinct from the criteria already discussed. Moreover, as I will show later, emotion has a critical part to play in explaining how duration is possible. It is largely through memory's ability to elicit emotion that the past exerts causal influence on the deliberations and actions of the rememberer; and it is largely through its ability to continue to elicit emotion that the past transmits this influence over time.

There is an obvious moral principle for how long to engage in commemorative activities: if a particular activity of remembrance has the moral values I have attributed to it, then ceteris paribus, it should persist for as long as it continues to have, and there is reason to believe it continues to have, these values. But the expressive values of remembrance discussed above are essentially not time limited. There are no precisely specifiable criteria by which we can determine that, from this point on, the expression of attitudes of self-respect, respect for victims, or keeping faith with the dead in commemoration no longer has value. There is no definite timetable for this, for how long to remember, and it is even unclear just what having such a timetable would mean. Values do not generally come prelabeled with a date of expiration and expressivist values typically remain in force for an indefinite period of time. Showing respect and keeping faith are not like paying off a debt or fulfilling the terms of a contract: they do not consist in the performance of a set of specific acts that releases one from any further demands related to the debt or contract in question.

Where consequentialist considerations are in play, it takes time (and much else besides) to find out how long one needs to remember. The institutional and social conditions that supported and facilitated injustice and oppression, and the bitterness and distrust fostered by them, are not likely to be remedied by short-term efforts alone. Political relationships may fray again, and once repaired must be made secure. If remembrance of wrongdoing is critical to the success of the transition, then the victims and perpetrators and their descendants will need to remember the wrongdoing for as long as the work of transition goes on, and transitions generally take considerable time, sometimes several generations. There is also the continuing instrumental importance of remembrance after the transition has been completed, for which provision must be made.

Thus, the expressive norms governing memorial activities are open-ended both in terms of what they tell us to do and for how long they tell us to do it. And if remembrance is valued for its consequences, these often take considerable time to materialize, given the tortuous course of many transitions. This gives rise to a critical question for what we might call a *moral politics* of memory: how can members and agents of the political community help remembrance last for as long as it should? This is a particularly pressing problem in transitional settings

196   FORGIVENESS AND REMEMBRANCE

where worries about rekindling past resentments and reigniting conflict might lead to the suppression of memories.

There are various ways to keep the memories of wrongdoing alive, of course. Section 4 gives *an* answer, an answer that is also intended to be a response to concerns about whether forgiveness is imperiled by memorialization. Commemorative rituals, I will argue, can help solve what I call the problem of the sustainability of memory and, as I will further claim in section 6, they can do this in a way that is compatible with forgiveness. It is in part because of the emotive character of these practices that collective memories of wrongdoing are strengthened and maintained over long periods of time. Of course, memorial practices can involve emotions incompatible with forgiveness and still have the same effect on the duration of memories of wrongdoing as those that involve other sorts of negative emotions. But we should prefer those that are compatible with forgiveness if forgiveness is warranted and part of a just political reconciliation.

(a) The sustainability of individual and collective memories

Let me start by clarifying the notion of durability. The durability of memory is a different feature of memory from its accuracy. Memories that are well-entrenched and long-lasting may nevertheless be distorted in various ways and in different ways at different times. As the behavioral neuroscientist James L. McGaugh observes about individual memory:

> We can, and certainly do, have memories that are both strong [i.e., last over time] and *inaccurate*. As we all know, our family members and close friends are often joyously helpful in noting and pointing out our mis-recollections.[20]

A similar distinction between durability and accuracy can be found with respect to collective memories. Mark Osiel describes one way in which the distortion of collective memory gains a foothold:

> Collective memory consists of past reminiscences that link given groups of people for whom the remembered events are important, that is, the events remain significant to them later on . . . As the events in question recede further into the past and those who experienced them directly no longer remain alive, the "memory" becomes, more precisely, a memory of a memory, that is, a memory of what others have told future generations about their pasts.[21]

"A memory of a memory," unchecked by the recollections of those with direct experience of the original event, is easily manipulated to serve political and other ends regardless of the truth of its representations. A memory of a memory—and as the generations stretch farther into the future, a memory of a memory of a memory, etc.—of momentous events in the history of a society is likely to construct the past along lines other than fidelity to the truth, and to do so increasingly with the passage of time. Past events may take on mythic overtones, and myth may be mistaken for literal truth. Yet though it misrepresents the past in important respects, such a narrative is capable of arousing the passions of its members and guiding their collective actions from one generation to the next. It may in fact be capable of these effects precisely because those who tell it are not terribly concerned about the accuracy of the historical record.

In societies with recent histories of violence and widespread human rights abuses, there are reasons to value both the long-term retention of collective memories of wrongdoing and the accuracy of these memories. Accuracy is important because the perpetrators and their supporters typically attempt to justify their actions by demeaning the victims and falsifying and misrepresenting the historical record; and durability is important because the expressive and instrumental values of remembrance require it. Both the content of the memories and their durability are important if remembrance is to promote the moral reconstruction of political relationships. Significant past wrongful acts and their victims should be well remembered over time, and collective memories of them should in salient respects be free of error as well as long-lasting. Hence, those in transitional societies who are tasked with or undertake responsibilities for memorializing the wrongs of the past, or who are in a position to influence those who have such responsibilities, should aim to ensure the sustainability of accurate memories, not just sustainability *simpliciter*. Even after the transition is completed—and it may be difficult to say exactly when this is—there may be reasons to value the durability and accuracy of memories of past wrongdoing, especially if the society in question has a long history of political upheaval and civil conflict.

Memory accuracy is a problem because memories are susceptible to interference, manipulation, and distortion, and it is a moral problem to the extent that there are moral reasons to resist or correct this. Memory sustainability is a problem because, to put it simply, events retained in memory are susceptible to forgetting, and there may good reasons, political as well as moral, why this should be prevented. Collective forgetting in particular has many explanations. It may result from state-imposed policies that discourage, stifle, or penalize critical reflection on past wrongs. Social and cultural transformations also shape attitudes toward the past in destructive ways. As a number of cultural critics have noted, they may direct attention away from the past by fostering the belief that there is nothing valuable to learn from it and that it is largely irrelevant to present interests and concerns. Thus, Eric Hobsbawm observes that "the destruction of the past, or rather of the social mechanisms that link one's contemporary experience to that of earlier generations, is one of the most characteristic and eerie phenomena of the late twentieth century."[22] And Andreas Huyssen points to "the undisputed waning of history and historical consciousness" as a product of central features of our culture.[23]

Apart from these features, there is a phenomenon on the collective level that resembles one on the individual: the accumulation over time of layers and layers of new memories that bury earlier ones and make them more difficult to retrieve. This happens in the lives of individuals, and for a similar reason life in common with others produces collective experiences that, in volume and significance, may be enough to weaken the impact of earlier collective memories. Memories, collective as well as individual, tend to lose vividness and strength over time and become increasingly difficult to retrieve as the time from the original event lengthens. Of course, while there are similarities between the two cases, there are also important differences: the processes and mechanisms that explain the decline of collective memory over time are different from those that explain the decline of individual memory. In the case of individual memories, their tendency to fade with time is explained ultimately in terms of the operation of psychological mechanisms and corresponding changes in underlying brain systems. In the case of collective memories, their waning is traceable to features of the political, social, and cultural contexts of remembrance. Still, the similarities just in terms of the significance of the passage of time are noteworthy.

The problem of the sustainability of memory presupposes that memories have already been formed, the question then being how to maintain them over time. But of course there is a prior concern, and this returns us to the issue of accuracy, for a problem relating to historical memory that arises in transitional contexts is precisely the absence of an informed, widely disseminated collective memory of wrongdoing. Ruti Teitel discusses what is needed to correct this problem in two different sorts of transitional contexts, one post-military dictatorship, the other post-Communist:

> In the postmilitary transitions, when the predecessor dictatorship acted with utter impunity, failing even to concede the fact of the wrongs committed, historical justice signified a *construction* of state history, a *building up* of documentation, largely through testimony witness by witness. In the former Communist bloc, such official narratives have largely been eschewed, for documentation abounds; historical justice implies a *tearing open* of amassed state history, file by file.[24]

Collective memories are formed by assembling documentation of wrongdoing, in the one case, and by opening up access to secret state archives, in the other.

The evident importance of these measures to enhance collective memory shows that the value of sustaining memories is not independent of their content and quality. Memories from which witness testimony has been precluded by a military dictatorship, or memories that a repressive Communist regime has seen fit to allow a society to have, might be sustained by public memorials of different sorts, including rituals, monuments, and museums, but they are hardly memories whose survival we should applaud. Even if there is some instrumental value in sustaining them for the short term, this hardly compensates for the wrong and harm it does.

The reasons to object to sustaining memories of this sort are several, and both consequentialist and expressive considerations are involved: among other things, it perpetuates and strengthens the repressive power of the state; dishonors the victims; denies them the opportunity for validation and vindication; and impedes the efforts of survivors to keep faith with their dead. Clearly not all memories are worth sustaining, only those that, especially in transitional settings, are reasonably accurate and that are not objectionable in one of these other ways. My focus on the importance of sustainability should not be construed as a denial of this. On the contrary, the moral argument for sustainability is a qualified one, restricted to memories that are accurate and for other reasons worth preserving.

(b) Sustainability and emotion

There has been considerable recent experimental and clinical research in psychology on the relationship between emotion and memory, more specifically the contribution of emotion to the retention and retrieval of memories.[25] The consensus view, borne out by ordinary experience, is that memories of emotional events, particularly those that generate strong emotional reactions, tend to persist longer than memories of emotionally neutral events. Although emotional memories are subject to fading over time, just like neutral ones, their deterioration is slowed down, perhaps for a considerable period of time, because of the emotional reaction at the time the memories are, in the language of cognitive psychology, laid down. Gail Goodman and Pedro Paz-Alonzo put it this way:

> There is evidence to indicate that memories of traumatic and emotional events tend to be well retained over time, especially compared to memory for more mundane events.[26]

Many cognitive psychologists and behavioral neuroscientists have made the same observation. Here is another from psychologist Daniel Reisberg:

Emotional memories also seem to be long lasting. More specifically, evidence suggests that emotion slows the process of forgetting, so that emotional episodes are eventually forgotten, but the rate of forgetting is slower than that for neutral episodes.[27]

For the sake of clarity we should distinguish here between different senses of "emotional memories." The above quotes are not referring to the emotional quality of the memories themselves, but to that of the episodes remembered. In other words, they are not imputing to the memories what Richard Wollheim calls an "affective tone." To be sure, as Wollheim notes and these authors perhaps assume, memories of emotional events may have an "affective tendency"; that is, there may be a "tendency for the original affective complex to set itself up anew in the mind of the rememberer."[28] But this tendency is not always actualized, one reason being the length of time between the experience of the event and later recall. It may happen therefore that the memory of an emotional event is not itself an emotional memory of that event, in the sense of "emotional memory" that I explained in chapter 2. Instead, the memory, when some retrieval cue triggers recall, may generate little or no emotional reaction in the rememberer and be largely devoid of feeling. Or it may generate a significantly diminished, less intense emotional response. Whatever the emotional quality of the memories themselves, psychological research tells us that the circumstances of their origin give memories of emotional events an advantage in terms of durability over memories of emotionally neutral events.

There is much discussion in the scientific literature about precisely why memories of emotional events last longer than memories of neutral ones. Some of the explanations are biological, referring to particular chemical processes in various regions of the brain.[29] Others are cognitive. Friderike Heuer and Reisberg offer the following account:

> It does seem likely that emotional events are more distinctive than neutral ones, and this by itself may promote memory. In particular, the distinctiveness may create a retrieval advantage, which would be particularly evident with the passage of time and so would be manifest as slowed forgetting . . . A final contribution to the slowed forgetting of emotional events comes from the extra attention and rehearsal that these events receive. Emotional events are, by their nature, often worth thinking about. Emotional events often have consequences for one's life and the lives of others, and these are also worth contemplation. For these reasons, emotionality may lead subjects to rehearse the material more than they otherwise might, once again leading to slower forgetting.[30]

The positive effects on memory of closer attention and fuller rehearsal tend to diminish with time, but empirical studies on memory retention give us some reason to think that this fading can be slowed if emotions periodically accompany the memories at the time of *recall*. These subsequent pairings may strengthen the memories and produce better long-term retention. In effect, the emotion–memory pair becomes a new emotional event, acting to bolster or compensate for the waning effects of the emotions that were experienced at the time the memories were laid down. As a consequence of these emotion–memory pairings, the original events benefit from renewed attention and rehearsal, and unless the process is somehow disrupted, this leads to more durable memories. If this is right, then emotion is connected to the sustaining of memories in two ways. Events with a strong emotional character tend to be more durably remembered than events without it; and emotions can retard forgetting if they are experienced in conjunction with memories of the original events and if these emotions are related to the original events in the right way.

These findings about the effects of emotion on memory suggest a possible approach to one of the moral challenges transitional societies confront in promoting political reconciliation, namely how to make it durable: they can enlist the social sharing of emotions in the service of remembrance. And they may be able to do this in such a way that remembrance is extended beyond the victims of wrongdoing and is given an enduring presence in the life of the larger society. Among the victims themselves, memories of the abuses to which they were subjected tend to be long-lasting, because they were traumatic and generated strong negative emotional reactions from them. Among these are powerful feelings of anger, resentment, and indignation that target the leaders, agents, and collaborators of the former regime and motivate violent, vengeful, or retaliatory actions. There are also likely to be other negative emotions intermingled with these, as I pointed out earlier, such as grief, fear, mistrust, and shame. The memories will partake of at least some of the "original affective complex" that ensures their persistence for some period of time. They will not just be *of* emotionally charged events, but will themselves *be* emotionally charged events. And as long as the emotions persist, which in the context of the wrongs that haunt transitional societies is likely to be some time, they sustain the memories of wrongdoing, fortifying and animating them.

As I noted in chapter 4, there is frequently a gap between the political process of political reconstruction and the emotional struggle of victims and survivors, and this is a core problem for societies attempting to repair political relationships that have been damaged by violence and oppression. The emotional responses of victims and survivors do not tend to lose their intensity in lockstep with significant progress on the national or political front and their memories of wrongdoing are sustained by them. But there is another problem as well, related not to the emotions of the victims but to the emotions that others share with them. The problem is that unless the emotions of others more broadly can be engaged, public memory projects are likely to have only a small base of genuine support in one segment of the larger society, where they will last only as long as the memories of wrongdoing retain their emotional force.

The duration of *obligations* to remember wrongdoing and the duration of *memories* of that wrongdoing, however, do not normally coincide, and this is true even if these memories are widely disseminated across the society. Emotions can make the memories of wrongdoing last longer, but the duration of memories does not determine the duration of obligations to remember it. It may be possible, however, for the two to be more closely aligned with each other and for the duration and locus of memories of wrongdoing (how long it is remembered and by whom) to more closely approximate the duration and locus of obligations of remembrance. This is what the social sharing of emotions can accomplish, since emotion seems to have significant memory-enhancing effects when it accompanies recall, and the more widely the emotions are shared the more widely these effects are felt.

It is still unclear, however, how the connection between emotion and memory enhancement can be utilized in transitional societies so that obligations of remembrance are taken seriously across the society and the moral work of memorialization is sustained over the long term. This is the subject of the next section. Before turning to this, however, I want to briefly note a concern about a presupposition of the argument there.

The studies about emotion and memory retention to which I have referred are from the literature of individual psychology and do not address the relationship between emotion as a collective phenomenon and memory retention. Yet the argument in the next section does assume, plausibly I think, that there is a relationship here that parallels the relationship noted in the psychological literature. So the question is bound to arise what it means to say that a group of people can be angry, or profoundly sad, or deeply disappointed, or ashamed, or grief-stricken. This is a question I have addressed before, so let me say just a word about it here.

Attributions of emotions to groups can be given either a reductive/individualistic or a holistic analysis. According to the individualistic analysis of group emotions, only individuals can feel anger, sadness, etc. They may feel these emotions because of what the group they belong to has done, but the emotions are still felt by individuals, not by them collectively as a group. However, when there are enough of them who have this feature in common, we can say that, in a manner of speaking, the group to which they belong feels them. Holism denies that collective terms referring to emotions are always analyzable as referring to the sum of the attitudes and emotions of constituent members of the collective. According to holistic analyses, the subjects of these emotions constitute genuine collectives: it is *we* who feel a certain way, not *me* and *you* and *you*. What licenses us to speak this way about groups is a subject of considerable debate within the philosophy of the social sciences, and it would be too much of a digression to enter into it here. (I discussed this briefly in chapter 3.[31]) Nevertheless, in my view it is only a holistic analysis that can properly explain how emotions are experienced within the context of commemorative ceremonies and rituals. Those who participate in commemorative ceremonies and rituals share their memories with one another and thereby form a community of memory; they collectively respond to what is being commemorated with whatever emotions the rituals elicit. If we can intelligibly speak about co-rememberers sharing their memories, as I believe we can, then we can intelligibly speak about the emotions that accompany these memories being shared as well.

4. Commemorative rituals and the persistence of memory

Whatever the complete psychological explanation of emotion's ability to slow the rate of forgetting, both as experienced in the initial encounter and at the time of remembering, sufficient empirical evidence exists to support such an influence, and we can plausibly attribute to collective emotion a similar influence on the retention of collective memories. If, as Reisberg says, "emotional events are well-rehearsed and often discussed with others, and this rehearsal and discussion promote memory,"[32] and if the rehearsal and sharing of emotional events among individuals makes the experience of those events a communal phenomenon, then the rehearsal and sharing should also promote a group's shared memory. (There is no assurance, of course, that a group's collective memories will be free of systematic error. As I noted earlier, duration and accuracy are features of memory that may come apart.) This, at any rate, is a possibility I want to develop in this section.

A brief word of clarification to avoid misunderstanding: to say that collective emotions can sustain collective memories is not to offer this as an all-things-considered reason to endorse these emotions. The point harks back to the one I made earlier in discussing the duration and accuracy of memory: longevity as such is morally neutral. There are multiple moral criteria by which to assess the value of long-term memories: they are good or bad depending on their content and the uses to which they are put. The badness of some memories might actually be exacerbated by their being long term.

Specifically, the social sharing of emotions, even if it does promote collective memories, is not always helpful to the process of restorative justice and political reconciliation. There are two issues to consider here: what emotions are shared and by whom. The sharing of hostile emotions, for example, may revive conflict and undermine prospects for establishing or reestablishing relations of respect and trust among former antagonists. Even if outright hostile behavior is not a consequence, the social sharing of emotions might create divided communities ruled by a kind of "us versus them" mentality and with not enough in common to collaborate on rebuilding the political and social order. The emotions that are shared among the perpetrators might only strengthen their refusal to accept responsibility for past wrongdoing or reinforce their unwillingness to cooperate in the rebuilding of political relationships. And those that are shared among the victims might heighten their defensiveness and prevent them from seeing that the perpetrators no longer pose a threat to them and are worthy of their trust. In the latter case, forgiveness may be warranted, and the social sharing of negative emotions could then be faulted for standing in its way.

The following discussion is intended to illuminate the particular contribution that commemorative ceremonies can make to restorative justice and political reconciliation in transitional societies emerging from civil conflict and political repression. The distinctive contribution is made possible by their prolonging the memory of wrongdoing over the long term and keeping the past from becoming an object of mere antiquarian interest; and if the ceremonies are inclusive, they may be able to help bridge intercommunal divisions in a period of sociopolitical upheaval and change. From the standpoint of actual transitional societies, the account of commemorative rituals that I will present is admittedly something of an idealization, but it is nonetheless useful because it sheds light on what needs to happen if actual commemorative rituals are to help sustain a just reconciliation over the long term.

(a) The nature of commemorative ceremonies and rituals

I now want to start making good on the suggestion that collective emotions, specifically negative emotions, can be generated to prolong collective memories of past wrongdoing across society. I have in mind a particular vehicle or mode of memorialization, different from monuments, memorial spaces, and memorial museums. These can influence the formation of a sense of the collective past, but their influence is commonly short-lived and socially limited, short-lived and limited, that is, unless and until they are accompanied and surrounded by civic ceremonies and commemorative activities. The incorporation of these memorials in civic ceremonies and commemorations sustains interest in the past by infusing public remembrance with shared emotion and making the remembering itself an emotional occasion. The historian Geoffrey Cubitt remarks on the peculiar character of this mode of memorializing, contrasting it with other practices that shape a community's sense of its past:

The emphasis that studies of social memory have frequently placed on the analysis of such [public commemorative] activities is not . . . completely misplaced: commemorative occasions and ceremonies do indeed contributive distinctively, and in many social settings vitally, to making the past an active rather than a passive element in people's social awareness.[33]

Commemorative activities and ceremonies are capable of doing this, of making the past an "active" and "vital" presence in people's lives, in part because they have an emotional character and make the past emotionally present. Through them, the past is relived emotionally, although not necessarily in the sense that the past is remembered with the very same feelings the participants experienced initially. This may happen, but the past can also be brought to life by emotions that serve as a kind of surrogate for the original feelings. In these cases, the experience of the participants in commemorative ceremonies shadows that of the original experience of the victims in the sense that some negative animating emotion (different from the original) still targets the wrongdoing. In any case, as follows from my earlier remarks about the connection between emotionality and long-term retention of memories, it is to the emotional character of commemorations that we should look for an explanation of how they can sustain remembrance over time.

In order to more fully explain how they can do what I claim they can do for memory retention, I want to focus on a particular type of commemorative ceremony that shows in the clearest way how commemorative activities can sustain interest in memorials of other sorts and counteract the erosion of memory over the long term. The notion of "commemorative ceremonies" encompasses a variety of activities: some are one-off occasions; some are repeated at regular intervals; some are rule-governed; some are loose and unstructured; some are idiosyncratic events having little in common with other ceremonies; and so on. I am concerned with one type of commemorative ceremony, the type that evokes the past through ritualized activity, what I call commemorative rituals. Commemorative ceremonies that are not rituals, strictly speaking, may nonetheless contain elements of and include references to commemorative practices that are.

Like Cubitt, Paul Connerton, in his influential book *How Societies Remember*,[34] maintains that commemorative ceremonies—by which he means commemorative rituals—have special significance as vehicles for the formation of social memory. Social memory is the memory that belongs to groups, ranging in size from "small face-to-face societies" to "territorially extensive societies" (1) and, he argues, it is embodied in and conveyed and sustained to a large extent by such ceremonies. By conveying and sustaining the collective memory of a group, commemorative ceremonies contribute to a sense among the members of the group that they form a collective. Connerton explains this sense of being a collective partly in terms of shared meaningful narratives linking present to past events, analogous to personal memory. Collective ceremonies remind a community "of its identity as represented by and told in a master narrative." They make "sense of the past as a kind of collective autobiography, with some explicitly cognitive components" (70). Connerton emphasizes, however, that commemorative ceremonies are not merely composed of cognitive elements and that competence in carrying out or participating in the ceremony is not simply a cognitive matter. The collective autobiography "is more than a story told and reflected on; it is a cult enacted" (70), a type of ritual performance.

Connerton follows Steven Lukes in defining ritual as "rule-governed activity of a symbolic character which draws the attention of its participants to objects of thought and feeling which they hold to be of special significance" (44). Commemorative ceremonies, located within the larger category of ritual, have two features in common with other sorts of rituals, "formalism and performativity; and in so far as they function effectively as mnemonic devices they are able to execute that function in large part because they possess such features" (61). Rituals are formalized in the sense that they tend to be "stylised, stereotyped and repetitive" (44) and therefore susceptible of little variation from one occasion to another. As Israel Scheffler puts it, "a ritual performance alludes to its own past kin, just as it may point back to a commemorated event."[35] That is, one performance of a ritual is the ritual equivalent or replica of another performance of the same ritual, and the evocation of this equivalence is one of the central functions of ritual performance. This allusion to past ritual performances helps to establish the legitimacy of the ritual in the minds of the participants by assuring them that they are engaging in a practice that has a long history.

Rituals, and so ritualized commemorative ceremonies, are also performative in character. The performativeness of rituals partly relates to the verbal utterances they involve, utterances that do not merely give a description of or convey information about an action, but rather constitute an action of some kind in being uttered. Criminal trials, which resemble commemorative ceremonies in being a kind of official construction of collective memory, have this ritualistic element among others: when a criminal tribunal issues a verdict of guilty, it is not merely making a statement about the culpability of the offender, but "finding" him guilty. Performatives are also "encoded in set postures, gestures, and movements" (59). In general, there must be some type of enactment in commemorative rituals, and it must have a symbolic relationship to and be expressly linked to an originating event in the past. Finally, according to Connerton, rituals are "as it were the place in which the community is constituted and recalls to itself the fact of its constitution" (59). The community-constituting character of commemorative ceremonies is also something Cubitt emphasizes,

Commemoration and the Moral Values of Remembrance 207

and I will return to it later. I will also come back to the feature of repetitiveness that partly defines what a ritual is, since this plays an important role in explaining how commemorative rituals are able to sustain the memory of wrongdoing over time.

First, however, I want to discuss the emotive dimension of rituals. Rituals have a number of functions with respect to emotion: generative, educative, and regulative. Rituals elicit emotions in participants (on an ongoing basis) by drawing their attention to emotionally laden events; they teach participants what emotions it is appropriate for them to have in relation to certain events; and they regulate the emotions that they elicit or that participants bring to the ritual activity by providing channels for their expression. I call the latter feature of rituals *disciplined emotionality*. To expand on these points, especially the last one, I want to turn to the work of two philosophers who have made important contributions to our understanding of ritual, whether from the standpoint of commemoration or more broadly: Edward Casey and Susanne Langer.

Expressing surprise that there has not been more philosophical discussion of this "most elusive" form of remembering, Casey in his book *Remembering*[36] offers a remarkably nuanced account of the nature, purposes, and modes of commemoration. There are, he notes, different commemorative vehicles or *commemorabilia,* such as rituals or texts. But whatever vehicle is adopted, what one does with it or through it (i.e., commemorating), "is an essentially *inter*-personal action. It is undertaken not only in relation *to* others and *for* them but also *with* them in a common action of communalizing" (225). Moreover, commemorating is a way of taking the past seriously, of "acknowledging its importance to oneself or others" (224). Not all ways of taking the past seriously commemorate or memorialize it, in Casey's sense of this term, however. What memorialization adds to taking the past seriously is "honoring" or "paying homage" to the past, which includes "paying fitting tribute" to it in words and deeds and seeking to do it "in a lasting way" (226). My primary interest here is what Casey has to say about one particular vehicle of commemoration, namely ceremonial observances that memorialize the past through ritualized activity.

Casey's account of commemorative rituals includes the features I have already noted, "repetitiveness in observance" (224) and "formality" (225), and his discussion of formality also makes mention of the emotional aspect of commemoration. It is not surprising that he should take it to have some sort of connection to emotion, given what he says about taking the past seriously. Commemoration, after all, is one way of taking the past seriously and this is "a matter of letting the past *matter*" (224), something that I assume often involves letting the past register emotionally in one's life (although, as Casey points out, "I can take the past seriously without having to assume a dour attitude"). But there is

208   FORGIVENESS AND REMEMBRANCE

a more specific function that ritual has vis-à-vis emotion, which he explains as
follows: "Formality serves to express and specify emotion while channeling any
tendency to excess. The formality of ritual solemnizes the expression of emotion
on the occasion" (225).

Commemorative rituals have various effects on the emotional states of the
individuals involved. By "specify emotion" I take it Casey is suggesting that the
formality of rituals helps participants identify the specific emotions it is appropriate or fitting for them to feel under the circumstances; and by "channeling
any tendency to excess," formality divests negative emotions of their dangerous
quality and teaches participants how they should express them in ways that are
socially acceptable and personally manageable. (As I note below, commemorative rituals can inflame emotions rather than discipline them. They may begin in
a disciplined way, but the power of the emotions cannot be contained by them.
They have failed to do what rituals are supposed to do, and so can be considered
defective instances of them.)

Consider one type of ritual that Casey discusses (239–245): mourning rituals celebrating loved ones who have died.[37] These rituals provide a forum in
which individuals can openly express and share their grief with others who are
also grief-stricken. On subsequent occasions, on anniversaries, for example, participation in the ritual can re-actualize that grief, although perhaps in a more
attenuated form. Moreover, while sharing grief can augment the grief each feels,
mourning rituals also regulate and moderate grief by prescribing particular performances, verbal as well as behavioral, for its expression.

The educative function of rituals, hinted at by Casey, is explicit in the following remarks by David Garland:

> They [rituals] arouse them [emotions] and organize their content; they
> provide a kind of didactic theatre through which the onlooker is *taught*
> what to feel, how to react, which sentiments are called for.

But it is not only onlookers who are taught this, as he makes clear:

> Rituals . . . are ceremonies which, through the manipulation of emotion,
> prompt particular value commitments on the part of the participants
> and the audience and thus act as a kind of sentimental education.[38]

Emotional responses to past events, especially traumatic ones, may be confused,
unfocused, insufficiently differentiated from one another, and poorly understood
even by those who experience them. Through a kind of "sentimental education,"
commemorative rituals help participants become clearer about and make sense
of what they are feeling, not so that they can experience an emotional catharsis

Commemoration and the Moral Values of Remembrance   209

but so that they can learn what is appropriate for them to feel and express within the regulative framework the rituals provide.

Susanne Langer's discussion of ritual also emphasizes their emotional character, but she has a more elaborate account of how rituals affect the emotional states of participants than Casey provides.[39] Rituals, she says, are not practices that encourage or permit the spontaneous "free expression of emotions" (153). Emotions that are freely expressed are labile and tend to lack rational structure, and it is one of the functions of ritual to supply it. Langer introduces the notion of "*articulation* of feelings" (ibid.) to denote this. What articulation ultimately produces "is not a simple emotion, but a complex, permanent *attitude*"—that is, an "emotional pattern which governs all individual lives" within the context of the ritual (ibid.). This articulation is not a discursive activity, for rituals are like works of art in that they essentially involve a form of nondiscursive meaningful experience. Nevertheless, Langer insists there is a "logic" to the way in which rituals articulate feelings, a logic that consists in the imposition of meaningful patterns on the expression of emotions and that is not represented by formal syllogistic reasoning. It is a logic that the mere spontaneous outpouring of emotions does not possess: "As soon as an expressive act is performed without inner momentary compulsion it is no longer *self-expressive*, it is expressive in the logical sense" (152).

To be expressive "in the logical sense" is not to be without emotion altogether. To be sure, rituals are symbolic activities or "gestures" (ibid.) that often involve a kind of psychic distancing from events that might otherwise provoke an intense emotional response.[40] But it is a distancing that moderates the power of the response and that substitutes "a disciplined rehearsal of 'right attitudes'"(153) for the spontaneous expression of emotions. What rituals accomplish, according to Langer, is the disciplining of emotions, by which they are transformed into ingredients of enduring attitudes and structured into meaningful patterns.[41]

Two connected distinctions are involved here: one between a spontaneous and a disciplined expression of emotions, the other between a simple emotion and a complex attitude. The latter distinction seems partly a temporal one, since Langer characterizes complex attitudes as "permanent": a simple emotion is transient, whereas a complex attitude is lasting. But the complexity of the attitudes that Langer alludes to is partly an emotional complexity that distinguishes them from other elements of the broader class of emotional response. Perhaps what she had in mind here can be clarified by this distinction from Lucy Allais:

> The word 'attitude' . . . picks out a specific group of emotional responses that have a complexity that simple or singular emotions lack . . . Emotions like disgust, anger, or joy primarily involve a singular way of feeling towards or seeing their objects, whereas an affective attitude towards

someone is more complex, in that it need not involve any one specific feeling, but rather involves being disposed to have a range of feelings in a range of circumstances.[42]

Interpreting "complex attitude" this way, and putting the two distinctions together, we arrive at the following characterization of commemorative rituals: commemorative rituals consist of activities that elicit and reinforce complex dispositions to have a range of feelings about events in the past and/or the people involved in them, feelings that are expressed in a disciplined manner in meaningful patterns that extend over time. The *permanence* of the attitudes explicitly directed toward events and people in the past is for Langer a general feature of ritual, and it is one reason why memorialization should be ritualized. This is because the explicit aim of memorialization is to ensure the persistence of memory, what Casey calls "perdurance" (228), and ritual, because it not only evokes the past but seeks to ensure continuity into the future, is an especially effective means of doing this.

This completes my account of commemorative rituals. I have emphasized their formal features of repetitiveness, invariance, and disciplined emotionality, and that they allow participants to share their memories and emotions with one another without being overwhelmed or controlled by them. Ritual commemorations are emotionally charged events, and they do not extinguish personal negative emotions associated with a commemorated event such as an outbreak of collective violence. In fact, participation in them tends to reactivate negative emotions.[43] But to the extent that they offer participants a channel for the disciplined expression of their emotions, commemorative rituals enable them to respond emotionally to past events in a safe and non-socially disruptive manner. Instead of the spontaneous expression of emotion in pursuit of emotional catharsis, rituals provide a framework for emotions that moderates their intensity and discourages those that tend toward expressive excess. I now want to relate these formal features of commemorative rituals to the problem of the previous section in order to show how this mode of memorialization can provide a solution to the sustainability of memory problem.

(b) Commemorations, repetition, and emotionality

Commemorative rituals retard the process of forgetting in two mutually reinforcing ways. One explanation has to do with disciplined emotionality. I remarked earlier about the mnemonic effect of emotion experienced at the time of retrieval of memories of emotionally charged events. If this is correct, then the emotive character of commemorative rituals at least partly explains why they are capable of promoting long-term retention of memories. Admittedly I am extrapolating here from evidence of the interaction of memory and emotion in the psychology of individuals, but it seems likely that there is a similar effect of shared emotion on collective memory.

When what is being commemorated is wrongdoing and its victims, the emotions at the time of recall, even if different from the emotions originally experienced, will typically be negative emotions that in some manner register the wrongness of what was done. Participants in rituals of commemoration may remember the original events with profound sadness and lingering grief rather than anger or vengefulness, especially if the events took place many years in the past or if social and political conditions have dramatically changed since those events occurred. Or the children and grandchildren of the perpetrators may commemorate the original events with a kind of lingering shame long after those guilty of the crimes have died. The sadness and the shame, shared by participants in commemorative rituals, can work to fortify their collective memories of wrongdoing and enhance their durability. It is also possible that positive emotions are elicited by commemorative rituals and that they have a strengthening effect on the memories of acts that did not initially provoke a positive reaction. Commemorations can instill hope and gratitude, for example, and these can both reinforce memories of wrongdoing and alter how the past is remembered.

The second explanation concerns repetitiveness, one of the defining features of ritualized commemorations. Laboratory studies provide evidence for the claim that their ability to sustain memory is to a significant degree due to this feature. Psychologists Henry Roediger, Franklin Zaromb, and Andrew Butler, discussing "specific processes by which . . . collective memories (indeed all memories) are created and maintained over long periods of time,"[44] remark on the powerful effect that "repeated retrieval" seems to have on long-term memory retention. They explain the effect this way:

> Retrieving information from memory is not a neutral event; rather, it leads to a modification of the memory trace. As a result, the act of retrieving information from memory produces a memory trace that is more resistant to forgetting. (146)

It stands to reason, therefore, and recent empirical studies they mention lend the conjecture support, that retrieving information *repeatedly* will, in the normal course of events, produce a stronger memory trace than retrieving information on a single occasion only. Roediger and colleagues then extend the lessons learned from laboratory experiments to the issue of collective memory formation and retention. Distinguishing between the effects on memory retention of conditions at the time of encoding and the effects on memory retention of retrieval, they argue for the important explanatory role of the latter. "Observed group differences in historical memory" are not solely "determined by . . . the initial impact of the event and the influence of group identification on that experience." Of "equal if not greater importance," they assert, "may be the role that retrieval plays in the formation and retention of memories across groups over time . . . Probably the repeated retrieval of events is critical to their long-term retention" (153). As examples of repetitive collective practices that promote long-term retention of historical knowledge, they mention "commemorative holidays such as President's Day, the Fourth of July, Veteran's Day, or Martin Luther King's Birthday in the U.S." (148).

If repeated retrieval plays the role in collective memory retention that experimental evidence suggests it does, then we have an additional explanation, besides disciplined emotionality, for the power of commemorative rituals to sustain collective memories, including memories of past and historical wrongs. The repeated invocation of memories of key events in a community's past that occurs through commemorative rituals, usually at more or less regular intervals, itself makes for better retention of those memories.[45] By contrast, monuments and dedicated public spaces, unless they are made a focal point of and are repeatedly revisited by commemorative rituals, are less able to preserve memory of important communal events over long periods of time.

Though important for retention, the mere repetitiveness of commemorative rituals is not sufficient to ensure that key events in a community's past will be remembered in the *right way*, that they will be well remembered. From this standpoint, religious commemorative holidays, like Easter and Yom Kippur, might serve as better examples of commemorations than the secular commemorative holidays that Roediger and colleagues mention, since the former are generally taken more seriously by their celebrants. Sometimes what is missing from commemorations, both commemorations of events in the distant past and commemorations of more recent events, is a certain solemnity, an appropriately somber attitude toward deeply painful or tragic events. But commemorations don't have to be somber and gloomy in order to be vital, vivid presences in the life of a social group or the larger society, instead of mere excuses for time off from work to enjoy recreation and relaxation. More generally, what is needed is an investment in the ritual and in the events and people it commemorates that appropriately engages one's emotions by befitting what is being commemorated. This suggests that the disciplined emotionality characteristic of commemorative rituals might not only be valuable because of its effects on memory retention. Harking back to the discussion of the evaluative significance of emotions in chapter 2, it might also show that the participants have a grip on the moral significance of what is being commemorated and that they not only care about it but care about it in the right way. Even if commemorative rituals are repeated

Commemoration and the Moral Values of Remembrance   213

again and again over long stretches of time, if they do not properly enlist the emotions of their participants, and enlist the right emotions, they are likely to become either perfunctory performances from the standpoint of commemoration or occasions for excessive displays of emotionality. In short, what is remembered will not be well remembered.

(c) Commemorative rituals in transitional societies

The issue I have just raised is how rituals introduced to commemorate past events can continue to serve this purpose over the long term, that is, how they can continue to have actual memorial content and import for their participants. Commemorative rituals can sustain memory for as long as they celebrated, but their continuing relevance in everyday social life as commemorative activities is not guaranteed. They may instead degenerate into marginal social activities that rarely engage people in reflecting on and honoring the past in appropriate ways. I now want to focus on commemorative rituals in transitional societies and address some of the challenges they confront as potential sources of meaning for their participants in the present and over the long run. I begin with commemorations in non-transitional settings that are meaningful in these ways and then consider what we can learn from them about commemorations in circumstances of sociopolitical upheaval and change.

Commemorative rituals in ordinary circumstances are maintained over the long term by becoming, in Geoffrey Cubitt's words, "part of the regular patterning of social existence."[46] I mean by this (I do not claim this is what Cubitt had in mind) that commemorative rituals are sustained by occupying an assured and symbolically significant place within a larger set of social activities and practices that constitute the community's way of life. "Social existence" is here understood broadly, to encompass more than the repeated socializing that commemorative activity itself involves. (Of course, commemorative rituals should also address significant or momentous events in a community's history, since events that have had little formative influence on a community's values and practices, or that do not shape a community's self-understanding, will not sustain participation over time.) Another factor helping to sustain commemorative rituals, also noted by Cubitt, is that participation in the rituals is difficult in practice to avoid because participation in them is regarded as a condition of membership in the community, so in a sense non-optional. When rituals of any sort meet these conditions, they help to establish a sense of social connectedness and to create a strong sense of community identity. In so doing they contribute to the making of a community. With respect to commemoration in particular, because collective identity is based in part on shared memories, joining with others in commemorative rituals that have these qualities has a similar effect. Even if this joining is not entirely voluntary, it can elicit in individuals the sense that they share membership in the same community. Though one-off commemorations can have some of these effects—Cubitt mentions "the state funeral of a recently deceased personage" as an example—they are "deepened and extended" (220) by ritualized commemorative performances that play a central, or at least non-peripheral, role in the life of the community.[47]

Of course, even if certain commemorative rituals are woven into the fabric of social life, in time they might no longer serve as sources of communal identification through the emotional invocation of a shared history. New ways of invigorating these rituals, of making them emotionally charged events, will need to be found. Nevertheless, insofar as they are part of the regular patterning of social existence, these rituals provide a framework for reconstructing and reconnecting with the past in meaningful ways, and the framework is more likely to endure than if it is not so integrated. No cultural vehicle for focusing attention on the collective past can be expected to resist the erosion of memory indefinitely, of course. But the proper criterion for assessing its value is not this in any case. It is rather whether it retards the process of forgetting for as long as it is possible and desirable to do so. Commemorative rituals, if they are broadly integrated into other areas of social life and backed by a sense of collective identity, have a better chance of doing this than others types of memorials alone.

When we turn to commemorative rituals or commemorations in many transitional settings, however, we see that being part of the regular patterning of social existence might only be partially realizable. The rituals may not provide participants the predictability and security of belonging that commemorative rituals in ordinary circumstances offer, since the regular patterning of social existence has been upset by the systematic abuses to which they have been subjected and which they may yet fear. Moreover, commemorative rituals' capacity to foster and undergird participants' feelings of social integration may be limited. Ritualized commemorative activity that could boost the morale of a particular community and improve social cohesion among its members may be difficult to organize, and social cohesion on a larger scale may be lacking or weak. This limits the socially transformative potential of commemorative activities in transitional settings, since this requires some common understanding among former enemies of who is responsible for what, and especially in the early stages of a transition, this is often hard to arrive at.

For these reasons actual commemorations of wrongdoing in transitional settings may be quite different from commemorative rituals in ordinary circumstances. The former may have difficulty sustaining themselves and may require considerable time to become part of the regular patterning of social existence, whether that of the community of survivors or the larger society that includes it. Nevertheless, it is still useful to reflect on what enables commemorative rituals to endure and flourish when they are not confronted with the challenges facing transitional societies. This is so if only to make clear how social and political conditions in these societies would have to change if commemorative rituals there are to fully have the effect I have been attributing to them.

5. Commemorative rituals and transitional justice: examples and problems

Memorialization initiatives for the victims of large-scale wrongdoing take a wide variety of forms, with monuments and memorial museums being prominent examples. However, the commemorative significance of these types of memorials, considered on their own, may dissipate relatively soon after the initial enthusiasm that accompanies their inauguration. Unless they are buttressed by commemorative activities that collectively evoke and focus attention on past events and experiences, the impact of those events on a society's sense of itself is likely to be transient and superficial because the memorials will fall to become ingrained in public consciousness. I have emphasized a particular type of commemorative activity, ritualized commemorative activity, because certain of its features seem best able to enliven and sustain collective remembrance over the long term. Typically these rituals are performed in a memorial landscape consisting of a monument or museum or public space that serves as a kind of stage, literally and figuratively, for the enactment of collective rituals.

I have also noted that commemorative rituals have a dark side, and this is especially worrisome in transitional societies where the rule of law is still tenuous and the conditions for peaceful coexistence among former adversaries are unsettled. The following passage from Jon Elster can serve to indicate the problem. Elster discusses various "mechanisms by which the decay of memory and emotion may be slowed down or even arrested altogether," and he gives these as examples:

> communication among the victims of wrongdoing, codes of honor that keep memory alive until the desire for revenge has been satisfied, visible physical reminders of the wrongdoing, and perpetuation of the state of affairs caused by the wrongdoing.[48]

I would add commemorative rituals to this list, since as I have argued, they can be a mechanism by which memories are strengthened and maintained over long periods of time. But putting commemorative rituals in the same category as these other mechanisms raises a disturbing possibility, namely that like codes of honor, they will entrench resentments and stoke the fires of hatred and revenge.

The problem is that there are various ways to slow down or arrest the decay of communal memories, and some of these exacerbate rather than ameliorate the conflicts that must be managed if political transformation and reconciliation are to be possible.

Let's look at a few examples of actual commemorative rituals in transitional societies for illustrations of how they can help rebuild political relationships damaged by large-scale wrongdoing, on the one hand, and on the other, how they can arouse strong emotions that impede or resist progress toward political reconciliation.

The demonstrations of the Madres de Plaza de Mayo. Starting in the late 1970s, the activist organization Madres de Plaza de Mayo carried out collective rituals of remembrance to keep alive the memory of their children who were abducted and disappeared during Argentina's "Dirty War" (1976–1983). Through weekly marches in the Plaza de Mayo, a location chosen partly for its symbolic significance, they converted a plaza in the central business district of Buenos Aires into an emotionally and politically charged memorial. The Mothers kept the problem of the disappeared before the public, pressed for answers to the kidnappings, and had an impact on the government's decision to seek prosecution of former junta members.[49]

Indigenous commemoration in Sierra Leone. There is no nationwide program for commemoration of the victims of Sierra Leone's brutal civil war, a war that lasted 11 years and claimed over 50,000 lives. However, it is remembered by rural communities in a number of ways, including the restoration of sacred sites, symbolic cleansing, and annual commemorative rituals. Traditional ceremonies in rural Sierra Leone, through which indigenous peoples sought to communicate with supernatural beings and ancestors, were adapted to new uses in the aftermath of the civil war: to remember its victims and to provide an environment for former enemies to interact and reconcile their differences.[50]

Commemorative marches in Northern Ireland. Parading has long been a major form of commemoration in Northern Ireland. Since 1981, when ten hunger strikers in Northern Ireland died protesting British rule, Republicans have engaged in these ritualized events to commemorate them as martyrs to their cause. The deaths of these hunger strikers had far-reaching consequences for the political future of Northern Ireland and launched Sinn Fein, the political arm of the Irish Republican Army. Protestant and Unionist groups have held their own parades, often in a deliberately confrontational manner, to honor the victims of IRA violence and to assert their claims to political hegemony. Hostility between the communities abetted by these parades led to sporadic outbreaks of violence, before and even after the ratification of the Good Friday peace agreement between Britain and Northern Ireland in 1998.[51]

War commemorations in the Balkans. A number of war events commemorating Croatia's war for independence in the 1990s are held there every year, organized by the state, local communities, and war veterans' associations. One of the most important is the commemoration each year of Operation Storm, a military campaign launched by the Croatian armed forces that officials characterize as the beginning of the rebirth of the Croatian nation. Commemorations are also organized each year in Serbia to honor the memory of Serbian civilians killed during and after the operation. These different commemorations create tensions between Croatia and Serbia and help to reinforce ethnic divisions between communities of Serbs and Croats. Reconciliation of these groups is precarious at best.[52]

These examples give some idea of the variety of types and uses of commemorative rituals, the actors who organize them, and the different relationships that these rituals have to the promotion of political reconciliation because of their content and execution. There is no simple or single answer to the question whether commemorative rituals in transitional societies promote political reconciliation, either in the sense of peaceful coexistence or mutual respect and trust. There are reasons to think they might and reasons to think they might not. Commemorative rituals provide occasions and opportunities for members of a group or community to assert their self-respect; to celebrate their heroic deeds; to press for recognition of their rights; and to commemorate and keep faith with those they have lost, all of which help to install them as equals within the political community. Rituals can also convey a warning and a lesson regarding the dangers of renewed violence and enable participants to appropriately celebrate their connection to the past in emotionally disciplined ways. This can facilitate the construction of a new common identity and new social relations that counter the dispersive influences of ethnic, regional, religious, and other group identities. Rituals have the potential to restore the trust that has been shattered by political violence, or to establish it for the first time, if all parties to the former conflict participate, and they can make it easier for victims on all sides of a conflict to forgive each other and can serve as symbols of a wider national reunification. But as the examples suggest, commemorative rituals divide communities from one another and fuel distrust as often if not more often than they build bridges across them. Memorializing is often enacted in purely separate or segregated activities that reflect and perpetuate divergent political loyalties and identities. In these cases, rituals are likely to mobilize passions associated with unresolved grievances and embolden participants to assert in deliberately confrontational and aggressive ways rights that they claim have been violated. Moreover, by failing to discipline emotion they can fragment identity. In short, the balance of considerations can argue either for or against commemorative rituals, depending on how they are used, their likely effects, and the political, social, and historical contexts in which they are performed.

Related to this, commemorative rituals can further a kind of moral blindness, especially in transitional contexts where wrongs are recent and the strong emotions they aroused are still raw. They do this by entrenching a victim mentality that prevents individuals from recognizing their own role in injustice and grasping the complex issues of innocence versus culpability that characterize many conflict situations. Individuals bound together by a victim identity may also have difficulty recognizing and sympathizing with the suffering of others and appreciating that they are entitled to the status of victim as well.

The verdict about commemorative rituals is therefore decidedly mixed. They can provide symbolic moral recognition of victims that could help repair relations damaged by violence and repression, but caution is warranted. How this potential might be realized, without lending support to competing claims of victimhood and risking the renewed outbreak of hostility, is an important challenge for any transitional state that takes its memorial responsibilities seriously and seeks to do justice to the past.[53]

The governments of transitional states play a crucial role in supporting, promoting, and monitoring commemorative rituals. As I will discuss in chapter 7, the state through its agents has a special responsibility to promote public memorial projects deriving from its unique ability to galvanize public support for such efforts and to lend them legitimacy. Agents of the state also have a responsibility to monitor commemorative rituals that are organized and promoted by nongovernmental groups and that have potentially explosive political implications. They might decide to ban certain commemorative ceremonies outright if they promote an extreme or nationalistic ideological agenda or are deliberately provocative and likely to spark violence. Or they may decide to permit ceremonies that, despite having a potential for violence, also secure important goods for the community involved, but only if they are tightly regulated. Other ceremonies might be officially encouraged and receive state resources if they commemorate wrongdoing without stirring up vengeful feelings and if they are thought to properly address the wrongs that were committed. The state's responsibility to monitor commemorative activities that originate in civil society flows from its responsibility to create the conditions that make the moral reconstruction of political relationships possible.

It is not only governments that have such responsibilities with respect to memorialization. Citizens and nongovernmental groups and agencies have responsibilities to oppose commemorative activities that foment intercommunal enmity and to monitor the activities of the state with regard to commemoration. These monitoring activities are particularly important. Commemorative rituals are able to foster and solidify a sense of national identity much more effectively than other sorts of memorials, so states use them to generate narratives that add legitimacy to their decisions and, in transitional settings, to bolster the authority of the new regime. Commemorative rituals that mark a break with the past give new leadership a way of building public support for the political measures it takes to deal with the crimes of the past. If these measures promote the aims of transitional justice, then the rituals that legitimize them serve a valuable social function. There is, however, another side to the transitional state's use of commemorative rituals: their very effectiveness in engaging the public can tempt states to use them for other less worthy purposes—for example, to lend official legitimacy to a self-serving and cursory acknowledgment of past wrongs. Civil society must remain alert to this possibility and to other abuses of the symbolic power of commemorative rituals.

6. Forgiveness and commemoration in transitional societies

The question I have so far explored in this chapter is how to sustain the memory of wrongdoing over the long term: if remembrance expresses intrinsically valuable attitudes and has socially beneficial consequences, then we ought to give serious consideration to modes of public memorialization through which collective memories are strengthened and maintained over long periods of time. The other question to which I now turn is whether in a transitional society where perpetrators have largely been forgiven for their crimes, or where this has not yet happened but where there is reason to hope that it could, memorializing the victims of their crimes could undermine or impede the process of forgiveness. The last section gave some reasons to take this possibility seriously.

There are two initial responses to what I will call the compatibility problem, neither of which provides a satisfactory solution. The first is to *refocus commemoration*: commemoration will not imperil forgiveness, it is claimed, as long as the focus of commemoration is the wrong and the victims, not the wrongdoers themselves. In this case I do not forgive and forget, or not exactly. Rather, I remember the wrong but forget the wrongdoer, and the role of the state is to help shape collective memory by directing attention to the victims and away from the perpetrators. I suppose something like this is possible, especially long after the wrongs have been committed: the memory of those responsible for the wrongs may fade, while the memory of those who were wronged and of what they suffered remains sufficiently intact. But this process of dissociating the wrong from those who committed the wrong, while it may be welcomed by the perpetrators, will hardly satisfy others who see commemorative ceremonies as providing an opportunity for the wrongdoers to take responsibility for what they have done and for the victims to hold them accountable for their actions.

The second response is to *delay commemoration*: efforts to memorialize should wait until it is "safe" to memorialize—that is, until the transition is complete and there is no longer any danger of arousing hostile emotions among former enemies. Until then, it may be said, commemoration is politically explosive. It is likely to be so divisive and fraught that whatever forgiveness has done to promote reconciliation will be ruined or whatever forgiveness might yet do to promote reconciliation will be put farther out of reach. The problem with this solution is that if the delay is long enough to avoid any risk of a renewal of hostility, it may be generations before it is safe enough to proceed, effectively robbing commemoration of much of its symbolic power as a reparative practice. Whatever commemorative activities can accomplish in terms of helping to make amends for past wrongs and reestablishing the dignity and self-worth of the victims will be too little too late. It will be a case of "justice delayed is justice denied."

The choice between forgiveness and commemoration is not necessarily as stark as this delaying strategy suggests, however, nor is the only way to ensure their stable coexistence the kind of separation of wrong from wrongdoer suggested by the first strategy. To see this, recall my earlier discussion of the emotional sequelae of forgiveness. As I have repeatedly noted in developing a sentiment-based account of forgiveness, forgiveness does not necessarily, or perhaps even ordinarily, wipe the slate clean of all negative emotions directed toward the offender. Negative emotions may persist. For example, forgiveness is not necessarily incompatible with occasional outbursts of anger or other retributive emotions. As long as the agent does not endorse her outbursts as warranted, works to control them, and seeks as her ultimate objective the elimination of any retributive emotions that remain, this condition of forgiveness has been satisfied.[54] In addition, there may be any one or more of a variety of nonretributive negative emotions, such as grief, profound sadness, hurt, and deep disappointment, that target the wrongdoer as their cause. As regards these emotions also, efforts must be made to moderate them if forgiveness is to be possible. The agent need not be committed to their ultimate elimination, as with retributive emotions, but only to their continued moderation. These are the necessary conditions under which the negative emotions exert an influence that is not incompatible with forgiveness, and the person who is in the process of forgiveness will strive to fulfill them.

Commemorative rituals are characterized by their moderating effects on the emotional states of the individuals involved, and this provides part of the explanation of a possible convergence between forgiveness and commemoration. It is a general fact about commemorative rituals that they are laden with emotion. Actual commemorative rituals often arouse hostile emotions and do not satisfy the condition of disciplined emotionality, as some of my earlier examples showed, and this poses formidable challenges for the possibility of forgiveness as well as of a convergence between it and commemoration. But if the transitional state and civil society work together to fulfill their responsibilities to support and monitor each other's commemorative activities, then the excesses of actual commemorations, and the fears they fuel, might be mitigated. And the more closely they resemble the ideal case, the less worrisome commemoration is from the standpoint of realizing forgiveness.

Clearly if commemorative rituals elicit and endorse retributive emotions, and direct them at the same wrongs for which the perpetrators have been forgiven, then the rituals threaten forgiveness. Forgiveness involves a commitment to ultimately let go of angry feelings, if any, whereas participants in commemorative rituals that evoke and sanction such feelings for the same wrongs do not have such a commitment. But commemorative rituals do not necessarily trigger resentment or other angry emotions, nor do they only moderate angry emotions that they nevertheless give participants permission to feel. Instead, they can—and certainly sometimes do—evoke memories of past wrongdoing that chiefly involve non-retributive emotions. They can also provide a "sentimental education" that rationalizes these emotions as the only appropriate ones to feel in response to particular past wrongs. Further, commemorative rituals can maintain these emotions at a level of moderation that does not threaten to subvert whatever forgiveness might have done to rebuild relations of respect and trust or that it might yet do. By eliciting only non-retributive emotions, moderating even these, and teaching participants that this is how they should react to past wrongdoing, commemorative rituals can even make it easier for victims to forgive.

Will perpetrators resent the participation of victims and survivor communities in commemorative rituals that keep alive the memory of wrongs for which they have allegedly already been forgiven? Will they see this participation as a sign that victims' claims to have forgiven them cannot be believed and that they must take steps to protect themselves against a renewal of hostility? This would indeed be likely if the emotions experienced because of participation in commemorative rituals were angry ones. But as I have argued, the emotional experience of participation in commemorative rituals may be very different: participants may instead experience negative emotions that address past wrongdoing without anger or hostility. Emotional memories of this sort are less likely to trigger a defensive response from perpetrators than emotional memories of the former sort. Perpetrators who have shown a willingness to remember what they have done are not likely to respond defensively to others remembering it too, if they perceive that others remember it with negative emotions other than anger. And related to this, whether or not perpetrators have been forgiven, non-retributive emotions may communicate a victim's moral objections more effectively to a wrongdoer than anger,[55] and therefore commemorative rituals that chiefly involve such emotions may be more effective as vehicles of moral protest against ill treatment.

I have been discussing the participation of victims and survivor communities in rituals commemorating wrongdoing. Often ceremonies commemorating wrongdoing are more or less entirely the affairs of particular communities, involving the victims and survivors, as well as their descendants, family members, and members of the community that suffered persecution in the past. Fellow citizens may express support for these activities as a gesture of respect and political inclusion, but they do not participate in them. Sometimes, however, the entire society actively participates with victims and survivor communities in these activities. This may include the perpetrators, although this is perhaps not terribly common, as well as citizens who were neither perpetrators nor victims but who may have shared responsibility for the wrongdoing or who may have resisted it. And there are their descendants as well. The involvement of other members of society in commemorative activities sends a powerful symbolic message that magnifies their reparative potential and assures victims that the wrongs of the past will not be repeated. The participation specifically of those responsible for wrongdoing is especially significant. It can be one way in which they take responsibility for what they have done, and the participation of their descendants can express the conviction that they were right to do this. The inclusion of perpetrators in commemorations is important for another reason as well. It can symbolize and exemplify the social reacceptance of perpetrators who, by their participation in these ceremonies and in other ways, express repentance and try to repair the harm they have caused.

6. A final note

The moral grounds for forgiving and the moral grounds for commemorating are not the same. Hence, commemorations—as well as other forms of memorialization, for that matter—can perform a valuable service whether or not there are grounds to forgive those responsible for the wrongs being commemorated; and they can continue to be important morally, psychologically, socially, and politically, whether or not there is even anyone still living who could be forgiven for the offenses being remembered. (Perhaps they can be forgiven after they are dead, if that is possible.) Commemorations have multiple moral functions: they serve as vehicles for moral protest and thereby express the self-respect of those engaged in them; they give tangible expression to the desire of survivors to keep faith with the dead; they help repair the harm done to the victims by acknowledging the legitimacy of their grievances; they symbolically reinstate the victims as equals in the political community; and they promote relations of mutual respect across society. Commemorations have the potential to do much good, especially in the context of societies in transition. Moreover, commemorative rituals in particular have this distinctive feature: they help maintain the memory of wrongdoing over time as a vital presence in the public life of a community or larger society, and when combined with other sorts of memorials, keep them from becoming mere relics of a bygone age.

Though I have focused on negative emotions in my discussion of commemorative rituals and political reconciliation, I should also note that they can help rebuild social relations insofar as they encourage *positive* affective attitudes in their participants. Of especial importance here is hope, specifically hope constituted by a belief in the possibility of a better future, a future free of violence and abuse and the fear they breed, in which all can live as equals in peace and security. Hope focuses on future possibilities and not, where wrongs have been committed, on their indelible reality, and it motivates individuals to help advance that future. Hope is also intimately related to trust, and the establishment of trusting relations is essential to political reconciliation. Margaret Walker comments on the interaction between hope and trust:

> A moral order requires a core of confidence in the shared understandings that make it up and trust in the responsiveness of its members to what the understandings require . . . repairing moral relations requires securing or restoring that trust, and that trust needs hope to stabilize or recreate it.[56]

Igniting or restoring hope, on the one hand, and paying tribute to the victims of wrongdoing and empowering those who survived, on the other, are distinct achievements of commemorative ceremonies. Each is critical for repairing moral relations in post-conflict and post-authoritarian societies.

Endnotes

1. For more on this, see chapter 5 of Jeffrey Blustein, *The Moral Demands of Memory* (New York: Cambridge University Press, 2008).
2. See Joel Feinberg's discussion of the rights of dead persons, in *Rights, Justice, and the Bounds of Liberty: Essays in Social Philosophy* (Princeton, NJ: Princeton University Press, 1980), pp. 173–176. I am not here endorsing the view that the dead have rights.
3. For an excellent discussion of the contribution of memorialization to building a culture of democracy, see Sebastian Brett, Louis Bickford, Liz Ševčenko, and Marcela Rios, *Memorialization and Democracy: State Policy and Civic Action*, available at ICTJ-Global-Memorialization-Democracy-2007-English.pdf.
4. Elizabeth Anderson, *Value in Ethics and Economics* (Cambridge, MA: Harvard University Press, 1993), p. 17. Page numbers appear in parentheses in text. A more inclusive conception of expressivism than Anderson's is not limited to favorable attitudes or attitudes expressed toward intrinsically valuable objects.
5. Elizabeth Anderson, "Practical Reason and Incommensurable Goods," in *Incommensurability, Incomparability, and Practical Reason* (Ruth Chang, ed.) (Cambridge, MA: Harvard University Press, 1997), pp. 90–109, at 95.

6. Gabriele Taylor, *Pride, Shame and Guilt* (Oxford: Oxford University Press, 1985), pp. 78–79.
7. Lester Hunt, *Character and Culture* (Lanham, MD: Rowman and Littlefield, 1997), p. 41.
8. Taylor, op. cit., p. 79.
9. Stephen Darwall, *The Second-Person Standpoint: Morality, Respect and Accountability* (Cambridge, MA: Harvard University Press, 2006). Page numbers appear in parentheses in the text.
10. Stephen Darwall, "Respect and the Second-Person Standpoint," *Proceedings and Addresses of the American Philosophical Association*, vol. 78, no. 2 (2004): 43–59, at 54.
11. Darwall, note 9, p. 126.
12. Loyalty and fidelity are often used interchangeably, although R. T. Allen ("When Loyalty no Harm Meant," *Review of Metaphysics*, vol. 43, no. 2 [December 1989]) considers them to be closely related cousins. Though there are shades of difference between these terms, I will not differentiate between them here.
13. Brandon Hamber, *Transforming Societies After Political Violence* (Dordrecht: Spring, 2009), p. 86.
14. Ibid., p. 87.
15. Quoted in Hamber, p. 86.
16. Janna Thompson, *Taking Responsibility for the Past* (Oxford: Polity, 2002), p. 114.
17. I take this last point from Margaret Gilbert's analysis of collective remorse. See "Collective Remorse," in *War Crimes and Collective Wrongdoing: A Reader* (Aleksandar Jokic, ed.) (Malden, MA: Blackwell, 2001), pp. 216–235.
18. See, e.g., Michael Bratman, "Shared Intention," *Ethics*, vol. 104, no. 1 (1993): 97–113; M. Gilbert, *Sociality and Responsibility* (Lanham, MD: Rowman and Littlefield, 2000); and Tracy Isaacs, *Moral Responsibility in Collective Contexts* (New York: Oxford, 2011).
19. Hunt, op. cit., p. 49.
20. James L. McGaugh, *Memory and Emotion: The Making of Lasting Memories* (New York: Columbia University Press, 2003), p. 86.
21. Mark J. Osiel, "Ever Again: Legal Remembrance of Administrative Massacre," *University of Pennsylvania Law Review*, vol. 144, no. 2 (December 1995): 463–704, at 475.
22. Eric Hobsbawm, *Age of Extremes: The Twentieth Century* (London: Vintage, 1994), p. 3.
23. Andreas Huyssen, *Twilight Memories: Marking Time in a Culture of Amnesia* (New York: Routledge, 1995), p. 5.
24. Ruti G. Teitel, *Transitional Justice* (New York: Oxford University Press, 2000), p. 102.
25. Two very useful volumes are: *The Handbook of Emotion and Memory: Research and Theory* (Sven-Åke Christianson, ed.) (Hillsdale, NJ: Lawrence Erlbaum Associates, 1992); and *Memory and Emotion: Interdisciplinary Perspectives* (Bob Uttl, Nobuo Ohta, and Amy L. Stiegenthaler, eds.) (Oxford: Blackwell, 2006). See also McGaugh, op. cit.
26. Gail Goodman and Pedro Paz-Alonzo, "Trauma and Memory: Normal versus Special Memory Mechanisms," in Uttl et al., pp. 233–257, at 241.
27. Daniel Reisberg, "Memory for Emotional Episodes: The Strength and Limits of Arousal-Based Accounts," in Uttl et al., pp. 15–36, at 17. See also Linda J. Levine and David Pizarro, "Emotional Valence, Discrete Emotions, and Memory," in Uttl et al., pp. 38–58.
28. Richard Wollheim, "On Persons and Their Lives," in *Explaining Emotions* (Amelie Oksenberg Rorty ed.) (Berkeley: University of California Press, 1980), pp. 299–321, at 308.
29. McGaugh is a leader in the field (see note 20). Other important contributors include Joseph LeDoux (see his contribution to the Sven-Åke Christianson volume, op. cit., pp. 269–288) and Larry Cahill in many papers, including L. Cahill and J. L. McGaugh, "Mechanisms of emotional arousal and lasting declarative memory," *Trends in Neuroscience*, vol. 21 (1998): 294–299. Many other references are found in the Christianson and Uttl et al. volumes.
30. Friderike Heuer and Daniel Reisberg, "Emotion, Arousal, and Memory for Detail," in Christianson, op. cit., pp. 151–180, at 170–171. See also Reisberg, "Memory for Emotional Episodes," op. cit.
31. One of the leading accounts is Margaret Gilbert's plural subject theory, according to which collectives can be said to have emotions when the parties to them enact a joint commitment to feel certain emotions as a body. She gives a holistic analysis of one sort of collective emotion, guilt, in "Collective Guilt and Collective Guilt Feelings," *Journal of Ethics*, vol. 6, no. 2 (2002): 115–143. For a critique of Gilbert's account of collective feelings, see Burleigh Wilkins, "Joint Commitments," in the same issue, pp. 145–155; and Tracy Isaacs, *Moral Responsibility in Collective Contexts* (New York: Oxford University Press, 2011), pp. 83–92.

Commemoration and the Moral Values of Remembrance   225

32. Reisberg, "Memory of Emotional Episodes," op. cit., p. 28.
33. Geoffrey Cubitt, *History and Memory* (Manchester: Manchester University Press, 2007), p. 219.
34. Paul Connerton, *How Societies Remember* (Cambridge: Cambridge University Press, 1989). Page numbers appear in parentheses in text.
35. Israel Scheffler, "Ritual and Reference," *Synthese*, vol. 46 (1981): 421–437.
36. Edward S. Casey, *Remembering: A Phenomenological Study*, 2nd edition (Bloomington: Indiana University Press, 2000). Page numbers appear in parentheses in the text.
37. Casey is interested in the intrapsychic dimension of mourning. I am here considering it as a type of social practice of commemoration. For an interesting discussion of the emotional effects of funeral rituals in the context of a post-conflict society, see Carlos Marin Beristain, Dario Paez, and Jose Luis Gonzalez, "Rituals, social sharing, silence, emotions and collective memory claims in the case of the Guatemalan genocide," *Psicothema*, vol. 12, Suppl. (2000): 117–130.
38. Quoted in Osiel, op. cit., p. 491. The main aim of Osiel's lengthy essay is to characterize and contrast two broad conceptions of legal rituals: one, which he calls "mechanical solidarity," he derives from Durkheim; the other, which he terms "discursive solidarity," emphasizes the give-and-take among individuals who may have deep disagreements about matters of value.
39. Susanne Langer, *Philosophy in a New Key* (Cambridge, MA: Harvard University Press, 1951). Page numbers appear in parentheses in the text. For a sympathetic discussion of Langer's theory of ritual, see Stanley J. Tambiah, "A Performative Approach to Ritual," in *Readings in Ritual Studies* (Ronald L. Grimes. ed.) (Upper Saddle River, NJ: Prentice-Hall, 1996), pp. 495–511.
40. Rituals provide conventional forms for expressing emotion, and it is because of this conventionality that participants can psychically distance themselves from the emotional events to which the ritual refer.
41. I do not endorse Langer's theory of ritual in full. One reason is that her theory relies on a questionable theory of the emotions, according to which even the most complex emotions are construed as felt bodily changes in the organism. For an elaboration of this criticism, see Malcolm Budd, *Music and the Emotions: The Philosophical Theories* (London: Routledge, 1992).
42. Lucy Allais, "Wiping the Slate Clean: The Heart of Forgiveness," *Philosophy and Public Affairs*, vol. 36, no. 1 (Winter 2008): 33–68, at 52.
43. For more on the relationship between collective rituals and the arousal of negative emotions, see Bernard Rime, Dario Paez, Patrick Kanyangara, and Vincent Yzerbyt, "The Social Sharing of Emotions in Interpersonal and in Collective Situations: Common Psychological Consequences," in *Emotion Regulation and Well-Being* (Ivan Nyklicek, Ad Vingerhoets, and Marcel Zeelenberg, eds.) (New York: Springer, 2011), chapter 9, pp. 147–163.
44. Henry L. Roediger III, Franklin M. Zaromb, and Andrew C. Butler, "The Role of Repeated Retrieval in Shaping Collective Memory," in *Memory in Mind and Culture* (P. Boyer and J. V. Wertsch, eds.) (New York: Cambridge University Press, 2009), pp. 138–170, at 141. Page numbers appear in parentheses in the text.
45. Roediger and colleagues argue that, in addition to repeated retrieval, the spacing of retrievals also has a bearing on long-term retention of memories. "When the repeated retrieval attempts are spaced over a period of time, much greater retention is produced than when the attempts are massed together" (148). This spacing effect is evident with respect to both secular and religious commemorative rituals.
46. Cubitt, op. cit., p. 220.
47. Though the state funeral of a particular government official may occur only once, it normally includes elements that have occurred, in similar form, in other commemorations of the same type and that are in turn repeated in future state funerals.
48. Jon Elster, *Closing the Books: Transitional Justice in Historical Perspective* (Cambridge: Cambridge University Press, 2004), p. 223.
49. See http://en.wikipedia.org/wiki/Mothjers_of_the_Plaza_de_Mayo.
50. Steven E. Kaindaneh, "Remembering the Past and Reconciling for the Future: The Role of Indigenous Commemorative Practices in Sierra Leone," in *Peacebuilding and Reconciliation: Contemporary Themes and Challenges* (Marwen Darweish and Carol Rank, eds.) (Pluto Press, 2012).

51. Jennifer Edwards and J. David Knottnerus, "The Orange Order: Parades, Other Rituals, and their Outcomes," *Sociological Focus*, vol. 43, no. 1 (February 2010): 1–23; Neil Jarman, "Not an Inch," *Peace Review*, vol. 13, no. 1 (2001): 35–41.
52. Tamara Banjeglav, "Conflicting Memories: Competing Narratives and Contested Histories in Croatia's Post-War Commemorative Practices," *Politicka misao*, vol. 49, no. 5 (2012): 7–31. PDF available from srce.hr.
53. For a discussion of some of the ways in which commemorative rituals can stir up retributive emotions and impede the process of political reconciliation, see Judy Barsalou and Victoria Baxter, "The Urge to Remember: The Role of Memorials in Social Reconstruction and Transitional Justice," *Stabilization and Reconstruction Series*, vol. 1 (January 2007): 1–24.
54. See Charles Griswold, *Forgiveness: A Philosophical Exploration* (New York: Cambridge University Press, 2007), pp. 42–43.
55. This point is made by Glen Pettigrove in "Meekness and 'Moral' Anger," *Ethics*, vol. 122, no. 2 (January 2012): 341–370, at 367.
56. Margaret Walker, *Moral Repair: Reconstructing Moral Relations after Wrongdoing* (New York: Cambridge University Press, 2006), p. 44.

6

The Nature and Value of Memorialization as Symbolic Activity

1. The symbolism of memorialization

Transitional measures whose purpose is to affirm the dignity of victims and help repair relationships damaged by violence and repression include public memorials of one sort or another. In the previous chapter, I focused on one way of memorializing, commemorative rituals, but here, and in the next chapter, I am not concerned to emphasize what is distinctive about them and what makes them particularly valuable adjuncts to monuments, museums, and dedicated public spaces. Commemorative rituals were my focus chiefly because I wanted to address the problem of the sustainability of memory, and focusing on these I also suggested how they could be compatible with forgiveness. For the purposes of this chapter, however, I regard commemorative rituals as just one among a range of public initiatives and practices that have as at least one of their main purposes preserving the memory of wrongdoing, in order to give the victims a dignified place in the collective memory and to aid present and future generations in the recall of significant wrongs committed in the past. These initiatives include, in addition to commemorating in ceremonies and rituals, establishing memorial museums, sites of conscience,[1] and archives documenting past injustices and rights violations; erecting monuments to victims of violence and crimes against humanity; and dedicating public spaces to their memory. These are all "commemorative" in the sense that they provide and are intended to provide opportunities for the sharing of memories, for co-remembering. But "commemorative rituals" refers to only one type of public memorial activity.

Truth commissions and legal tribunals, the most frequently discussed transitional justice practices, are dependent on and have important relations to memory as well. The former elicit memories of wrongdoing from victims in order to help them move beyond trauma and preoccupation with loss and injury; and both truth commissions and legal tribunals depend on the memory of wrongdoing by witnesses and others in order to be able to hold the perpetrators accountable for the harms they inflicted on others. Truth commissions also collect and analyze materials and elicit testimonies that can be invaluable for further memorialization initiatives, and a number of them have included recommendations for memorialization in their reports.[2]

To be sure, these transitional justice mechanisms have additional purposes beyond simply preserving the memory of victims and wrongdoing. But one reason not to draw too sharp a line between truth commissions and public trials, on the one hand, and the memorials mentioned above, on the other hand, is that to some extent even the latter have purposes in addition to memorializing and truth telling about the past. For example, monuments and commemorations potentially play a constructive role in helping establish a culture of respect for human rights and democracy, and they are sometimes promoted on these grounds, among others. There are additional reasons not to draw too sharp a line. The proceedings of truth commissions can be thought of as rituals of social memory whose purpose is to construct narratives of the past that counteract the evasions, distortions, and falsifications of the predecessor regime, and public trials, national as well as international, may have a similar purpose. These are mechanisms that can officially correct collective memory through a more accurate or thorough accounting of past events, and they often provide public opportunities for collective mourning. What's more, for the survivors and the families of the victims, the reports issued by truth commissions are often themselves a kind of memorial to the dead that has some, albeit limited, reparative value. So though public trials and truth commissions may not be what first come to mind when we speak of memorialization, there is sufficient overlap with more standard cases to justify including them in a discussion of transitional memorializing activities and practices.

Memorializing activities and practices, whether they take place in transitional or ordinary circumstances, do not simply depend on memory or incidentally promote its retention. Rather, they have remembrance as one of their central and explicit aims. They take the past seriously, but there are different ways of taking the past seriously and memorialization does this in a particular way: it pays what is thought to be fitting tribute or homage to significant past events or the people affected by them, and it seeks to create an enduring memory of them, to render it immune to the passage of time and the social, political, and other forces that, if not resisted, generate a kind of social amnesia.[3] Truth commissions in their own way aim to construct a public record of wrongdoing that has a similar purpose, and public trials, depending on their stature and national or international visibility, can do the same.

Memorials, an umbrella term for public processes or products that serve to keep remembrance of persons or events alive, are commonly justified by their

The Nature and Value of Memorialization as Symbolic Activity   229

founders, promoters, and supporters on the grounds that they are morally imperative or obligatory or a solemn moral responsibility. This is certainly how victims, families of victims, and survivor communities typically regard them: remembering injustice and its victims is not just a good thing to do that we cannot be morally criticized for not doing. The notion of "a duty to remember" (I do not distinguish between duty, obligation, and responsibility) has acquired considerable currency in recent years, both in the political arena and in scholarly writings on transitional justice, and I myself am drawn to this way of thinking of it.[4] But whether we think of remembering as morally obligatory, supererogatory, or just a decent thing to do, what we are urged to do, or praised for doing, or expected to do, is to *engage* with the memory in various ways, to respect it, promote it, keep it from being tarnished, and so on. I call these various modes of engaging with memory doing the work of remembering, and public memorial practices of different sorts carry out this work with greater and lesser success. When memorialization is employed as a tool of transitional justice, the work of remembering may arouse intense emotions and occasion hostility, recriminations, and denials of responsibility. But as a practice that also has significant restorative potential, it deserves more attention than it has received in the literature, at least as much if not more attention than forgiveness has received.

Memorialization, the public process of creating material as well as non-material vehicles and markers of remembrance, is one way that societies respond to injustice and wrongdoing during and after periods of sociopolitical upheaval and regime change, and depending on how the memorials are fashioned and implemented, it has the potential to further the cause of justice for those whose human rights were violated by violence and repression. Specifically, memorialization, like public apology, does this by providing a type of symbolic engagement with the past, importantly but not exclusively in order to repair the harm that was done. (Not exclusively because symbolic engagement also provides an opportunity and platform for historical dialogue that can promote reconciliation.) To be sure, this is moral as distinct from material reparation. Yet rather than being a weakness, there is a sense in which moral reparation is more fundamental than material. If the harm caused by wrongdoing is in part moral harm, as it surely is, then material reparations are not fully reparative if they aren't also morally reparative in just the way that memorialization can be. It is reparative insofar as it serves as a kind of symbolic acknowledgment of wrong done and affirmation of the dignity and equal moral and civic standing of its victims. It may be accompanied by, motivate, and bring about tangible changes in the life circumstances of victims. But insofar as memorialization repairs the harm caused by wrongdoing, it does so essentially symbolically, in the form of gestures and practices that carry symbolic meaning.

It is the aim of this chapter to explore the nature of this process and to understand the value it possesses as a type of symbolic activity. This value is symbolic value and I will examine the relationship between the symbolic value of memorialization and its moral value. (I speak interchangeably of the symbolic value of x and the value of x as symbolic.) To clarify my interest in the former notion, there are different criteria that one can use to assess the value of symbolic actions or objects. They can be *apt* symbols of what they are attempting to symbolize. For example, shortly after the overthrow of Egyptian President Hosni Mubarak, a Cairo court ordered that images of him and his wife and their names be removed from all "public squares, streets, libraries and other public institutions around the country." The removal of their images and names was an apt symbol of their removal from positions of power.[5] Another example: the massive Nazi party rallies held annually at Nuremberg, and so memorably recorded in Leni Riefenstahl's film *Triumph of the Will*, were an apt symbol of the grandiosity of Nazi ambitions. Their monumentality also effectively conveyed in symbolic terms the utter insignificance of the individuals who participated in them. In each case, the actions possessed symbolic value because there was a good fit between the symbol and what it symbolized. But whether they also had moral value as symbols is another matter. Indeed, in the Nazi rally example, the symbolism was from this standpoint disvaluable. In one sense, then, we can say that the rallies were valuable as symbols—that is, they were good symbols because they were apt. However, in another sense, we can say they lacked value as symbols—that is, they were bad symbols because they stood for or expressed something immoral. Aptness and moral value, in other words, are distinct criteria of evaluation and they can come apart. (The same could be said about aptness and the possession of other sorts of values, such as religious or aesthetic value.) My aim in this chapter is to explore whether and how actions that are apt symbols of what they symbolize also have moral value as symbols.

Part of what motivates this chapter is that there is a fair amount of confusion about just what symbolic value is and how it relates to other sorts of value, and part of this chapter will be spent exploring these matters. One indication of this confusion is a tendency in ordinary discourse to downgrade the evaluative status of actions with symbolic value by using the adjective "mere" to qualify it. Calling an action "symbolic" or "symbolically meaningful" is often intended as a kind of evaluative criticism of it, effectively removing it from contention as a serious or weighty sort of value. Consequentialist moral theories support this way of thinking about symbolic value, although the derogation of symbolic value is not confined to those who, even on reflection, would consider themselves consequentialists. To counter this, I will consider the sort of evaluative import and weight that symbolic value can have by relating it to a kind of value that is generally regarded as supremely important if not overriding, namely moral value. The claim that I will be defending is not only that symbolic actions can have moral value in the *same way* that non-symbolic actions can have it, because of their consequences, but that actions can be morally significant and have moral value *due to* the fact that they are symbolic, and that their being symbolic is an essential part of the explanation of their moral value. This is, at base, because in so acting we put ourselves on record as standing for or allying ourselves with something of moral value, and there are different ways of doing this. This account will in turn lead to a better understanding of the evaluative significance of memorialization when it is employed as a practice of transitional justice as well as in ordinary circumstances.

In order to get clearer on how memorialization functions symbolically and what can explain its moral value as symbol, a number of general issues relating to the nature and moral significance of symbolic value need to be addressed. I begin in section 2 by asking whether symbolic value is a type of intrinsic or extrinsic value that actions possess. I will argue that there are different sorts of extrinsic value, instrumental and non-instrumental, and that symbolic value should be classified as extrinsic but non-instrumental. Whatever value acts may have qua symbolic is not due to the fact that they bring about, or even that they are expected to bring about, intrinsically valuable states of affairs. Since the symbolic value of actions is not explained by their effects, symbolic value is not a type of instrumental value. Moreover, if actions have a distinctive sort of moral value because they are symbolic, the explanation cannot be an instrumentalist one. It may even be possible for symbolic actions to possess moral value though they are non-optimal from an instrumental standpoint, or instrumentally disvaluable, at least if the costs are not too great. I say more about conflicts of this sort toward the end of the chapter.

After discussing the nature of the "standing for" relation that is a defining feature of symbolic action and symbolism in general, the rest of section 2 illustrates how individuals and groups can be misguided in thinking that their symbolically meaningful actions have the value that they take them to have.

The failure or inability of symbolic action to bring about change in the world is commonly given as one of the reasons for discounting the moral significance of such action, and I take up this challenge in section 3. A crucial distinction here is between symbolic acts having moral value (for some reason or other) and symbolic acts having moral value *in virtue of* being symbolic. Consequentialists can straightforwardly explain how symbolic acts might have moral value, depending on their actual or expected utility, but they have difficulty explaining how symbolic acts can have moral value because they are symbolic. The difficulty arises from a tension between a consequentialist account of the moral value of actions and a conception of symbolic value according to which it is essentially not linked to (good) consequences. The section ends by asking why we should accept the evaluative ranking of sorts of value reflected in this discounting, but it does not offer any positive arguments for the moral value of symbolic action.

This is the task of sections 4 and 5. One suggestion is to group symbolic value with deontological rather than instrumental value. On this view, symbolic actions might be valuable from a deontological standpoint, because they satisfy principles commonly held by deontologists. The account I mainly offer is, broadly speaking, non-consequentialist, and in the sense of the term "deontology" that refers to any theory that rejects consequentialist theories of act evaluation, it *is* a kind of deontology. However, deontology, more narrowly construed, is only part of the explanation of the moral value of symbolic actions: conformity to deontological principles can provide a moral argument for symbolic action in some cases, but symbolic actions are not fully characterizable as a type of deontologically obligatory or permitted actions. They cannot be exhaustively evaluated in these terms because they are morally valuable for reasons not all of which are recognized within the usual versions of deontology. Rather, there are multiple sources of the moral value of symbolic actions, and therefore of activities of memorialization, several distinct though non-mutually exclusive grounds for attributing moral value to those symbolic actions that possess it. There are the principles they stand for; the evaluative attitudes they symbolize and express; their relationship to the character or virtue of the agent; and their importance for the actor's self-understanding and identity, individual as well as collective, though I focus on the latter. The relation to character and identity is explored in section 5.

Section 5 argues that the relationship between symbolic actions and identity, both individual and collective identity, can provide an explanation of the moral significance that symbolic actions possess. When it does so, the connection to identity *augments* the moral value that the actions possess on other grounds. Section 6 investigates what this means in practical terms by examining how the connection to identity may affect decisions about what to do in cases where actions that are morally valuable for symbolic reasons are suboptimal from a consequentialist standpoint.

A final general point that is implicit in much of the following and that is critical to explaining the moral significance of memorialization: symbolic action normally has a communicative purpose. Symbolic action is typically a social activity, implying both an agent who intends to convey something via some representational form and a recipient toward whom this is directed. Symbolic acts of memorialization also embody communicative intentions of the agent and, in transitional contexts, these are directed to the victims and survivor communities, to the perpetrators and their supporters, and to other citizens. It is in part because of the communicative dimension of symbolic action that activities of memorialization have the potential to repair the harm caused by

The Nature and Value of Memorialization as Symbolic Activity   233

violence and oppression. It should also be noted that in some versions of non-consequentialism, namely those that endorse Kant's formulation of the Categorical Imperative, we are likewise required to attend to the evaluative attitudes toward others that we express in our actions and communicate to them. As we will see in section 4, there are recognizably Kantian elements in my account of the moral value of symbolic action.

2. The nature of symbolic value

(a) Remembrance and symbolism: Lincoln at Gettysburg

Louis Bickford draws a distinction between two overlapping paradigms for dealing with past injustices in transitional societies.[6] One, the "transitional justice paradigm," emphasizes the legal responsibilities of the transitional state to promote the rule of law. These responsibilities include truth telling about the past; prosecuting perpetrators; securing reparations for victims; and guaranteeing non-repetition of past injustices through reform of the legal, political, and other institutions of society. The other is the "memory paradigm," which applies to transitional societies that seek to promote a culture of democratization in large part through practices that elicit and preserve memories of wrongdoing. Remembrance, according to this paradigm, is essential to the establishment of democracy and a bulwark against the recurrence of past injustices, since it keeps the past alive and fosters a "never again" mentality. The memory paradigm emphasizes the importance of honoring those who suffered or died during conflict as a means of promoting educational efforts to involve the public in dialogue about the past.

The distinction between these paradigms for dealing with past wrongdoing, and the splitting off of memory from transitional justice, might reflect the relatively recent history of the development of the field of transitional justice. However, it is not a theoretically helpful way of dividing up questions about our moral relations to the past. Transitional justice is not only concerned with restoring the rule of law, although this is one of its key functions: remembrance can itself be an instrument of transitional justice, although commonly it is conjoined with other corrective and compensatory measures. Another problem is that the description of the memory paradigm is too focused on what memory can achieve in the future: the value of memorialization in transitional contexts is not solely accounted for by its capacity to serve the social interest in political transformation. But particularly important here is Bickford's alerting us to the significant role of remembrance in transitional contexts. I would revise his point this way: the so-called memory paradigm is not an alternative to transitional justice but an aspect of it. Transitional justice concerns the legal responsibilities of transitional regimes and the steps they ought to take to reestablish the rule of law, but also the various sorts of reparatory measures, material as well as symbolic, that should be instituted to rehabilitate victims and restore them as equals within the political community. Memorialization has the potential to contribute to this in a way that has particularly deep significance for victims and survivor communities.

The example that I start with to show the symbolic function of memorialization, although it pertains to a society very much in a process of sociopolitical transition, is not like common cases of memorialization in transitional societies. The activity of memorializing does not occur after a truce has been declared, or peace terms have been agreed, or violence has ceased, but while conflict and violence continue to rend the society. However, there is sufficient similarity between the example and the common cases—for example, memorialization in the example is part of a campaign to establish a more democratic political order—to warrant using it to illustrate how remembrance can function symbolically as a response to conflict and social disintegration. There is also the advantage that the details of the case are sufficiently well and widely known so that there is no need to provide extensive background information to set up the example.

The example is the establishment of the Gettysburg National Cemetery, dedicated by President Lincoln in November 1863. The address Lincoln delivered there, which Gary Wills has argued "remade America,"[7] was in part an honoring gesture, a way of dignifying the "brave men, living and dead," who fought to preserve the Union. It was an act of memorialization, and Lincoln used the occasion for a larger purpose as well. He did this by transforming a scene of carnage into a potent symbol, a symbol of the struggle to realize the ideals of liberty and equality for which the American Revolution was fought. In so doing, the cemetery not only became a means of preserving memory of the honored dead, but also, because the War was still going on, an inspiration for the living to continue the struggle and refound the republic through "a new birth of freedom." The symbolic significance of the cemetery did not only derive from the dedication that turned it into a symbol, however. The design of the cemetery itself, in its configuration of graves, sent a powerful symbolic message, as Drew Gilpin Faust notes:

> The cemetery at Gettysburg was arranged so that every grave was of equal importance; William Saunders' design, like Lincoln's speech, affirmed that every dead soldier mattered equally regardless of rank or station. This was a dramatic departure from the privileging of rank and station that prevailed in the treatment of the war dead.[8]

The cemetery at Gettysburg, like all cemeteries, was intended to "mark a site in the landscape where time cannot merely pass through, or pass over"[9]—to be, in other words, a place of enduring remembrance. Its symbolic meaning consisted in its being allied with the values of the founding fathers and in its affirming the equal worth of all who died in defense of the Union, regardless of military rank or social status. This is what the cemetery came to stand for or symbolize as a result of the eloquence and power of Lincoln's words and the democratic way in which the graves were arranged. The memorial became, through Lincoln's oratory, a potent symbol of the rightness of the Union cause and the country's rededication to the principle that all men are created equal. In time, the values enunciated at Gettysburg became the dominant ones of a unified nation, and today the cemetery still represents for many the core democratic principles and values of the American republic.

Designing, constructing, dedicating, and visiting the national cemetery at Gettysburg were all elements of a process of memorialization, a process that, precisely because of its powerful symbolism, aroused strikingly different emotional reactions from Northerners and Southerners. It was welcomed by and raised the spirits of those in the North and in the border states who supported Lincoln and his aims and valued what the memorial stood for. But it was not symbolically valuable to the Southerners who did not share these beliefs and repudiated what the memorial stood for and the values its accompanying dedication upheld. Moreover, since Southern soldiers were not included among the dead who were reburied at Gettysburg, many in the South regarded this as an insult to the young men who had bravely given their lives in defense of a cause they deeply believed in. This symbolic insult further embittered the South and strengthened its commitment to fight on.

The example of Lincoln at Gettysburg illustrates how memorialization can work symbolically by putting forth a conception of national identity that can be the basis of a reconstructed polity. This is one reason why memorialization is important from a symbolic point of view, and as we will see, there are others as well. Memorialization can have symbolic value, however, without having *moral value* as a symbolic activity. Whether it does so or not depends on what is being symbolized; on the content of the beliefs, ideals, and principles the actions stand for; and on how it is being symbolized. It also depends on what the symbolic actions reveal about the agents, about their commitments and attitudes, and about the sorts of identities that are bound up with their actions. But before turning to this, there are some preliminary issues about what it means to symbolize and about the nature and significance of symbolic value that need to be covered. These occupy the rest of this section and section 3.

(b) Symbols and the relation of "standing for"

The symbolic value of actions, as well as of objects and events, although here I am concerned chiefly with actions, is value that is derived from their association with something else that has value.[10] Because it is derived from association with something else, it is in one sense of the term a kind of extrinsic value. "Association," however, is ambiguous. There is an instrumental or causal kind of association that confers value on something because it has desirable *effects*. There is another type of association that is conceptual of symbolism in general: the association that one thing has with another by virtue of *standing for* it. This is a crucial distinction. The standing-for relation that one thing has to another is not the same as the relation that one thing has to another in virtue of producing it, bringing it about, or promoting it. Hence, the value that is proper to symbols and that accords with their nature as symbols is not causal utility. It is rather value that derives from a non-causal relation of standing for something else that has value, and the value of what it stands for can itself be at least partly symbolic. Guido Pincione and Fernando Tesón make this point about symbolic value in discussing how agents conceive of what they are doing when they act symbolically:

> The agent performs an act because it has symbolic value for him and others. That the act is symbolic means that it stands for something else—a principle, or value, or something desirable. Crucially, however, the act does not cause the state of affairs recommended by the principle, the value, or the desirable thing. What the act symbolizes (that "something else") has value for the agent and that value is imputed back to the act.[11]

The value of what is symbolized is, in Robert Nozick's words, "imputed back" to the act that symbolizes it,[12] and in this way the former serves as a source of value for the latter, irrespective of whether the act causes what it symbolizes.

Those who act for reasons of symbolic value are not necessarily indifferent to what their actions cause or to the consequences of the policies their actions might support. They may in fact believe that these deserve serious consideration, and they may be right. However, it would misconstrue the point of what they do to regard it as aimed chiefly at the production of intrinsically valuable states of affairs and as deriving its value for them mainly from the effects it brings about or promotes. This would misconstrue both their intentions and their understanding of the significance of what they are doing. This distinction between standing-for and causing, moreover, applies to both the value an agent believes his act has and the value that it has irrespective of the agent's belief. An agent may be correct or incorrect in believing that his act has positive symbolic value, depending on whether the relation between his act and what it stands for is "objectively" value conferring. There may be good reasons of symbolic value to perform certain acts, the force of which the agent fails to appreciate; and acts believed to be symbolically valuable along some dimension may nevertheless be flawed symbols along the same dimension.

The Nature and Value of Memorialization as Symbolic Activity   237

There is a possible objection, however, to the claim that symbolic value is not instrumental or utility value that I want to briefly mention in order to further clarify what I take symbolic value to be. The objection essentially argues that by construing the relationship between symbolic action and outcome in a particular way, the claim that symbolic value is not instrumental value collapses.

Consider commemorative ceremonies that the participants are emotionally invested in and that have deep memorial significance for them. What, we might ask, is the point of such ceremonies? One answer might be that commemorative ceremonies keep us vigilant against the recurrence of wrongdoing: it fosters a "never again" mentality, as Bickford's description of the memory paradigm has it. This is a consequence of the first sort. But for the agents themselves, I have already said, the value of symbolic acts does not solely derive from the further consequences they may cause. Nevertheless, as Pincione and Tesón note, "an agent may derive utility or value from doing A, where *his doing it* is the outcome he intends."[13] Hence, it would not be quite correct to say that those who act for symbolic reasons find value in what they do regardless of whether it has a good outcome. Rather, they may believe that their act does indeed have a good outcome, namely the outcome of symbolizing itself.

The objection to the claim that symbolic value is non-instrumental would then be that even if symbolizing has no *further* valuable consequences, symbolizing can *itself* be a valuable consequence of his action. Someone who wants to minimize the significance of this distinction in order to bring symbolic value into the domain of instrumental value, it seems, would in effect be arguing that symbolic acts are or can be components of intrinsically valuable states of affairs brought about by the acts themselves. The value of symbolic acts would not consist in something further that they bring about, the argument would go, but just in its being good to have them occur as ingredients of such state of affairs. But here is the problem. One can hold that symbolizing may itself be the outcome one intends without holding that symbolic acts are therefore to be regarded as constituents of states of affairs, or that the value of these acts derives from being constituents of intrinsically valuable states of affairs. Indeed, in my view this cannot be an adequate understanding of the standing-for relation. To regard them solely in this way is to fail to appreciate where their value distinctively lies, which is in the particular non-detachable relation they have to the agents who perform them and in the importance because of this that the acts have for them.

The standing-for relation, however, is somewhat obscure, and it would be important to unpack it in order to understand how memorialization functions symbolically. Nelson Goodman has provided some suggestive categories that are a good stepping-off point. "'Reference,'" he says, "is a very general and primitive term, covering all sorts of symbolization, all cases of *standing for*,"[14] so to understand symbolization, and how memorializing actions in particular symbolize, we need to understand the various relationships between a symbol (which can be a word, an object, event, or act) and its referent. According to Goodman, one species of reference is *denotation*, "the application of a word or picture or other label to one or many things" (121). Another species is *exemplification*: "exemplification is reference by a sample to a feature of it" (124). That is, a symbol exemplifies a property if and only if it refers to that property *and* possesses that property. He gives the example of a tailor's swatch, which in normal use exemplifies the color, weave, and thickness of the full fabric. Exemplification differs from denotation: in denotation, a symbol refers to an object but is not an instance of what it refers to.[15] Finally there is *expression*, in which, according to Goodman's usage, a symbol refers to a property and possesses the property metaphorically or figuratively.[16] Aesthetic symbols are expressive. What they express, he says, is a property of the symbols themselves, not of the person or persons who employ or engage with the symbols. The distinction here is familiar from philosophical discussions of the role of expression in art, between "being expressive of" and "expressing."[17] An artwork can be expressive of sadness, for example, without itself expressing the emotions of the artist: it exemplifies the feeling of sadness metaphorically rather than literally.

In contrast to Goodman, Elizabeth Anderson and Richard Pildes do not focus on the figurative or metaphorical qualities of expression but characterize it more broadly as referring to the ways that a statement, action, object, or other vehicle of expression manifests a state of mind.[18] On this view, aesthetic symbols, in which an expressive medium manifests a state of mind metaphorically, represent one but only one type of expression, and in what follows I will adopt their more inclusive characterization. States of mind include beliefs as well as "moods, emotions, attitudes, desires, intentions, and personality traits," and these can be expressed by both individuals as well as collective bodies, such as organizations and states, through the officials who represent them.[19] Anderson and Pildes mention three features of the relationship between states of mind and their expressions. First, the same state of mind is expressible in different ways, by more than one expression; but an expressive mental state must be embodied in, take shape through, some expressive medium or other to be "fully realized." Respect for others, for example, can be expressed in many ways. But it is an expressive mental state in the sense that it must be expressed in some medium or other to count as genuine. Second, when mental states are expressed they are made manifest—that is, brought into the open for oneself and others to recognize. In order to recognize the mental state being expressed—and this is true both when the recognizer is oneself and others—one will have to engage in interpretive activity, and this could be quite straightforward or require considerable effort. It may also happen that in bringing one's mental state into the open, one discovers it is not what one thought it was prior to expressing it. Expression can in this way

The Nature and Value of Memorialization as Symbolic Activity 239

foster self-understanding. Third, media of expression can be assessed in terms of how well they express particular mental states, and there are various terms of evaluation that may be appropriate in this context. Expressions may be apt or inapt; perspicuous or confusing; ambiguous or unequivocal; and so on.

Symbolic actions are often expressive actions—that is, they embody and make manifest for an audience some state of mind (metaphorically or otherwise). Nozick says of these cases that "what flows back along the symbolic connection to the action is (the possibility of) expressing some particular attitude, belief, value, emotion, and so on."[20] The symbolic action may express commitment to or support for a principle or value or cause, possibly one that is implicated in the actor's very identity; attitudes of respect, honor, reverence, or admiration; or emotions of compassion, grief, and love. Symbolic actions that are expressive have expressive *meaning*, and this is given by the mental state to which they give expression and the manner in which it is expressed.

Further, we can distinguish between what a symbolic action stands for and what it expresses: it *stands for* "a principle, value, or something desirable,"[21] but what it *expresses* is a state of mind. For example, it may stand for the principle that "amends should be made for the harm done or sanctioned by the former regime" and express the successor regime's awareness of its responsibility to provide it and dedication to the task of doing so, perhaps by memorializing the victims. However, I don't want to belabor this distinction. For if the object of an affective attitude is worthy of being valued in this way, then the valuing can itself be considered "something desirable," and often what an act stands for and what it expresses are closely intertwined. The cemetery at Gettysburg, for example, stood for the principle that those who gave their lives in defense of the Union should be honored because they died in pursuit of a noble cause. But its construction and dedication honored them at the same time that it symbolized the value of doing so, so we can say that as a symbol, it did two things: it expressed a state of mind that it stood for as a principle.

In general, there is a difference between, on the one hand, engaging in symbolic acts that express one's allegiance to a principle, say, and on the other, regulating one's action by it, beyond the symbolic show of support itself. The former does not ensure or even necessarily dispose one to the latter, since one can symbolically support a principle without doing much else besides to instantiate the principle in one's actions. The gesture may have some value in itself. However, our estimate of the sincerity of the agent's commitment to the principle will often depend on other things the agent does. There are often, though not always, a number of concrete ways to demonstrate this commitment. It is perhaps as a result of thinking of this sort that the adjective "mere" often gets affixed to symbolic value. A symbolic action might be taken by the agent, or be socially seen, to show support for a principle and may give some indication of where one's sentiments lie and the direction of one's concerns. But this can ring hollow or be perfunctory if it is not a sample or representative instance of a larger set of acts supportive of the principle. In cases like this we might say, in a disparaging way, it's only a symbolic gesture.

This is not to say, to reiterate a previous point, that symbolic acts have value only insofar as they bring about, or are expected to bring about, valuable consequences. Symbolic acts that stand for a principle are typically taken to stand for a pattern of supportive acts that extend into the future, acts that, if carried out, show continuing adherence to the principle. If the acts are not forthcoming, then there might be reason to question whether the agent is truly committed to the principle or value in the name of which he claims to be acting. But symbolic value does not become a species of instrumental value simply because symbolic acts point beyond themselves to a range of actions that we expect the agent to carry out, if possible, as assurance of the genuineness of the agent's commitment. In addition, the fact that symbolic acts can have consequences, psychological, social, and political, for others that are serious enough to cancel their purported symbolic value does not entail that symbolic value is just a species of instrumental value. Sometimes symbolic acts convey a message that is hurtful, insensitive, or insulting to its recipients, whether intended or not, and the symbolic acts would be disvaluable because of this message. What this shows is that the good or bad effects of the symbolic acts depend on their symbolic meaning, not that symbolic value is a function of consequences, assessed apart from it. Thus, consequences are relevant to the assessment of an action's symbolic value, but not in the way consequentialists propose. Rather, they are relevant because of their bearing on its meaning: the consequences for the target audience may be such as to communicate a particular meaning that undermines the action's purported symbolic value.

(c) How attributing symbolic value can misfire

I earlier alluded to the distinction between the symbolic value that a person takes an act to have and the symbolic value that it has, whether or not he regards it as valuable in this way. The distinction can be drawn with respect to values of all sorts, so that, for example, an act or practice can have symbolic religious value, or symbolic moral value (my concern here), or symbolic aesthetic value, or lack such value, whether or not the agent or someone else recognizes it and values it accordingly. Various combinations of value and valuing are possible, and this holds for symbolic acts of memorialization as well: an act can be valued by the agent or by another because of what the agent or another takes it to symbolize, but the act might nevertheless lack symbolic value or the symbolic value he took it to have or it might be symbolically disvaluable; it might

The Nature and Value of Memorialization as Symbolic Activity   241

be symbolically valuable but not be valued that way or might be disvalued by the agent or another; etc. Some act may have symbolic value for moral or other reasons although it is not recognized to have it, or some act may be symbolically disvaluable because it lacks moral value but is thought to possess it. The general explanation of these different possibilities is plain: a person's perceptions of symbolic value and the reasons for it do not always reliably and accurately track the symbolic value that something actually has, whatever the source of this value. The agent's assessment of the symbolic value of an action is one thing; the agent's being right about this and about how to value it, as judged from a standpoint that transcends the agent's actual responses, is another.

I start with a symbolic action believed to have moral and social value because of what it symbolizes, but where this indicates a failure to understand the action in all of its moral and social dimensions. This is not a case where the agent thinks a symbolic action has one sort of value, say, religious value, but where from an "objective" perspective it lacks another sort of value, say, moral value, because it is morally repugnant. Rather, this is a case where both subjective and objective standpoints assess an action using the same type of evaluation.

Consider then the controversy surrounding the flying of the Confederate flag over the statehouse in South Carolina.[22] To commemorate the Civil War Centennial, the state of South Carolina hoisted the Confederate flag above its state capital building as a symbol of pride in its Southern heritage and as a way of honoring the Confederate dead. But in recent years, sentiment has changed: many South Carolinians (and Americans) now want it to come down. It is not difficult to justify this stand: the values and principles that the flying of the flag symbolizes, or more charitably those that are inextricably tied up with what the act symbolizes, are morally repugnant. The flag is not just a symbol of an idyllic way of life or state's rights, but arguably of slavery and racism, even if those who fly it refuse to accept this interpretation. To fly the flag, associated as it is with a history of racial subjugation, is, at the least, grossly insensitive to the descendants of slaves and to those who still suffer the effects of racial discrimination. To be sure, continuing to fly the flag cost South Carolina economically. But the problem with flying the flag that I am highlighting is with the symbolism, not its consequences: supporters of flying the flag just got it wrong about the value of what the act, all things considered, symbolizes. They took its symbolism to be unequivocally morally valuable because of the particular virtues it honors. But they overlooked, willfully or otherwise, the potent message of racial superiority it conveys. It does not have the symbolic meaning they took it and intended it to have. It is, in fact, a deeply morally flawed symbol.

In another sort of case, agents might not be mistaken in this manner but rather misguided in the way they choose to symbolize their values. Another example involving memorialization that can illustrate this is the controversy surrounding the design and construction of an official 9/11 memorial in Lower Manhattan. Not all of the controversy, to be sure, had to do with the symbolism of rebuilding on the World Trade Center site, but the strong emotions it evoked have to be explained in part by reference to it. There were two impulses behind the rebuilding effort with different symbolic implications, and there was some tension between them.[23] On the one hand, construction on the site was to symbolize America's resilience in the face of terrorist attack and to evoke an optimistic future. On the other, since thousands died in the attack on the World Trade Center, their deaths had to be properly commemorated; and since the site was the final resting place of many hundreds of victims whose remains could not be identified, their deaths had to be commemorated there, not someplace else. These different intentions for the World Trade Center site sometimes clashed. Thus, initial construction plans called for rebuilding the towers as a symbolic show of defiance to terrorists, and soon developers also urged the inclusion of retail shops in the new towers to demonstrate that life goes on as before. But vocal family members insisted that the footprints of the original towers remain untouched out of respect for those who died and as a symbol not of defiance as much as of the loss they had suffered. Moreover, the commercialization of the site was deeply offensive to them. Though family members did not necessarily object to having the site serve as more than a memorial to their dead loved ones, they objected to, and arguably had a legitimate case against, how this goal was being pursued. In their view, celebrating American values and American resilience might be an important symbolic function of a rebuilt World Trade Center site, but the memorial to the victims had to be given priority.

Actions may be undertaken to symbolize certain moral or other values, but the agent or others might be mistaken in thinking that they are values, or that their actions symbolize them, or they might be insensitive to alternative meanings the acts might convey, or wrong about how to show support for them. Though this is obvious enough, explanations of these divergences tell us something important about the nature of symbolic value. I propose two explanations. According to the first, two facts account for the divergences: (1) symbolic meaning does not reside solely in the mind or intentions of the agent but in public space; and (2) the symbolic value of action depends on its symbolic meaning. (I could just assert that symbolic value is located in public space, but I think it is helpful to ground the publicity of symbolic value in something recognizably public like meaning.) These propositions entail that the agent does not have unrestricted free choice with respect to endowing an action with symbolic value. Given that the agent's choice is constrained, when it is not clear to others what the symbolic meaning of an action is, or when it has an ambiguous symbolic meaning and reasonable alternative interpretations of its meaning are possible, or for some other reason, its symbolic value may be called into question, regardless of the

The Nature and Value of Memorialization as Symbolic Activity   243

agent's intentions. And when there is disagreement over the symbolic value of an act—as, for example, in the case of the flying of the Confederate flag—the agent's interpretation of it is not necessarily dispositive.

A second explanation, or perhaps it is an elaboration of the first, stresses the communicative function of symbolic action. Symbolic action is commonly communicative action or action that is intended to communicate something to a recipient. Communicating differs from merely expressing oneself: though expression brings mental states into the open, this is not the same as intending to communicate these mental states or something else to others. Communication is a *transaction* between agent and recipient and it is constituted by various norms that specify the conditions for success or failure in the activity.[24] Thus, communicative transactions ought to be sensitive to the recipient's interests and to how she is likely to interpret the agent's intent, given her current circumstances and background. Otherwise the so-called communication simply fails as communication. If standards for successful communication are violated, then either nothing will be conveyed to the recipient or what is conveyed will not be what the agent intended to convey. An example of this is when symbolic reparations intended to acknowledge and make amends for a wrong instead leave victims feeling insulted, outraged, or bitterly disappointed, as a result of the agent's failure to properly assess how the gesture would be received by its intended beneficiary. This can happen in other contexts too—for example, when a church introduces a new form of religious worship intended to be inclusive and respectful of all members of the congregation but that is deeply offensive to some of them. The possibility of a mismatch between agent intention and recipient interpretation offers a further explanation of why an act that has symbolic value for the agent might not have symbolic value for the recipient and why, since symbolizing is a mode of communicating, the agent might be mistaken in attributing symbolic value to the act.

However, it is one thing to say that the symbolic meaning and value of an act are not determined solely by the agent, and quite another to hold that the agent's reasons and motives for performing it are irrelevant to the symbolic value that the act possesses. The latter is plainly false. In particular, the agent's reasons are not irrelevant to the *moral* value that the act of symbolizing has: not just the moral value the agent takes it to have, but the moral value it has from a standpoint independent of the agent's perspective. The following simple example should suffice to show this. As generally understood "in public space," the act of giving one's wife a wedding anniversary gift symbolizes and expresses commitment to the value of fidelity to one's spouse. Suppose, however, that one's reason for giving the gift is to appear to be committed to this, in order to ward off suspicions that one is having an affair. In other words, the agent's reasons do not align with the gesture's generally accepted, conventional symbolic meaning as an expression of fidelity. Misleading communications of this kind are possible not only in interpersonal situations, but also in the political arena of official communication—for example, when groups that have been the victims of wrongdoing are led to believe, falsely, that acts of official contrition will be followed by substantive changes in the material conditions of their lives. Even though the acts promise substantive changes by virtue of their generally accepted symbolic meaning, the agent's reasons have a bearing, specifically in these cases a negative bearing, on the symbolic value of the act viewed through a moral lens. The symbolic value of the acts consists in their standing for a moral commitment, but there is no commitment of the right sort.

3. Against the moral value of symbolism

I made a suggestion in the previous section that can be reformulated as follows. A symbolic act that stands for a value or principle or cause, that expresses support for or appreciation of it, is commonly viewed as issuing a kind of *promissory note* with respect to future acts that refer to or stand for the same value, principle, or cause. If these acts are not forthcoming, we may have grounds to question whether the agent's professed endorsement of the principle, value, or cause means that he is really determined to see it realized. Importantly, however, this does *not* show that the symbolic value of an action is value derived from its effects. Moreover, it does not imply that symbolic acts have no value as symbols or no symbolic moral value, *until* they are followed by additional acts exemplifying support. After all, further acts may not be possible, or they may be problematic in other ways for reasons that do not impugn the sincerity of the agent's commitment. In some situations, a single symbolic gesture might be potent enough to have considerable moral weight.

I will in fact argue in sections 4 and 5 that there can be moral value that inheres in symbolic action because of what it is—that is, because it symbolizes something and does not cause it and also expresses (literally or metaphorically) mental states of one sort or another. Assuming this, and given that symbolic value is not instrumental value, a number of combinations of value seem to be possible. An act may have both types of moral value or lack both; or an act may have moral value qua symbolic but be lacking in instrumental value because it has suboptimal or negative consequences; or it may have the best consequences that can be achieved in the circumstances but not much moral value from the standpoint of its symbolism. My interest here is how to rank the two types of value in general and in situations requiring a choice between them. This will set the stage for my account of the moral value of symbolic value by presenting an approach that is antithetical to it.

The Nature and Value of Memorialization as Symbolic Activity   245

A common view about symbolic value is that it can't compete with the value of achieving good outcomes, of actually producing good in the world, and that by comparison with the latter, it is what we might call a "lightweight" kind of value.[25] There are different ways to explain what this might mean. One is that symbolic actions have no specifically moral value at all. Symbolic value is a type of non-moral value—perhaps sentimental or aesthetic value—and as such the moral value of achieving good outcomes is always overriding when the two values are in competition. This may be a kind of moral value monism. Another possibly somewhat more plausible view is that even if it has some sort of moral value, symbolic value is always overridden or swamped by the moral value of achieving good results, when they are in competition and even when the good results are not substantially greater than the bad. This allows for a kind of moral value pluralism, where "symbolic moral value" refers to the moral value that symbolic acts have for a reason other than that they produce good consequences. Whichever view one takes, I call this *the thesis of lesser value*.

Here is one way to present it. We act symbolically partly because there is nothing better that we can do under the circumstances, and it would *be* better if, instead of just symbolizing some value or principle or goal, we could do something to actually achieve the goal or to bring about the state of affairs enjoined by the principle or sanctioned by the value. According to this way of thinking, symbolic acts are simply to be regarded as surrogates or stand-ins for the real thing, what we do only because we are powerless or insufficiently imaginative or too risk averse to do something better, and what we are only permitted to do if and because we are not forgoing the possibility of achieving good or better outcomes by so acting. They do not themselves have or have much moral value.

This or something like it is what we might say about symbolic compensation, for example. Symbolic compensation is commonly contrasted with "real" or fully adequate compensation and valued as a kind of approximation to it. "Real" compensation is what we would provide if we could, but for various reasons we can't, so compensation that is symbolic will just have to do. Another example is symbolic opposition to an oppressive regime. Here it might be argued that symbolic opposition is a second-best alternative to actually overturning or contributing to overturning the regime. If the regime could be toppled, there would seem to be little point or value in symbolically opposing it—unless, that is, by symbolically opposing it others would be inspired to join the cause and this would make the overthrow more likely. Symbolic opposition, when "real" political change is possible, seems pretty pathetic by comparison, and this might be taken to show that symbolic opposition itself has little moral value.

The thesis of lesser value holds that whatever our moral reasons might be for engaging in symbolic acts, if there is something reasonably available to us that would be better to do in the circumstances, "better" not in the sense of symbolically better but in terms of consequences, then we are only permitted to perform the symbolic acts if they can be done without compromising the achievement of those consequences. I mean better consequences to include better consequences *for the principle* in the name of which the agent acts. Thus, in general, it is preferable, other things being equal, to bring about or contribute to bringing about the state of affairs enjoined by a principle than just to symbolically exemplify and express support for it, when the issue is what we should do to support the principle. Of course, other things are not always equal, in which case symbolic ways of expressing support for the principle, assuming they have some moral value, might be better than nothing. This isn't saying very much for the importance of symbolic value, however.

What these assessments reveal is that symbolic value, as a distinct type of value, has a lesser normative weight or significance than instrumental value, and this holds even in cases where there is not in fact something reasonably available to the agent that would be better to do. We might explain this on the ground that there is a notion of a *better* way to do what symbolic acts are (only feebly) doing, say, supporting a principle—better because it accomplishes what symbolic acts are unable to do, which is to make an actual difference in the world. Though existing circumstances may not permit doing what is better, circumstances might have been different, in which case the symbolic act should have been abandoned or done only if it did not stand in the way of more efficacious action. And if, under existing circumstances, we cannot do better, we should at least be on the lookout for a (consequentially) better way to show our support for the principle and be prepared to so act.

With respect to the ranking of memorialization initiatives, proponents of the thesis of lesser value would make something like the following case. Acts of memorialization can symbolically express adherence to the principle that amends should be made for past wrongdoing and in this role can stand for other acts whose purpose is to make amends. But there are other and not just other but *better* ways of showing support for this principle than memorialization. Memorialization, after all, is "just" symbolic. These should be pursued vigorously; and where social resources are limited, they should not be siphoned off to support memorial projects, because whatever good they might do, practical policies of social reconstruction and victim assistance can do more. If you really want to show that you take your responsibility to make amends seriously, it might be said, then enforce the rule of law and punish the perpetrators; promote democratic values and a culture of human rights; establish medical facilities to care for survivors; and reform key institutions that sanctioned and facilitated past injustices. To be sure, memorial projects can have effects that contribute somewhat to transitional goals, and if there is nothing else that can be done, then such projects would have some special importance. But surely there is almost always

The Nature and Value of Memorialization as Symbolic Activity 247

something more and better that can be done, more than engaging in symbolic gestures, however well intentioned, and memorial projects should only be pursued if they leave enough resources for more worthy measures. Moreover, the sacrifices required of society to produce public memorials are relatively minor by comparison with those needed to make the other necessary changes, and they attest to less of a commitment on society's part to make amends for past wrongdoing. Even taking into account its possible psychological benefits, memorialization exemplifies and fulfills the principle less fully than performing acts of amends making that realize non-symbolic values.

To be clear, those who make this argument need not deny that practical policies of social reconstruction and victim assistance carry symbolic meanings and that because of these meanings they can advance these ends. Symbolic acts can produce certain effects, some of which bear specifically on the possibility of realizing the state of affairs enjoined by the principle that the acts symbolize, as I noted above in discussing the notion of "better consequences," and some of which do not. The consequences might be positive or negative, or less positive than what would result from other courses of action. If the symbolic act has positive consequences and does not interfere with worthwhile social projects of other sorts, then the thesis of lesser value would not object to its performance. But if the overall consequences of its performance are negative or less good than those of other available acts, the thesis would hold that it should not be done. (According to a slightly different version of the thesis, the act should not be done if the anticipated negative consequences are above a certain threshold, or the consequences are less good by a certain margin than other courses of action, regardless of whether the act would constitute a significant departure from symbolic values. As a version of the thesis of lesser value, this modification would subscribe to the same evaluative ranking of symbolic and instrumental values as the original formulation of the thesis.) These general points about how the thesis of lesser value assesses the moral value of symbolic actions apply, of course, to symbolic acts of memorializing as well: what counts or counts most is whether the world is made better or worse by practices of memorialization. It is not that the consequences of memorialization are good in virtue of the relation they have to symbolically valuable meanings, but rather that the value of symbolism is assessed in terms of the consequences it produces.

Because meanings are not socially inert but have real effects of various sorts, good as well as bad, on those to whom the acts are directed, proponents of the thesis of lesser value will not be indifferent to the symbolic meanings that memorialization can have for the victims and others, including perpetrators. Moreover, proponents will only accept memorial projects whose likely overall negative consequences, including their opportunity costs, are outweighed by their positive ones. Of note in this regard, as writers on transitional justice have pointed out, is the process of arriving at and implementing decisions about what should be memorialized and how it should be done. Specifically, the risk of some of the negative consequences of carrying out acts of memorialization in transitional societies can be greatly reduced if these decisions are not made unilaterally and imposed from above but result from a broad-based community consultation process. The report of the South Africa's Truth and Reconciliation Commission emphasizes the importance of having the right process:

> Symbolic reparations such as monuments and museums are important but should ideally be linked with endeavors that improve the everyday lives of victims and their communities. One way of combining the two aims is to involve victims prominently in the design and manufacture of monuments.[26]

Monuments and museums are likely to be meaningless, offensive, or socially divisive if the needs of victims and their communities are not taken into account in constructing them and if they are not actively involved in the memorializing process and in determining priorities among social initiatives. Proponents of the thesis of lesser value, for whom creating monuments, museums, and other memorials is morally permitted only to the extent that it promotes or does not interfere with achieving the best state of affairs under the circumstances, will likely insist on these measures if they are going to allow memorials at all. Whether it symbolizes a moral principle or value is otherwise irrelevant.

It might seem quite plausible in some cases, such as those of symbolic compensation and symbolic protest against an oppressive regime, that symbolic acts are warranted only as a kind of substitute, only because there is no way at all or no feasible way under existing conditions to do something better, better, that is, in an instrumental sense. From a consequentialist standpoint, the value of symbolic action in these cases consists in their supporting dispositions that can be put to better use under more favorable conditions. But these examples, while appearing to fit the thesis of lesser value, do not really support the moral claims of the thesis. In other words, they do not show that the thesis correctly assesses the respective moral weights of symbolic and instrumental considerations. What the examples show is that we need to take note of and not gloss over the essential and ineradicable limitations of symbolic action. However, the thesis of lesser value goes too far in the other direction, by holding that symbolic value is relatively insignificant from a moral standpoint, compared to the value that actions have in virtue of their consequences.

At this point, we might wonder with Nozick: "Why is actually leading to something so much better than symbolizing it that symbolization should not count at all? "Because that's the bottom line, what actually occurs; all the rest is talk." But why is this bottom line better than all other lines?"[27] We *talk*, presumably, when and because we cannot *do*; and when we can do, we stop or should stop talking. The thesis I have been discussing takes a less extreme position: it does not assert that symbolization should count for nothing, only that it should count for less or is a lesser kind of value. But we can ask with the same sense of perplexity that Nozick's question reflects why symbolic adherence to a principle should be regarded as having less value or as being a lesser sort of value by comparison with "what actually occurs"—that is, with the causal utility of the act. Certainly, the fact that act-tokens bearing one type of value (symbolic) can sometimes be overridden by act-tokens bearing another type of value (causal utility) does not by itself entail that, as a type of value, the former ranks less highly than the latter.

If we were to leave the case against the thesis of lesser value here, we would have accomplished something, but not enough. For it is one thing to challenge the claims of the thesis and to ask why we should accept them, and something else to show why we shouldn't. To show the latter, we need to have a better grasp of the moral values that symbolic acts can possess. Once this is made clear, we will be in a better position to challenge the thesis's ranking of value-types and its discounting of the value of symbolic acts, including those of memorialization. We will see that there is moral value in symbolic acts that the thesis of lesser value does not acknowledge, and while the issue of ranking may not be finally resolved, the implausibility of the thesis should become more apparent.

4. Memorialization and reasons of respect

This question I am pursuing, "What is the moral value of symbolic action?" is an instance of the larger question, "What value does this action have, considered from the standpoint of its symbolism?" The first question asks about the moral value the action has in virtue of what it stands for or the moral value to which it refers. In addition, since symbolic actions are often expressive actions, it asks about the moral value of the emotions or attitudes that are expressed in and by them. The second question encompasses values of different sorts, including religious and aesthetic values, as well as the value of aptness or suitability. Thus, among other things, it asks about how well the action functions as a symbol, how fitted or qualified it is to serve as a symbol of what it is alleged to be a symbol of and how effectively it symbolizes it. As noted in section 1, the action may be a good symbol in this respect, even though it is not a symbol of what is good or of one's allegiance to it. These symbols are not my concern here, however: I am only interested in symbols that are good because of fit and moral value.

In what follows, I discuss two non-rival ways of addressing the question of the moral value that symbolic actions in general, and symbolic acts of memorialization in particular, can have. The results of these two approaches, especially when combined, provide a strong case for the non-instrumental moral value of these acts. One approach assesses them from the standpoint of the evaluative attitudes that are expressed by symbolic means. This is what I will discuss in this section. The other assesses them from the standpoint of what they reveal about the character of the agent and of their importance for the agent's identity, individual as well as collective. This I take up in the next section.[28] The arguments are meant to provide a counter to the thesis of lesser value, and while I will not attempt to "prove" that the thesis is mistaken in the ordinary sense of that word, the combined weight of the considerations I adduce speaks strongly against it and should make us considerably less willing to embrace its value ranking.

(a) Respect for value

This explanation consists of two claims: (a) symbolic acts can express and communicate respect for value; and (b) respect for value is morally valuable when the value is moral. The idea of "respect for value" is taken from Joseph Raz's discussion of respecting people in *Value, Respect, and Attachment*.[29] "Respect in general," he says, "is a species of recognizing and being disposed to respond to value" (160) that is non-optional for practical reason. There are "three stages of correct response to value, and to the presence of good-making properties" (161) in things that have value (including objects, states, and activities). The first is recognition: "regarding objects in ways consistent with their value, in one's thoughts, understood broadly to include imaginings, emotions, wishes, intentions, etc." (161). Raz regards the "expression of recognition of value in language and other symbolic actions as also belonging with the first stage of relating to value" (162). The other two stages are preservation (objects of value are not to be destroyed and are sometimes to be preserved) and engagement, which can take various forms, depending on the nature of the valuable object. Because not everyone is competent to fully engage with value or can reasonably be expected to devote the resources needed to do so, reasons of respect are often only reasons for the first two stages of response to value.

Following Raz, I propose that actions that are (objectively) symbolically valuable respond to what is of value and respect value by recognizing it through the symbolic meanings with which they are invested. The reasons we have for performing symbolic acts, on this account, are reasons of respect. There are different kinds of values that symbolic actions might recognize, as I noted before— religious, aesthetic, political, and so on—and the requirements for respecting them will vary depending on the kind of value it is and the context of action.

I am interested here in the relationship between symbolic value and moral value, as indicated in (b).

To illustrate how the notion of respect for value can explain the moral value of symbolic action, I turn to memorialization. Acts of memorialization, such as erecting a monument or constructing a memorial museum or instituting days of commemoration, can manifest respect for moral values of different sorts and for the values that things possess, and respecting the moral values things possess entails that the respecting itself has moral value. There is the value of life and of protecting it from assault. There is the value of a way of life that is on the verge of extinction because of the genocidal policies of an authoritarian regime. There is the value of making amends for wrongdoing; of repairing the harm that was done by injustice and wrongdoing and restoring the dignity of those whose rights were violated; and of taking responsibility for having committed or supported or acquiesced in wrongdoing. And there is the value of morality itself as the regulative standard governing social and interpersonal relations.

Memorial projects can manifest respect for these various values, as can other kinds of symbolic action. But memorials do this in a special way and in so doing, respect another value that is unique to them: the value of remembering itself. In the case of memorial projects that commemorate the victims of wrongdoing, this is the value of keeping their memory alive and making certain that future generations do not forget them and what they suffered. Remembering them in the right way is itself of moral value, and respecting the moral value of remembering the lives lost is distinct from respecting the value of those lives. The two are connected, however: failing to respect the value of remembering the lives lost is itself a way of failing to respect the value of the lives themselves. In relation to all of these moral values, memorial activities acquire a moral character by respecting them: they become morally valuable activities. This is an instance of the general truth that respecting moral value or the moral value that something has is itself morally valuable. (Analogously, respecting things that have religious value is religiously valuable, and so on.)

I do not limit this account to individual agents. Collectives too, by which I mean individuals considered together as interacting parts of a functioning whole and not merely as an aggregate, are capable of having beliefs and intentions and engaging in actions that together express respect for value. Public memorial projects are collective enterprises and, adapting claims (a) and (b), they have moral value as collective enterprises to the extent that they collectively express respect for what is of moral value. However, collective memorialization is more complicated from the standpoint of symbolism than acts of remembrance carried out by individuals acting individually, so a word about this is necessary.

The reason it is more complicated is that there may be proxies or surrogates who are authorized to *represent* the collective, in which case there is a second layer of symbolism on top of the symbolism of the memorials themselves. The actions of those who speak for or represent a collective entity, when they have legitimate authority to speak for it and their actions fall within its scope, symbolize the actions, beliefs, and sentiments of the collective they represent.[30] So, for example, when state officials of this sort confer legitimacy on memorial projects, symbolizing takes place on two levels: state action symbolizes the political community's endorsement of these projects and the projects themselves are a kind of symbolic reparation. Of course, not all political regimes have the authority to represent their community in such a way as to symbolize its endorsement of memorial projects, so the argument only applies to certain states, including those that have more or less open political processes and are broadly democratic in character. Democratic regimes symbolize the political community's views about and attitudes toward all sorts of issues, including but not limited to whether and how to memorialize the victims of wrongdoing. Indeed, it is a characteristic feature of democratic regimes that because of their representative relationship to the political community, they have the ability and the license to symbolize its views and attitudes across a broad spectrum.

There are different sorts of responses to moral value and objects of moral value that can count as respectful, and among these are acts, individual and collective, that have a symbolic relationship to them. As T. M. Scanlon observes, "to value something is to take oneself to have reasons for holding certain positive attitudes towards it and for acting in certain ways in regard to it. Exactly what these reasons are, and what actions and attitudes they support, will be different in different cases. They generally include, as a common core, reasons for admiring the thing and respecting it, although "respecting" can involve quite different things in different cases."[31] I agree with Raz and Scanlon that practical rationality admits of different rational and moral ways of responding to and respecting value. One way is to promote its existence: those who seek to promote intrinsically valuable states of affairs can be said to express respect for the value of those states of affairs by so doing. But respecting value does not always involve this, and believing that something is valuable does not involve believing that there is only one way to properly respond to it. In particular, respecting value can also involve engaging in acts—such as acts of memorialization—that in different ways have a symbolic relation to that value. Indeed, in some situations this might be the only or the best way to express respect for important moral values, since other ways of doing so are foreclosed or excessively costly to others or extremely dangerous. However, to repeat an earlier point using the language of respect, this is not to say that the respect for value shown by symbolic acts is only a stand-in for something of greater value and that it has a lesser value than the respect for value that is shown by bringing about states of affairs possessing it. Moreover, even if the symbolic act does promote the existence of the value it symbolizes, it

The Nature and Value of Memorialization as Symbolic Activity   253

does not follow that the symbolism of the act adds not at all or only marginally to the overall moral value that the act possesses.

At this point an advocate of the thesis of lesser value will likely have the following rejoinder: I have only shown that there are different ways of respecting value and different sorts of values corresponding to these, not that these different ways of respecting value are of equal value. The issue, however, is whether there is an evaluative ranking of values such that symbolic ways of respecting a value are ranked below respecting that value by promoting states of affairs with it.[32] A definitive response to the thesis of lesser value, therefore, would not only consist in making the case for a *pluralism* of values but would also need to challenge its claim about their *ranking*. According to one version of the thesis, symbolic actions are allowed to have some moral value, but if there is a conflict between them and doing something that is instrumentally valuable, the latter always wins. The question of what criteria to use to compare and rank different sorts or sources of moral values is obviously larger than the one I am confronted with here, and I cannot properly address either this larger issue or the particular one concerning the relation of symbolic and instrumental value. But at least a few brief comments are called for.

First, the idea that there is some general ranking of values that assigns priority to one of them has one apparent attraction: by telling us that one value is more normatively significant and that we should always give priority to it conflict situations, it removes uncertainty and ambiguity from the decision-making process. But if it does this by imposing an artificial hierarchy that distorts and oversimplifies the complexity of moral life, then this alleged advantage can no longer be considered a point in its favor. And in my view, this is just what the thesis of lesser value does. It is a fundamental fact about human beings that we are complex creatures who can view the world and our relation to the good in different ways and who inevitably face conflicts of value for this reason. These conflicts speak to the complexity of human nature, a complexity that is deep and in basic respects largely unalterable, and the prioritizing of one sort of value over others seems arbitrary in light of this. Some reasons for acting are reasons of symbolic value. These are ubiquitous and central in human life, and one way that we relate to the good is by acting on the basis of reasons of this sort. Other reasons pertain to the production of good. We respect value by doing good in the world when we can, when we take as a reason for doing something that it will bring about intrinsically desirable states of affairs. Proposals that reduce the former sort of value to the latter or that subordinate the former to the latter are simply not plausible as responses to this diversity of values. Rather than rank them, the more sensible course is to think of them as representing different kinds of ethical considerations, neither of which regularly outweighs or overrides the other and both of which may need to be taken equally seriously if one is to make moral decisions responsibly.[33]

In further support of this position, there is a phenomenological argument against the thesis of lesser value: it can be faulted for failing to do justice to our intuitions concerning moral experience in circumstances of moral complexity and conflict. A pluralistic account of value that accords neither instrumental value nor symbolic value unwavering priority over the other in such circumstances better captures the phenomenology of moral responsiveness than the view expressed by the thesis of lesser value.

(b) Respect for persons

I turn now from respect for value to respect for persons who possess value. Memorial projects and practices can express this and be a fitting response to wrongdoing that deprived individuals of their most basic rights as persons. Respect for persons, conveyed through acts of memorialization and in other ways, is also an evaluative attitude that can serve as the basis of a reconstructed political community.

Before discussing what I mean by respect for persons and how memorialization can express it, I want to return to last chapter's discussion of three moral values of remembrance and explain why I focus on one of them, respect for persons, here. One of the values I discussed there is self-respect: memorial activities can express the self-respect of victims whose rights were violated and who were excluded from equal membership in the political community. Another value is fidelity to the dead: survivor communities, and others with particular ties to the dead, can express their continuing loyalty to the dead by engaging in memorial activities in their honor. Creating memorials and museums can be significant symbolic acts because they embody and exemplify these values. They can also express and exemplify respect. As a value, respect for persons is different from the others because it does not presuppose or require membership in a particular subgroup of society or the existence of a particular normative relationship with others (excluding the relation of fellow citizen). In a political community, respect for persons, in this case meaning respect for those who were the victims of wrongdoing, is owed by citizens generally—not just those who were themselves the victims of wrongdoing or who had a relationship with them that grounds obligations of fidelity—and it is owed toward all who were wronged by the breakdown of political and legal institutions in their society. In this sense it has the most inclusive implications of the three values.

Another reason for dwelling on respect is a similarity between the scope of its associated imperative and the scope of reparative obligations. It is not only the imperative of respect that is inclusive. The harm done by wrongdoing must be repaired, and reparative obligations that are owed to the victims of wrongdoing and that may be partially fulfilled through memorial practices can be quite

The Nature and Value of Memorialization as Symbolic Activity   255

inclusive as well. These obligations are not simply owed by those responsible for the wrongdoing: they can also adhere to individuals as a condition and consequence of membership in a political community. As such, they are part and parcel, as W. James Booth puts it, of "belonging to an enduring mesh of relations of justice characteristic of a political community." As he explains:

> We attribute to political communities an identity understood as a cross-generational enduringness of some broadly normative aspects of their existence: for example, a shared perception of justice, a constitution to express it, and its correlated institutional arrangements. That persistence makes a community the bearer of the past and the steward of its future, and gives it an enduring relationship to the absent denizens of both domains.[34]

Thinking of a political community this way, as an "enduring mesh of relations of justice," its members can be obligated to make reparation since membership carries with it a moral involvement in its past. This obligation is discharged in part by engaging in memorial activities that are expressions of respect for the victims[35] because respect is of sufficient scope to be an appropriate basis for public memorial activities that are reparative in nature.

What is next to be discussed is what respect for persons and hence for victims requires, and how it is shown to the victims of wrongdoing, many of whom are not alive to appreciate it.

Raz conjectures that respect for persons is a special case of a more general obligation to respect value. It is not, he argues, a special kind of respect, but rather, respect for a special kind of object. The argument I consider now does not follow Raz in this and may in fact rely on a conception of respect for persons that cannot easily be squared with his. However, it is not important for present purposes to decide whether it can or not.[36] Rather, I will simply assume what seems to me a very plausible and compelling account of respect for persons, the one elaborately worked out by Stephen Darwall.[37] I will then contend that symbolic acts of memorialization can express respect for persons thus understood, whether the persons are living or dead, and that they have moral value as a consequence of their doing so. Of course these symbolic actions do not always express and show respect for persons; they may instead express disrespect or have other purposes unrelated to respect for persons. But respect for the victims of wrongdoing who were denied it seems to be part, indeed an essential part, of the point of memorialization in transitional societies, and it is in terms of respect that the moral value of such acts in transitional contexts is commonly defended.

Respect for persons, according to Darwall, involves recognizing that they have authority to make demands of oneself equal to one's authority to make demands of them and holding oneself accountable to them for complying with these demands. Wronging another person disrespects him because in so acting one regards him as having no authority to make demands of oneself, or as having less authority than oneself to make demands of others. It disrespects him because one does not hold oneself accountable to him for complying with demands that he has the authority to make. Now under the right conditions, some of which are highlighted by the restorative justice movement discussed in chapter 4, those responsible for wrongdoing might come to recognize their victims' authority to make demands and might take responsibility for their failures to comply with them. When this happens, and especially when this recognition and responsibility taking are enacted in the presence of the community—the community to which the wrongdoers belong as well as that to which the victims belong—the standing of victims as moral interlocutors (that is, as persons with the authority to make demands of others, including those who have mistreated them, and to hold them accountable for their mistreatment) is acknowledged, and the wrongdoers' intent to do justice is communicated. By assenting to the victims' second-personal authority and holding themselves accountable to them for failure to respect this authority, the victims receive a kind of validation, and validation can be reparative: it can help repair the harm caused by wrong and violence.

We can learn more about the meaning and importance of respect in the context of memorialization if we turn to the psychotherapeutic literature, where validation is described as a critical aspect of psychoanalytic and cognitive-behavioral therapies.[38] Though validation through memorialization in transitional societies is not a matter of one person providing validation for and of another, but an entire community validating many or perhaps a few of its members, and though the validation that is provided by memorialization is only symbolic, there is considerable similarity in how validation works and what it communicates in both the therapeutic and the memorialization settings.

Validation in the therapeutic encounter, according to Mark Schechter, involves responding "to the patient's feelings, thoughts, or behaviors as understandable, justified, and legitimate in the context of the patient's past experience" (112), acknowledging her feelings, thoughts, or behaviors as valid responses in light of what she experienced in the past and not discounting them as hysterical, exaggerated, or irrational. The central meaning of validation is something more basic, however: it conveys to the patient that she is worthy of attention and that her perspective, thoughts, and feelings are worth taking seriously for this reason. "The essence of validation," as Schechter succinctly puts it, "is the experience of having been perceived, understood, and accepted as legitimate by an important other" (106), so it is not just specific feelings, thoughts, or behaviors that are validated, but also the individual who has them. The patient's sense of self

The Nature and Value of Memorialization as Symbolic Activity   257

and identity receive confirmation or, if her sense of self has been impaired, she is supported in her efforts to rebuild it. In transitional contexts, the "patient" includes the direct victims who survived the violation of their rights (primary victims); the families of the victims who also suffered from what was done to them (secondary victims); and the communities to which the victims belong and that were damaged by the wrongdoing targeted at their members (tertiary victims). For all of these, the feelings, thoughts, and behaviors are those that are associated with or caused by wrongdoing.

A full account of validation through memorialization would incorporate these insights from the psychological literature, but it would also contain moral elements. Psychologically speaking, validation of the victims of wrongdoing involves their having the sense that they are accepted as legitimate by an important other, and it is therapeutic to the extent that it manages to undo the effects of a prior refusal by an important other to accept them as such. But to account for memorialization as an activity with *moral* effects—that is, an activity that not only heals wounds but that repairs wrongdoing—we need to explain what being "accepted as legitimate" means in moral terms. Here is where Darwall's analysis of respect is extremely useful. As I have explained it, respect validates in a specifically moral sense when one's authority to make demands of others and to hold them accountable for complying with these demands is recognized by those others as legitimate, and they communicate their intention to take responsibility for past wrongdoing. But validation through memorialization raises the question of how respect in this second-personal sense is expressed and communicated in decisions about and policies related to memorialization, and more specifically, how they can be construed as expressing and communicating respect for victims who are dead. For the victims of wrongdoing who have not survived, it is too late for them to experience validation from the wrongdoers' acknowledgements of culpability, and if they cannot "experience" the validation that respect provides, then one might wonder what sort of validation of them is possible at all. Can acts of memorialization nevertheless symbolize respect for these victims? And if so, how?[39]

Respect is a particular evaluative attitude that differs from other attitudes that activities of memorialization can symbolize, including love, appreciation, admiration, and reverence. It is also not the same as honor, with which it is sometimes used interchangeably, for honor, in one of its senses, differs from respect in being bound up with conferring a symbol of distinction on another, with singling another out for special acknowledgment or praise. One can honor the victims of wrongdoing, for example, by publicly reading their names at annual commemorative ceremonies or by naming public spaces such as streets and plazas after them. The issue at hand, however, is how memorialization can symbolize the particular attitude of *respect*, when this is understood in the second-personal sense of recognizing the standing to make demands of others and hold them accountable for compliance with them.

For memorialization to validate victims, and this, I take it, is a key function of memorialization in societies emerging from periods of violence and repression, it must recognize a standing in those it memorializes to demand compliance with norms adherence to which is demanded by the dignity of persons. Memorialization can be reverential and solemn and appreciative and more without respecting the victims in this specific sense. To be sure, memorializing recognizes this standing symbolically: the question is how. That is, we need to explain how memorialization can symbolically accord this standing to those who can no longer make demands of any kind. This is a critical question for a theory of the moral value of memorialization in transitional contexts, where many victims of human rights abuses have not lived to demand respect.

One way to think about this is to include persons related to the dead in some way within the ambit of respectful treatment. Memorialization can show respect for those who did not survive the violence and repression of the past if respect is shown their survivors. This can be done by linking memorialization to transitional programs and projects that involve survivors in a way that expresses and communicates respect (in the second-personal sense) for them. If these public programs and initiatives manifest and communicate respect for survivors in their design and implementation, *and* if the survivors have the sort of relationship with the dead that morally authorizes them to represent them, then memorialization symbolizes respect for the victims who did not survive. On this view, survivors are thought of as legitimate surrogates for or unofficial representatives of victims who did not survive, and the way the former are treated by the state and by civil society actors who collaborate with it conveys a message, belatedly, about the rightful claims of the latter and exemplifies how the latter ought to have been treated. The inclusion of memorial projects in a package of official measures that express concern and respect for survivors has the effect of conveying to them that the new regime is serious about restoring their status as equals within the community and is ready to take steps beyond memorialization to ensure this.

It is not only survivors who suffered a direct violation of their rights who can play this representative role; there are other sorts of "survivors" too. There are secondary victims, such as family and close friends, who suffered indirectly as a result of the wrongs done to the former. And there is also a tertiary victim, when the broader community that includes the primary and secondary victims is harmed. When individuals are targeted because of their membership in a particular religious, ethnic, or cultural group, or acts of violence attack its central symbols and traditions, or community leaders are killed, this harms the community as a whole, not just the individuals directly affected by these actions.[40]

The Nature and Value of Memorialization as Symbolic Activity   259

Including survivors of all sorts in transitional programs and projects evinces respect for them when they are given the real opportunity to play a significant role in their design and execution and have the recognized authority to veto or demand revision of those that do not meet their needs, as they understand them. Including them in this way can also serve as an indirect and symbolic means of expressing respect for the victims who did not survive.

It is also vital that survivors be involved in the design and execution of the memorial projects themselves. In theory these projects can pay *homage* to the victims who did not survive even if those who did survive and may legitimately represent them are not consulted. But as I said earlier, honor and (second-personal) respect are different evaluative attitudes, and this is another way in which they differ: respect requires that survivors play a more robust and normatively consequential role. The reason why memorial projects that exclude or marginalize them disrespect them—and through them disrespect the victims who did not survive and whom they represent—has to do with the attitudes that are thereby expressed toward them as *rememberers*.

To respect the survivors as survivors is in part to respect them as rememberers of their own suffering and the suffering of those close to and affiliated with them. It is to acknowledge the legitimacy of how they remember the past and what they choose to remember about it, and the necessity of taking their views seriously in this regard since they are the ones who have been harmed. Having been harmed does not mean that the statements they make about this wrongdoing are always factually accurate, or more factually accurate than those of more dispassionate reporters. It does, however, give them a kind of moral authority to testify to the wrongs that they and their relatives and fellow community members have suffered, an authority that derives from their speaking from a privileged (but not unimpeachable) vantage point.[41] Deference is shown to this moral authority only if deference is shown to them as rememberers of salient events in their past, if their competence as rememberers is acknowledged and their authority to testify is recognized by others as legitimate. It precludes, among other things, discounting their memories on the grounds that they are overly emotional or excessively parochial or biased, hence in some way or another untrustworthy.[42]

Respecting victims in the design and execution of memorial projects conveys a message of social inclusion of those formerly excluded from the political community by respecting them as rememberers. Brandon Hamber also remarks on a connection between involvement in memorials (and symbolic reparations in general) and social inclusion, but he understands this in psychological terms. "If symbolic reparations such as memorials and apologies are delivered," he says,

> individuals generally but not always need to feel that their suffering, or their relative's suffering, is adequately reflected in these measures. This

260 FORGIVENESS AND REMEMBRANCE

can be difficult to achieve and cannot be assumed without adequate participation and public involvement of key stakeholders in the development and conceptualisation of the symbolic reparations.[43]

Memorial projects are most likely to be successful as reparation and valuable to those who receive it, Hamber claims, when they come from the affected communities themselves and the survivors, relatives of victims, and survivor communities are involved in making key decisions about memorializing. Success is measured by whether memorials are able to effectively "serve as bridge between troubled internal feelings and feelings of social belonging."[44]

The argument of this section is a way of understanding this goal in moral terms. That is, the notion of second-personal respect provides a particular interpretation of what social belonging means and how memorials can promote feelings of social belonging for survivors and their relatives and communities. The feelings of social belonging that respect makes possible and justifies are not merely a result of passively receiving the benefits of social and economic life, including guarantees of protection from further harms, benefits that, in transitional contexts, recipients were formerly denied. Even if they are recognized as entitled to receive such benefits, this is not the same as being recognized to have second-personal authority to demand them and to hold others accountable for complying with these demands. The latter is what we might think of as "social belonging" in the full moral sense. It is what second-personal respect entails, and when it is expressed through memorials and other measures to redress past wrongdoing that accompany them, it promotes feelings of belonging to a political community of a certain sort, namely a community of mutually accountable equals.

Finally, as regards symbolizing respect for the dead by means of memorialization, it is of course the case that one of the reasons respect is so important is that people are alert to being treated with respect or disrespect and are hurt and offended by the latter. This would obviously not apply to those who did not survive wrongdoing: memorializing the dead (depending on how the process is carried out) can only symbolize, but not literally give them, respect in the second-personal sense. But the moral value of respect for persons is not entirely accounted for by its psychological effects on those who are respected (or not). Nozick makes the following observation that is relevant here: "Treating people with respect and responsiveness puts us "on the side of" that value, perhaps allying us with everything else on its side, and symbolizes our intertwining with this . . . The moral acts get grouped with other possible events and actions and come to stand for and mean them."[45] Normally, one puts oneself on the side of the value of respect for persons by respecting persons who are or are capable of being aware of respect and disrespect. But one can put oneself on the side of that value by engaging in acts that, while not conforming to the usual circumstances of respect for persons, nevertheless symbolize respect by being intertwined with actions of the same type that can be appreciated. Thus, acts of memorialization can put one on the side of the value of respect for those who perished, insofar as they stand for or are grouped with other actions that treat living victims with the respect the dead were denied. (Part of what gets them grouped with other actions that treat living victims in this way is the special relation that these victims have to the dead as their representatives.) By being grouped with other actions that recognize the authority of the living to demand respect from others, memorialization symbolizes the respect the dead were owed but did not receive.

5. Memorialization, character, and collective identity

The account so far has focused on the intrinsically valuable attitudes that agents symbolically express toward others in the process of memorializing them. I now want to consider the moral value of symbolic actions from the standpoint of their relationship to the agents themselves, their characters, identities, and self-understandings. This will be in two parts. I begin with how such acts can reveal the moral *character* of the agent and then discuss how they are intertwined with the agent's normative *identity*.

(a) Symbolic action and virtues

Symbols, and symbolic actions, stand for something, and that something can be a deontological principle. The principle represented by memorialization in the context of transitional societies is chiefly a principle of justice—more specifically, not punitive or compensatory but restorative justice. All of these principles are deontological because as commonly understood, they impose substantive restrictions on the achievement of desirable states of affairs. This contrasts with views holding that these are not substantive moral principles that can have independent significance in assessing the value of states of affairs.

In addition to principles of justice there is also a virtue of justice, and this can refer to a trait of individuals or of a group of individuals. There are in fact many different conceptions of the virtue of justice put forward by different theories of virtue. Some but not all of these are virtue ethical theories in that they regard virtue as the basis for understanding all of morality. They differ from the non-virtue ethical theories in that they do not give principles the same prominent and critical justificatory role as they have in these. There is also a distinction between (indirect) consequentialist and non-consequentialist non-virtue ethical accounts of virtue. I set aside the former since the current explanation is part of a non-consequentialist alternative to consequentialist understandings of the moral values of memorialization. Aside from this, I will not comment on these different ethical accounts of virtue. For what matters for present purposes is not how virtues are justified but only that, however justified, they are another source of the moral value of symbolic actions.

Robert Merrihew Adams, in one of the few discussions in the moral philosophy literature of symbolic value, asks the following question, intended to be rhetorical:

> If we take for granted that the value of what we cause, or at least of what we intentionally cause, is important for the moral quality of our lives, why should we not assume that the value of what we stand for symbolically is also important to the moral quality of our lives?[46]

The thought seems to be something like this. A person's actions can contribute to the goodness of her life in different ways. A good life is a life well spent, and we judge how well spent a person's life is partly by how much good she does or intentionally does in the world, when she has the opportunity or ability to do it. Actions can also contribute to the goodness of a human life in a different way, not by what they cause, but by "expressing symbolically an allegiance to the good or an opposition to the bad" (219). By "an allegiance to the good" I take Adams to refer to a habitual disposition to act well. One natural way to interpret this remark is as an endorsement of the important role that virtues play in moral life, since this would show that consequentialism is not a complete account of the moral value of human actions. Interpreted this way, symbolic actions could express, for example, virtues of hope, courage, loyalty, solidarity, or sympathy, and each would be valuable to the extent that it constitutes a way of being an ally of the good or an enemy of the bad—or "for the good and against the bad," as Adams puts it (218). Symbolic actions would flow from well-entrenched dispositions to act, feel, and will rightly, as these are determined by the aretaic norms for the particular virtue to be expressed.

Two examples will illustrate how one can symbolically be "for the good" by exhibiting virtue. Consider moral courage. It is especially evident that it may take moral courage to memorialize the victims of wrongdoing in the early stages of a political transition, or in politically repressive conditions, when remembrance confronts perpetrators and their supporters with the truth about their involvement in human rights abuses. Remembrance can speak truth to the guilty, but if the guilty also have the power to harm the speakers and to prevent others from hearing them, it takes courage to remember. Another virtue is hope. Memorials commemorating those who died from political violence are often undertaken with the aim of ensuring that such abuses do not recur, and those who participate in them are sustained by the hope that they can make a difference in

The Nature and Value of Memorialization as Symbolic Activity   263

this regard, that they will move others to establish political and legal safeguards, so that the wrongs of the past are not repeated. Hope works in another way as well, not to sustain efforts to prevent repetition of wrongdoing, but to sustain the commitment to engage in the work of memorialization itself. Those who are engaged in this work may lack assurance that later generations will actually remember the wrongs of the past because of what they do now or the conviction that their efforts have much chance of succeeding. But as a demonstration of something admirable in the character of those who persevere—allegiance to a worthy end (preserving the memory of wrongdoing) and hope that it may be realized—their efforts still have moral value.

Adams links symbolic actions to the moral quality of individual lives, but as a political act in transitional settings, memorialization is a response of the political community or part of it to past wrongdoing. It is a collective response because its members are jointly committed to the goal of memorializing and act in concert to achieve it, or because officials with authority to represent them symbolize this joint commitment through their decisions and policies. Nevertheless Adam's remarks may be relevant here too.

Virtues are traits of character, well-entrenched dispositions with multiple dimensions. They are not exhausted in the performance of an individual act but are exhibited in patterns of action, feeling, perception, and willing that provide a connecting thread among different moments of the agent's life. Moral virtues in particular are traits of moral character, so attributions of moral virtues to collectives presume that we can sensibly speak of them as having a moral character. But it is not clear what licenses us to do this. Notions such as "national character" and "the character of a people," for example, have frequently been viewed with considerable suspicion by social scientists. They have been criticized for being merely metaphorical or, more objectionably, for connoting some ahistorical, fixed essence of social systems. In order for virtue to explain the moral value of collective symbolic action, therefore, we need other concepts, or specifications of character concepts, that capture the distinctiveness of belonging to a particular nation, household, association, etc. for the individuals who belong to it, but that involves no problematic essentialist assumptions.

One sociological concept that fits the bill is habitus, popularized in recent decades by Pierre Bourdieu[47] and Norbert Elias in the concept of national habitus.[48] On one characterization, a habitus is a set of socially learned cognitive and affective dispositions, skills, and ways of acting that are acquired through activities and experiences conditioned and shaped by living within a particular social system. It refers, in short, to a historically specific personality structure. Looked at from a different point of view, it is a property of the social system itself that shapes these dispositions, skills, and ways of acting and gives them a distinct psycho-cultural specificity.

On this interpretation, group character refers to the features of a social system that explain how individuals develop and why they manifest certain typical and distinctive forms of feeling, thinking, doing, and interacting in virtue of belonging to it. The social system loosely structures these dispositions that together constitute a distinct psycho-cultural personality structure. The system gets its character from specific social and cultural developments and contexts. It is shaped and sustained by historically conditioned social conventions and institutions, and it is manifested in habits that are transmitted through time and constitute a particular way of life that people share in common. These habits are preserved in and transmitted by collective memory, a collective memory that, as James Booth describes it, is not "just the intentional, willed acts of remembrance, of a sort of national/political storytelling," but "habit-memory, being habituated or accustomed to act, to respond in certain ways, a way of life in the most basic sense."[49] The character of a political community, for example, is not only revealed in self-conscious commemorative ceremonies and rituals. It is also revealed in the habit-memory of citizens, in habits of feeling, thinking, doing, and interacting that for the most part constitute a political community in an un-self-conscious fashion.

Some of the habits that are structured by the social system provide grounds for moral appraisal of the system and its impact on those who are included within it. The moral character of a group refers to the cluster of these aspects of a group's character that have moral import, and it is embodied in the group's values and sentiments and in the principles it stands for, to those who belong to it as well as to outsiders. It can be manifested in different ways: in the good or bad the group brings about in the world, in the collective symbolic acts of the group, and in the symbolic acts of those who are authorized to speak for the group and to serve as its proxy. In the latter case, it is important for those in leadership positions to consider the symbolic meaning of what they do when they act in an official capacity, because those they speak for see themselves reflected in these actions. It is also important because the actions of officials can symbolize the character of those they represent to others outside the group and perhaps to the world at large. (The latter is particularly relevant in relation to the concerns of the next chapter, where I discuss the reactions of the international community to national memorialization efforts.)

An account of the moral value of symbolic acts in terms of virtue focuses on the character traits of those who perform them, the possession of which is needed for persons to be good and to live well, whether individually or together with others in a collective body. In Adams' words, they show the agent's individual or collective "allegiance to the good and opposition to the bad." On this account, symbolic acts of memorialization have moral value if they flow from traits of character constituting individual or group moral virtues, and they are

The Nature and Value of Memorialization as Symbolic Activity   265

morally disvaluable if they flow from traits of character constituting vices. The moral virtues or vices exhibited in symbolic action are not reducible to the principles the action stands for, nor are they simply dispositions to produce good or bad consequences. For example, public memorials whose purpose is mainly to entrench feelings of victimhood and fuel hatred do not just fail to promote peace and reconciliation. They also reflect negatively on the moral character of those who establish and support them, because in memorializing individuals collectively show "allegiance" to the wrong values. Alternatively, establishing memorials can demonstrate a community's determination to right the wrongs of the past and to promote peace, and together these are part of the virtue of justice. Activities and practices of memorialization can be mean-spirited, self-serving, and malicious; or they can be hopeful, generous, and empathic. And there are other vices and virtues as well.

(b) Symbols and the normative bonds of community

There is a connection between group character and group identity, by which I mean the identity that a group has as a collective body. One connection that has been noted in the virtue ethics literature is that character provides a criterion of identity in a metaphysical sense: it is what persists through changes in a person's physical (and some psychological) characteristics.[50] This is not, however, the sense of identity that I will be discussing here. Rather, as I construe it, identity refers to the characteristics that make us who we are or that we consider most important to who we are, and it is associated with self-conceptions and self-understandings that are "pervasive, important and relatively stable."[51] Character, when it provides material for one's self-conception, is an ingredient of identity in this sense. Moreover, the identity is either individual or collective, as is the nature of the memory that partially constitutes it. I now want to argue that the collective self-conception of a community, the shared conception that individuals have of themselves as members of the same particular community, is often implicated in complex ways in symbolic acts of memorialization carried out by it. I will argue further that this points the way to another explanation of the moral value of memorialization.

Gerald Postema's brief discussion of the relationship between symbolism and collective values is helpful in developing this argument.[52] Postema argues that there are certain symbols, public symbols, that are bound up with the character of a community and that are important for the self-understanding of its members. Taking issue with accounts of symbolic value that dismiss it as mere sentimentalism, he claims that some symbols play a vital role in "communities bound by important collective values"—that is, by values that are held collectively and "express a view of who and what we are," and so involve matters of genuine public concern:

> These symbols express in concrete and concentrated form the common convictions of the community. They concisely summarize what the community stands for and how its members view themselves. They are not so much a vehicle of communication with the rest of the world as a lens for focusing the attention of members on community matters. They also serve to remind them of their commitments, to call them to recommitment, and to teach these commitments to new generations. (431)

The actions of the members of a community that have a publicly symbolic role and that treat public symbols with respect and protect them from harm and desecration take significance from the various roles that the actions and symbols play in the lives that the individuals lead together. They figure in a shared understanding of themselves as members of the same community and, since the community extends across generations, this shared understanding is transmitted to new generations through these same actions and symbols. The symbolic actions and the symbols they respect and protect are essential ingredients of the present generation's self-conception, and they provide a unifying thread of collective memory and identity over time, both toward the future and toward the past.[53]

Postema wants to argue that in light of all this—the role that public symbols play in encapsulating the collective values of a community, focusing the attention of its members on them, and inspiring rededication to them; and the importance of these symbols as vehicles for ensuring the community's continuity over time—the symbols and the actions that respect and safeguard them have a kind of normative significance that is weightier and more profound than what the label "sentimentalism" suggests.[54]

The relationship between public symbols and collective commitments to which Postema refers can provide the basis of an additional argument for the moral significance of memorialization, but only with the following stipulations. First, "profound" doesn't entail morally commendable or even morally permissible; the symbols can be profound and also profoundly morally repugnant because of what they stand for, and these must be excluded. Second, there is the problem, as Postema points out, that "symbols can become the focus of attention to the exclusion of the values they are taken to express, or they can be taken to be symbols of absolute, unalterable, and ineffable values. This would be a distortion of their nature and role" (ibid.). For example, there might be a group of people more concerned with symbolic than material forms of reparation, excessively focused on the former while they neglect the material needs of those who were victimized by the very policy that is being symbolically repudiated. A

The Nature and Value of Memorialization as Symbolic Activity   267

proper, undistorted understanding of the nature and role of symbolic acts would take them to be important expressions of a community's attitudes and values, but would also put them in proper perspective so that they do not hinder or frustrate the realization of the very values in the name of which the community claims to be acting. I argue for the moral value of memorialization only under these two conditions.

What Postema says about public symbols and, by implication, the acts that respect them, is also true for symbolic acts of memorialization. They can be bound up in complex ways with the collective values of a community and with the self-conceptions of those who identify with it, self-conceptions that combine to form one self-conception that is not just yours and mine, but that belongs to *us,* that is *ours*. Memorialization is often like this. It serves as a way for the members of a community, directly or through their representatives, to identify with salient or momentous events in their common past and appropriate them into their shared self-understanding as a community. These projects might commemorate events in a group's past that are a source of pride for its current members if they see themselves and their praiseworthy or noble predecessors as belonging to a single transgenerational community. Or they might commemorate events in a group's past that its current members are prepared to accept responsibility for and to make amends for in some way. Either of these purposes can implicate the collective identity of those who memorialize.

Activities and practices of memorialization are not only media for expressing beliefs and attitudes that are important for collective self-understanding. Equally important, they can also facilitate critical reflection on these beliefs and attitudes, a process that can either validate or cast doubt on them. For societies emerging from a period of violent conflict and repression, monuments, commemorative ceremonies, and memorials of other kinds can be an integral part of their attempt to come to terms with their own history. As powerful reminders of a burdened past, they might shatter illusions many of its members have had about their nation's moral goodness or innocence and stimulate them to consider anew what their nation and their national identity mean to them. To those who were victimized, individuals as well as communities, the establishment of memorials can be a way of responding to the indignities they suffered, a demand that history be rewritten to give them the recognition they were denied, and an assertion of pride in their collective identity. Memorials of different sorts can also assist in the formation of a new collective identity, for both victims and perpetrators, one that includes the memory of past wrongdoing but also attempts to integrate it into a vision of a transformed future. In these cases, historical wrongs that have harmed a group and attacked its way of life are acknowledged, but the ceremonies, monuments, and the like serve mainly as beacons of a transformed identity.[55]

The intersection of memorialization with issues of identity is an evolving and dynamic process. It is in part by memorializing significant events in their past that individuals jointly work out the meaning of their history and its implications for their collective identity, and particular self-understandings are provisional, subject to revision in the light of new information and new insight. As new generations interact with the symbols that relate to their collective past, they may come to challenge or even repudiate earlier self-understandings. In the words of historian Geoffrey Cubitt, activities of commemoration "offer occasions for communities to take stock of, to debate, and perhaps to adjust the meanings they find in their own history and the shapes they give to their collective identity."[56] In cases where the purpose is to repair (symbolically) the harm caused by wrongdoing, commemoration is a vehicle through which groups, from local communities to entire nations, articulate and possibly modify their sense of a collective past, in order to provide validation for victims, their families, and survivor communities.

The taking stock, debating, and adjusting Cubitt speaks of are communal activities that can help clarify and transform a community's relationship to its past and self-understanding and lead to a kind of moral progress. But importantly, this could not happen because of memorialization if it did not have a symbolic relationship to collective identity. It is because of this relationship that memorialization can be intertwined with collective identity and encourage a community to examine how it sees itself in relation to its past and hence how it understands itself in the present. What's more, memorialization does not have symbolic moral value because or to the extent that it promotes moral progress and social enlightenment. This would collapse the distinction between symbolic and instrumental value. Rather, the symbolic moral value of memorialization derives from its non-causal association with constitutive ingredients of a group's identity, with values, principles, traditions, and practices that are or that come to be seen as central to it. This identity may evolve in the ways Cubitt describes, and there may be doubts and disagreements among those who are taking stock and debating about what their collective identity consists in. However, assuming that some aspects of this identity are at least provisionally agreed upon, it is the symbolic relationship to them that serves as the basis of an argument for the moral value of memorialization.

Monuments, commemorations, and other memorials that are related in this way to collective identity play an especially significant role in the collective memory of a group across generations. Memorials are commonly intended to endure, or to convey a message that endures, and to transmit symbolic meaning from one generation to the next, and their symbolic connection to collective identity makes this more likely. To the extent that they succeed at this—and I discussed in the last chapter the conditions that make this possible —memorials become an enduring presence in the public life of a community, capable of

The Nature and Value of Memorialization as Symbolic Activity   269

galvanizing and sustaining public attention and interest over long stretches of time. They become focal points for ongoing efforts to understand a common past and its bearing on the group's sense of itself and the values by which it defines itself, efforts that are often tortuous and generate competing interpretations of past events and their continuing relevance.

(c) The identity dimension of memorialization

Not all public projects of memorialization are especially important for the self-understanding of a group and its identity, even if they are socially significant in other ways. Some may be of little consequence or be unrelated or only distantly related to features of the group's identity. That said, commemorations and monuments commonly play a prominent role in transitional societies, and this is to a large extent explained by their connections to collective self-understanding and identity. This connection enables memorialization to contribute to the reconstruction of political relationships in newly emerging post-authoritarian societies by stimulating debate about collective memory and identity.[57] It can do this in a conspicuous, absorbing, and focused way.

Collective identity, as I have been using the term, is a holistic notion that refers to a feature of a collective entity: it belongs to the collectivity of a collective. But it can also refer to the collective dimension of individual identities. Paige Arthur notes that collective identity in this sense is often a factor in the conflicts addressed by transitional justice: "since an individual's personal sense of worth is tied to the collective identifications he or she has, denial of the value of those identifications through discrimination, repression, and worse should be seen as a root cause of conflict."[58] The denial of the value of these identifications typically takes the form of what Ernesto Verdeja calls "a strongly binary logic of identity. In-groups use language that constructs a tightly knit community while simultaneously disparaging and dehumanizing out-groups."[59] Transitions effect a change in the politics of identity in two ways. First, "the most salient forms of political identity that characterized the era of violence . . . no longer mobilize the passion and viciousness they once did."[60] Second, identities that were despised and stigmatized are now put forward by disparaged and dehumanized groups as sources of positive value. When individuals are exploited, tortured, disappeared, or excluded from political participation because of their membership in a particular ethnic, religious, racial, or social group, the transition to a more democratic regime is commonly accompanied by a vigorous assertion of the value of the identity on the basis of which earlier wrongs were perpetrated. Those who were previously wronged individually and collectively demand recognition of their identity and their claims for reparation are forcefully couched in terms of it. At the same time that this revaluation of formerly stigmatized ethnic, religious, and other communal identities signifies a resurgence of community pride, it also creates special obstacles to political reconciliation. This is because identities become highly politicized and tend to be mobilized in ways that give them a relatively fixed, entrenched quality, and this is an impediment to working together with former enemies.

The political context in which identities have this particular character is only one of the contexts in which identity considerations play a practically significant role. Richard Pildes' observation about identity explains why: "identities are less a matter of fixed, profound, fundamental psychological and affective attachment than fluid and contingent possibilities that become mobilized by specific circumstances."[61] Especially in the earlier phases of a transition, when societies are emerging from a period of political violence and repression, or when transitional gains have not been consolidated, identity considerations tend to have a particular urgency and refractory quality, and this is reflected in the way that wrongdoing is remembered. But this, Pildes persuasively argues, is only one of the contingent manifestations of identity, and it would be a mistake to think it a fundamental feature of it. The mistake may become clear after the immediate crisis has passed, for then, while identity may still be a normatively significant category of self-understanding for formerly oppressed and marginalized groups, the character of appeals to it may change and its fluid and contingent nature become apparent. Ethnic, religious, or other identities that were formerly a pretext for political violence and social marginalization may continue to be tied up with a sense of self-worth for many, but their invocation in political life may become less polarizing and confrontational. Memorialization can contribute to this softening of the stridency of appeals to identity.

These remarks about how identity functions in circumstances of substantial political change suggest that identity can be a sufficiently adaptable concept to be useful for social analysis. I believe, in addition, that it can be useful for moral analysis. To be sure, there have been distortions and oversimplifications in both theoretical literature and popular debates about identity. But these are not inevitable when employing the concept. Or so I shall argue. By attending to the ways in which the notion of collective identity has been misused and misunderstood, we can learn what to avoid to make it more serviceable in political and moral argument.

Two critics of the concept of identity in social science, Rogers Brubaker and Frederick Cooper, have leveled a number of criticisms against it, and by so doing they have also indirectly indicated how we need to understand it in order to avoid them.[62] Especially problematic in their view are these common uses of the term in social science discourse (and, I might add, in some philosophical writing on collective identity as well). Identity is understood as a "fundamental and consequential *sameness* among members of group" (7) or sameness over time that implies "a sharp distinctiveness from nonmembers, a clear boundary

The Nature and Value of Memorialization as Symbolic Activity   271

between inside and outside" (10); as a *"deep, basic, abiding, or foundational"* (7) feature of a group that is relatively unchanging; and as the necessary result of "efforts to build a collective self-understanding" (16). Feelings of "commonality, connectedness, and groupness" (20) that characterize group membership from the participant standpoint may be treated as attributes of some core essence that all members share and that they "can have without being aware of it" (10).

Brubaker and Cooper admonish us to be wary of reifying identity and to avoid ways of talking and thinking that suggest these "substantialist understandings of groups and essentialist understandings of identity" (10). Their criticisms suggest how to understand it so that we have an appropriately complex picture of how processes of memorialization and collective identities are intertwined. For one thing, we should not think of the collective identities that are implicated in and shaped by practices of memorialization as fixed essences but as composed of collective self-conceptions that can be reconfigured in light of new insights into the group's past by current and later generations. We should also allow that the identity-constituting features of one group may be shared to some extent with those of another, so that while group boundaries are not dissolved, they become somewhat permeable. Since collective identities are not impervious to one another, the identity of one society or social subgroup concretely encapsulated in its memorial practices may overlap that of another. Additionally, we should recognize that there is room within particular collective identities for differing and even conflicting interpretations of their meaning and the responsibilities they entail. Memorials often provide occasions for and sometimes even encourage alternative readings of a common history among those who nevertheless share a collective identity. These are the ways we should understand identity and memorialization's relation to it, for the idea that there is a single, unambiguous, rigidly bounded collective identity that is statically projected by memorial projects cannot survive close examination of social and political reality.

The conception of identity outlined here differs from what is reflected in many contemporary political and cultural invocations of the notion, including some of the debates about multiculturalism, but it is nonetheless an important and potentially fruitful category of social analysis.[63] The concept of identity has explanatory relevance and utility, I would argue, because individuals commonly think of themselves as sharing membership with others in groups that have a collective character and identity, and because this identity is a source of strength and meaning for many. We should not get rid of the concept of identity but use it in ways that better accord with how identity functions in the lives and self-understandings of those who share in it.

Though memorialization is often symbolically bound up with a society's sense of itself in transitional settings, it is also significant outside these settings for the same reason. Commemoration of important historical events can be an instrument of social cohesion and a locus of collective identity in societies that have more or less successfully made a transition to democracy or that do not have a recent history of undergoing radical political change. In multicultural democratic societies where cultural, religious, and ethnic groups often struggle to maintain their distinctive identities, activities of memorialization often have particular importance as rallying points for a shared collective identity for their members. How important memorialization is in these different contexts, and what factors explain the forms it takes and its social uses, are obviously matters for empirical investigation. But it is evident that the intensity, salience, and social meaning of the symbolic connections between memorialization and collective identity vary and fluctuate. Appeals to collective identity, and reliance on the symbolic resources of memorialization to express, adjust, modify, and safeguard this identity, are of greater moment in some times and places than others, depending on an array of social, political, and historical factors. In transitional societies, for example, concerns and questions about collective identity often loom large, and memorialization may be especially useful in addressing them.[64]

(d) The moral significance of identity

It is one thing to claim that identity can be a useful descriptive concept in the social sciences and quite another to do what I want to do here, namely invoke a connection to collective identity in order to explain why memorialization has moral value.[65] Indeed, it might be denied that identity can explain this, on the following grounds. Collective identity involves activities and attachments that are important to the self-conception or self-understanding of a group. It also involves ideals to which the members of the group aspire and standards to which they hold themselves. These are general facts about collective identity, true of all groups whose members are bound together by a sense of shared membership. Hence, they are true of groups whose identity is founded on and constituted by moral as well as immoral attachments, ideals, and standards. So the connection to identity per se can't provide an explanation of the moral value of memorialization. Rather—and here is the crucial step—it is the character of these attachments and the content of the ideals and standards alone that determine whether the "identity" of a group is to count in moral argument. Identity itself drops out of the picture since it does no moral work. Its invocation is otiose, at best a kind of rhetorical flourish, since the burden of the argument is entirely borne by the attachments, ideals, and standards themselves. Though identity-expressing and identity-constituting acts are often valorized, there is a confusion lurking here, the objection claims: the moral value of action flows from the moral principles it embodies, the virtues it exhibits, or the attitudes it expresses, whereas the fact that an action implicates identity adds nothing to and cannot help ground the action's moral value.

The Nature and Value of Memorialization as Symbolic Activity   273

There are additional reasons to question whether identity really has the moral importance I am claiming for it. Certainly the quality of a community's self-understanding, how openly and conscientiously it deals with its past, for example, is a critical factor in assessing whether its identity warrants moral consideration and deference. Identity can be compromised or damaged by a failure or refusal to acknowledge, give proper weight to, or give an accurate accounting of significant events in a group's past, just as it can for individual identity. It is how identity is formed and maintained that matters here, it may be said, and we can give an argument for why these factors matter morally without having to introduce the concept of identity at all. So again, the claim is that the appeal to identity serves no useful purpose: it is unnecessary and, worse, obfuscating.

Samuel Scheffler's remarks about the normative authority of cultural identity are relevant here. He maintains that appeals to it as a source of moral authority rest on a confusion, and though he confines his discussion to culture, we might consider extending his argument to ethnic, racial, and other communal identities as well:

> cultures are not perceived sources of normative authority in the same sense that moral, religious, or philosophical doctrines are . . . The relation between culture and identity does not support an extrapolation from the case of moral, religious, and philosophical convictions to the case of cultural affiliations.[66]

For example, one can invoke a moral principle asserting an obligation to make amends for wrongdoing to justify establishing a memorial to its victims. By contrast, the fact that public memorials may be cultural and political activities by means of which a community makes sense of, affirms, or renegotiates its identity does not confer normative significance on memorialization in the same way that conformity with a moral principle does. Hence we might conclude from this that identity can safely be discarded as a morally significant construct.

This deflationary view of identity echoes what Avigail Eisenberg claims is "the widely held position that identity and identity claims have no moral force."[67] It should be noted, however, for what it's worth, that this flies in the face of the fact that cultural and other identities—and memorialization's connection to them— are often thought to warrant some sort of moral recognition and respect. International law, for example, registers this idea by incorporating the principle of a "right to protection of identity," which Arthur explains as "preserving the freedom of minorities to practice their culture, religion, and language in the public and private spheres, and taking measures to enable minorities to develop these aspects of their identity."[68] How should we understand this? More generally, what is it for a collective identity to matter, from a moral standpoint?

The answer I propose is that while identity, simply as such, may be a doubtful source of moral value, this does not preclude the possibility that practices that are important to identities have heightened moral significance because of this. It is a mistake to suppose that a conception of identity that avoids the oversimplifications Brubaker and Cooper warn us about must be "too protean and variable a notion"[69] to be a significant consideration in moral argument and deliberation. Memorial activities, for example, might both symbolize moral principles and values and symbolically implicate the identity of the group engaged in them, and the latter could magnify the moral standing that the acts have in virtue of the former. Indeed, the fact that practices that are bound up with the identity of a group are profoundly important to its members and that the failure of the state to make room for or respect these practices is regarded by them as deeply injurious is enough of a reason to take seriously the possibility that identity has a morally magnifying effect under certain conditions.

Identities do not justify in the same way that moral principles and values do; and morality may be a basis for disqualifying some identities as undeserving of our respect. Identity can augment the moral significance of actions that are important for it only if other conditions are met, including that the identity is a morally permissible one and the attachments, principles and values, standards and beliefs that constitute it are themselves worthy of endorsement. Also important here is that the identity not be built on self-deception or historical fabrication. The principles, values, and so on, by contrast, confer moral significance directly. However, the fact that some action implicates a collective identity—assuming at least that it is not disqualified on moral grounds and that it is not formed and sustained by burying or denying the past—gives it moral weight that is not entirely accounted for by the principles and ideals themselves that constitute it. In other words, while identity (and this true for individual as well as collective identity) has no independent moral weight,[70] it makes a difference, when it does, by supplying reasons for action whose normativity is not completely explained by the normative force of its constituent elements. Its contribution to the moral value of action depends upon the presence of other values, ideals, and principles that belong to the identity in question, and also on the quality of the general self-understanding. But under the right conditions, it does contribute. And memorialization's symbolic relationship to collective identity contributes to its moral value, if this identity meets those conditions.

6. Identity claims and moral conflict

What does the prescriptive moral weight added by identity come to, practically speaking? How is it acknowledged and manifested in the deliberations and

The Nature and Value of Memorialization as Symbolic Activity   275

actions of individuals and groups in morally complex social situations? Before answering these questions, I want to propose a number of conditions that identity claims must satisfy if they are to have the magnifying effect I discussed above. These will make clear that "identity" is not some single undifferentiated feature of an individual or group, all of whose elements contribute equally to the force of claims made on its behalf; and they will also make explicit that for various reasons identities are not always worthy of respect. The following conditions address these concerns.

One I have already mentioned and I will not dwell on it here: practices and activities whose moral standing is enhanced because they are important for group identity cannot valorize or sanction immoral conduct. For example, commemorations that celebrate the oppression of one group by another do not gain moral value merely because what they celebrate is claimed (even if correctly) to be integral to a group's self-conception. This is closely related to what Eisenberg calls "the safeguard condition" according to which "the strength of a claim [is to] be assessed in terms of whether it threatens to generate significant harm."[71] Two additional conditions for assessing the strength of claims made on behalf of identity, what Eisenberg calls "the jeopardy condition" and the "validation condition," deserve some comment.[72] Each of the three conditions is necessary to account for when the link to collective identity heightens the moral value of memorialization. Together, they serve as a standard by which to assess the moral significance of claims about practices that are important for identities, including those involving memorialization. Specifically, my proposal is this: claims advanced on behalf of identity have moral force only to the extent they satisfy these three conditions, and the strength of the identity argument for the moral value of memorialization depends on the extent to which it satisfies these conditions.

"The jeopardy condition," Eisenberg says, "gauges the strength of a[n identity] claim in terms of its importance to the identities of those advancing the claim" (32). Some identity claims are made with regard to practices, traditions, or values that are "central and integral" to the identity of the individual or group making the claims; others relate to practices, etc. that have the status of being part of an individual's or group's identity but are ranked lower in the individual's or group's hierarchy of values and concerns. Global references to "the" collective identity of a group mask these differences. One measure of the strength of an identity claim is the result for those whose make the claim of a failure to honor it. If it causes "serious jeopardy" (33) and not mere inconvenience, then its centrality is confirmed. As applied to memorialization and the claims made for it, the jeopardy condition would attribute differential moral weight to it based on the centrality of what is being commemorated to the identity of those engaged in it. The more central the object of commemoration, the more serious are the consequences for those who want to memorialize but are prevented from doing so, whether by the state or by non-state actors. It might seriously disrupt a way of life; or deny an oppressed group a crucial means of protesting against the status quo; or further disparage those who were treated as inferiors by denying them the opportunity to express pride in their history. It might in these and other ways display profound disrespect or contempt for those advancing identity claims. On the other hand, the repercussions might be relatively minor because more peripheral values and concerns are affected.

The validation condition is necessary because the legitimacy of identity-constituting practices or activities depends in part on how they became part of the group's identity and how they are sustained by the group. Practices or activities that are integral to a group's identity may nonetheless lack moral standing because the processes by which they have come to be and continue to be accorded importance in the group fail to be "fair, inclusive, or otherwise legitimate" (40). Decision-making processes do not have to be democratic to count as validating: traditional methods of communal decision making, even if non-democratic, might count as well. But there are other cases in which, though practices are part of a group's identity, members have no meaningful political role in making decisions about them, or are not permitted to deliberate about or question them, or have no means of abandoning them if they should wish to without risking serious harm to themselves. The fact that they cannot do these things does not mean that these practices are not part of the group's identity: group identities, after all, can be formed and sustained in all sorts of morally questionable ways. At the same time, this fact undercuts the moral force of any identity claims people might make respecting those practices. Presumably identity claims can be so weak according to the validation condition that they count for little or nothing, morally speaking. With regard to activities and practices whose purpose is to memorialize, their symbolic relationship to collective identity confers moral legitimacy on them only insofar as they satisfy the validation condition. So like other practices claimed to be important for a group's identity, those that are commemorative in nature are only fully worthy of respect and protection if they are legitimated by those who are subject to and participate in them.[73]

These three conditions—safeguard, jeopardy, and validation—provide a framework for assessing one sort of argument made on behalf of activities and practices of memorialization. They do this by addressing the legitimacy of the identity claims that are made on their behalf and are supposed to show that they have moral value. What I now go on to suggest assumes that these conditions are satisfied to such a degree that the memorializing activity in question is worth upholding and protecting, as judged from the standpoint both of participants and of nonparticipants in the activity.

There are at least two explanations of how reasons of identity add moral weight to memorialization in conflict situations. First, reasons of identity

The Nature and Value of Memorialization as Symbolic Activity   277

justify *increased resistance* to abandonment of symbolic actions in the face of countervailing moral considerations. For example, suppose the issue is whether to erect some monument, or construct a memorial park, or declare a day of national commemoration. According to this explanation, when they are important for the collective identity of a group (and the three conditions are satisfied), considerations against performing these symbolic acts have less weight, relative to the value of performing them, than they otherwise would have. How much less will likely depend on the nature of the countervailing considerations. The considerations might be instrumental ones if doing these things would have negative social consequences, or if performing the actions would preclude achieving better social consequences. In cases of this sort, the threshold for refraining from identity-implicating symbolic actions because of countervailing instrumental considerations would be higher than it would be if identity were not implicated (and certainly higher than any version of the thesis of lesser value would countenance). One threshold is higher than another when it requires that the negative consequences be more severe or more probable before refraining from acting symbolically, or when the consequences that are foregone are considerably better than the ones that are produced. "More severe," "more probable," and "considerably better" are obviously vague, and "important for collective identity" is not specific about the ways in which it is important and how important it is. Nevertheless, the point is clear enough and seems plausible. Considerations of identity can make a difference in moral deliberation because they are capable of altering the significance of conflicting moral considerations in the overall assessment of what should be done.

When considerations of symbolic value conflict with other morally relevant factors, the former will not always trump the latter, nor the latter the former.[74] However, dealing with conflict is not always just a matter of determining which takes precedence over the other. A second explanation of how a symbolic relationship to identity affects deliberation relative to memorialization involves the notion of symbolic *interchangeability*. There may be alternative ways of realizing the same symbolic value, alternative activities that equally well satisfy the safeguard and validation conditions and symbolize central features of a group's identity and that present less of a conflict with other weighty moral considerations. If there are, and if there is an important moral principle or moral value at stake in acting symbolically, then the agent should explore the possibility of other modes of symbolic expression. For example, a transitional regime might decide that establishing a monument or a museum that can have a significant impact on the collective memory, while certainly a valuable sort of commemorative activity, would detract from the implementation of worthwhile development projects and the fulfillment of urgent social obligations. Other measures, like designating and supporting a national day of commemoration, might have

278   FORGIVENESS AND REMEMBRANCE

roughly equivalent symbolic memorial value and be less costly than constructing a museum or monument. In saying this, I am supposing that it makes sense
to claim that two different acts or projects can be roughly interchangeable in
terms of symbolic value and that there are means of determining whether this
is the case. The issues here are complex since there are several factors to be considered in making this assessment and they vary considerably in relevance and
weight from one political and cultural context to another. But intuitively at least,
symbolic interchangeability is sometimes a viable strategy for resolving conflicts
between symbolic moral values and other values.

When a symbolic act or measure with memorial intent not only stands for a
morally valuable principle, or expresses an intrinsically valuable attitude toward
the victims of wrongdoing, but is important for a group's collective identity,
there is plainly more at stake in the search for a substitute symbolic act than
when it is not. If a symbolic act has particular importance for a group's collective
identity, situations of serious moral conflict put pressure on agents to consider
whether there are symbolic substitutes for the act in question that can satisfy
their identity claims. A symbolic relationship to collective identity, therefore,
can not only justify increased resistance to refraining from acting symbolically.
It can also powerfully motivate the search for alternative symbolic acts that have
(roughly) equivalent importance for the identity of the group when there are
compelling non-symbolic values at stake. The normativity of collective identity
can affect moral deliberation in conflict situations in both ways.[75]

7. Conclusion

Though much of this chapter has been about memorialization and its functions
within societies transitioning from a period of violence and repression, I have tried
to frame the discussion by examining the nature and significance of symbolic value
in general. I took this approach because memorialization essentially operates in
the realm of symbolism and because we need to clarify the nature of symbolic
value and expose some of the misconceptions about the value of symbolic actions
before we can proceed to properly consider the moral significance of memorialization in particular. Because these misconceptions are not uncommon, they need to
be dispelled before moving on to a positive account. The first task of clarification
took up section 2, and I took a tentative step in the direction of questioning certain
dismissive views of the symbolic value of symbolic actions in section 3. Sections 4
and 5 went further and contributed a positive account.

From certain theoretical standpoints, the idea that symbolic actions as such
might have moral value or much moral value is ruled out from the outset. On
some of these views, if symbolic actions have moral value at all, it is only in virtue

The Nature and Value of Memorialization as Symbolic Activity 279

of their bringing about or embodying intrinsically desirable states of affairs. On other views, symbolic actions have some independent moral value, but this is always trumped by the value of actions that bring about such states of affairs. Both sorts of views pose a challenge to what I have argued for in this chapter, and while I am not claiming that it is the only challenge that can be mounted, it is arguably the one that proponents of the moral value of symbolism most commonly face. It is for this reason that I used the thesis of lesser value to set the stage for my defense of the moral value of memorialization. In my view, an account of the moral value of symbolism that is faithful to the kind of importance that it has in people's lives shows in an especially convincing way the inadequacies of those theoretical standpoints that deny or discount its moral value.

Memorialization is a symbolic activity, so we can learn a great deal about it just by considering the nature of symbolism and symbolic value in general. But as a specific type of symbolic activity in extraordinary circumstances of political transition, memorialization also has its particular uses. These include, as I have emphasized, its employment as a restorative justice practice by democratizing societies seeking to make amends for the wrongs of a violent and repressive past. It does this by showing respect for victims and symbolically restoring their reputations and civic and moral standing. Memorial activities in transitional societies can also express a sense of collective identity and assist in its transformation. They can provide a common ground where former enemies meet, reach some consensus on the meaning of their shared history, and reconcile their differences, although other less fortunate outcomes are certainly possible as well.

Contexts of violent conflict and deep social division are often ones in which there is a strong identity dimension to the antagonisms. Perpetrators may stereotype their victims and use this as a justification for discrimination or repression,[76] and victims may respond by stereotyping the perpetrators and/or by attempting to defend their own identity and protect it from further assault. Perpetrators in one context may be victims in another, and vice versa, with alternating identity claims fueling their ongoing hostilities. Memorialization cannot by itself resolve these conflicts, and might even make them worse. But collective identities are socially constructed over time, and memorials of various sorts—ceremonies, rituals, monuments, memorial museums—can help forge a new collective identity by encouraging less divisive forms of identification. They can serve as settings for and provide opportunities for education to engage the public over time in reflection on their common past and its ever-changing significance for contemporary social life. This new collective identity may be able to accommodate former identities, but only to the extent that doing so does not threaten to revive violence and conflict.

Whatever memorialization accomplishes it accomplishes through symbolism whose value is conditioned by the meanings that it has for the agent and others, meanings that are affected by the reasons for which it was performed and the relationship between the agent and the audience. One might have the view that symbolism is all or mostly show and no or little substance, and so discount its evaluative importance. The various arguments presented in this chapter—formulated in terms of notions of respect for value and persons; virtue and the moral character of individuals and groups; and the self-identity of a community—represent my attempt to counter this dismissive view. What I hope to have shown is that it is no objection to memorialization that it is symbolic or, if reparative, that it is a type of symbolic reparation. Indeed, even when victims receive material compensation for the wrongs they suffered, the compensation is morally reparative only because, and because of what, it symbolizes.

Endnotes

1. According to the website of the International Coalitions of Sites of Conscience, sites of conscience are "sites activating the power of places of memory to engage the public in connecting past and present in order to envision a more just and humane future." Sites include the District Six Museum in South Africa; the Gulag Museum in Russia; the Liberation War Museum in Bangladesh; the Lower East Side Tenement Museum in New York; Maison Des Esclaves in Senegal; Memoria Abierta in Argentina; the Terezin Memorial in the Czech Republic; and the Workhouse in the United Kingdom. See http://www.sitesofconscience.org/about-us/.

   For an extremely illuminating discussion of the nature of memorial museums, and what distinguishes them from history museums, war museums, and art museums, see Paul Williams, *Memorial Museums: The Global Rush to Commemorate Atrocities* (Oxford: Berg, 2007). A memorial museum, according to Williams, is a "specific kind of museum dedicated to a historic event commemorating mass suffering of some kind" (8).

2. As noted in Judy Barsalou and Victoria Baxter, *The Urge to Remember: The Role of Memorials in Social Reconstruction and Transitional Justice* (Washington, DC: The United States Institute of Peace, January 2007). Available at www.usip.org. Truth commissions have issued recommendations for memorialization initiatives, but sometimes memorialization initiatives have substituted for official truth commissions in countries that are not ready to establish them. For example, the Colombian Historical Memory Group, an independent academic group, was created in 2005 by the National Commission on Reparations and Reconciliation. It was tasked, among other things, with documenting the memories generated during periods of violence and giving voice to the victims. This was a laudable step, but it did not amount to the establishment of an official truth commission.

3. These features of memorialization are explored by Edward Casey, in *Remembering: A Phenomenological Study*, 2nd edition (Bloomington: Indiana University Press, 2000), pp. 223–230.

4. The duty or imperative to remember was a major theme of my previous book, *The Moral Demands of Memory* (New York: Cambridge University Press, 2008).

5. As reported by Sarah E. Bond in the article "Erasing the Face of History," *New York Times*, Sunday, May 15, 2011.

6. Cited in Barsalou and Baxter, op. cit.

7. Gary Wills, *Lincoln at Gettysburg: The Words that Remade America* (New York: Simon and Schuster, 2006).

8. Drew Gilpin Faust, *The Republic of Suffering* (New York: Alfred A. Knopf, 2008), p. 100.

9. The line comes from Robert Pogue Harrison's philosophically oriented study of the history and human significance of burial practices, in *The Dominion of the Dead* (Chicago: University of Chicago Press, 2003), p. 23.

10. I formulate it this way for now without stopping to distinguish between actions that are subjectively and those that are objectively symbolically valuable.

The Nature and Value of Memorialization as Symbolic Activity   281

11. Guido Pincione and Fernando Tesón, "Self-Defeating Symbolism in Politics," *The Journal of Philosophy* (2001): 636–652, at 640.
12. Robert Nozick, *The Nature of Rationality* (Princeton: University Press, 1993), p. 27.
13. Pincione and Tesón, op. cit., p. 641.
14. Nelson Goodman, "Routes of Reference," *Critical Inquiry* (Autumn 1981): 121–132, at 121.
15. In Goodman's words, "exemplification, far from being a variety of denotation, runs in the opposite direction, not from label to what the label applies to but from something a label applies to back to the label (or the feature associated with that label)" (ibid., p. 124).
16. Again, in Goodman's words, expression "involves exemplification of a label or feature that metaphorically rather than literally denotes or is possessed by a mark or other symbol" (ibid., p. 126).
17. On the distinction between "expressing" and "being expressive of" in art, see "Expression Theory of Art," in *Encyclopedia of Aesthetics* (Michael Kelly, ed.) (Oxford University Press, 1998); and "Artistic Expression," in *Routledge Encyclopedia of Philosophy* (Edward Craig, ed.) (Routledge, 1998).
18. Elizabeth S. Anderson and Richard H. Pildes, "Expressive Theories of Law: A General Restatement," *University of Pennsylvania Law Review*, vol. 148, issue 5 (2000): 1503–1576.
19. With regard to public apologies, officials who perform them might not themselves have any of the sentiments or affective attitudes associated with apologizing in interpersonal contexts, or be personally responsible for the wrongs that were committed; and likewise for many members of the society whom they represent. This doesn't mean, however, that official apologies must be insincere, hollow, or meaningless. Official acts can instead signal a commitment on the part of those who make it, and on the part of those on whose behalf the commitment is made, to make amends for past wrongs. Moreover, when this is the meaning of the apology, it can have considerable restorative power with respect to a society's moral, political, and social health. The moral force of interpersonal apologizing, by contrast, is not independent of the sentiments of the apologizer. Sincerity in this context demands that the apologizer be troubled in some way because of his wrongdoing, that he feel remorse or guilt for it, that he manifest it, and so on. Unlike political apologies, interpersonal apologies must actually involve the proper emotions and attitudes to count as genuine apologies and to have moral force.
20. Nozick, op. cit., p. 28.
21. Pincione and Tesón, op. cit., p. 640.
22. For information about the Confederate flag controversy, see www.solidarity-us.org/site/node/ 1677; www.huffingtonpost.com/news/confederate-flag-controversy/; www.researchomatic. com/The-Confederate-Flag-36769.html.
23. The tension is discussed in David Simpson, *9/11: The Culture of Commemoration* (Chicago: University of Chicago, 2007), 55–85.
24. For more on communicative norms, see Neil C. Manson and Onora O'Neill, *Rethinking Informed Consent in Bioethics* (Cambridge: Cambridge University Press, 2007), especially pp. 41–42, 57–64, 84–90.
25. It has been pointed out to me that I adopt an overly defensive tone in my discussion of symbolic moral value and take too seriously the claims of opponents who dismiss the value of symbolic action as mere symbolism or sentimentalism. This will certainly seem to be the case to those who are already convinced of the moral significance of symbolism. There are many who are not, however. Some of these are consequentialists, and my unhappiness with the thesis of lesser value can be viewed as part of a larger critique of the adequacy of consequentialist accounts of many aspects of moral life and human flourishing, including but not limited to symbolic action. However, I do not want to portray my defense of the moral value of symbolic action solely as a philosophical response to a particular moral theory. For it seems to me as well that in a utilitarian culture like our own, the discounting of symbolic value is not confined to those who consider themselves to be consequentialists. Even those who do not discount the moral importance of symbolic action often have difficulty explaining why.
26. Report of South Africa's Truth and Reconciliation Commissions, vol. 6, section 2, chapter 6, paragraph 4.
27. Nozick, op. cit., p. 30.
28. Margaret Walker, in "Truth Telling as Reparations," *Metaphilosophy*, vol. 41, no. 4 (July 2010): 524–532, and again in "The Expressive Burden of Reparations: Putting Meaning into Money,

Words, and Things," *Boston Studies in Philosophy, Religion, and Public Life*, vol. 1 (2003): 205–225, explores the symbolism of reparations and sets out four criteria for assessing the adequacy of particular reparative gestures. There is considerable agreement between the views she presents in these articles and those in this chapter as regards making amends for past wrongdoing, and I have learned much from her writings. However, in two respects my discussion departs from hers. First, and most obviously, I am concerned with remembering the victims of wrongdoing, including those who did not survive, and Walker does not single this out for special attention. Second, as I go on to discuss in the next section, I am also interested in the symbolic connection between memorialization and collective identity, and she does not address this in her articles.

29. Joseph Raz, *Value, Respect, and Attachment* (Cambridge: University Press, 2001). Page numbers in parentheses.

30. For the idea that persons in leadership positions can, by their actions, symbolize the views and traits of those over whom they exercise authority, see Gregory Mellema, "Symbolic Value, Virtue Ethics, and the Morality of Groups," *Philosophy Today*, vol. 43, no. 3 (fall 1999): 302–308. He writes:

> The symbolic value of actions by people in positions of [leadership within a formal organization, such as a corporation] . . . are likely to take on exaggerated significance. When corporate leaders perform acts of virtue while acting in an official capacity, these acts symbolize virtuous patterns of actions throughout the organization. (306–307).

31. T. M. Scanlon, *What We Owe to Each Other* (Cambridge, MA: Harvard University Press, 1998), p. 95.

32. Advocates of the thesis of lesser value might want to extend it by ranking instrumental value higher than other types of values besides symbolic values, but I will confine myself to the narrower version of the thesis.

33. This paragraph closely follows Thomas Nagel's view in his essay "The Fragmentation of Value," *Mortal Questions* (Cambridge: Cambridge University Press, 1979), pp. 128–141.

34. W. James Booth, "'From This Far Place': On Justice and Absence," *American Political Science Review*, vol. 105, no. 4 (November 2011): 750–763, at 757.

35. They can also be regarded as expressions of respect for the values that were subverted by the injustices of former regimes.

36. Stephen Darwall takes this up in "Authority and Reasons: Exclusionary and Second–Personal," *Ethics*, vol. 120, no. 2 (January 2010): 257–278.

37. Stephen Darwall, *The Second-Person Standpoint* (Cambridge, MA: Harvard University Press, 2006).

38. A useful article on the role of validation in the psychoanalytic process, with numerous references to discussions of validation in the psychoanalytic and cognitive-behavioral therapy literatures, is Mark Schechter, "The Patient's Experience of Validation in Psychoanalytic Treatment," *Journal of the American Psychoanalytic Association*, vol. 55, no. 1 (March 2007): 105–130. Page numbers in text reference this article.

39. According to Margaret Walker "all reparative gestures . . . are a kind of representation by exemplification of the 'right relationship' that wrongdoing has denied or broken" ("Truth Telling as Reparations," op. cit., pp. 530, 532). I will now argue that activities of memorialization manifest and communicate respect for the dead insofar as they are part of an effort to establish the "right relationship" with those who survive and represent them.

40. For more on how groups can be harmed or wronged, see Jeffrey Blustein, op. cit., pp. 132–138.

41. Lawrence Thomas, "Moral Deference," *The Philosophical Forum*, vol. 24, nos. 1–3 (Fall–Spring 1992–1993): 233–250.

42. For a pertinent discussion of how rememberers can be disrespected as rememberers, see Sue Campbell, *Relational Remembering: Rethinking the Memory Wars* (Lanham, MD: Rowman and Littlefield, 2003).

43. Brandon Hamber, *Transforming Societies after Political Violence* (Dordrecht: Springer, 2009), p. 114.

44. Ibid., p. 111.

45. Nozick, op. cit., p. 29.

The Nature and Value of Memorialization as Symbolic Activity   283

46. Robert Merrihew Adams, *Finite and Infinite Goods: A Framework for Ethics* (Oxford: Oxford University Press, 1999), p. 219. Page numbers in parentheses in text.
47. Pierre Bourdieu, *The Logic of Practice* (Stanford, CA: Stanford University Press, 1990).
48. Norbert Elias has written extensively about the phenomenon of a national habitus. See *The Civilizing Process*, vol. 1 (E. Jephcott, trans.) (New York: Urizen Books, 1978); *The Civilizing Process*, vol. 2 (E. Jephcott, trans.) (Oxford: Basic Blackwell, 1982). See also two papers by Andreas Pickel: "The Habitus Process: A Biopsychosocial Conception," *Journal of the Theory of Social Behavior*, vol. 35, no. 4 (2005): 437–461; and "Homo Nationis: The Psychosocial Infrastructure of the Nation-State Order," *Global Society*, vol. 18, no. 4 (2004): 325–346.
49. W. James Booth, *Communities of Memory: On Witness, Identity, and Justice* (Ithaca, NY: Cornell University Press, 2006), p. 27.
50. See, for example, Christine McKinnon, *Character, Virtue Theories, and the Vices* (Ontario, Canada: Broadview Press, 1999), especially pp. 63–66.
51. From Ross Poole, *Nation and Identity* (London: Routledge, 1999), p. 66.
52. Gerald Postema, "Collective Evils, Harms, and the Law," *Ethics*, vol. 97, no. 2 (January 1987): 414–440, at 430–433.
53. An example that illustrates a connection between symbols, symbolic action, and collective identity is the case of the stolen Ethiopian artifacts. In 1868 a British expeditionary force of 30,000 laid waste to the stronghold of the Ethiopian emperor at the time after removing thousands of sacred texts and other items of great religious and national significance, including crowns and chalices. As soon as Ethiopia was able, it asked for the return of the artifacts, but to date, repeated calls from the Ethiopian church, government, academic institutions, and citizens have succeeded in getting the British to return only some minor treasures. It is reasonable to suppose that the stolen objects were Ethiopia's cultural property, property that they were unjustly deprived of and that was significant to Ethiopians because of its symbolic relationship to their national identity. Return of the artifacts would symbolically recognize Ethiopians' right to maintain that identity intact. See R. Pankhurst, "Ethiopia, the Askum Obelisk, and the Return of Africa's Cultural Heritage," *African Affairs*, vol. 98, no. 391 (1999): 229–239, and Janna Thompson, "Cultural Property, Restitution and Value," *Journal of Applied Philosophy*, vol. 20, no. 3(2003): 251–262.
54. Postema's target here is Joel Feinberg's discussion of public symbols in his book *Offense to Others*.
55. The South African Freedom Park project is an example of this. Barsalou and Baxter describe it as follows (op. cit.):

> [this project] is being built opposite the Voortrekker Monument in Pretoria. Freedom Park seeks to negotiate the triumphant nature of the Voortrekker Monument by depicting a variety of stories, ranging from the Anglo-Boer War to the anti-apartheid struggle in South Africa. In doing so, Freedom Park acknowledges the survivors, broadly defined, of the conflict but focuses mainly on drawing together different racial, ethnic, and cultural narratives of a richly diverse country in an attempt to portray a nation moving forward into a transformed future.

56. Cubitt is actually referring only to commemorations, but the observation can be extended to other kinds of memorial activities as well. See *History and Memory* (Manchester: Manchester University Press, 2007), p. 221.
57. In a fascinating paper on the role of national symbols in Baathist Iraq, Benjamin Isakhan considers the relation between symbols and national identity from a different direction. Remarking on the role that memorials, monuments, and museums play in creating a sense of national identity, he then asks: "Could the destruction of the symbols and institutions of the state also destroy the nationalism and social cohesion they were designed to promulgate?" Isakhan answers in the affirmative and describes in considerable detail the various ways in which the invasion of Iraq by coalition forces in 2003 dismantled the Baathist state by destroying the memorials and monuments it erected ("Targeting the Symbolic Dimension of Baathist Iraq:

284   FORGIVENESS AND REMEMBRANCE

Cultural Destruction, Historical Memory and National Identity," *Middle East Journal of Culture and Communication*, vol. 4, no. 3 [2011]: 257–281). These effects are possible because of the symbolic relationship between memorialization and collective identity. In this case, the *destruction* of memorials associated with prior regimes undermines dominant notions of national identity, leaving in its wake a society bereft of any united and cohesive national identity.

58. Paige Arthur, "Identities in Transition: Developing Better Transitional Justice Initiatives in Divided Societies," *International Center for Transitional Justice*, November 2009.

59. Ernesto Verdeja, *Unchopping the Tree: Reconciliation in the Aftermath of Political Violence* (Philadelphia: Temple University Press, 2009), p. 63.

60. Ibid., p. 64.

61. Richard H. Pildes, "Identity and Democratic Institutions," draft presented for the New York University Legal, Political, and Social Philosophy Colloquium, September 12, 2007: 1–45, at 7.

62. Rogers Brubaker and Frederick Cooper, "Beyond 'Identity,'" *Theory and Society*, vol. 29, no. 1 (February 2000): 1–47. Page numbers of quotations appear in parentheses.

63. For discussions specifically about the usefulness of the concept of national identity in the social sciences, see Richard Handler, "Is 'Identity' a Useful Cross-Cultural Concept?" pp. 27–40; and David Lowenthal, "Identity, Heritage, and History," pp. 41–57, both in *Commemorations: The Politics of National Identity* (John R. Gillis, ed.) (Princeton, NJ: Princeton University Press, 1994).

64. For more on the relationship between memorialization and collective identity, see Brian S. Osborne's excellent article, "Landscapes, Memory, Monuments, and Commemoration: Putting Identity in Its Place," commissioned by the Department of Canadian Heritage for the Ethnocultural, Racial, Religious, and Linguistic Diversity and Identity Seminar, Halifax, Nova Scotia, November 1–2, 2001. Available at Canada.metropolis.net/events/ethnocultural/publications/putinden.pdf.

65. One may be tempted to do what a number of philosophers have done and draw a distinction between ethics and morality proper, then locate issues relating to the normative authority or obligations of identity in the former domain. This is the approach taken by Kwame Anthony Appiah in *The Ethics of Identity* (Princeton, NJ: Princeton University Press, 2005), pp. 230–237. Closer to the subject of this chapter, Avishai Margalit also draws the distinction in *The Ethics of Memory* (Cambridge, MA: Harvard University Press, 2002), pp. 7–8, 14–15, 45–46, 84–91, where he claims that "while there is an ethics of memory, there is very little morality of memory" (7). Whatever the usefulness of this distinction for certain other purposes—and I myself have employed it elsewhere—introducing it here would only complicate and not enlighten.

66. Samuel Scheffler, "Immigration and the Significance of Culture", *Philosophy and Public Affairs*, vol. 35, no. 2 (Spring 2007): 93–125, at 120, 122.

67. Avigail Eisenberg, *Reasons of Identity: A Normative Guide to the Political and Legal Assessment of Identity Claims* (New York: Oxford University Press, 2009), p. 15.

68. Arthur, op. cit., page number not given.

69. The phrase is Scheffler's, op. cit., p. 122.

70. Here I may disagree with Eisenberg. See op. cit., p. 25.

71. Ibid., p. 37.

72. Ibid., especially pp. 32–42. Parenthetical numbers in the text refer to page numbers in the book.

73. In section 4 of this chapter, I quoted Brandon Hamber on the importance of "adequate participation and public involvement of key stakeholders in the development and conceptualization of symbolic reparations." Such participation and public involvement could count as satisfying the validation condition with respect to memorial projects that implicate collective identity.

74. I hold that memorials, at least those that involve a community's collective identity, will sometimes be of such weighty symbolic value that they will trump considerations of the instrumental disvalue of implementing them. Thus, while I defend a pluralism of values, I do not endorse an *incommensurability thesis*. That is, I do not take the view that there is no rational basis upon which to adjudicate conflicts between symbolic value and other fundamental evaluative considerations at play in a given situation.

The Nature and Value of Memorialization as Symbolic Activity   285

75. There is another argument involving identity considerations that I will mention that might throw light on the moral value of memorialization, although this would require more explanation than I can give it here. (Some) memorials, the argument goes, embody how a culture or society regards itself, what it takes to be important to its sense of itself, and understanding this is an important part of understanding the culture and society. Memorials have value because they facilitate this cross-cultural understanding and this is important because it facilitates cultural self-examination. That is, they provide others a window into understanding how people organize the lives they lead in common, the manifold possibilities of human sociality. And understanding this enlarges our own vision of what is possible and challenges the familiar tendency to regard our own way of life as the only acceptable or worthwhile one. Grasping the meaning of symbolic acts of other cultures and societies "from the inside" can undercut the parochialism of our own. I thank John Greenwood for this observation.

76. See the discussion of stereotyping group identity and its role in contexts of civil conflict and social division in Colleen Murphy, *A Moral Theory of Political Reconciliation* (New York: Cambridge University Press, 2010), pp. 114–118.

7

Human Rights and the Internationalization of Memory

1. The human rights focus of memorialization

The discussion in the previous chapter aimed to rescue memorialization from the deflationary charge that it is, after all, *merely* of symbolic importance, implying by this that it has relatively little or no moral value. I had already provided some of the materials for my defense in chapter 5, where I considered the expressive dimension of remembrance and the evaluative attitudes of self-respect, respect for persons, and fidelity implicit in it. The last chapter added to my rebuttal in two ways. I pursued a suggestion by Robert Adams that engaging in symbolic activity is important to the moral quality of our lives, specifically because it manifests our moral allegiances. I then developed a view suggested by Gerald Postema that symbolic action can express the common convictions of a community and be bound up with its sense of itself and its identity. Though identity cannot morally justify action on its own, or make what is morally indefensible defensible, it can heighten the moral significance of action that is morally acceptable or commendable on other grounds.

These chapters were not chiefly concerned with the issue of what might be called the *political locus* of memorialization. I did address this issue to some extent when I spoke about remembrance as a restorative justice practice. Remembrance has as one of its purposes to repair the harm caused by wrongdoing, so relative to that purpose it is only the responsibility of those who are obligated to make or assist in making repair. But more specifically, who are those to whom this rationale for responsibilities associated with remembrance applies? That is, what political entities are charged with fulfilling them or ensuring that they are fulfilled and why? The rather abstract statement that reparative remembrance is incumbent on those agents with reparative obligations does not provide the answers. My goal in this chapter, therefore, is to supply some. In brief, what I will argue is that the responsibilities related to memorialization

Human Rights and the Internationalization of Memory 287

exist on two levels. They exist first, and perhaps most obviously, on the *domestic* level: they belong to the states that committed or allowed the wrongs and those that succeed them and to whom these responsibilities are passed on. Second, they exist on the *international* level: they belong to international actors—whether regional or global in scope—as the guarantors of those responsibilities. Responsibilities also transcend national boundaries if regional or global actions contributed in a significant way to domestic violence and instability.

The focus of this chapter is the role of state, regional, and global actors with respect to the establishment and maintenance of memorials to the victims of wrongdoing in transitional societies. I am interested in memorialization as a practice that can address a *specific type* of wrong, the type of wrong that transitional societies commonly confront, so I will need to say something about what this specific type of wrong is. First, however, I will provide some context with a few remarks about the circumstances of transitional justice and the means that have been adopted for achieving it.

Since the 1970s, some 60 countries have made a transition from authoritarian rule to nascent forms of democratic governance.[1] In almost every case, the authoritarian rule was characterized by a record of human rights violations, whether as part of a campaign of organized and systematic repression or during the course of war and civil conflict, confronting transitional regimes with complex and often highly sensitive political and moral questions about how they should respond to this legacy of egregious wrongdoing. They had to decide how to restore respect for the rule of law and to balance a number of possibly competing political and social objectives, including restoration of peace and stability, economic reconstruction, punishment of the guilty, and assistance for the victims. As part of this task, transitional governments had to assess their own strengths and weaknesses, capabilities and limitations in order to determine what sort of official response from them was likely to be effective and would not jeopardize the prospects for reconciliation (even if only in the minimal sense of non-lethal coexistence) and social reconstruction. Transitions are not always from authoritarianism to democracy: they can be from one authoritarian government to another with perhaps a brief period of democracy in between. But as I will understand it, transitional justice refers to the doing of justice in societies whose transition to democracy depends on their confronting the human rights abuses of the past.

Some transitional governments criminally prosecuted individuals who belonged to or were collaborators of the prior regime. Some opted to expose former elites to public condemnation and humiliation and ban them *en masse* from public office. In still other cases, transitional governments adopted formal amnesties or pardons of the perpetrators. Truth commissions also became an increasingly popular alternative to punitive methods. Which of these or other approaches is appropriate or best in a period of substantial political upheaval is not a question that can sensibly be asked in the abstract, since the answer depends on the particular social, political, and historical circumstances of the transitional society, and these vary considerably from country to country. There is, however, one constant among all the various measures adopted in furtherance of transitional justice: they are conceptualized as responses to violations of human rights, especially systematic and/or gross violations of them. The reference to human rights in the definition of transitional justice has important implications for the allocation of responsibilities relating to memorialization, as we will see. It provides a moral foundation for the involvement of the international community in domestic memorialization efforts.

Human rights are thought to be a particular sort of rights with special moral weight and with distinctive implications for which parties have reason to or an obligation to respond to their actual or potential violation. There is considerable debate in philosophy and law about human rights, about how to understand and ground them, and I can only suggest something of the variety of positions that have been taken.[2] One issue is whether human rights even exist, in the sense of universally valid moral norms for the treatment of human beings generally. Some philosophers have argued that attempts to defend human rights are plagued with difficulties and inconsistencies, and they want to jettison the notion of human rights altogether and replace it with something else. This is Douglas Husak's view:

> Philosophers have dreamed of specifying rights which human beings share regardless of their race, religion, sex, or nationality . . . But when such philosophers attempted to answer the question of why all human beings possessed rights by specifying their ground or basis, they identified a characteristic(s) that is not shared by all human beings. Thus their projects are better understood as defenses of the rights of *persons* rather than of *human beings*. As so construed, their projects remain interesting and important.[3]

A more radical position is taken by moral relativists who argue that the morality of human rights has only local validity, depending upon whether a particular community happens to include these among its moral norms, and that human rights (or rights that persons have as such), in the sense of norms that are valid in all communities regardless of their local mores, do not exist. Others retain the language of human rights, perhaps partly out of fear of what consequences would follow from repudiating them, and ground them in a notion of agency, humanity, or dignity. Or they see human rights as falling within an overlapping consensus of diverse political moralities. Still other philosophers focus on how the language of human rights functions in international law and global affairs

Human Rights and the Internationalization of Memory   289

and in this way try to bring some order to the array of things that are called by this name. They construct a conception of human rights from the practice of human rights in international political life. Disagreements about the ground or basis of human rights are also reflected in disagreements about which particular rights are to be included on the list of human rights, about whether for example certain political rights are human rights.

This chapter retains the language of human rights in recognition of the central place it occupies in international doctrine and practice. It does not attempt to derive human rights from certain basic nonpolitical moral values, such as human dignity, because of the difficulty of finding a philosophical foundation that has real explanatory value, that is robust enough to ground the variety of rights that have been called human, and that will also be embraced by the world's diverse cultures. Nevertheless it supposes that there is a notion of human rights that can be successfully defended against skeptical attacks and that has sufficient normative force to be action guiding in political life, domestic as well as international. It supposes as well that various particular rights proposed as "human" can be tested by reference to it.

The feature that is distinctive of human rights, and the one that will loom large in this chapter, is their nation-transcending character, their spanning of territorial and national boundaries. According to Daniel Levy and Natan Sznaider, for example, human rights norms are "a globally available repertoire of legitimate claim making" that sets moral if not legal limits to the sovereignty of states and their representatives.[4] For Charles Beitz, a distinctive feature of human rights practice, perhaps its most distinctive feature, is that their observance and breach are matters of "international concern."[5] The manner in which such international concern can and should be expressed depends on many factors, including the scale of human rights violations; the domestic political climate of the state where the breaches occurred; the resources available to outside agents; and the costs to them of preventive or remedial action. I will return below to the different modalities of international involvement in maintaining respect for human rights, including both juridical and non-juridical mechanisms for affecting the responsiveness of states to human rights violations. But the justification of any of these possibilities hinges on what I take to be a basic feature of human rights—namely, they are norms whose validity does not depend upon the interests that persons have as members of particular political, religious, or ethnic communities. What's more, their observance is increasingly being viewed as a necessary condition of the legitimacy of state governments themselves.

One response to human rights violations, the one that concerns me here, is *memorialization*, a term that refers to a range of public initiatives at least one of whose explicit and central aims is to preserve the memory of past abuses for present and future generations, by such means as monuments, memorial museums, sites of conscience, commemorative ceremonies, and rituals. (There are private acts of memorialization as well, of course, but they are not my concern here.[6]) As noted in chapter 6, this definition of memorialization is broad enough to include initiatives that are not solely memorial in intent but that have the preservation of memory as an integral part of their mission. Truth commissions and even trials therefore could qualify as kinds of memorials, under a description that emphasizes this aspect of their work.

Since the basic form of a human rights norm X is, "X governs how persons should be treated whatever the local community to which they belong," conceptualizing transitional justice in terms of their violation has moral implications for the involvement of international actors in processes of memorializing. Memorialization is one sort of response that societies in transition can employ to deal with human rights abuses of prior regimes, and many have established memorials of one sort or another. But transitional societies are not always willing or able to undertake the work of memorialization, and even if they have made significant efforts to address past harms through memorialization, they might be able to benefit from outside assistance. There may be elements within the transitional society, such as civil society actors, that support memorializing initiatives but others that resist it, including members of the political elite. In some cases, it is only through the constructive involvement of outside agents that a fitting memorial to those who were harmed by repression and violence can be mounted and sustained. As with other sorts of domestic failures and shortcomings in acknowledging and respecting human rights and doing justice to the victims of human rights abuses, unwillingness or incapacity to properly memorialize them is not only a domestic problem of political morality. It is, in addition, an occasion for practical reflection by international actors about what they can reasonably do to advance the work of memorialization. In other words, the political locus of memorialization—characterized as having the violation of human rights as its generic target—is international, its implementation and maintenance a legitimate concern of agents outside the states primarily responsible for redressing the rights violations.

Recognition and protection of the human rights of persons is not merely the legitimate concern of the state in which they reside: it is also its responsibility. The responsibility, however, does not solely belong to it. The same is true for memorialization. Memorializing the victims of human rights abuses is one of the approaches that states can adopt to deal with past abuses, and arguably transitional states have a moral responsibility to do this, to establish public memorials to the victims of prior regimes and the wrongs done to them, among other transitional justice measures. But the moral responsibility for memorializing is not restricted to the state that is responsible for causing those abuses or for repairing them. It extends beyond these political borders. This is not to say, however, that actors on the international stage, or certain ones of them, have a moral obligation, all things considered, to initiate, facilitate, or augment memorialization in transitional societies. It is to say rather that such efforts do not fall outside the scope of possible international responsibility. Still, there may be situations in which action by regional and international actors to preserve the memory of victims of human rights violations is their responsibility, and not only a domestic responsibility.

Triggers for the involvement of international actors in memorializing the victims of human rights violations include the unwillingness of transitional states to fulfill their moral responsibilities with respect to memorializing them and the inability of transitional states to memorialize them with the resources they have at their disposal. If transitional states have made notable strides but have not been able to mount memorials that do justice to the nature of the crimes that were committed, they may seek outside assistance and other states, individually or jointly, may respond positively. But the morality of involvement by outside actors in memorial activities and practices within transitional societies is not always dependent on first receiving an invitation from the transitional regime. Moreover, when public officials are authorized by a community to represent it, their shortcomings with respect to memorialization are not theirs alone: they also symbolize the shortcomings of the community itself and are attributable to it.

In making these assertions about the triggers for international involvement, I am plainly presupposing the truth of two other claims for which I will need to argue, one about responsibilities and the other about who bears them. The first is that there is a moral responsibility or imperative to remember the victims of human rights violations, a topic that I have already addressed and about which I will have a few more things to say in section 2. Incorporating discussions from previous chapters, I present a number of grounds for claiming that memorializing the victims of wrongdoing, especially wrongdoing that consists in violations of human rights, is morally imperative. In section 3, I turn to the second claim and consider memorialization from the perspective of the political agents for whom violations of human rights provide grounds for such a responsibility. There I give a number of reasons, moral as well as pragmatic, for assigning states a primary and prominent role in memorialization.

Section 4 looks at the role of international actors, including international governmental and nongovernmental bodies with a global or regional character, in the memorializing efforts of transitional societies. Though individual states have primary responsibilities to respect and protect human rights, these are also necessarily matters of international concern and responsibility. In the case of memorialization, I argue that international actors of global or regional scope have default responsibilities that track whether transitional states fulfill their responsibilities with respect to memorializing the victims of human rights abuses.

I devote most of this section to a discussion of various mechanisms of implementation that global and regional actors might employ to promote memorial initiatives. These might target transitional states that are not willing to invest the resources that it would take to properly commemorate and do justice to the victims, although they may have adequate resources to do so. Some might also be employed to assist regimes and domestic groups that lack the resources but take their memorial responsibilities seriously. Whether international actors, including those of sufficient scope to be called *the* international community as well as those that are not as inclusive, have compelling reasons to act in support of or to further memorial projects in transitional societies depends on various factors, including the domestic political situation, the urgency of this as compared with other transitional justice measures that they can assist with, and the role that they might themselves have played in fostering repression and conflict within those societies.

The conclusion in section 5 includes a brief discussion of what I call the problem of contextualization and relates it to the internationalization of memory. Violations of human rights generate remedial responsibilities, including responsibilities to memorialize, in particular political, historical, and cultural settings, and these constrain the sorts of memorializing initiatives that are possible and appropriate for registering human rights violations at a given time and in a given place. For moral as well as political reasons, general notions of responsibilities to promote memorialization must be adjusted to and specified by the contexts in which they are applied. This is something that international actors, who are contemplating some type of involvement in processes of memorialization in transitional societies, need to take seriously as they decide whether intervening furthers the goals of transitional justice and how they can be most helpful in this regard.

There is also an appendix to this chapter that contrasts my view about an international presence in national memorial initiatives with Avishai Margalit's much more ambitious notion of a universal community of shared memories. The international role, as I describe it in section 4, involves many different sorts of actions by different sorts of outside agents, but what is not required for effective international intervention is an international collective memory of human rights violations, analogous to nation-centered collective memory only on a larger scale. There sometimes is such a memory, of course, most notably Holocaust memory.[7] But an international collective memory of human rights abuses is only one manifestation of what I call the *internationalization of memorialization*. In fact, collective memories are normally associated with groupings of considerably smaller size, such as families, religious associations, and nations with or without states of their own, where a sense of shared history provides the medium for shared collective memories.

I have a number of aims in this chapter: (1) to establish that primary responsibility for memorialization belongs to the states that have committed or failed to prevent human rights violations and their successors; (2) to present the moral case for an international role in the domestic memorializing efforts of transitional societies; (3) to give some examples of how international actors can further these efforts; and at the end and very briefly (4) to describe some of the challenges that international actors confront in doing this. The role of memorialization in the conduct of international and global political life—more specifically, the implications of human rights norms for involvement of regional and global actors in processes of memorialization—is a topic that has not received much attention in the memory studies or the transitional justice literature. Nor has enough been said about the international implications of the fact that international actors may have contributed to domestic human rights violations. Few scholars have written about how the normative discourse of human rights displaces the concept of historical memory from its usual home in nations and nation-states delimited by clearly defined borders to the international arena, where memorialization is not confined to territorially bounded nations but may be promoted and sustained in new ways by international actors. This chapter explores this neglected topic by showing how the discourse of human rights and the dynamics of international power politics change the frame of reference for memorial responsibilities. They shift attention away from the nation and the nation-state as the locus of memories of genocide, atrocity, resistance, and persecution, and provide the moral underpinnings of an enlarged practice of public historical memory in which international governmental and nongovernmental organizations play a critical role.

2. Memorialization: the moral argument

Is there a moral responsibility—duty or imperative or obligation, the exact words and their different significations are not critical here—to remember wrongdoing and its victims? More precisely, is there a moral responsibility for some party x to remember victims y of some wrongdoing z, and if so, why? Moreover, what value does memorialization have with respect to promoting the aims of transitional justice? In this section I want to return to the question of the moral foundations of memorialization and focus on the grounds of a moral imperative of remembrance related to wrongdoing. Other questions are which entities have moral responsibilities to carry out or promote memorial projects and the bearing on this of what I have described as the generic target of memorial initiatives in transitional societies, namely human rights violations. These questions deal with the role of governments and civil society actors in supporting and promoting these

294 FORGIVENESS AND REMEMBRANCE

practices, as well as that of international actors. I take up these questions in sections 3 and 4.

(a)   What and who should be remembered

My topic here is not the duty of remembrance in general: the objects of remembrance, and the reasons agents have to engage in or promote private or public acts of remembrance, are too varied to be able to say anything very informative about the duty without considering cases. The specific issues that concern me in this chapter are whether there is a responsibility to remember or promote remembrance of wrongdoing, more specifically still violations of human rights, and who is tasked with this responsibility. Though wrongdoing is certainly not the only possible ground of a duty to remember, and the victims of wrongdoing—both those who were actively involved in resisting it and those who were simply caught up in its web—are not the only ones who plausibly should be remembered, I will disregard these other possibilities in what follows.

If there is a moral duty to remember wrongdoing, then at least three conditions must be met in order for it to be activated in any particular situation: (1) the victims must be identifiable; (2) the duty-bearer must be specifiable and must also exist; and (3) the wrongdoing must cross a threshold of seriousness by some objective measure. It would be implausible and counterintuitive to claim that persons can have a responsibility to remember or promote remembrance of wrongdoing, regardless of the seriousness of the wrongdoing. The degree of seriousness matters, and it depends on various factors. Most obviously, there is the importance of the interests of the victim that are harmed and, related to this, whether the harm is such that the victims can be restored to their original condition. Another factor is the numbers of victims whose interests have been set back. The mental state of the offender is also relevant, since accusations of wrongdoing commonly involve two sorts of judgments: one that the offender did something that objectively he should not have done, and the other that he is blameworthy for doing it because of the reasons for which and the motives out of which he acted. Putting these factors together, wrongs and wrongdoings differ along a number of dimensions. They range from, at one end, minor offenses that result from mistake or carelessness and that affect few people to, at the other, deliberate violations that harm the most basic human interests of many people. Where in this range the wrong falls should surely make a difference to whether there is a duty to remember it.

(3) should not be taken to suggest, however, that there is a single threshold for all cases in which there are duties of remembrance. On the contrary, since responsibilities of remembrance are relative to the kind of the relationship, if any, between the victim and the one who may be called upon to remember, this

Human Rights and the Internationalization of Memory   295

can result in variable thresholds. Personal relationships generate special obligations of care and concern, and it seems likely that there is a lower threshold for
remembering wrongs done to them than wrongs done to those to whom one
does not have such special obligations. It is not just the seriousness of the wrong
that matters, therefore, but also how the agent was antecedently related to the
person or persons to whom the wrong was done.

One sort of wrong that would plainly meet the third condition for an imperative of remembrance is the particularly serious wrong that consists in the violation of a person's or group of persons' human rights. The special importance of
this sort of wrong can also be expressed conditionally by saying that if there are
any duties to remember the victims of wrongdoing, then surely duties to remember the victims of this sort of wrong qualify. The reasons have to do with the
distinctive normative force of human rights norms and with the gravity of the
assault on the dignity of the victims inflicted by human rights violations. Human
rights violations do not exhaust the whole domain of moral wrongdoing: persons might be treated unjustly or unfairly, for example, and as James Griffin
observes, "there is no inference from something's being a matter of justice or
fairness to its being a matter of human rights."[8] The inference doesn't even necessarily go through when the injustice or unfairness is extensive and persistent.
Violations of human rights are wrongs of a different order, and if any wrongs are
serious enough for their victims to be remembered, these must be.

There is a wide range of views, and wide-ranging disagreement, about what
gives human rights their distinctive normative force. One common explanation is that they are grounded in and derived from some fundamental feature
of persons, variously identified as intrinsic moral worth, dignity, humanity, and
normative agency, to name a few. Prominent advocates of such a view include
James Griffin, according to whom human rights are protections for the exercise
of "personhood,"[9] and Martha Nussbaum and Amartya Sen,[10] who propose that
human rights are protections for certain "basic human capabilities." Another
philosopher in this vein is Seyla Benhabib, who maintains that a human right is
"the claim of each person to be recognized and to be protected as a legal personality by the world community."[11] An alternative approach is to claim that human
rights constitute the core of an "overlapping consensus" among persons with
diverse moral, political, cultural, and religious values. They are standards upon
which persons with diverse conceptions of the good can converge.[12] For Rawls,
who originated the idea of an overlapping consensus but who does not use it in
this way, human rights are limited to those rights that "set a necessary . . . standard for the decency of domestic political and social institutions."[13] An explanation different from any of these, one that does not try to derive human rights
from abstract foundations or intercultural agreement, offers a practical conception of human rights. Charles Beitz proposes such an account. On this view,

"international human rights is the name of a collective political enterprise—a practice—with distinctive purposes and modes of action. An understanding of these purposes and modes of action is essential to a grasp of the nature of human rights."[14] According to Beitz, neither "naturalistic" theories (e.g., Griffin) nor "agreement theories" (e.g., Taylor) give the right sort of account of why human rights merit the special protection of being a political priority.

All of these accounts regard human rights as a special category of moral rights and their violation as a special category of moral wrongs, and it is this general view rather than any account in particular that I take as my point of departure. Moreover, among the rights that have been included in this category, some are arguably more *basic* than others, and the argument for a duty to remember wrongdoing is strongest with respect to violations of these rights. I mean by a basic right, following Henry Shue, a right without which "no one can fully enjoy any right that is supposedly protected by society." Basic rights include rights to physical security (that is, rights not to be subjected to "murder, torture, mayhem, rape, or assault") and rights to subsistence or to "minimal economic security."[15] Not all the rights that have been classified as human rights, such as some welfare rights as well as some political rights, are basic in this sense.

The most serious sort of injustice consists in violations of human rights, but not all instances of injustice set the same priorities and justify the same kinds of interventions as violations of human rights do. Elimination of injustice or unfairness in social life may or may not be reasonably regarded as a political priority; protection of human rights, by contrast, cannot be set aside until other political priorities have been met. The special normativity of human rights partly consists in their having transnational reach, such that their violation might be grounds for legitimate intervention in the affairs of otherwise sovereign states. Injustices committed by a political regime are not necessarily objects of legitimate international concern and involvement in the same way that violations of human rights are.

(b) Why remembrance

Establishing the distinctive normativity of human rights is only the first step in a philosophical account of duties of remembrance in transitional societies and internationally. The next step is to ask why, as I have assumed, it is both appropriate and imperative to respond to violations of human rights specifically with activities and practices of public *remembrance*—that is, by memorializing the victims. And the step after that is to ask *whose responsibility* it is to engage in or promote such acts and practices. Human rights norms require that persons' enjoyment of these rights be protected, and if it is not protected, that the violations be dealt with by appropriate measures, including punishment as well as material

Human Rights and the Internationalization of Memory 297

compensation. Can memorializing the victims of wrongdoing also count as a kind of redress for violations of their human rights?

"Redress," of course, is ambiguous. According to the dictionary definition, it can mean any of the following: "to set right or remedy," "to compensate," "avenge," and "heal."[16] In order to answer the question whether memorialization can redress wrongdoing, therefore, we need to clarify the expectations we have concerning what redress should be able to accomplish. There is obviously a great deal that remembrance cannot do. It cannot make good the loss that was caused: there is no way to make the wrong disappear by transforming a wrong into a right. It cannot restore the victims to the state they were in prior to the violation, as expropriated possessions or their equivalent might be restored to their rightful owner. It may or may not help them to heal. It cannot literally compensate the victims for what they suffered, and even as symbolic compensation, it is not by itself a fully adequate response to the grievances of survivors and victim families. The remedy or redress that remembrance itself provides, insofar as it does, may seem to be relatively modest, and it is only partial. But especially when combined with other sorts of remedial action, it can convey a powerful moral message and have significant psychological and social effects for the victims whose suffering is memorialized as well as for their families and communities.[17]

As I discussed in the previous chapter, it does this by virtue of what it symbolizes: memorialization can serve as a symbolic means of expressing intrinsically valuable evaluative attitudes, including belated respect for those who suffered from wrongdoing. On the most basic level, the respect expressed by remembrance is expressed by just being remembered—that is, by counting for something in the eyes of others and being taken by them as important enough not to be forgotten. (This differs from respect as discussed in chapters 5 and 6, since it is not second-personal.) This needs to be sharpened, however, since there are many ways of being important and many kinds of importance. A moral monster too may be important enough to be remembered, since it is important to remember the atrocities he committed and that he was the one who committed them. What I have in mind here is a sort of recognition of importance that acknowledges what I earlier called "the dignity of one's having existed"[18] and that is a way of valuing another intrinsically, for himself, and appreciating the basic goodness of his being. It is distinguished from respect for another as a being with moral dignity in a Kantian sense as well as from respect for another in virtue of his merits. Moral monsters do not possess this sort of dignity, although wrongdoers may. It can be that despite what the perpetrators did, the dignity of their having existed is not extinguished by their wrongdoing, and one way to acknowledge this dignity is by remembering them and so rescuing them from oblivion. Motivated forgetting of another, by contrast, is disrespectful in the most basic sense, for it says, "it would have been better had you never been born, since the fact of your having existed has no value in itself whatsoever."

What else can memorialization accomplish symbolically vis-à-vis the victims? Memorialization is a process of creating and using social artifacts of various sorts to tell stories that focus attention on the past. What it can accomplish for victims, therefore, depends on the story or stories that memorials tell about the circumstances of past wrongdoing and the parties that contributed to, suffered from, and resisted it. It depends also on how, by means of these stories, the memorials refer beyond themselves to patterns and structures of social interaction, to the broader political and moral life of the community. Whatever else these stories may do, one of their critical functions is to address the victims' needs for, and rights to, public acknowledgment that what was done was wrong and that they did not deserve it. Material means of redressing the wrongs do not provide full satisfaction. It is true that perpetrators may not be moved to provide compensation and will not in any case willingly commit to positive change if they don't acknowledge that they committed wrongs. But this is not the only reason for telling such stories.

It is also, importantly, because affirming the victims' entitlement to redress and right to demand it of others and communicating this to them is a sign of respect, and respect is lacking if the perpetrators and society at large fail to acknowledge that the victims were harmed undeservedly. Affirmation of their right to redress and authority to demand it of others is a necessary condition of their standing in relationships of political and moral equality with others, relationships from which they have been wrongfully excluded. Public memorials (monuments, museums, commemorations, etc.) can contribute, in a limited but important way, to undoing the wrongs of the past and to restoring their equal status in society. Through them also responsibility for past wrongdoing may be acknowledged and taken, and this can help to promote more trusting relationships. But as I explained in previous chapters, for second-personal respect of victims, many of whom have not survived, the views of survivors and their communities about the design and implementation of memorial projects must be solicited and respected, and these projects must be integrated with other reparative measures to which survivors have also contributed. Under these circumstances, memorials have what I called a validating function.

Memorials also have the capacity to vindicate. This is related to validation, but vindication specifically aims to refute allegations that the victims were somehow to blame for what was done to them. Perpetrators commonly try to justify their violations of human rights by claiming that the victims were a threat to social order and the rule of law and had to be eliminated in order to maintain peace and safeguard the stability of society. The exposure of these self-serving fabrications gives the lie to official histories that minimize the culpability of state agents and demonize the victims as traitors who deserved whatever they received. For the victims, this righting of the historical record can provide a measure of vindication, although it may not entirely free them from blame if there were victims and perpetrators on both sides. Vindication can accomplish even more: it can show not only that the victims were not traitors, but that they were the true patriots who resisted the injustices of the former regime. In their vindicatory function, memorials also symbolize the reintegration of the falsely accused into the political community.

Public memorials validate and vindicate victims in part by telling the truth about the nature and extent of the wrongs that were committed and about those who bear responsibility for them. Indeed, they can have considerable influence with respect to conveying the truth about the past because truth telling is often one of their central aims and they provide a prominent vehicle for its dissemination. (Of course, they sometimes also have as one of their central aims altering the truth to serve political ends.) They might tell the truth about the past in fragments of narrative or in more elaborate ways, and they often stimulate a broader interest in exploring the past to provide a fuller accounting of the wrongs that were committed.

Truth telling about serious wrongs done to individual victims and victim groups, especially when truth is told in a public forum and with the official support and encouragement of the state, affirms the reality of their suffering by making it difficult for others to avoid hearing it, something that might not have been possible before because the truth was covered up and denied by the same regime that engaged in widespread violations of human rights. It is not only their suffering that was denied: these regimes may have tried to obliterate any memory of the victims having existed at all, the ultimate act of disrespect, as I have suggested. In addition, memorials do not just convey the truth: they also involve survivors themselves in its telling. When they do so, victims who may have tried to tell the truth about their suffering but were silenced are given an opportunity to tell their own stories in their own way and a public forum for demanding public acknowledgment of their suffering as a crucial political and moral expectation. This gives them credibility as testifiers of and to their own suffering and contributes to restoring their sense of self-worth and establishing their standing as members of the political community with the same rights as all other members.[19] Families and survivor communities, not only individual victims, can also experience a measure of vindication from truth telling about the crimes of prior regimes.

Disseminating truth about past wrongdoing, and finding effective vehicles for doing so, are particularly important in the aftermath of a period of violence and repression. In these circumstances officials and members of the political elite not only frequently lie and deceive— deny that wrongs were committed, minimize their significance, fabricate excuses for them, or falsely portray themselves as innocent victims—but also insulate these lies and deceptions from challenge by promoting policies of deliberate forgetting and focusing exclusively on forward-looking measures of social reconstruction. Further, since future generations may be vulnerable to a recurrence of similar abuses, preserving and transmitting the truth about the past can prime them to watch for early warning signs.

The truth telling function of memorialization, and its inclusion of victims in the telling, is one of its main contributions to transitional justice. However, truth telling, whether by means of memorialization or in some other way, is not an end in itself. It operates in the service of other important values and aims, and these determine what sort of concern for truth it is reasonable to have. Its value may consist in the validation and vindication of victims through the open and public acknowledgment of the reality of past crimes, as I have said; the promotion of respectful and trusting relations between victims and perpetrators through transparency about past wrongdoing; and the support it provides for the establishment of a culture of respect for human rights in political life. There are both consequentialist and non-consequentialist arguments for truth telling and hence for memorialization as a vehicle of it.

Cutting across both sorts of arguments are questions about what truths about the past should be selected in creating memorials and how they should be combined to construct a coherent narrative about political responsibility. How much truth is required, and for what purpose, are questions whose answers depend on the political and social context, the nature of the events being related, and the needs of victims. Sometimes in some settings it may be critical to record the truth about past events in meticulous or exhaustive detail, if for example an oppressive regime has engaged in massive and systematic efforts to suppress the truth, or if the truth about a particular instance of political atrocity has been covered up. Nothing less than "full" disclosure might suffice in these cases. At the same time, the concern with details can become excessive if the search for truth becomes a distraction from the core of the historical record and fails to promote the moral ends of remembrance.

Of course, for many victims, those who died from the wrongs committed against them, telling the truth about long-hidden and -denied suffering comes too late to literally restore their sense of self and reinstall them in the political community. Still, it may not be too late for others. Moreover, widespread and systematic human rights abuses harm not only the direct victims but their families and immediate survivor communities as well, and truth telling may contribute to their sense of self-worth and enhance their standing within the larger political community. Survivor communities, as well as individual survivors, can experience a kind of moral regeneration from the social recognition and opportunity for truth telling provided by memorialization and other means.

Human Rights and the Internationalization of Memory   301

For this to happen, the stories that memorials tell need to get enough of the historical details right to be at least substantially true, although many specifics may be omitted. There is a flipside, however: memorials, precisely because they have the potential to inform and shape a community's understanding of its history, are tempting targets for abuse by those in positions of political power. They can be exploited by officials and members of the political elite who want to whitewash the past and promulgate a story with little relation to actual historical events. Those involved in the fabrication may even lose their grasp on the difference between truth and fantasy.

Memorialization can have validating and vindicating functions and can be an important component of societal reconciliation, but of course it is not unique in these respects. There are other practices that can reaffirm the dignity of victims and their place as equal fellow citizens (e.g., inclusion in the political, economic, and social domains of society); other measures for disclosing the truth about past wrongdoing (e.g., criminal trials and official investigations); and other ways of promoting relations of trust and respect among former adversaries (e.g., institutional reform of the rule of law). The claim that I want to advance here, however, is not only that activities of remembrance constitute a *valuable* transitional justice practice, but that it is *imperative* for (as yet unspecified) agents to engage in or support them. How can this particular claim be defended? One could argue that truth telling about past crimes, for example, is morally imperative, and that memorialization, as a vehicle for eliciting and transmitting truth, belongs to a category of morally imperative activities. One might also argue, although this is more dubious, that memorialization occupies a special place in this category because it is likely to be the most effective in promoting truth telling. Is there anything else we can say about why activities of remembrance specifically are morally imperative?

I believe there is. First, the dead cannot be rehabilitated or validated except symbolically and it is only by being remembered that this can happen: they cannot be given the recognition they were denied if they are not made the focus of public remembrance. Second, reparations are essentially backward-looking. They are given to repair the harm that was done in the past, not to rectify current injustice which is not necessarily the legacy of a pattern of past injustice. They are only intelligible as reparations, therefore, if they are understood in relation to past events, memory of which provides the moral rationale of the practice. Moreover, memorial activities and practices to help focus public attention on why reparations are given are imperative to the extent that the social commitment to reparations is likely to wane without them. Third, a duty to remember and to establish practices and activities to foster and sustain remembrance can be defended on the ground of its precautionary effects. We must remember, it is often said, so that we—our society or the world—are alert to the danger of

302 FORGIVENESS AND REMEMBRANCE

a recurrence of wrongdoing and adopt measures to prevent it. To be sure, the power of remembrance to protect against future wrongdoing has been exaggerated. "Never again" commonly only expresses a weak resolution to take preventive action. Nevertheless, it has some influence in political decision making as a counter to unopposed wrongdoing.

Finally, there are some vital needs that only memorialization can meet, and there are responsibilities associated with remembrance because of these. Daan Bronkhorst explains how a monument has special significance for the relatives:

> In addition to rehabilitation, it also has a humanizing function. Victims of human rights violations from the past are often anonymous: the dead, the 'disappeared' person. A monument turns this abstract category into concrete and personal victims. The victims become people of flesh and blood.[20]

By turning victims into flesh-and-blood people, memorials help meet a basic human need of the living to be left with some concrete remnant of the dead in their particularity, and they provide a measure of compensation to those survivors who will never have the corpse itself to bury. The very concreteness of memorials serves as a symbol of the concrete human being who was lost and in some limited way repairs the harm caused by his wrongful death. They also provide a kind of lifeline for the living that helps them to keep faith with the dead.

This completes my argument for the first of two claims presupposed by my remarks about triggers for international involvement in domestic memorialization. The next question is who bears the moral responsibility to see to it that the victims are remembered. I will turn to it after a brief examination of some objections to my account.

(c) Objections and complications

I have argued that public memorials in transitional settings can advance the aims of transitional and restorative justice in multiple ways. By acknowledging that serious wrongs were done to certain people and by securing them a dignified place in the collective memory of the community, memorials provide a kind of reparation (symbolic and partial, to be sure) for the victims and their families and communities. They can show respect for those who have been wrongfully harmed, in both second-personal and non-second-personal ways, and they can also vindicate them. This is both intrinsically and potentially instrumentally valuable, since it can facilitate the process of social reconstruction and political reconciliation. Memorials also do this by bringing hidden violations to light and providing opportunities for the development of a more accurate accounting of past wrongdoing. However, my arguments for the value of memorialization in transitional societies might be criticized in two ways. First, with respect to political reconciliation, it might be objected that we should not conceptualize memorialization initiatives in terms of redressing the violation of human rights, since their individualistic character clashes with the aim of rebuilding political relationships. Second, it is conceded that the claims I have made about the role of memorialization in achieving the objectives of transitional justice may be true in the abstract. Nevertheless, the objection is that they gloss over a number of highly contentious and morally freighted issues in the actual design and execution of memorial projects.

The first objection maintains that there is a lack of fit between features of the discourse of human rights and the moral ideas behind reconciliation, and also between the discourse of human rights and the focus of memorial initiatives in transitional societies. Human rights, the objection goes, are grounded in features that individuals share with all persons, entitlements that *individuals* have simply because they are persons or in virtue of their humanity, whereas the ethics of reconciliation deals with how to build or rebuild political *relationships* on moral foundations in communities that have been damaged by violence and repression. Human rights belong to individuals; the ethics of reconciliation, by contrast, has a communal frame of reference and is fundamentally relational. The same can be said about memorialization. It seeks symbolically to repair the harm done to some by their ostracism or permanent exclusion from a particular political community and to restore them as equal members of that community. In aiming to advance reconciliation, its objectives are relational, and these are not well articulated in terms of redressing violations of individualistic human rights.

The contrast that is drawn here, however, is extremely misleading about both political reconciliation and human rights. First, all reasonable views about the moral legitimacy of states require that they protect their citizens and look after their welfare, and this includes preventing and remediating violations of their human rights. Indeed, one of the clearest indications that individuals are not considered equal members of the political community is that their state fails to respond to violations of their human rights or actively participates in their violation. To be sure, reconciliation cannot be achieved only by memorializing human rights violations, since memorializing these violations is insufficient to establish relations of trust and respect in the aftermath of systematic wrongdoing. Other steps must be taken, including addressing the political and economic inequalities that made these violations possible. Nevertheless, since the context for discussion of reconciliation in transitional societies includes serious violations of human rights, processes of reconciliation have to address them. Thus, in addressing them, memorialization does not work at cross-purposes with reconciliation. Rather, it focuses on and reaffirms the minimally necessary conditions for membership in any legitimate political community, including the one that the transition is constructing.

Second, even if human rights are individualistic and protect the interests of individuals, they also have a collective dimension, by which I mean that reference to an individual's membership in a group is required to fully explain the importance of the right.[21] This is in part because the point of human rights is not simply to protect the fundamental interests of individuals, considered in isolation from one another, but also to protect the interests of individuals in having a certain standing in their society and in belonging to communities that, as Rawls puts it, provide "a secure basis for the sense of worth of their members."[22] This is an aspect of the protection afforded by a regime of human rights, and from this standpoint they do have a relational dimension. The rights still belong to individuals, but their importance for them has to be explained in part by reference to their interests in not being treated as inferiors within the political community and not being prevented from having a secure place in the smaller communities that structure their lives. Memorialization does not necessarily bring about reconciliation, but there is no incompatibility, or even pronounced tension, between memorialization that has this as one its aims and memorialization that targets human rights violations.

A second objection to my account of the morality of memorialization that is worth taking more seriously is its incompleteness. To this I plead guilty. It is incomplete because it does not address a number of critical normative issues relating to the creation of memorial projects. These include the following: When there are many different events that can be memorialized, or different parties who were involved in these events as victims or resisters, what and who should be memorialized? Material and financial resources for memorialization are not unlimited and must be shared with other vital reconstruction and developmental projects of transitional societies, and some difficult choices between alternative memorial projects will have to be made for this reason.[23] But it is not only because of scarce resources that these choices will have to be made. Questions will remain about who should be remembered and why—that is, who should be remembered for what undeserved suffering or resistance to repression or involvement in human rights abuses; and these matters are often extremely contentious because they are approached from multiple perspectives reflecting diverse collective memories of historical wrongdoing. Additional questions concern who has the standing to be involved in the design and implementation of public memorial projects, a topic that needs more discussion than I gave it before, and how and in what capacity they should be involved.[24] Finally, public memorials can only promote a culture of human rights if they are and remain relevant to the experiences and concerns of new generations. Hence, questions about how memorials can achieve this, and how they can involve young people in critical reflection on their history and promote civic participation, are not just narrowly technical. They are also, because of the potential of memorials to support a culture of resistance to human rights abuses, of critical moral importance. All these matters require further investigation.

While these are important moral questions, there is not much that can usefully be said in a general way to answer them. Clearly those who should be remembered, and who have standing to be involved in the development and execution of memorial projects, include the victims of human rights violations and their families and communities. But this does not resolve the problem of what to do if there are disagreements within the transitional society, as there often are, over who is properly considered a victim or whose suffering merits social recognition. In these circumstances, procedural solutions have obvious appeal. We can look to processes of democratic deliberation, debate, and negotiation between diverse stakeholders for at least provisional solutions to problems of who, what, and how to memorialize, when there is no prior social consensus on these matters. An added benefit is that a democratic process for the creation of memorial projects can itself have reparative effects in addition to the reparative effects of the memorials themselves, once they are established. Broad-based participation in discussions and debates about the form and content of memorial projects includes those who were formerly excluded from public decision-making processes, and this can help damaged communities come together and signifies recognition of the victims' standing and dignity. Deliberation, negotiation, and debate about memorial initiatives can also have *memorial* effects of their own, for they can reinforce and strengthen the collective memory of past wrongdoing. The democratic process should not necessarily exclude perpetrators, but arguably the minimal condition for participation is their acknowledgment that the victims were wronged and that they played some role in it. Otherwise, their participation in the democratic process is likely to subvert the process of memorialization.

3. The memorial responsibilities of states

Repair of the harm caused by the violation of one's human rights is usually thought to be a right of the one who was wronged, a right that derives from the primary right to have one's human rights respected. So perhaps we should also say that since remembrance can be a duty and can promote repair of the harm caused by the violation of one's human rights, even if only symbolically, the bearer of these rights has a right to be remembered for having been the victim of such a violation. An affirmative answer may be plausible in some cases, but it also runs up against philosophical problems connected with the idea that the dead can have rights, since at least some of those who are remembered have died as a result of the violation of their human rights, killed in the massacre of a village, starved through forced displacement, or tortured to death. This is obviously quite common in transitional settings. However, my focus here is not the right to redress but the duty to provide it, not the right to be remembered but the duty to remember or to promote remembrance, and there can be a duty to remember persons whether or not they can claim this as their right. In this way, I avoid the philosophical controversy over whether and in what sense the dead can have rights to be remembered.

I turn now to the question of who the duty-bearers are, and I approach this by asking the following question: as a general matter, which agents have primary responsibility to respect and protect human rights and to provide redress to those whose human rights have been violated? This in turn will help us to answer the narrower question of which agents have primary responsibility to engage in or promote remembrance of human rights violations.

Given the global reach of human rights, it might be supposed that the agents with primary responsibility for their protection and remediation are international in character, including international nongovernmental organizations (NGOs) as well as intergovernmental international or regional organizations. This is not reflected, however, in contemporary human rights practice. As Charles Beitz notes: "The human rights treaties all place the primary responsibility for compliance on states . . . The formal mechanisms for monitoring human rights violations are overwhelmingly constituted of states."[25] Assuming that an adequate account of human rights should reflect the contemporary practice of human rights, at least in major respects, the agents with primary responsibility to protect human rights and remediate their violations are *states*, each of which is composed of a set of political institutions that govern a political community or nation.

It might be argued against this that using contemporary practice as the benchmark merely reinforces the status quo and neglects or downplays the transformative normative power of human rights norms. But this is not a very compelling reason to reject the requirement. For even if the primary responsibility resides with individual states, this does not preclude other actors, in particular international ones, from having responsibilities of their own in the event that individual states do not fulfill theirs. It may be permissible in some circumstances for these others actors to involve themselves in the internal affairs of states, perhaps even obligatory for them to do so, because of human rights violations that occur within those states. This is the normative challenge that human rights norms pose to an international order of sovereign states, and it is also reflected to some extent in contemporary human rights practice (although perhaps not to the extent that critics would like). So the charge that this criterion of the adequacy of a conception of human rights is unacceptably conservative in the above sense is not terribly persuasive. If assigning primary responsibility for protection of human rights and remediation of their violations to states is objectionable, we should try to find some other reasons.

If the protection of human rights and redress of their violation is primarily a state responsibility, and if memorialization can be classified as a type of redress, as I have argued it can be, then it seems that states should have primary responsibility for that too. However, this conclusion might still be resisted by pointing out that in any given jurisdiction there may be various non-state actors who can promote and contribute to the memorialization of victims of human rights violations. Often these have the seeming advantage over the state of being closer to the communities in which the violations occurred, so they are better able to determine what an appropriate form of memorialization would be. Aren't we, by assigning primary responsibility to the state, overlooking the important contribution that these non-state actors can make?

I want to answer this by first acknowledging the importance of their contribution, but then continuing to insist on a "first responder" role for the state in regard to memorialization. In societies where human rights violations have occurred, there may be many individuals and non-state actors who can promote public remembrance of the victims. There are NGOs, a term that has no generally agreed legal definition but that usually refers to nonprofit organizations that operate independently of government and that are formed to further political or social goals. They may be funded totally or partially by government; however, they maintain their nongovernmental status by excluding government representatives from their membership, and this independence may win them the trust of a broad section of society. These organizations may help shape public perceptions of human rights abuses and exercise significant influence over state policies relating to how they will be memorialized. Other civil society actors, distinguished from NGOs, such as churches, labor groups, and professional associations, can perform similar functions.[26] In various ways, then, civil society actors can be effective in helping determine whether memorialization takes place at all, as well as the form, content, and scope of memorialization efforts. They do not do this as state actors, and if they only act with the approval of the state, their efforts to secure an appropriate memorialization may be compromised.

Nevertheless, it is the state that has jurisdiction over the political community in which the violations occurred, that may even have caused these violations or human rights violations outside of its jurisdiction, that has a special responsibility with regard to memorializing the victims. In transitional societies, where the political order is undergoing change, the successor regime that takes on the task of managing the transition acquires this special responsibility: the responsibility goes with the assumption of governance. Though non-state actors can encourage and influence public memorialization in significant ways—by applying pressure on the state to establish memorials to address rights violations; by challenging the selective and self-serving accounts of "official" memorials; and by imparting whatever social prestige they enjoy to these efforts—there are a number of reasons why states are chiefly responsible for securing adequate memorialization.

The reasons are as follows. According to one argument, citizens of a political community have a collective obligation to make reparation for the wrongs committed by their government, an obligation that includes activities related to memorializing the victims and their suffering. It is the responsibility of the state, as proxy for the people, to ensure that this obligation is discharged. Other supporting arguments focus on the impact that the state and its representatives have on how receptive the society at large will be to memorialization and to the reflection it occasions. These arguments claim that the impact is likely to be significant, and greater than that of civil society or international actors. There are at least two reasons for this: state actions have a kind of symbolic power that public actions by non-state actors lack; and the actions of states, those whose legitimacy depends on their claim to represent a nation, can give expression to and safeguard an important kind of identity of its members, namely national identity. The symbolic power of state action, and the linkage between state action and national identity, give the state a special capacity to influence historical memory and public understandings of past wrongdoing. This special capacity in turn grounds a special responsibility, a responsibility that includes at least some of the following: establishing, promoting, supporting, stimulating, and coordinating public memorials of different sorts. The arguments do not purport to show that the state is obligated to take a leadership role with regard to memorialization at any particular stage of the transitional process. Indeed, the transitional state may have weighty reasons not to try to do so, if political conditions are unsettled, its authority is tenuous, and its ability to survive political or military challenge is uncertain.

The basic moral argument for assigning the state primary responsibility in matters of memorialization has, as its fundamental premise, that citizens of a political community have obligations to help repair the wrongs committed against their fellow members, even if they were not directly responsible for them. These obligations extend over time, so they include reparation for wrongs that may have been committed or allowed by their political predecessors years before. Admittedly, this claim is not uncontroversial. Many deny that citizens in general can have responsibilities to remedy wrongs to which they have not contributed in some way, and citizens may not have contributed to past or present wrongdoing as perpetrators, collaborators, or supporters. Currently existing people who are burdened with the task of making reparation for past wrongdoing might not even have been alive at the time the wrongs were committed. This criticism

Human Rights and the Internationalization of Memory

could also apply to certain transitional situations, since transitions go through different phases and take time to become stabilized, in some instances several generations. But even in transitions of shorter duration, it may be doubted that citizens in general are responsible for redressing the wrongs committed by their leaders and officials now or in the past, especially if they took steps to distance themselves from those wrongs. To be sure, memorialization is not always burdensome and may require little of the average citizen, but the objection is not to its cost but to its fairness. How can we justify a general obligation of reparation for wrongs that citizens may not have been personally responsible for and that may have been committed under very different political circumstances, and in particular an obligation of reparative remembrance?

Why citizens have this obligation, and what moral reasons they have for accepting it, have been explained by philosophers in various ways.[27] The argument I present, in rough outline, starts by asking what is entailed morally by membership in a political community. (I assume that the members are citizens in a state so constituted that its actions can be attributed to them as their responsibility.) A political community does not just exist in the present. It is made up of a structure of interlocking practices and institutions that extend over time and across generations. A citizen, therefore, normally takes her place within a social order constituted by practices and institutions that have existed before her birth and that will endure after her death, and the obligations she has *as a citizen* are conditioned and shaped by the cross-generational framework of practices she is a part of. Being a citizen entails accepting this basic normative fact, whether it is done eagerly, as individuals do who identify strongly with their state, or reluctantly, as is the case with individuals who are not especially patriotic. Obligations associated with citizenship, therefore, are not confined to those that are voluntarily assumed and they do not require some direct or indirect contribution from those who have them. They are rather obligations with which citizens are invested in virtue of their belonging to an enduring, ongoing political community. (This removes the earlier objection to general reparative obligations.) In a well-ordered political community, citizenship entails responsibilities to maintain the political integrity of that community, and when it has been damaged by repression or violence these include providing material and symbolic reparations to its victims. The issue of guilt is not determinative here: in particular, citizens may inherit responsibilities to provide reparations, symbolic as well as material, for wrongs for which they have no rational grounds to feel guilty.

Though citizens are encumbered with an obligation of reparation for the wrongs committed, sanctioned, or permitted by their political leaders, they cannot fulfill this obligation directly. Instead, the obligation must be fulfilled by a proxy, and this is a role for a state. In assuming the role of proxy—and to some extent it does so just by being in a position to function as such—a state speaks and makes decisions as though it were the people. Among the critical decisions it is called upon to make in transitional circumstances is how to fulfill the people's obligation to make amends for wrongs for which their political predecessors are responsible. Memorial initiatives should be considered and, absent overriding countervailing considerations, implemented, since memorialization is a form of symbolic reparation that has immense value for victims, families, survivor communities, and the larger political community. Simply put, the transitional state's obligations with respect to memorialization have the following grounds: (a) citizens' reparative obligations include the obligation to memorialize and (b) the state functions as their proxy in the matter of providing reparations. Its efforts on behalf of memorialization are significant both as a form of official and symbolic acknowledgment of the citizens' obligations to make reparation and as a means by which these obligations can be discharged.

This argument holds that the exercise of state authority for the purpose of supporting and promoting memorialization has special moral and not merely political significance, since it is grounded in the reparative obligations of citizens and the moral values of memorialization. In transitional contexts, the harm has often been committed by a former regime, or it has been complicit in it, and it may take years to uncover evidence of its crimes. But when wrongdoing is clear, those who have been harmed by wrongdoing are entitled to redress, material as well as symbolic. By anchoring the special memorial responsibilities of states in the reparative responsibilities of their citizens and in the relations between states and their citizens, the argument gives citizens a moral reason—on top of whatever other reasons, moral or not, they might also have—to participate in processes of memorialization and to respond positively to state efforts to promote it.

When states fulfill their obligations as proxies for their citizens, or when they take responsibility for actions that they may or may not have been responsible for, this can have the effect of lending considerable prestige to memorialization efforts. This introduces a new element into the account and it brings us to the next argument. This argument and the next focus on the state's ability to galvanize public support for and to motivate citizens to engage in memorial initiatives.

The notion of symbolic power is key to understanding how this is possible. State action in general has symbolic power insofar as the fact of its being the *state's* action is taken to confer a particular kind of *legitimacy* on it by those who are subject to and recognize the state's authority. And they are justified in taking it this way only if the state is in fact a legitimate one, an important point to which I will return. Under these circumstances, the symbolic power of state action derives, in part at least, from recognition of the state's authority to act as legitimate. As Mara Loveman puts it, "symbolic power is a sort of *meta*power that accrues to the carriers of specific forms of power to the extent that their particular basis of power is recognized as legitimate."[28] States do not merely exercise a monopoly of coercive power over individuals who reside in them. They also exercise a kind of power that enables them to influence behavior not through threat but by affecting the meaning or significance that those who are subject to state authority attribute to their own actions. The ability to affect meaning in this way, by conferring legitimacy, is a defining feature of the symbolic dimension of state power.

With respect to memorial projects in particular, this conferral of legitimacy is important for a number of reasons. Through it, society *at large* shows that it acknowledges and takes seriously its obligation to make amends for past wrongdoing. State legitimacy can be conferred in different ways, but however it is done, memorial projects that receive it symbolize the entire society's recognition of the standing and dignity of those who were denied equal membership in the political community. Moreover, these projects, the reflections and debates on the past that they encourage, and the participation of citizens in them, acquire a meaning for them that they otherwise lack, and they come to see them in a special light. The projects are now officially legitimized, and if they recognize the legitimacy of the state, this gives them a weighty reason to view these efforts favorably. Public memorial projects that lack the official legitimacy conferred by state action do not have the same symbolic and expressive meaning, although of course such projects undertaken by particular survivor communities can still be extremely meaningful for those communities and perhaps others with similar histories of wrongdoing.

This power to legitimate can be misused, of course. Even legitimate states can use the symbolic power of state action to neutralize disagreement about the past in order to create a unified national narrative.[29] But state power can also be used in other ways. Especially if prodded by civil society and international actors with a human rights agenda, states may seek to promote memorial projects in order to foster critical debate about past wrongdoing and to help repair the harm it caused. At any rate, legitimate states, as proxies for citizens in fulfilling their reparative obligations, have a special responsibility to use their symbolic power to legitimize memorial projects for this end. It is "special" because the potential impact of the symbolic power of state action on the attitudes and behavior of citizens gives agents of the state a responsibility to use that power for morally worthy ends that is of a different order from that of non-state actors.

An additional reason that states have a special status and responsibility with respect to memorializing the victims of human rights abuses stems from conceiving of the state as agent and guardian of a nation. (This is connected to the previous argument in that the state's symbolic power derives in part from this role, but the arguments are worth discussing separately.) Of course, not all nations are states or have states of their own, and if a nation is conceived of as a group of people united by a common history, language, and culture, then some states are multinational. But I am conceiving of a nation as a collection of citizens in whose name and by whose authority a state acts and with the political and legal structure of a state, and I am supposing that if there is more than one nation (in one sense of the word) within the territory of a given state, their members belong to the same political community and share a common national identity in virtue of this. Further, and by way of clarification, I am not supposing that the legitimacy of states is entirely dependent on their having certain normative relations to the nations they represent. Indeed, because of the emerging practice of international law, their legitimacy is increasingly dependent on their relations to the overall international system.[30] Rather, I am simply supposing what is fairly obvious, namely that there is no genuine and effective world government; that the world is still divided into separate states; that states not only result from but play an active role in creating nations; and that membership in a particular state supplies many across the world with an identity that exerts considerable influence in their lives.[31] (Whether it should or not is a question I will address shortly.) Ross Poole describes the centrality of this identity this way:

> A major source of the strength of national identity has been in its inescapability. For much of the modern world, the nation has appropriated to itself the linguistic and cultural means necessary for the articulation of the self and its members. The fusion of language, culture, and polity defined by the nation has so entered our conception of ourselves that it becomes difficult to address the question of who we are except in terms which presuppose that we already have a national identity.[32]

As the sociologist Andrew Thompson notes, echoing Poole, "'Nation' and 'national identity' . . . are fundamental sociological categories with which each of us as individuals work in order to make sense of our social world."[33] A state that is also a nation or whose boundaries are approximately coterminous with that of a nation, therefore, has a relationship to a form of identity that strongly influences the actions and choices of those who reside in it. Non-state actors may be able to draw on other sources of identity, such as religious affiliation and family membership, to inspire dedication to political or social objectives, including the creation of memorials of various kinds. But their ability to speak to and motivate others from different religious, ethnic, and cultural groups may be limited. The state that governs a nation, on the other hand, is composed of institutions whose agents can tap into the motivational power of a kind of identity that is more widely shared and that can galvanize civic engagement on a large scale, namely national identity. It is a kind of identity that the state can draw upon in order to further social projects with widespread appeal, including for the purpose of memorializing the victims of human rights abuses. Given that memorialization warrants collective effort or at least the support of the majority of citizens, then arguably the state ought to use its connection to national identity to promote it, a connection that, once again, non-state actors do not have.

Against this, it might be argued that even if citizens do have reparative obligations, including moral obligations to memorialize the victims of past human rights abuses, this is not the right way to go about ensuring that they fulfill them. The state's ability to inspire action based on appeals to national identity cannot be a *good* reason to give states a prominent role in memorialization, since appeals to national identity are fraught with peril. After all, throughout history authoritarian and totalitarian regimes have invoked national identity to justify wars and unspeakable crimes of all sorts, and they have used memorials and commemorative ceremonies to establish the legitimacy of their aims. National identity may have the kind of galvanizing power that I am attributing to it, but this is something to lament, not to welcome for its ability to inspire dedication to memorial projects.

However, the wholesale rejection of appeals to national identity would be too sweeping. There are a couple of reasons for this. First, democratic or nascent democratic states are less likely to appeal to national identity for malign purposes, to motivate wars of national aggression, for example, than authoritarian ones, and in those political contexts national identity can excite public support for morally worthwhile projects and policies. By capitalizing on their connection with national identity, such states may be able to provide the political conditions necessary for the promotion of projects that involve constructive forms of memorialization, for example, and in this way advance the process of political reconciliation in societies that have been torn apart by violent and deadly conflicts. Where the linking of memorialization to national identity promotes memorial projects that are socially polarizing and destructive, other actors, including domestic and international ones, may be justified in exerting pressure to prevent or redirect those projects.

Second, and related to this, the objection overlooks the fact that in transitional circumstances national identity can itself be constructed through a regime's insistence on respect for human rights. It is when national identity is conceived in narrowly nationalistic terms that a state's appeal to it to generate public support for state initiatives is most troubling. But the national identity that a transitional state invokes to generate public support for reconstructive and reparative projects of different sorts is not only shaped by the particularisms of ethnicity, culture, or tradition. It can also be shaped in part by the state's efforts to create a political culture of human rights, and this weakens the force of the objection.[34]

Memorialization can play an important role in fostering such a culture and in the construction of a new national identity around human rights. In transitional societies, the serious wrongs perpetrated or permitted by the prior regime raise troubling questions about how citizens should relate to their national history and understand their role in it. Many will no doubt ask themselves how the nation they took pride in and identified with could have committed such wrongs or allowed them to take place. In the process, assumptions about the meaning of citizenship as they understood it, their conceptions of themselves as members of a particular nation, are challenged. In the circumstances of political transition, memorialization often plays a significant role in fostering such questioning and self-examination. It forces citizens, or perhaps only gives them an opportunity, to critically reflect on their identification with the nation, and it might facilitate the forging of a new national identity. There is a complex reciprocal relationship between memorialization and national identity: national identity has normative implications in that it carries with it special responsibilities to make reparation for and remember wrongs that belong to the nation's past; and national identity may be reconfigured in response to the human rights abuses that are remembered.

The preceding arguments for assigning states a prominent role with respect to memorialization do not imply that these should be entirely state-run or that the state should dictate the specific direction they take. Indeed, the suggestion that the state should usually be the exclusive or dominant party in memorialization efforts risks alienating those whose suffering is being memorialized. The arguments contend only that states should exercise their distinctive symbolic power to legitimize remembrance, but do not imply that they should take control of its implementation. Thus, state responsibility in this matter is compatible with creating state–civil society partnerships of various kinds and with assigning considerable responsibility for conceptualizing, designing, locating, and implementing memorials to local communities most harmed by the violations.[35]

To be sure, memorialization in transitional settings often has national significance. In these cases, the museums, monuments, and ceremonies established to commemorate the victims of human rights abuses and to warn against their repetition embody sentiments that are shared by the larger political community, and they speak to an entire nation's sense of the trauma and devastation it has suffered. These projects address the nation as a whole and are national in character, but they can have national scope even if they are largely local in origin and design. The involvement of civil society groups and local survivor communities in designing and implementing memorial projects does not mean that memorials will necessarily end up being of significance to survivor communities only. Moreover, even when it is appropriate for memorial projects to largely be the work of local communities, the state's role with respect to them is not merely that of an uninvolved observer. Rather, it can act as the "strategic facilitator"[36] of projects that were initiated locally and exploit its symbolic connection to national identity to generate wider support for them.

The above arguments assume that states are capable of conferring official legitimacy on memorialization efforts, and they suppose that states have, and are regarded by their citizens as having, legitimacy. Both arguments presuppose this, for otherwise states will lack the symbolic power to motivate commitment to and participation in memorial projects, whether by appealing to national identity or in some other way. Thus, the state's special responsibility with respect to memorialization in transitional contexts is premised on its sharing to some extent at least a feature that many states in more settled and ordinary circumstances have. When there is too great a dissimilarity, so that the transitional state does not have, and is not recognized to have, sufficient legitimacy to confer legitimacy on memorial projects, the arguments cannot get off the ground.

This brings us to a problem that confronts many transitional regimes in the aftermath of widespread human rights abuses: they come into power facing very real obstacles to establishing their legitimacy. New regimes are typically weak and inherit a state in crisis, with unstable, illegitimate, and impaired institutions.[37] Prior regimes have eroded respect for the rule of law and violated human rights with impunity, leaving transitional regimes with the task of "manufacturing legitimacy"[38] for their new state institutions. To do this, they must demonstrate a commitment to respect for human rights, to transparency in disclosing responsibility for past abuses, to the creation of a criminal justice system independent enough to reliably deliver justice, and to the control of violence. Transitional states have attempted to manufacture legitimacy by establishing human rights bodies such as truth commissions to investigate past abuses and conducting criminal trials to prosecute the most flagrant perpetrators. They have also mobilized state resources to create monuments and museums. Having achieved a degree of legitimacy, transitional regimes are then in a better position to pursue a range of state objectives that can further consolidate state power. In particular, memorials, perhaps tentative and modest at first, can be established with greater confidence and on a larger scale. Memorialization thus has a double relationship to political reconstruction in the aftermath of widespread human rights abuses: it can both contribute to strengthening the legitimacy of a new transitional regime and benefit from the regime's having achieved legitimacy.

For the arguments from symbolic power and national identity to work, there must be a strong enough and developed enough state apparatus for the state to govern effectively and to secure the obedience of its citizens. But this is only a necessary, not a sufficient condition of legitimacy, and transitional regimes may acquire and hold power that those over whom it exercises control do not regard as legitimate. When transitional regimes lack sufficient legitimacy to generate public support for memorial initiatives, non-state domestic actors may step forward to fill the vacuum and spearhead these efforts, at least on a temporary basis. Outside states and regional and international actors might try to do the same, but they may also face daunting challenges convincing others of the legitimacy of their own efforts.

4. Memorialization as an international phenomenon

(a) Failures to memorialize and international response

There are any number of reasons why states within which violations of human rights occurred might not memorialize or adequately memorialize their victims. Some explanations make mention of the survivors themselves. Survivor communities might be too fragmented to effectively advocate for memorialization; or survivor communities may be divided over how or whether to memorialize the wrongs that were committed against them. Or they may have pressed the transitional regime to postpone memorial projects in favor of other reconstruction needs that are felt to be more urgent, such as caring for victims and their families and rebuilding the shattered infrastructure of their communities. The transitional regime might have adopted their agenda as its own.

Explanations can also focus on the state. State facilitation and coordination are often critical to the success of memorial initiatives. Without them, community efforts to memorialize victims may have little resonance in the broader society. But circumstances of radical political transition are often such that regimes are unable or unwilling (or both) to do what only states can do to promote memorialization efforts. The transitional regime may be struggling to reform social and political institutions and to restore respect for the rule of law, but it may only have achieved limited success. Its ability to promote social projects of various sorts, including memorials, may therefore be hampered because citizens do not regard it as having (sufficient) political legitimacy. Related to this, the new regime might not have the military strength to secure the peace and might, with good reason, fear that support for memorialization will ignite a return of violence that it will not be able to control. If there are deep disagreements within the society over the meaning of national identity, there will be no unifying notion of national identity to which a transitional regime can appeal in order to generate public support for memorialization. There may also be disagreements among the members of the transitional regime over the wisdom of memorializing the wrongs of the past, preventing it from establishing a unified policy concerning this. This may be because some of the members of the new regime are carryovers from the former discredited one. In a different scenario, a transitional regime might have succeeded in establishing its credentials as an agent of democratization and be strong enough to prevent a resurgence of socially destructive violence. Nevertheless, it chooses not to exercise its power to confer legitimacy on memorial initiatives because it believes this conflicts with its pursuit of an agenda of national unity and reconciliation. And in yet another situation, the state may not lack the political will to memorialize, and may even have made significant efforts to address it. But it may lack the financial resources and the expertise to organize memorial projects that do justice to the victims of human rights abuses and to mount memorial projects whose scale is commensurate with the gravity of the wrongdoing.

The inability or unwillingness of a transitional regime to establish memorial projects for the victims of wrongdoing, or to act as strategic facilitator of memorial initiatives it does not initiate, does not mean that the victims of human rights violations will be left without any type of public recognition. Survivor groups and other agents of civil society may have some success memorializing victims even without state approval or support. Moreover, this is not necessarily a regrettable situation. State involvement in memorial efforts, after all, does not always give victims the recognition they deserve or promote truth telling about the past. But on the other hand, without the resources, material as well as symbolic, that a state may be able to provide, the ability of civil society actors to mount memorials that shape the collective memory of an entire nation so that victims are recognized and truth is told is likely to be limited. Without at least state approval, the good that memorialization can do to promote political reconciliation is also likely to be hindered.

International actors may be able to provide the support for memorialization efforts that transitional regimes will not or cannot. But the kind of support that will be constructive, that will enable memorialization to advance transitional justice in post-conflict societies, and that these actors should therefore render, is not always clear. It will vary depending on the political conditions of those societies and the particular attitudes that the transitional regimes in those societies have adopted toward their memorial responsibilities. For example, transitional regimes whose political agenda does not include memorial initiatives present different moral and strategic problems for international actors than regimes that are willing to memorialize but do not have the information and resources to do so adequately or effectively. Generally speaking, the timing and type of international response must be carefully calibrated to the reasons for the state's shortcomings with respect to memorialization, and international actors may for this reason hesitate to intervene.

I am of course supposing that what a transitional regime does with respect to memorialization is legitimately a matter of international concern and that international intervention to promote memorialization in transitional societies is sometimes justified. Indeed I would also argue that there can be an international obligation to intervene. There are two arguments for these claims: one focuses on the type of wrongdoing in virtue of which memorialization is called for in transitional societies, namely human rights violations, and what this entails internationally; the other addresses the contribution that foreign powers might have made to the occurrence of this wrongdoing. I discuss them in turn.

According to the first argument, the moral and legal norms for human rights have universal reach and exert normative pressure to restrict the traditional scope of state sovereignty. Given this, the protection of human rights and remediation of their violation is not *exclusively* the moral responsibility of individual states. The significance and reach of human rights are such that the international community and international actors have responsibilities as well, specifically default responsibilities that can get activated, depending on how human rights are treated in those states. Among these default responsibilities are those pertaining to memorialization of the victims of wrongdoing, because memorialization is among the moral responsibilities of states. That is, it is an implication of focusing on *human rights* violations as the specific sort of wrongdoing to be memorialized that international actors are stakeholders with respect to memorialization with default responsibilities for its implementation. Of course memorialization in post-conflict societies cannot meet the basic needs of individual victims and communities for education, health care, housing, and the like. Nevertheless, it is an essential part of a comprehensive reparations program to meet the material, social, and psychological needs of victims and survivor communities. For this reason too, memorialization must be included among the range of responses to human rights abuses that agents with an international scope of power or influence should entertain.

Even if international indifference to memorialization in transitional societies is not morally acceptable, there are better and worse, justified and unjustified, ways to express international concern and fulfill international obligations when states either fail to memorialize or lack the resources to do so. It may be unclear, however, how international actors should use their influence in these circumstances. For example, compelling a state that refuses to erect monuments to the victims of the previous regime may or may not be an effective means of getting that state to acknowledge the wrongs of the past, depending on the political conditions in the transitional society and the larger international political context. Failures to memorialize may be disrespectful and wrong, but coercive intervention as a means of promoting memorialization might only create resentment toward international agents and strengthen resistance to it. At the same time, recalcitrant states may be brought to accommodate themselves in other ways to international demands for memorialization, and this may enhance the prospects of political reconciliation. I will say more about this in the conclusion.

The second argument for an international responsibility in relation to memorialization in transitional societies focuses on cases in which foreign states played a causal role in generating and sustaining domestic conflicts in those societies. Opposing international powers may have contributed to domestic human rights violations by using states as third-party substitutes for fighting each other directly; or they may have signaled that they will not restrain states that violate the rights of their citizens in order to win their cooperation in global politics. The moral principle underlying this argument is uncontentious: agents are morally blameworthy for foreseeably and avoidably contributing to conditions that they know or can be expected to know will result in the violations of people's human rights, and they should take responsibility for undoing or mitigating the effects of their involvement. What may be contentious, however, is whether, in light of the empirical evidence, we can make a plausible case that in a given set of circumstance these states are truly at fault for behaving in this way. At any rate, the principle blurs the domestic/international boundaries of memory work by imputing (partial) responsibility to outside agents for the wrongs that call for memorialization.

Two examples illustrate how the involvement of groups of states in domestic affairs can contribute to the destabilization of societies and the repression and violence that characterize it: Angola and Mozambique. Both of these countries suffered from decades-long civil wars in which different sides were used as proxies for regional and world powers who were antagonists during the Cold War. The Angolan civil war lasted from 1975 to 2002, claimed the lives of an estimated 500,000 people, and displaced over a million internally. The contest was perceived by the United States and the Soviet Union as a critical strategic conflict in the Cold War, and opposing factions, both former liberation movements, were supported by each.[39] In Mozambique, the civil war lasted from 1977 to 1992, claimed the lives of about a million people, and displaced five million civilians. The civil war pitted a liberation movement supported by the Soviet Union against a group sponsored by South Africa and Rhodesia, then aligned with the West.[40] In both Angola and Mozambique, domestic civil wars were fomented and fueled by international powers pursuing their own national interests. Of note, both countries have resisted establishing truth commissions to investigate human rights violations committed during their civil wars, and both have passed general amnesty laws covering that period, the former for "crimes against the state," the latter for war crimes.[41]

These are the grounds of the principle that international actors have a legitimate interest in, and obligations concerning, the memorial activities of transitional states. But how can those actors have an impact on or augment those activities? Here we move from abstract principle to questions of implementation. The modalities of international involvement in this area can be divided into two types: those that involve the inclusion of protections for human rights—with implications for memorialization—in international law and their enforcement by international courts (juridical approaches); and those whereby international governmental and nongovernmental bodies seek to stimulate a commitment

320   FORGIVENESS AND REMEMBRANCE

to and provide support for memorialization initiatives, including assistance to states in their efforts to memorialize (non-juridical approaches). I will try to describe these briefly in what follows, drawing on actual examples from international human rights practice to illustrate.

(b) International criminal trials and collective memory

In thinking about memorials and memorialization, it is common to focus on museums, monuments, and commemorative ceremonies. These are among the standard examples of how events and persons are memorialized. But I have argued that we should take a larger view of this. Other types of responses to human rights violations, for example, such as national and international criminal trials and truth commissions, also have memorial effects, and it is somewhat artificial to draw a sharp line dividing these from monuments and the like. There may be some pragmatic justification for drawing a distinction here: memorials like monuments and commemorations might be more politically feasible and less likely to reignite violence than trials. Nevertheless, I do not want to press the distinction. For in seeking retributive justice, criminal trials assemble documentary evidence of crimes that establishes a public record that shapes a society's understanding of its history and informs subsequent memorialization efforts. Trials as part of a process of political transition and reconciliation thus influence the collective memory of a nation. But more than this, they also operate as exercises in remembrance, as public rituals of collective remembrance in which crimes previously hidden or unknown are exposed, acknowledged, and documented.[42] In short, there are good reasons to include criminal trials in a discussion of the internationalization of memory.

One way in which the international community is involved in processes of transition in societies attempting to create the conditions for peace and the rule of law after a period of conflict or repressive rule is the establishment of international criminal tribunals. International criminal tribunals take different forms. Some are ad hoc, like the International Criminal Tribunal for the former Yugoslavia (ICTY) and the International Criminal Tribunal for Rwanda (ICTR), both bodies of the UN; there is also the permanent International Criminal Court (ICC), established by international treaty in 2002. Criminal prosecutions conducted by these tribunals may or may not have the cooperation of the states where the violations occurred; they are officially based outside these states, although their proceedings may take place anywhere. There are also hybrid tribunals, as in Sierra Leone, Timor-Leste, Kosovo, Bosnia, and Cambodia, that include national and international judges and prosecutors and that are governed by national and international regulations. These hybrid tribunals operate in the location where the violations occurred, and they may be viewed as legitimate by certain groups within society and not by others.[43] International criminal prosecutions of any sort remediate violations of human rights by applying what Charles Beitz calls a "juridical paradigm of [human rights] implementation."[44]

Criminal proceedings with an international dimension generally have significant memorial effects. They not only dispatch justice; they also create a historical narrative that may survive long after the tribunal has finished its work. The materials assembled, scrutinized, and recorded by these tribunals are often essential in creating and shaping a shared memory of past atrocities, both within the countries where the rights violations occurred and more widely, atrocities that may have been officially denied or about which little may be publicly known. Though the immediate purpose of criminal trials for human rights violations is to assign guilt, punish perpetrators, end the impunity enjoyed by them, and deter future violations, international involvement also establishes a forum in which truths about the past are expressed and recorded and, potentially, made available to future generations.

Speaking of trials in general, James Booth notes a connection between the justice they aim for and the persistence of memory, a connection he calls "memory-justice":

> The fear for memory-justice is that the memory of the injury will not endure, that the crime will be allowed to slip into oblivion, into the forgotten; that the passage of time will, like a natural solvent or a willed forgetting, free the perpetrators and loosen the already weak hold of the hands of justice in the world. The trial is one forum of resistance to this, seeking the victory of the memory of justice over the becoming of time and the will to forget.[45]

Trials, according to Booth, function as a remedy for amnesia, as a site for and as a type of remembrance. Publicly conducted, they can serve broader educational and moral purposes, "as contributions to the shaping of the collective memory of a community and to the instruction of future citizens in their history and struggles for justice."[46]

If trials enact and promote collective remembrance, as Booth maintains, then international trials enact and promote remembrance with a scope that is potentially global in its dimensions. The growing importance of international criminal tribunals for the perpetrators of human rights abuses, therefore, holds out the promise of the emergence of a form of memory that is very different from memories delimited by the boundaries of a particular state. It is a memory that is international because it is rooted in international law and enforced by international legal procedures, and it differs in domain and often in content from the historical memories that a national state constructs for itself. Memories of this sort not only differ from collective memories centered in national states: they can and often do have a critical function as well, since these procedures may challenge the veracity of the collective memories that the members of a nation or nation-state have constructed of their shared past and that partially constitute their identity as a collective body.

In addition to being a forum for the enactment of an international form of memory, international criminal tribunals can be related to memorialization in another way: they can order reparations from convicted individuals to their victims. Among other measures, this could include contributing to the establishment of memorials to honor the victims of human rights violations, perhaps by paying into a fund for this purpose. In a discussion of the relationship between the permanent ICC and memorialization, Frédéric Mégret argues that the promotion of memorialization is a legitimate and useful interpretation of one of the main functions of the ICC:

> Neither the Statute [the Rome Statute of 1998 that created the ICC], Rules, and various other sources particularly anticipate symbolic reparations, satisfaction, or indeed anything as specific as the Court ensuring that reparations are used for the construction of commemorative monuments. However, . . . it does seem as if such reparations could be read into the Statute, and more importantly that encouraging "sites of conscience" is just the sort of focused, well-thought victims reparations policy that could maximize the ICC's impact.[47]

Linking memorialization to the court's judicial process of international accountability could also enhance the impact of memorialization. By including commemorative projects among other victim reparation measures ordered by the Court, the ICC would bring to bear the moral and legal authority of the international criminal justice system to promote the work of memorialization. It thereby adds normative weight to the claim that memorialization is of critical importance in attending to the needs of victims and repairing the harm caused by human rights abuses. What's more, it drives home the point that remembering the victims of human rights violations, no less than determining guilt and punishing perpetrators, is inseparable from an aspiration to justice for the victims.

International criminal trials, whether the permanent ICC or ad hoc tribunals established to deal with the legacy of human rights abuses in particular countries, play an important role with respect to protecting human rights. They do this in part by ensuring that those abuses become part of the collective historical memory of the society in which they occurred as well as that of the world more broadly. At the same time, their contributions to the collective memory of human rights violations can also damage the prospects for political

Human Rights and the Internationalization of Memory   323

reconciliation. As Michael Humphrey cautions, "one effect of the polarization between 'guilty' and 'innocent' [in criminal trials] is that while it may mobilize support for justice it can undermine the need for people to draw lessons from events in which they were morally implicated but now forget."[48] Trials, while establishing and preserving a collective memory of past crimes, can also provide warrant for a denial of responsibility for human rights violations by those who are not being prosecuted. The collective memory that emerges in the wake of criminal trials may be compromised by selective forgetting.

(c) International courts of human rights

International criminal tribunals do not exhaust the possibilities for a juridical model of international human rights remediation. Other international courts are regional and do not hear cases that can come from anywhere in the world, focusing instead on alleged human rights violations that occur within a geographically circumscribed set of states. They supplement the UN system for the protection of human rights and include the European Court of Human Rights, established in 1959, and the African Court of Human and People's Rights, established in 2006. Of particular importance for the purposes of this chapter is the Inter-American Court of Human Rights, since it illustrates how international institutions can further the work of memorialization in transitional societies. Latin America is notable not only for being home to some of the most substantial truth commissions for investigating human rights abuses, but also for having a court whose decisions one author has called "an innovative international best practice"[49] in the area of memorialization.

The inter-American system for the promotion and protection of human rights was born with the adoption of the American Declaration of the Rights and Duties of Man in Bogotá, Colombia, in April 1948. This was the first international human rights instrument of a general nature, and it predated the ratification of the Universal Declaration of Human Rights by the UN General Assembly later that year. (The close proximity between the American Declaration and the Universal Declaration is more than temporal: the latter was clearly influenced by the same ideas and sources that helped to shape the American Declaration.) The system consists of two permanent bodies, the Inter-American Commission on Human Rights and the Inter-American Court of Human Rights. The Inter-American Commission was established in 1959 under the Charter of the Organization of American States (OAS) to supervise human rights in its member states; 20 years later, after revisions in the OAS charter, the Court was created to enforce and interpret the American Convention on Human Rights, which entered into force in 1978. Both the Commission and the Court are authorized to handle complaints of human rights violations allegedly committed by any state party to the Convention, with the Court having both adjudicatory and advisory functions. Cases can only be referred to the Court by the Commission or by a state party, but any person, group of persons, or NGO may present a petition to the Commission alleging human rights violations. In addition, the Commission can only process cases where it is alleged that one of the member states of the OAS is responsible for the violations and the victims have either exhausted all means of remedying the situation domestically or were otherwise unsuccessful in obtaining redress.[50]

Commonly the Inter-American Court addresses the issue of memorialization under the heading of "other forms of reparation" or "obligations of repair" and refers to it as a type of "non-pecuniary" or "symbolic" or "moral" reparations or damages. The Court entertains a range of memorial initiatives. States found guilty of authorizing or tolerating human rights violations have been ordered to create public markers to territorially inscribe memories—for example, to "erect a memorial monument" (*Barrios Altos v. Peru*[51]; see also *Miguel Castro-Castro Prison v. Peru*[52]); to "build a monument of atonement" and install a "memorial plaque . . . during a ceremony attended by representatives of the National Government and local government" (*Villatina Massacre v. Colombia*[53]). In the case of *Myrna Mack Chang v. Guatemala*,[54] the state was told to do this and more, to "ensure remembrance of the victim through . . . measures of satisfaction and non-recidivism," including "publish[ing] a book on the history of Myrna Nack Chang's life," "build[ing] a monument to honor the victim or nam[ing] a square or avenue after her," and "establish[ing] a scholarship in her name." In the *Trujillo Oroza v. Bolivia* case, the Bolivian government was ordered to declare a specific day as "'National Day of the Detained-Disappeared' and accord suitable importance to this date with public acts and ceremonies in educational establishments, among other activities."[55] Court orders have been very specific, as when they direct a state to name a school after the victim "as a way of preserving his memory" (*Trujillo Oroza*), and also more open-ended, as when they instruct a state to engage in "public acts or works that seek, *inter alia*, to commemorate and dignify victims, as well as to avoid the repetition of human rights violations" (*Moiwana Village v. Suriname*[56]). The victims who are commemorated may be some prominent or emblematic individual (*Myrna Mack Chang; Carmelo Espinoza v. Chile*[57]; *Trujillo Oroza*); or they may constitute a community or other group of individuals (e.g., *Miguel Castro-Castro Prison; Villatina Massacre*). Sometimes the victims propose constructing a monument and the Court subsequently supports the request; sometimes the Commission initiates the idea; and sometimes the states themselves volunteer the building of monuments as part of compliance agreements, which are then enforced by the Court.

The Court includes memorials among the reparations it orders states to provide victims and their families because it recognizes that states, left to themselves,

Human Rights and the Internationalization of Memory   325

may be unwilling to initiate and/or support memorial projects or to follow through on whatever agreements they may have made to do so, without the sanctions that a court can impose. This concern is sometimes quite reasonable, especially with respect to societies in transition where new regimes may be too willing to make political compromises with former adversaries or may be misguided in believing that forgetting facilitates the consolidation of democracy and the rule of law. Not all transitional regimes are unreceptive to projects memorializing the victims of former regimes. However, whether or not a transitional state needs to be prodded to memorialize, the fundamental significance of the Court's involvement in memorialization in transitional contexts lies elsewhere. It lies in the principle on which it implicitly relies in its decisions and that it announces to all the states under its jurisdiction and others that follow its example. The principle asserts that memorialization of the harm done to individuals, families, and communities by violations of human rights is a form of (symbolic) reparation that is of such critical importance to their well-being and that of the society at large that states must take publicly visible steps to ensure it is provided; and that it is a legitimate function of international bodies to see to it that states fulfill their reparative memorial obligations. The Court effectively asserts that memorialization is not just a matter of local or national responsibility and concern. And in so doing, it assumes responsibility for giving legitimacy to the provision of symbolic reparations for human rights violations.

(d) Other types of international involvement in memorialization

I have focused on the juridical model of human rights implementation, specifically how international criminal tribunals and regional human rights courts can promote remembrance of the victims of human rights abuses nationally and beyond. However, the operation of such courts does not exhaust the range of ways in which international agents can affect the initiation, character, and viability of memorial projects and practices in transitional societies. The modes of international involvement and influence are varied in part because the agents who exert it are varied. International actors who can influence whether and how memorialization occurs in post-conflict societies include the following: the UN and its agencies; coalitions of states for whom respect for human rights is an important part of their political agenda; and NGOs with an international scope of action.[58]

Norm Articulation. The UN, potentially including all states in the world, has been involved on several fronts in the promotion of national transitional justice and, in particular, memorialization as an aspect of it. It has adopted international standards that call upon states to memorialize victims as a type of reparation for gross human rights violations. The Joinet/Orentlicher principles, formulated in

2005 at the behest of the UN Commission on Human Rights, include, among collective measures of reparation that the state has a duty to provide, symbolic acts, such as an annual homage to the victims, the establishment of monuments and museums, or public apologies by the state.[59] The following year the UN General Assembly adopted *The Basic Principles and Guidelines on the Right to a Remedy and Reparation for Victims of Gross Violations of International Human Rights Law and Serious Violations of International Humanitarian Law*, which include among the remedies for violations of human rights to which victims have a right "commemorations and tributes to the victims." Though these principles are not legal standards in the strict sense, but only guiding principles, and though practice has lagged behind them, they still have considerable potential to influence both international jurisprudence and state policy.

Advocacy. International actors might be able to promote memorialization by involving themselves as advocates in political and social processes within transitional societies. They might work with civil society actors to apply political pressure on the new regime to establish and support public memorials to the victims of human rights abuses. This pressure may be necessary for two reasons. First, transitional regimes may try to minimize the significance of past abuses by portraying them as aberrations. Second, even if they don't engage in this kind of historical revisionism, their political agendas may be directed chiefly to the promotion of national reconciliation and the revival of democratic institutions, and the needs of families and local communities for memorial projects that address their concerns may get insufficient attention. However, domestic actors may be successful in persuading their governments to change their policies so that victims receive the recognition they deserve, particularly if international actors partner with them and enhance the legitimacy of their efforts by framing their political activity as not just a local effort but as a struggle on behalf of human rights.

Facilitation and collaboration. International action on behalf of national memorialization need not be adversarial. It can instead provide vital assistance to fledgling transitional regimes and civil society organizations that are receptive to international help. For example, several bodies of the UN include efforts to promote memorialization among their objectives, in principle if not always in practice. The UN Human Rights Council, the primary UN forum for addressing human rights issues, established in 2006 as the successor to the UN Commission on Human Rights,[60] and the UN Peacebuilding Commission,[61] which also became operational in 2006, work with national governments and civil society actors to design, implement, and coordinate strategies for promoting transitional justice and recovery in post-conflict societies. As parts of the UN system, they are guided by the normative standards set out in the UN's *Basic Principles on Reparation*, which, as noted above, include memorialization initiatives among their recommended reparative measures. In addition, UNESCO's Memory of the World Programme, established in 1992, serves as coordinator and catalyst to sensitize governments and NGOs to the need to preserve valuable archives, museums, and libraries threatened, among other things, by human rights abuses that occurred within their borders. Though victims are not memorialized, these efforts may have some (limited) reparative effect.[62]

Outside the UN system, Barsalou and Baxter report that "affinity groups, such as the International Coalition of Historic Site Museums of Conscience, which has thirteen member institutions in eight countries, have organized to share knowledge and best practices internationally."[63] The International Council on Monuments and Sites (ICOMOS) is an international NGO whose mission is to "promote the conservation, protection, use, and enhancement of monuments, building complexes, and sites." Drawing on a network of experts from diverse fields, it provides advice to UNESCO on the designation of culturally specific historic sites and works with domestic architects and historians to facilitate the conservation of cultural heritage places, including those that serve as monuments and memorial museums.[64]

In addition to providing necessary resources, information, and training, and straddling the line between advocacy and facilitation, international actors can function as conduits for mobilizing and organizing people on the community level to participate in discussions about memorialization. They can facilitate processes of national and regional consultation on measures for social reconstruction and recovery, including the sorts of memorial projects that are appropriate on local as well as national levels.

Naming and shaming. Finally, there is the limited but not insignificant influence that the international community can exert through the pressure of world opinion. The UN is an obvious forum for publicly naming and shaming countries based on their violations of human rights and failure to participate in cooperative endeavors, including memorialization of the victims. UN resolutions that publicly condemn states for their human rights record could include their record on initiating or supporting memorial initiatives.[65] In addition, international NGOs play an increasingly important role in public practices of naming and shaming. They serve as watchdogs and monitors to ensure that states adhere to human rights norms,[66] and these norms can be elaborated to include memorialization of the victims of their violation. With this enlarged understanding of their mission, international NGOs could monitor how and whether states have fulfilled their legal and moral obligations with respect to memorialization; issue public reports about noncompliance; and censure states that have failed to establish memorial projects or have done little to support them. The data collection and monitoring function of NGOs, international as well as national, would create a historical record that is specific and difficult to dismiss as unsubstantiated.

This ends my brief overview of mechanisms by means of which international actors and the international community can extend their reach into the "internal" affairs of states to help remediate and repair violations of human rights through memorialization of their victims. Memorialization potentially has two important transformative effects. First, it may influence the prospects for political reconciliation within transitional societies. Memorials of different sorts, depending on the conditions under which they are implemented and their symbolic and expressive meanings, can help repair relationships that have been damaged by violence and repression and establish relations of mutual trust and respect among former adversaries. Fostering remembrance of victims of human rights abuses, therefore, is one way that human rights courts and other international organizations and bodies could help facilitate the transformation that is constituted by relations of this sort.

Second, the impact of these memorials may be transformative in another way. Even if not always intentionally designed for this purpose, memorials tend to involve individuals in, as one author puts it, "an active practice of remembering which takes an inquiring attitude toward the past and the activity of its (re) construction through memory."[67] Received views of national history may be revised; a new understanding of the past and altered identities, collective as well as individual, may emerge. International actors obviously cannot force a people to engage in such critical self-examination or to revise their thinking about their collective past and what defines them as a people or nation. They can, however, sow the seed for it through their connections to and instantiations of social practices of remembering. This is true of international agents with specific legal authority to act, but not only them. International actors of various sorts may be able to help shape collective and individual identities in transitional settings by promoting activities that influence the memories on which they are built.

5. Conclusion: Contextualizing human rights and memorialization

Collective historical memories are typically thought of as the construction of what Avishai Margalit calls "natural communities of memory,"[68] such as families, tribes, or nations. Within communities of this sort, collective memories embody shared understandings of significant events in the community's past that carry meaning for its current members. How the past is remembered, and what about it is remembered, are not fixed, of course: they change, and the change can be profound. In transitional circumstances, distortions, exaggerations, and omissions in the historical record may be exposed by former so-called enemies of the state and others who gain access to previously repressed history; a more accurate historical narrative may emerge that serves as a powerful corrective to prevailing self-understandings. In general, there is much at stake in what memories these communities have and how they hold them, since collective memories of momentous events in their past partially constitute their identities as distinctive communities. So it is not surprising if the process of uncovering hitherto repressed or neglected truths about such events and constructing an account to accommodate them is difficult and wrenching for the affected communities. Yet new representations of the truth do emerge, under ordinary as well as transitional circumstances, and as a consequence the community's understanding of itself and its defining norms shifts.

All this is true as far as it goes, but what it fails to mention is the role that outside agents play in influencing the formation and retention of communal memories, whether those of a family, a clan, a religious community, or a nation. Outside agents are invisible in these accounts. But as a descriptive matter, this is certainly mistaken. Communal memories are not only controlled and shaped by processes internal to those communities; and in this sense they do not belong exclusively to the natural communities that harbor them. Moreover, in at least one area, where human rights are involved, this is wrong normatively as well. As I have argued, these constitute a distinct class of moral norms, and while adherence to them is the primary responsibility of states, international actors have a stake in this as well and a responsibility to underwrite their observance. Among these responsibilities are those concerned with redress for the violations of human rights and repair of the harm they caused. And among responsibilities of repair are those concerned with preserving the memory of these violations and their victims through appropriate public practices of memorialization.

Uplifting though the language of human rights may be, the responsibilities associated with human rights cannot guide action if they remain merely a set of abstract aspirational goals. The authoritative demands of universalistic human rights must be made capable of guiding action within particular political, historical, and sociocultural contexts, and so must be formulated in a way that takes account of the circumstances of their implementation. These include the extraordinary circumstances of post-conflict societies where reparations for violations of human rights is or ought to be a paramount concern. Given the diversity of these contexts, respect for human rights will not be expressed in the same way everywhere, nor will practices of reparation for human rights violations. They will vary, and should vary, according to what is available for that purpose in a given setting, the needs and priorities of victims, and the meanings that different reparative measures have for victims and others in the community.

This chapter has addressed the question of the political locus of memorialization and, more generally, reparation of human rights violations. I have offered arguments for assigning states primary responsibility in these matters and the international community and its agents oversight responsibility with respect to its fulfillment. For both domestic and international actors, human rights must be contextualized in order to determine what can reasonably be done to fulfill the responsibilities associated with memorialization. For international actors, attending to the context of transitional societies is necessary to determine whether they should intervene at all in the internal affairs of those societies in order to promote memorialization. If a transitional regime's efforts to memorialize are reasonably construable as meeting their memorial responsibilities, constrained as those efforts may be by the particular political and social conditions it confronts, then what is called for from international actors is something like watchful waiting, unless there is a specific request for assistance from elements of the transitional society.

Context also has a bearing on the options for international actors at the point of intervention. Outside agents who want to effectively influence or direct such projects in transitional societies should investigate conditions bearing on this and consult with those who have most knowledge of and greatest familiarity with them, including members of the transitional regime, domestic civil society actors, and survivor communities. Information from these and other sources can help international actors determine which interventions have a reasonable prospect of success in promoting the goals of memorialization under the political and social conditions prevailing in the transitional society. Without knowledge of these conditions, the implications of human rights norms for memorialization initiatives are uncertain, for international as well as domestic actors. And without knowledge of how interventions will affect a society's willingness and capacity to memorialize, international intervention could well prove counterproductive.

The conditions internal to transitional societies provide context for their memorialization efforts, and international agents overseeing these efforts should assess them in light of those conditions. But the relevant context is larger than this, for international agents act on the world stage. They are embedded in a web of relations in which their interests and actions affect, and are affected by, the interests and actions of states and other international agents. In some cases, promoting respect for human rights in transitional societies might be costly to international actors with a human rights agenda politically and economically, and they might be under political pressure to abandon it. They also have their own domestic responsibilities to consider.

These factors are part of the context of human rights practice in general and memorialization in particular from an international perspective. To decide whether there is sufficient or compelling reason to involve themselves in the internal affairs of transitional societies and how to do so, a general claim that human rights are matters of legitimate international concern is plainly of little use to international actors. It has no determinate implications for memorialization without the addition of premises describing the domestic context that conditions and constrains the implementation of human rights and the remediation of their violation in particular cases. And even then, the conclusions are conditional on a specification of the global context in which the international actors operate.[69]

Appendix: Margalit on global collective memory

In an earlier discussion of Avishai Margalit's account of obligations of memory,[70] I argued that it is best understood as exemplifying what Robert Goodin dubs "the assigned responsibility model" of special duties. According to this model, "special responsibilities are . . . assigned merely as an administrative device for discharging our general duties more efficiently."[71] Margalit's account illustrates this model in the following way. There are, he claims, general moral obligations for humanity to remember certain especially egregious acts of wrongdoing, such as violations of human rights. However, he goes on, it is unrealistic to expect "humanity" to be able to fulfill these obligations. Instead, he turns to smaller types of community, such as political communities, to do the work of discharging these obligations. The responsibilities that are assigned to these communities to remember wrongdoing are, to use Goodin's expression, "devices" whereby obligations that humanity has to remember the victims of human rights violations anywhere in the world get assigned to particular agents.

I want to revisit Margalit in order to compare elements of his account of global collective memory and its limitations with my account of the internationalization of memory. As I will show, his understanding of what it would mean for memory to be international is different from my understanding of what it means for memory to become internationalized. Further, because he focuses on international memory that is global in scope—a type of memory that he himself regards as visionary—he does not address the ways in which international actors and the international community may be able to assist or influence individual states to properly memorialize human rights violations. I bring out these differences between Margalit and myself not to fault him for what his account of remembrance as part of human rights practice leaves out. After all, he is not precluded from acknowledging that the international community could contribute to domestic memorialization efforts without sharing a global memory of wrongdoing. Rather, I advert to Margalit chiefly to bring into sharper relief how I see international actors playing a role in promoting remembrance of human rights abuses and their victims.

First I need to rehearse the main elements of Margalit's account.[72] Central to it is the notion of a community of shared memories. Communities of this sort are typically what he calls "natural communities," composed of "families, clans, tribes, religious communities, and nations" (69). These communities are networks of "thick relations" that grow out of and are constituted by sentiments of caring; and those who belong to these communities are connected to one another through the memories they share of significant events in their collective past. Here caring and memory are intertwined: mutual caring creates shared memories and shared memories sustain caring. Margalit believes that human psychology being what it is, there are limits to who can be included within the ambit of those we care about. We care about our children, co-religionists, neighbors, and even compatriots. But though it is not logically impossible, it would require a radical transformation of our psychology to care about "bare human beings" (37)—that is, persons who have no particular relationship to ourselves. Hence, a universal community of shared memories based on caring for human beings as such, what Margalit calls a universal ethical community, is unlikely. Nation-centered shared memories, by contrast, are a common if not always welcome phenomenon.

Margalit considers whether another sort of universal community of shared memories is possible, one that is based on "some minimal shared moral memories" (78) and a sense of moral obligation rather than mutual caring. This community would be a truly global one too, encompassing "humanity," so would have much wider scope than natural communities. It would involve a shared sense among human beings that they belong to a community, the community of mankind, as we might put it, grounded in the inherent dignity and worth of all people. Were such a community possible, it would be like a community of compatriots who have a shared sense of themselves as belonging to one nation, minus the caring. Margalit, however, calls such a universal community "utopian," as he does a universal ethical community. "Memory," he says in a curious argument, "is too tied to the idea of immortality to expect that anonymous humanity can serve as a community of commemoration" (79). He therefore "believe[s] that the most promising projects of shared memory are those that go through natural communities of memory" (82). There are, in short, three sorts of communities of shared memories in Margalit's typology: (a) a universal community of shared memories based on mutual caring; (b) a universal community based on a commitment to certain basic universal moral standards; and (c) natural communities composed of thick relation. He places his trust largely in the last of these.

Margalit dismisses the former two as utopian and casts his lot with smaller natural communities. However, there is what we might think of as a middle ground between the first two and the last. That is to say, there are various sorts of constructive action that international agents and the international community can engage in to promote remembrance in societies confronting a legacy of large-scale wrongdoing. International influence and assistance, and even pressure, can be deployed to help counter the distortions and evasions to which nations and political regimes are often prone in their constructions of the past; to dignify the victims of human rights violations; and to create and maintain memorials that contribute to these ends and to the moral reconstruction of political relationships. There does not have to be a universal moral community of shared memories in Margalit's sense for international actors to be able to influence and shape social practices of remembering that affect a nation's collective self-understanding. Moreover, there is nothing utopian about the kind of international concern over violations of human rights that is expressed in the ways I discussed before. The international community, and international agencies, institutions, and organizations, can make a difference to whether and how violations of human rights are memorialized in transitional societies, even if a truly universal or global moral community of shared memories remains a largely unrealized hope.

Margalit's typology is incomplete for another reason: there can be communities of shared memories that transcend national and state boundaries but that are not global in scope, embracing all of humanity. They could instead be regional. Countries in a particular geographical region may share a common commitment to human rights that transcends borders, and it seems entirely plausible that an international, if not universal, narrative about the protection of human rights can grow out of this common concern. This narrative can be embedded in the historical memory of each of the involved countries, although none of them acting alone to memorialize the victims may be able to do justice to the magnitude of the wrongs that were committed.

Though Margalit is not hopeful about the possibility of creating a truly universal community of shared memories, he claims that "a thin notion of memory shared by the whole of mankind is desirable and important," even if "the politics of constructing this memory is immeasurably difficult" (79). This thin notion encompasses "striking examples of radical evil and crimes against humanity, such as enslavement, deportation of civilian populations, and mass extermination" (78), all involving gross violations of human rights. To Susie Linfield, however, the claim that it would be desirable and important for humanity as a whole to remember these wrongs is extremely problematic:

> This seems to pose more questions than it answers: Why, and how, should a victim of the Rwandan genocide remember those of the Gulag? And why should a comfortable 25-year-old citizen of, say, Amsterdam—or Cairo or Beijing—remember either? What, in such cases, would "remembrance" mean, and how would it manifest itself?[73]

Linfield is suggesting that there are conceptual and moral, and not just practical political, problems with Margalit's account. Whether or not she is right about

Margalit, my account is not vulnerable to her critique. For the idea that the victim of human rights violations in one country has an obligation to remember the victims in another, or that a comfortable person in one country has an obligation to remember victims elsewhere in the world, is not implied by my account of the internationalization of memory or even suggested by it. What I have claimed is that the international community and international bodies of various sorts, not individuals, might have good and possibly compelling reasons to become involved in some way in the internal affairs of transitional societies in order to ensure that the victims of human rights violations in those societies are properly remembered. Nothing follows from this about what well-off individuals ought to remember, or about what victims in one state have reason to remember about the wrongs suffered by citizens of a state distant from their own.

This foray into Margalit's discussion of communities of memory is aimed at clarifying what I mean by the expression "the internationalization of memory." It is not identical to Margalit's related notion, since it includes additional options than the two he highlights for international involvement in the memorialization of human rights abuses. It is not part of my intention, however, to argue against his claim that certain kinds of wrongs are so heinous that the world community has a moral obligation to remember them. In fact, I am inclined to agree with him about this. What's more, though creating a truly global moral community of shared memories of human rights abuses may not be a particularly promising project, as Margalit correctly notes, such a community is not unheard of. Holocaust memory is the best, and arguably the only, example of collective memory of human rights abuses realized on a global scale.[74] The global community of Holocaust memory would be an example of a universal moral community of memory in Margalit's sense. It is, however, only one manifestation of the internationalization of memory, and though communities of this type are not impossibly ideal, they are rare enough for us not to pin our hopes for the internationalization of memory on them.

On a smaller than worldwide scale, memorialization conducted on an international level may be morally obligatory for another reason. International responsibility for memorialization can be grounded in the culpable causal contribution of international actors to the human rights violations that occurred in particular countries. Their culpability gives those international agents a strong reason to promote and support memorialization in those countries, as part of their transitional process. But by the same token, it gives them reason to participate in memorialization themselves. Admittedly, since these actors are somewhat removed from the actual scene of conflict and repression, memorialization might have less traction internationally than memorialization has in the societies where the rights violations took place. Still, if responsibilities regarding memorialization flow from responsibilities for the wrongs that are memorialized, then in the causal circumstances I have described, the former responsibilities are not just discharged by international agents facilitating memorialization elsewhere. They are also discharged by international agents engaging in a type of internationalized remembrance.

Endnotes

1. S. Huntington. *The Third Wave: Democratization in the Late Twentieth Century* (University of Oklahoma Press, 1991).
2. The literature is vast, and I only mention a few recent philosophy books and articles that I have consulted. Charles R. Beitz, *The Idea of Human Rights* (Oxford: Oxford University Press, 2009), and "Human Dignity in the Theory of Human Rights: Nothing But a Phrase?" *Philosophy and Public Affairs* vol. 41, no. 3 (2013): 259–290; Seyla Benhabib, "Is There a Human Right to Democracy? Beyond Interventionism and Indifference," working paper presented at American Political Science Association Meetings, Seattle, Washington, September 4, 2011. Available at papers.ssrn.com/so13/papers.cfm?abstract_id = 1899956; James Griffin, *On Human Rights* (Oxford: Oxford University Press, 2008), and the special symposium on his book in *Ethics*, vol. 120, no. 4 (July 2010); James Nickel, *Making Sense of Human Rights*, 2nd ed. (Malden, MA: Blackwell, 2007); Martha C. Nussbaum, "Human Rights Theory: Capabilities and Human Rights," *Fordham Law Review*, vol. 66 (1997): 273–300; John Rawls, *The Law of Peoples* (Cambridge, MA: Harvard University Press, 1999); Amartya Sen, "Elements of a Theory of Human Rights," *Philosophy and Public Affairs*, vol. 32 (2004): 315–356; Henry Shue, *Basic Rights* (Princeton, NJ: Princeton University Press, 1996); Charles Taylor, "Conditions on an Unforced Consensus on Human Rights," in *The East Asian Challenge for Human Rights* (Joanne R. Bauer and Daniel A. Bell, eds.) (Cambridge: Cambridge University Press, 1999); Bernard Williams, "Human Rights and Relativism," *In the Beginning was the Deed* (Princeton, NJ: Princeton University Press, 2006).
3. Douglas N. Husak, "Why There Are No Human Rights," *Social Theory and Practice*, vol. 10, no. 2 (Summer 1984): 125–141, at 139.
4. Daniel Levy and Natan Sznaider, "Sovereignty transformed: a sociology of human rights," *The British Journal of Sociology*, vol. 57, issue 4 (2006): 657–676, at 659.
5. Beitz, *Idea of Human Rights*, op. cit., p. 32.
6. For more, see Jeffrey Blustein, *The Moral Demands of Memory* (New York: Cambridge University Press, 2008), especially chapter 5.
7. Each year on January 27, the day the infamous Auschwitz-Birkenau concentration camp was liberated, the international community unites in memory of the Holocaust and reflects on its lessons. On this occasion, the memory of the Holocaust is a collective experience of the international community at a global level.
8. Griffin, op cit., p. 198.
9. Ibid. See the response to Griffin by Rainer Forst, "The Justification of Human Rights and the Basic Right to Justification: A Reflexive Approach," *Ethics*, vol. 120, no. 4 (July 2010): 711–740.
10. Nussbaum and Sen, op. cit.
11. Benhabib, op. cit., p. 4.
12. Nussbaum also relates human rights to an "overlapping consensus," op. cit.; Taylor, op. cit.
13. Rawls, op. cit.
14. Beitz, *Idea of Human Rights*, op. cit., pp. 103–104.
15. Henry Shue, *Basic Rights* (Princeton, NJ: Princeton University Press, 1996), pp. 20–23.
16. *Merriam-Webster's Collegiate Dictionary*, 11th edition (Springfield, MA: Merriam-Webster Incorporated, 2005).
17. In the United Nations' *Basic Principles and Guidelines on the Right to a Remedy and Reparation for Victims of Gross Violations of International Human Rights Law and Serious Violations of*

International Humanitarian Law, adopted by the General Assembly on December 16, 2005, "commemorations and tributes to the victims" are an example of a type of reparation the declaration calls "satisfaction," and this is distinguished from "restitution," "compensation," and "rehabilitation." Available online at http://www2.ohchr.org/english/law/remedy.htm.

18. Blustein, op. cit., pp. 272–273.

19. For more on the relation between truth telling and moral recognition, see Margaret Urban Walker, "Truth Telling as Reparations," *Metaphilosophy*, vol. 41, no. 4 (July 2010): 525–545. See also the discussion of truth in Ernesto Verdeja, *Unchopping the Tree: Reconciliation in the Aftermath of Political Violence* (Philadelphia: Temple University Press, 2009), pp. 33–41.

20. Daan Bronkhorst, "Truth and justice: A guide to truth commissions and transitional justice," *Amnesty International Dutch Section*, 2nd edition (2006), 58.

21. Beitz also comments on the collective dimension of human rights in *Idea of Human Rights*, op. cit., pp. 112–113.

22. John Rawls, *A Theory of Justice* (Cambridge, MA: Harvard University Press, 1971), p. 442.

23. Related to this, see the discussion of the interchangeability of symbols in section 6 of chapter 6.

24. For example, the importance of the full participation of women in the design of memorials is noted in Sebastian Brett, Louis Bickford, Liz Ševčenko, and Marcela Rios, *Memorialization and Democracy: State Policy and Civic Action*, a report based on a conference of the same name held on June 20–22, 2007, in Santiago, Chile. Available online at ICTJ-Global-Memorialization-Democracy-2007-English.pdf.

25. Beitz, *Idea of Human Rights*, op. cit., p. 124. See also p. 109: "human rights apply in the first instance to the political institutions of states, including their constitutions, laws, and public policies."

26. On the role of civil society groups in promoting memorialization, see Verdeja, op. cit., pp. 154–155. For more on civil society actors and NGOs, see Marie Törnquist-Chesnier, "NGOs and international law," *Journal of Human Rights*, vol. 3, no. 2 (June 2004): 253–263; David Backer, "Civil society and transitional justice: possibilities, patterns and prospects," *Journal of Human Rights*, vol. 2, no. 3 (September 2003): 297–313.

27. The account sketched here belongs to a family of philosophical arguments defending non-voluntaristic political cross-generational obligations. See W. James Booth, *Communities of Memory: On Witness, Identity, and Justice* (Ithaca, NY: Cornell University Press, 2006), pp. 55–66, and "'From This Far Place': On Justice and Absence," *American Political Science Review*, vol. 105, no. 4 (November 2011): 750–763; Armen Marsoobian, "The Crime of Genocide: The Moral Imperative to Remember, Acknowledge, and Repair," paper presented at the 9th Biennial Conference of the International Association of Genocide Scholars, Buenos Aires, Argentina, July 20, 2011; Ross Poole, *Nation and Identity* (London: Routledge, 1999), pp. 67–74; and Janna Thompson, "Historical Obligations," *Australasian Journal of Philosophy*, vol. 78, no. 3 (2000): 334–345; also "Apology, Justice, and Respect: A Critical Defense of Political Apology," in *The Age of Apology* (M. Gibney, R. Howard-Hassman, J, Coicaud, and M. Steiner, eds.) (Philadelphia: University of Pennsylvania Press, 2008), pp. 31–44.

28. Mara Loveman, "The Modern State and the Primitive Accumulation of Symbolic Power," *American Journal of Sociology*, vol. 110, no. 6 (May 2005): 1651–1683, at 1656.

29. See the discussion of "challenges for state projects," in Brett, et al., *Memorialization and Democracy: State Policy and Civic Action*, op. cit., pp. 23–24.

30. See Ronald Dworkin, "A New Philosophy for International Law," *Philosophy and Public Affairs*, vol. 41, no. 1 (Winter 2013): 2–30. At 17, he says: "If a state can help to facilitate an international order in a way that would improve the legitimacy of its own coercive government, then it has a political obligation to do what it can in that direction."

31. See Mostafa Rejai and Cynthia H. Enloe, "Nation-States and State-Nations," *International Studies Quarterly*, vol. 13, no. 2 (June 1969): 140–158. Jeffrey Olick and Brenda Coughlin, "The Politics of Regret: Analytical Frames," in *Politics and the Past* (John Torpey, ed.) (Lanham, MD: Rowman and Littlefield, 2003), pp. 37–62, argue that the nation-state has declined in importance as a source of social identity for many in the contemporary world, but its influence nevertheless remains strong.

32. Poole, op. cit., p. 69.

Human Rights and the Internationalization of Memory   337

33. Andrew Thompson, "Nations, national identities and human agency: putting people back into nations," *The Sociological Review*, vol. 49, number 1 (2001): 18–32, at 24. Thompson also notes that we tend to reify and objectify the nation and national identity in our commonsense assumptions about them, and he cautions against overlooking "the interactional work that underpins how individuals position themselves in relation to national symbols or national narratives, about how we make sense of, interpret or renegotiate what our nation and our national identity mean to us" (27). "National identity," he says, "is produced by individuals in the course of social relations" (ibid.). See my discussion of Brubaker and Cooper in the last chapter.

34. Richard A. Wilson claims that the South African Truth and Reconciliation Commission was engaged in this effort: "In the 'new South Africa' national personhood became tied up with how to respond to past human rights abuses." In *The Politics of Truth and Reconciliation in South Africa: Legitimizing the Post Apartheid State* (Cambridge: Cambridge University Press, 2001), p. 14.

35. See also Brett, et al., *Memorialization and Democracy*, op. cit., pp. 24–26.

36. Ibid., p. 26.

37. See Luc Huyse, "Justice after Transition: On the choices successor elites make in dealing with the past," *Law and Social Enquiry*, vol. 1: 51–78.

38. The expression "manufacturing legitimacy" comes from Wilson, op. cit., pp. 17–18.

39. The United States provided covert aid to the forces of Jonas Savimbi and the group he headed, the National Union for the Total Independence of Angola, since he was seen as a key ally in the U.S. effort to counter Soviet-backed governments around the world. The Soviet Union, along with its Cuban and Eastern bloc allies, provided both combatants and support personnel for the People's Movement for the Liberation of Angola. See "Angolan Civil War," http://en.wikipedia.org/wiki/Angolan_Civil_War.

40. "Mozambican Civil War," http://en.wikipedia.org/wiki/Mozambican_Civil_War. Also "How was Mozambique used in the Cold War Proxy War?" at http://answers.yahoo/com/question.index?qid = 20090329172041/AAVtv5Y.

41. On Mozambique, see Priscilla Hayner, *Unspeakable Truths: Facing the Challenge of Truth Commissions* (New York: Routledge, 2002), pp. 186–195. On Angola, see David Backer, "Civil Society and transitional justice: possibilities, patterns and prospects" *Journal of Human Rights*, vol. 2, no. 3 (September 2003): 297–313; Joris van Wijk, "Amnesty for War Crimes in Angola: Principled for a Day?" *International Criminal Law Review*, vol. 12, no. 4 (January 2012): 743–761.

42. As Ruti Teitel puts it, "trials are traditional ceremonies affording a ritual to publicly contextualize and share past experience of wrongdoing." *Transitional Justice* (Oxford: Oxford University Press, 2000), p. 75.

43. For a description of types of international criminal tribunals and their political uses, see Teitel, ibid.; and Colleen Murphy, *A Moral Theory of Political Reconciliation* (New York: Cambridge University Press, 2010), pp. 177–182.

44. Beitz, *Idea of Human Rights*, op. cit., p. 32.

45. Booth, op. cit., p. 123.

46. Ibid., p. 126.

47. Frédéric Mégret, "Of Shrines, Memorials, and Museums: Using the International Criminal Court's Victim Reparations and Assistance Regime to Promote Transitional Justice," *Social Science Research Network*, working paper (May 13, 2009), available at SSRN-id1403929(3).pdf. A version is also published in the *Buffalo Human Rights Law Review*, vol. 16 (2010). See also Mégret, "The International Criminal Court and the Failure to Mention Symbolic Reparations," available at SSRN-id1275087.

48. Michael Humphrey, "From Victim to Victimhood: Truth Commissions and Trials as Rituals of Political Transition and Individual Healing," *The Australian Journal of Anthropology*, vol. 14, no. 2 (2003): 171–187, at 182.

49. Mégret, op. cit., p. 1.

50. For more on this two-pronged system for promoting and protecting human rights, see Thomas Buergenthal, "The Revised OAS Charter and the Protection of Human Rights," *American Journal of International Law*, vol. 69 (1975): 828–836; Cecilia Medina, "The Inter-American

338 FORGIVENESS AND REMEMBRANCE

Commission on Human Rights and the Inter-American Court of Human Rights: Reflections on a Joint Venture," *Human Rights Quarterly*, vol. 12 (1990): 439–464; "Inter-American Court of Human Rights," available online at http://en.wikipedia.org/wiki/Inter-American_Court_ of_Human_Rights; "Inter-American Commission on Human Rights," available online at http://www.cidh.oas.org/what.htm.

51. *Barrios Altos* Case, Judgment of November 30, 2001, Inter-Am Ct. H.R. (Ser. C) No. 87 (2001).

52. Case of *Miguel Castro-Castro Prison v. Peru*, Judgment of November 25, 2006 (Merits, Reparations and Costs).

53. *Villatina Massacre v. Colombia*, Case 11.141, Report No. 105/05, Inter-Am. C.H.R., OEA/ Ser.L/V/II.124 Doc 5 (2005).

54. Case of *Myrna Mack Chang v. Guatemala*, 2003, Inter-Am Ct. H.R., (Ser. C) No. 101 (November 25, 2003).

55. *Trujillo Oroza* Case, 2002, Inter-Am. Ct. H.R., (Ser. C) No. 92 (February 27, 2002).

56. Case of *Moiwana Village v. Suriname*, 2005, Inter-Am Ct. H.R., (Ser. C) No. 124 (June 15, 2005).

57. *Carmelo Espinoza v. Chile*, Case 11.725, Report No. 19/03, Inter-Am. C.H.R., OEA/Ser.L/V/ II.118 Doc. 70 rev. 2, at 588 (2003).

58. David A. Crocker discusses different ways in which "international civil society" and international regimes can assist states in transition. International civil society, he says, "can promote transitional justice by providing to [sic] domestic civil groups and democratically elected governments with material resources, lessons learned by other new democracies, international legitimacy, and moral support. Such assistance may be indispensable as domestic civil groups and fledgling democracies face the forces of revenge or appeals to social amnesia" ("Truth Commissions, Transitional Justice, and Civil Society," in *Truth v. Justice* [Robert Rotberg and Dennis Thompson, eds.] [Princeton, NJ: Princeton University Press, 2000], pp. 116–117). In this chapter I am interested specifically in one way agents of the international community can help fledgling states resist social amnesia: by assisting and engaging with societies in transition to establish memorials to the victims of human rights violations.

59. See Jonathan Sisson, "A Conceptual Framework for Dealing with the Past," *Politorbis*, vol. 3, no. 50 (2010): 11–15.

60. See the website of the UN Human Rights Council, www2.ohchr.org/English/bodies/hrcouncil/; also "Transitional Justice in the United Nations Human Rights Council,"*International Center for Transitional Justice* briefing paper, June 2011, available at ICTJ-Global-TJ-In-HRC 2011-English.pdf.

61. On the Peacebuilding Commission, see Renske Heemskerk, "The UN Peacebuilding Commission and civil society engagement," *Disarmament Forum*, no. 2 (2007). Available at www. isn.ethz.ch/Digital-Library/Publications/Detail/?id=47087.

62. From the Memory of the World Programme website, at www.unesco/org/new/en/communication-and-information/flagship-project-activities/memory-of-the-world/about-the-programme; and the Wikipedia entry http://en.wikipedia.org/wiki/memory_of_the_ world_programme.

63. Judy Barsalou and Victoria Baxter, "The Urge to Remember: The Role of Memorials in Social Reconstruction and Transitional Justice," *Report of the Memorialization Working Group of the United States Institute of Peace*, Stabilization and Reconstruction Series No. 5 (Washington, DC, January 2007). The International Coalition has created a Project Support Fund that provides financial as well as technical support to the building of memorial sites.

64. The ICOMOS website is at www.icomos.org/en/.

65. James Lebovic and Erik Voeten discuss the naming and shaming practices of the UN Council on Human Rights in "The Politics of Shame: The Condemnation of Country Human Rights Practices in the UNCHR," *International Studies Quarterly*, vol. 50, no. 4 (December 2006): 861–888. Though they do not include memorialization among the determinants of targeting a country, I am suggesting that a country's record of memorializing the victims of human rights violations is a suitable target for the commission's work.

66. See Törnquist-Chesnier, op. cit.

67. A. Kuhn, "A journey through memory," in *Memory and Methodology* (S. Radstone, ed.) (Oxford: Berg, 2000), pp. 183–186.
68. Avishai Margalit, *The Ethics of Memory* (Cambridge, MA: Harvard University Press, 2002). p. 69.
69. Contextualization of universalistic human rights is essential, but it is also a matter of considerable moral and political significance how and by whom they are contextualized.
Seyla Benhabib describes what she believes is the ideal process. It is what she calls "democratic iteration," and she explains it this way:

> By democratic iterations I mean complex processes of public argument, deliberation, and exchange—through which universalistic rights claims are contested and contextualized, invoked and revoked, posited and positioned—through legal and political institutions as well as in the associations of civil society. A democratic iteration is never merely an act of repetition. Every iteration involves making sense of an authoritative original in a new and different context. ("The Legitimacy of Human Rights," *Daedalus*, vol. 137, no. 3 [Summer 2008]: 94–104.)

A process of democratic iteration could also determine how the victims of human rights violations should be memorialized. This contextualizes them, which is necessary because even though all projects memorializing the victims of human rights violations derive their moral warrant from a common value framework that has universal reach, they can nevertheless justifiably differ from one transitional society to another. Of course the circumstances of transitional societies may make it difficult to realize an iterative process that is completely just in Benhabib's sense. That is, it may be unlikely that deliberations about memorialization will be "carried out by the most inclusive and equal participation of all those whose interests are affected" (ibid.). Still, the deliberative process can have some legitimacy, and transitional justice can be advanced, even under these circumstances, and one indicator of how the transition is progressing is whether the process is moving in the direction of becoming more inclusive and equal.
70. Blustein, op. cit., pp. 204–211.
71. Robert Goodin, "What Is So Special about Our Fellow Countrymen"? *Ethics*, vol. 98, no. 4 (July 1988): 663–686, at 685.
72. Margalit, op. cit., page numbers appear in parentheses.
73. Susie Linfield, "Memory's Lair," *Boston Review* (Summer 2003).
74. See Daniel Levy and Natan Sznaider, *The Holocaust and Memory in the Global Age* (Philadelphia: Temple University Press, 2006). However, the belief expressed by them that Holocaust memory fosters a culture of human rights by contributing to transcultural understanding can be challenged. A. Dirk Moses argues that Holocaust memory does not have the cosmopolitan effect that Levy and Sznaider suppose, in "Genocide and the Terror of History," *Parallax*, vol. 17, no. 4 (2011): 98–108.

INDEX

Adams, Robert Merrihew, 262
Allais, Lucy, 209–210
amnesia, collective, 119–120
Anderson, Elizabeth, 183
Anderson, E. and R. Pildes, 238–239
anger. *See* negative emotions
Angola, international role in civil war, 319
apologies, public, 158–160, 229, 281n19
Arthur, Paige, 269, 273
associative network theories of mood,
    112–113
attentional deployment. *See* emotion regulation,
    techniques of
autobiographical past-directed emotions
    empathic and non-empathic, 77
    and forgiveness, 77–78

Barsalou, J. and V. Baxter, 327
Beitz, Charles, 289, 295–296, 306, 321
Bell, Macalester, 68n68
Benhabib, Seyla, 295, 339n69
Bennett, Christopher, 37, 66n38, 67n50
Bickford, Louis, 233
blame. *See also* forgiveness
    after forgiveness, 44–47, 67n50
    emotions accompanying, 21–22, 39, 40,
        66n38
    Scanlon on, 40–41, 44–45, 46
    Sher on, 39–40, 46–47
    and suffering, 37–38
Blewitt, Mary Kayitsei, 1–2
Boleyn-Fitzgerald, Patrick, 124
Booth, W. James, 255, 321
Bourdieu, Pierre, 263
Boxill, Bernard, 57–59
Bronkhorst, Daan, 302
Brubaker, R. and F. Cooper, 270–271
Brudholm, Thomas, 154

Brison, Susan, 131
Butler, Joseph, on forgiveness, 18

Calhoun, Chesire, 103–104, 126–128. *See also*
    emotion regulation, techniques of
Care, Norman, 107, 113
Casey, Edward
    on commemoration, 183, 207–208, 210
character, of community and nation, 263–264,
    265
cognitive reappraisal. *See* emotion regulation,
    techniques of
collective identity. *See also* identity claims,
    assessment of
    conceptions of, 270–271, 337n33
    as dimension of memorialization, 269–270,
        271–272, 279, 283n55, 283n57, 313–314
    moral significance of, 272–274
    role of in moral conflict, 276–278, 284n74
(the) compatibility problem, 181. *See also*
    memorialization (commemoration)
    commemorative rituals as response to, 220–222.
        (*See also* rituals, commemorative)
    compatibility of commemoration and
        forgiveness, 3–4, 174–175, 193–194
    two unsatisfactory responses to, 219–220
Connerton, Paul, 119–120, 174, 205–206
criminal tribunals. *See also* internationalization
    of memory
    international, 320–321
    and remembrance, 227–228
Crocker, David, 338n58
Crocker, Lawrence, 160
Cubitt, Geoffrey, 204–205, 213–214, 268

Darwall, Stephen, 187–188, 255
Debus, Dorothea, 77, 98n10

INDEX   341

De Grieff, Pablo, 162
(the) differentiation problem, 72–73, 87–88
  forgiveness and affect on hybrid emotions, 94
  forgiveness and positive emotions, 94–95
  forgiveness and restoration of psychological
    equilibrium, 91–93
  proposals to solve, 89–95
disciplined emotionality, 207, 208, 209, 225n40.
  See also rituals, commemorative
Digeser, P.E., 154, 176n4
Duff, R.A., 28

Egypt, 230
Eisenberg, Avigail, 273, 275–276
Eisenberg, N. and T. Spinrad, 123
Elias, Norbert, 263
Elster, Jon, 215
emotion regulation, techniques of, 100–101,
  103–104, 122–129. See also forgetting
emotional memory
  as epistemically special, 76–77, 98n8, 98n10
  evaluative significance of, 72. (See also emotions)
  as a kind of emotional experience, 78
  three senses of, 75–77, 200
  type of declarative, episodic memory, 75–76
emotions
  background vs. situational, 90
  cognitive theory of, 78–79
  distinct from affective attitudes, 209–210
  evaluative significance of imparted to memories,
    80, 185–186
  of groups, 134–136, 202–203
  and moral appreciation, 80–84, 212–213
  social sharing of, 201, 203–204
  and valuing, 84–87
Ethiopian artifacts, theft of, 283n53
expressive actions, 238–239
expressivist theory of morality, 179, 183–184

Faust, Drew Gilpin, 234
Feinberg, Joel, 50, 166
fidelity to dead
  as collective attitude, 193
  expressed by remembrance, 179
  how shown, 191–192
  meaning of, 190–191
  virtue of, 190
Fisher, Philip, 54–55
forgetfulness, virtue of
  and emotional response, 110
  and ethics of forgiveness, 104, 129–132
  as multi-track disposition, 108–109
  Nietzschean inspiration for, 101–102
  paired with virtue of remembrance, 107–108
  teleological account of, 109

forgetting
  meanings of, 103, 114–115, 117–118
  role in psychology of forgiveness, 100–101, 102,
    121, 134. (See also emotion regulation,
    techniques of, rumination)
  collective, 119–120, 132–133
  social and cultural factors in, 119–120
  as value-laden term, 120
forgiveness. See also blame, (the) compatibility
    problem, forgetting, moral insult, negative
    emotions, political forgiveness, self-respect
  and blame, 21–22
  collective, 6–8, 104, 134
  expanded emotive account of, 1, 17, 20–22, 36
  and insulted feelings, 27, 29
  inadequacy of exclusively emotive account of,
    96–97
  memory as foundational to, 70, 99, 178
  and non-retributive emotions, 41–44, 55. (See
    also negative emotions)
  objections to expanded account, 52–53
  relational conception of, 149–151
  and resentment, 18, 30–31
  and restorative justice, 146, 148. (See also
    restorative justice)
  in the restorative justice literature, 149
  standard account of, 2, 17–20, 70–71, 99–100
Franklin, Christopher Evan, 52
Freud, Sigmund, 103,115–116

Garland, David, 208
Garrard, Eve and David McNaughton, 29
Gilbert, Margaret, plural subject theory, 135–136
Goodin, Robert, 331
Goodman, Gail and P. Paz-Alonzo, 199
Goodman, Nelson, 237–238, 281n15, 281n16
Govier, Trudy, 33
Griffin, James, 295
Griswold, Charles, 48, 64, 148
Gross, James, 122, 123

Hamber, Brandon, 189, 259–260
Heuer, Friderike, 200
Hobsbawm, Eric, 197–198
hope, 223, 262–263
Hughes, Paul, 34, 64n7, 80
human rights
  accounts of, 288–289, 295–296
  contextualizing, 328–329, 339n69
  nation-transcending character of, 289, 306
  state responsibility to protect and remediate
    violations of, 307–308.
  as suitable for an ethic of reconciliation, 303–304
  transitional justice concerned with violations of,
    288

Humphrey, Michael, 323
Hunt, Lester, 194
Hursthouse, Rosalind, 108
Husak, Douglas, 288
Huyssen, Andreas 198

identity claims, assessment of, 275–276
Ignatieff, Michael, 189
Inter-American Court of Human Rights, 323–325
International Criminal Court, 320, 322
internationalization of memory, 286–287, 292–293
  contextualizing international involvement, 317, 318, 330–331
  impact on domestic affairs of states, 328, 338n58
  international courts of human rights and, 323–325
  international criminal trials and, 320–323
  Margalit on, 331–334
  modalities of international involvement in, 319–320
  moral grounds for, 318–319, 334–335
  non-juridical mechanisms, 325–327
  triggers for international involvement, 291, 317

Joorman, Jutta and T.B. Tran, 111
Johnstone, Gerry, 169

Kandel, Eric, 74
Klapwijk, Jacob, 173

Langer, Susanne
  on rituals, 209–210
Leary, Mark and C. Springer, 35
Levy, Daniel and N. Sznaider, 289, 339n74
Loveman, Mara, 310–311

Maier, Charles, 133
Malamud-Goti, Jaime, 163
Margalit, Avishai, 97, 105, 114, 150, 328, 331–333
M.L. King and Gandhi, 38–39, 56
McKenna, Michael, 50–51
Mégret, Frédéric, 322
memorialization (commemoration), 173, 193.
  See also collective identity, human rights, respect for persons, respect for value, symbolic value
  civil society responsibilities with respect to, 218–219, 307–308, 311, 314
  and collective self-understanding, 267–269, 283n55

international responsibilities with respect to, 290–291, 311, 317–319, 334–335.
  (*See also* internationalization of memory)
modes of, 172–173, 227–228, 280n1, 290
national significance of, 314
and normative bonds of community, 265–267
official acts of, 251–252
as response to human rights violations, 289–290
and restorative justice, 146–147, 172, 173–174, 298
state as strategic facilitator of, 314
state responsibilities with respect to, 218, 290, 308–314. (*See also* state action)
as symbolic, 229, 239, 279
unresolved issues for an ethics of, 304–305
memorialization, state failures with respect to, 316–317. *See also* internationalization of memory
memories, repeated retrieval of, 211–212, 225n45. *See also* rituals, commemorative
memories, unconscious, 73–74, 116–117
memory and ethics of forgiveness, 178
memory, durability and accuracy of. *See* sustainability of memory, problem of
memory dampening drugs, 80–81
memory, goods of, 95–96
memory, semantic and episodic, 75, 97n5, 97n6
memory retrieval, inhibition of, 100
mindfulness, 124–125, 139n38. *See also* emotion regulation, techniques of
moral insult. *See also* forgiveness
  emotions accompanying, 21, 29–30, 33–35
  pain caused by disappointed expectations, 27
  objective sense of, 29
  and sense of self-worth, 24–27
  seriousness of, 31
moral protest. *See also* negative emotions, self-respect
  functions of after forgiveness, 60–62
  features of, 55–57
  and non-retributive emotions, 55, 59
  and retributive emotions, 22, 54–55
  and victim-offender conferencing, 169–170
  and self-respect, 22, 57–59
  types of, 49
moral virtues and memorialization, 262–263, 264–265. *See also* symbolic value
moral wrongdoing
  communicative conception of, 28–29
  insulting wrongs, 21, 27, 29–30, 30–31
  non-insulting wrongs, 28, 29–30
  safeguarding moral values, 52–53
Mozambique, international role in civil war, 319
McGaugh, James, 196
McGeer, Victoria, 63, 67n46
Muldoon, Paul, 165

Murphy, Jeffrie, 28, 48
Musil, Robert, 177n40

negative emotions
  after forgiveness, 71–72
  anger, 18, 54–55, 63–64, 66n30
  causal relations of retributive and
      non-retributive, 35–36
  constitutive desire of, 32–33
  directedness of, as objection to expanded
      emotive account, 41–42
  hurt feelings, 35, 66n33
  hybrid emotions, 35, 66n36
  non-retributive emotions, 34
  and protest, 53–55
  not moral emotions, as objection to expanded
      emotive account, 42–43
  retributive emotions, 18–19, 21, 31, 33–34, 37,
      64n7
  retributive emotions in transitional settings,
      166–167
Neu, Jerome, 31, 33–34
Nietzsche, Friedrich
  on (active) forgetting and remembering,
      101–107, 120–121
  forgiveness in, 23–30
  ressentiment, 23, 65n12
  and virtues of remembrance and forgetfulness,
      101–102, 137n6
Nozick, Robert, 81–82, 236, 248–249, 260
Nussbaum, Martha, 90, 92, 295

Osiel, Mark, 196

Pettigrove, Glen, 42, 67n47
Pildes, Richard, 270
Pincione, Guido and F. Tesón, 236
political forgiveness, 2, 134. See also forgiveness,
    memorialization (commemoration)
  conceptions of, 144–145, 152
  as instrument of national reconciliation, 153–154
  standing of officials to dispense, 155
political reconciliation, 160
  and democratization, 162–163
  forgiveness not primary vehicle of, 165, 167–168
  non-lethal coexistence as inadequate account of,
      161–162
  three conceptions of, 160–161
Poole, Ross, 312
Postema, Gerald, 265–266

Rawls, John
  on human rights, 295
  on moral emotions, 42–43

on non-ideal theory, 156
  and self-respect, 304
Raz, Joseph, 150, 250, 255
redress, meaning of, 297
Reisberg, Daniel, 199–200, 203
remembrance. See also fidelity to dead,
    memorialization (commemoration),
    respect for persons, self-respect,
    sustainability of memory, problem of
  collective, 6
  consequentialist arguments for, 181–182
  duties of, 5–6, 109–110, 229, 294–295, 301–302
  erosion of, psychological and social factors,
      179–180, 197–198
  ethics of, 4–6
  expressivist moral values of, 179, 182–183,
      192–193. (See also expressivist theory of
      morality)
  personal and political, 3
  as reparative, 229
  virtue of, 109–110. (See also forgetfulness,
      virtue of)
respect for persons. See also validation
  expressed by remembrance, 179, 188
  how shown for dead, 188–189, 258–259, 260–261
  most basic sense of, 297–298
  as second-personal, 187–188, 255–256, 260
respect for value, 250
  expressed by remembrance, 251
  how shown, 252
restorative justice, 145. See also forgiveness,
    political reconciliation, transitional justice
  in contemporary criminal justice, 157
  distinctive features of, 157–158, 163
  structured opportunities for forgiveness and,
      168–169
retributivism
  and significance of suffering, 18–19
  teleological and non-teleological, 81–83
rituals, commemorative
  in the Balkans, 217
  challenges in transitional societies, 213–215
  dark side of, 180, 215–216, 217–218
  and Madres de Plaza de Mayo, 216
  of mourning, 208, 225n37
  nature of, 204–210
  in Northern Ireland, 216
  in Sierra Leone, 216
  and sustainability of memory problem, 180,
      203–204, 210–213. (See also sustainability
      of memory, problem of)
Roediger, Henry, F. Zaromb, and A. Butler,
    211–212
rumination (dwelling on), 110–111
  collective, 133
  effects on duration and intensity of memories,
      111–113, 138n19

effects on effective agency, 113
  relation to forgiveness, 113–114
Rustig, Cheryl L. and S. Nolen-Hoeksema, 112
Rwanda, 163

sadness, 50, 52
Scanlon, T.M., 40–41, 44–45, 46, 252
Schechter, Mark, 256–257
Scheffler, Israel, 206
Scheffler, Samuel, 84–85, 273
self-respect. *See also* moral protest
  expressed by remembrance, 184–187
  individual and communal, 186, 193
  non-retributive emotions and, 22, 49–51
  resentment and, 22, 47–48
  violations that trigger, 47
  virtue of, 194
Sen, Amartya, 295
Shapiro, Shauna, 125
Shue, Henry, 296
Singer, Jefferson and M. Conway, 117–119
Smith, Angela, 55–56
social groups, types of, 7–8, 134–135
Solomon, Robert, 33
South African Truth and Reconciliation
    Commission, 153, 248
South Carolina Confederate flag controversy, 241
state action
  legitimacy of in transitional regimes, 315
  and national identity, 311–313
  symbolic power of, 310–311
Strawson, P.F., 4, 67n42
Stroud, Sarah, 129
sustainability of memory, problem of, 179–180,
    194–196. *See also* rituals, commemorative
  durability and accuracy of memory, 196–197,
    198–199
  importance of emotion for, 199–201
  problem for transitional societies, 178,
    201–202
symbolic action
  communicative purpose of, 232, 243
  expressive nature of, 239
  and "standing for" relation, 237, 239
symbolic value, 230. *See also* collective identity,
    moral virtues and memorialization, respect
    for persons, respect for value
  and consequentialism, 230, 231, 240, 278–279

and deontological principles, 232, 261
  as lightweight kind of value, 245. (*See also* (the)
    thesis of lesser value)
  Lincoln at Gettysburg, as example of,
    234–235
  misfiring of, 240–244
  and moral value, 231–232
  non-consequentialist accounts of, 261–262
  relevance of agent's reasons to, 243–244
  not utility value, 236–237, 240, 244, 268
  as type of extrinsic value, 231

Taylor, Gabriele, 184
Teitel Ruti, 198
(the) thesis of lesser value, 245–248
  inadequacy of, 250, 253–254. (*See also* respect
    for persons, respect for value, collective
    identity)
Thompson, Andrew, 312, 337n33
Thompson, Janna, 158, 191
transitional justice, 145, 155, 233–234, 287. *See
    also* restorative justice
  relation to Rawlsian non-ideal theory, 156
  restorative and retributive approaches to,
    145–146, 287
transitional regimes, challenges confronting,
    287, 315
truth commissions, 147, 227–228, 280n2, 290
truth telling and memorials, 299–301
Tutu, Desmond, 1–2, 145, 155
(the) unforgivable, 129–130

validation, 256–257, 298. *See also*
    memorialization (commemoration),
    respect for persons
valuing and emotions. *See* emotions
Verdeja, Ernesto, 269
vindication, 298–299. *See also* memorialization
    (commemoration)

Walker, Margaret, 45, 64, 223, 281n28, 282n39
Wallace, R. Jay, 18, 38, 41, 65n8
Wills, Gary, 234
Wilson, Richard, 153
Wolheim, Richard, 200
World Trade Center site, symbolism of, 242